Typical and atypical development in early childhood

TYPICAL AND ATYPICAL DEVELOPMENT IN EARLY CHILDHOOD

The Fundamentals

Ayshe Talay-Ongan

BPS
BOOKS

The British Psychological Society

First published in the UK in 1998 by BPS Books (The British
Psychological Society), St Andrews House, 48 Princess Road East,
Leicester LE1 7DR, UK.

A catalogue record for this book is available from the British Library.

ISBN 1 85433 269 4

Cover illustration: Anna-Lisa Doumani
Cover design: Toni Hope-Caten

Set in 10/12pt Garamond by DOCUPRO, Sydney
Printed by KHL Printing Co. Pte Ltd, Singapore

10 9 8 7 6 5 4 3 2 1

Dedicated to the memory of Dr Nurbike Talay, MD, in awe of her passion for healing children which knew no bounds and in agony for a life cut short senselessly in its prime, while her dreams must live on,

and to the memory of my brother, Haluk Mehmet Talay, who met his wife in their final embrace within months—your legacy is in good hands,

and to the rest of my family, Beraat Etem Talay, Aydin and Deniz Ongan (the lights of my eyes), Selin Talay and Doruk Ongan.

Contents

About the author

Ayshe Talay-Ongan, PhD, is currently a lecturer in child development at the Institute of Early Childhood, Macquarie University, Sydney. She obtained her BS (Hons) in psychology at Middle East Technical University, Ankara, Turkey, her motherland. She then studied speech and language pathology at Columbia University, New York (MS), and obtained an interdisciplinary PhD degree in neurolinguistics and developmental psychology.

Aiming to combine academic teaching and research with clinical practice, she has endeavoured to do all three concurrently over the past 20 years, maintaining a keen interest in delivery of services to young children and their families within a multidisciplinary, family-centred framework. Among her innovative practices, she co-founded the first private psychology clinic in Istanbul, Turkey, the Asam Child and Family Development Centre, which has since served as a model for dozens of similar establishments. She also founded the Center for the Competent Child, a community service therapeutic preschool in Berkeley, California, and has served as its executive director for many years. Dr Talay-Ongan was special consultant in early childhood to Berkeley and Oakland Public School Systems in California, during the years when the rights of *all* young children, regardless of the extent of their support needs, were being addressed by the public school system as a result of Public Law 99–457. She taught at Montclair State College, New Jersey, and Holy Names College, Oakland, California, before coming to Macquarie University.

Her research interests include infant auditory processing markers for later language skills, social emotional contexts of attention-related disorders, and preventive intervention with at-risk children. With over 30 professional publications, many national and international conference presentations and invited keynote addresses to her credit, this is her first book.

Although Dr Talay-Ongan has made Sydney home for the past nine years, she still travels and teaches intercontinentally. She was a research associate at University of California, and a visiting scholar at Bosphorus University, where she was granted the Docent (associate professor) Award in 1993.

Acknowledgments

To Assoc. Prof. June Wangman, for giving me the opportunity to take a semester off from formal teaching commitments, and for her review, support and wise guidance of the project.

To Prof. Alan Hayes, Dr Marija Radojevic, and those nameless colleagues who have been so generous with their time and enheartening with their comments in reviews of the manuscript.

To my undergraduate students, who have read and commented on the manuscript chapters, for making me feel validated.

To all those researchers and writers whose work and materials I have essentially synthesised into a personal tapestry.

To David Sun and Ahmet Ajara, who fought valiant battles with many a computer bug, saving my sanity and many nights of work.

To Elizabeth Weiss, Colette Vella, Kate Ormston-Jeffrey and the Allen & Unwin staff, for a lovely working relationship.

To Michael Perkins, for his wise counsel and facilitation.

To Mum, Mem, and all those priceless close personal friends near and far who gave me a pat on the back or a bright e-mail just when I needed it, and renewed my commitment to this work.

And, of course, to my one and only, who put up with it all and kept me well-fed, humoured and loved . . .

A heartfelt thank you.

Preface

This volume is assembled for students and professionals working with young children and their families. I hope that many parents will find it a useful reference as well, particularly those with children who have special needs. It is meant to bring a fresh perspective to the reader in its approach, by drawing not only from the field of developmental psychology but from various other disciplines, such as early childhood education, developmental disabilities, speech and language pathology, developmental neuropsychology, paediatrics and early intervention. I have focused on the period of life from birth to eight years as the formal definition of early childhood—those magical years that have such an indelible influence on the rest of our lives.

The book is written with two broad aims: the first is to present up-to-date information in an easy-to-access form in all domains of child development, so that the reader can obtain an overview of how normal development is conceptualised and investigated, and of how this foundation relates to our understanding of and providing for the needs of those children whose developmental trajectories are affected by various conditions. Intervention in atypical development takes normal development as its yardstick; I felt it was important to weave one with the other. Second, it should serve as a common currency of communication for all persons involved in the care, treatment, education or welfare of young children, whose interests converge, despite the differences in approach or professional language employed by each group. In the era of *inclusive* education for all children by the *collaboration* of all professionals, it should serve as a helpful reference.

This is not an exhaustive volume in the field; rather, it is intended to serve as a desktop reference with potential multiple uses: students in professional training in fields related to young children and their families (e.g. early childhood education, special education, psychology, speech and language pathology, occupational and physical therapy, social work, paediatrics and nursing) may find it helpful as a textbook in consolidating their understanding of a developmental era or domain, and possible disorders therein; professionals may use it as a reference to check on a particular area of child development, disability or syndrome. To many workers in the field who do not have a formal degree but have substantial interest and experience in working with young children, it may serve as a basic, multifaceted reference text. Many parents who make rounds with countless specialists and consultants for their child are often baffled by the terminology used to enlighten them; many professionals, too, share the parents' plight in deciphering each others' reports. I hope this book makes some contribution towards demystifying some of the professional communications.

Having said that, I have to admit that my mental audience as I was writing has been the students and practitioners in the field of early childhood, and for good reasons. First, as an educator of the future educators of young children, I sustain the fallibility of wanting to share with them all which I feel is important in their professional training. Many of my colleagues will rightfully disagree. Second, I have a strong belief that within today's inclusive and often resource-limited early childhood special education context, the early childhood educator plays a pivotal role in coordinating the various multi- and transdisciplinary intervention strategies, planning and implementing educational experiences that will best benefit the child in their care, and attending to the families' various and often complex support needs. I feel I owe them the assistance.

The errata, omissions and biases are all mine. Any value the reader may derive is attributed to my teachers: my students, who always inspire me; the children and families, who enrich me through the privilege of working with them; and my daughter, who has made it all real.

TO THE READER

The reader is urged to find auxiliary sources for more fully developed discussions of key concepts, as this book is meant to provide a compilation of fundamental issues and facts. For web-based material related to this book, please refer to www.mq.edu.au/academic/books/atalayon

A decision has been made to use alternating gender pronouns in consecutive chapters to reduce bias and to ensure more equal representation of boys and girls, though occasionally this can seem misleading.

AYSHE TALAY-ONGAN
SYDNEY, MARCH 1998

PART I

Setting the stage

1

Basic questions, frameworks and methods in child development

A baby is conceived. At that magical moment, her[1] genetic make-up has already been determined—from the colour of her eyes, to her height and certain preferences in life. The fetus will have to bear the influences thrust upon her in intrauterine life: her characteristics may be altered if rubella strikes her mother, for example. The baby will be born into a family, and perhaps the characteristics of the families are as diverse as the genetic make-up of the baby; yet the family will have an enormous effect on the kind of person she becomes. The family will function in a social matrix and environment. The experience of living in the country will probably be quite different from that of the inner city for the developing child. And all communities exist within a cultural heritage in which the social institutions, from child-rearing to the role of the elderly, will have been laid out. How can we ever study child development given this infinite variability in the forces acting on the individual?

> The basic questions posed and the theories put forth in child development are attempts to find regularities and make predictions. They enable us to have assumptions about pathways of development in this complex, multivariate network of influences.

SOME BASIC QUESTIONS

As we embark on the journey towards understanding the process of child development, we need to look at change as well as stability; similarities as

---

1   In fairness to both boys and girls, their respective pronouns are used in alternating chapters.

3

well as differences. A child born with Down syndrome will be in some ways different from her peers (her IQ scores may be lower, for example), yet what she shares with them in terms of similarities will by far outweigh the differences (her sleep cycles, rate of growth, ability to swim). While all babies will change by growth measures from infancy to adolescence and beyond, early characteristics of temperament, for example, tend to be stable over time.

Nature or nurture?

Questions regarding children and the influences shaping their growth, development, personality and the kind of person they become have occupied the minds of philosophers from antiquity onwards. Looking at some historical views, Plato and Descartes favoured the *nativist* explanations: most characteristics are shaped or determined by the time the child is born. John Locke took the *empiricist* view: a child's mind at birth is like a blank slate, and is shaped by the influences and experiences faced after birth.

The argument about *nature* (biological, genetic or hereditary influences; innate) versus *nurture* (environmental or child-rearing and caregiving influences) lingers to this day in developmental psychology, although the debate tends to bridge the gap, rather than widen it, by acknowledging an interaction between the two forces. Perhaps neither of these forces by itself can explain any one aspect of development. Development may best be explained by the *interaction* of these forces, and the relative contribution of each may be a topic of debate within different frameworks.

Twin studies

Let us illustrate the relative effects of nature and nurture in a paradigm that examines twins, commonly used in assessing these influences. The relationship between the IQ of identical (same-egg) and fraternal (those who are no more similar than any other siblings in their genetic make-up) twins is expressed by a correlation measure, where 1.00 indicates a perfect direct relationship, the strength of the relationship decreasing with a diminishing score, until zero, which shows no relationship at all. When many such studies are combined, the results indicate the following (Bouchard & McGue, 1981, p.1056):

- identical twins reared together   .85
- identical twins reared apart   .67
- fraternal twins reared together   .58
- siblings and fraternal twins reared apart   .24

Note that while identical twins reared together show a very strong similarity (which supports the *nature* end of the argument), when they are brought up in different environments their IQ scores are not so strongly related. There is still a pretty strong relationship—much stronger than non-identical twins or siblings—but we can attribute the lessening relationship to the effects of *nurture,* or the influence of different environments on similar IQ scores.

Obviously, we can extend the argument to children who are biologically constrained in some area of development. Given the limitations of nature, nurture will determine the realisation of the full extent of that potential. (What better example than the Paralympians?)

Heredity can influence behaviour

The closer we are able to look, the more we discover about the genetic coding of behaviour, especially if it is considered aberrant. Recent research seems to have discovered genetic influences on alcoholism, excessive aggression, antisocial behaviour, schizophrenia and anorexia (Gottesman & Goldsmith, 1994), and the list is growing. More important for our purposes, there seems to be a significant genetic influence on child temperament in such dimensions as the tendency to get upset easily (emotionality), the tendency to engage in high levels of movement (activity), and the preference shown for interacting with other persons (sociability).

Can environment be affected by heredity?

Interestingly enough, there are interactions in which the child's environment is affected by heredity. Plomin (1995) presents two avenues by which this would be possible.

- Parents not only share their genetic pool with the child but create the environment in which to sustain it. Highly intelligent children of intelligent parents often find themselves in enriched, stimulating, challenging home environments.
- Children, by virtue of their own characteristics, such as sociability or easy temperament, influence and alter the parenting characteristics of their parents.

Furthermore, nature–nurture interactions may vary from one child to another, such that *the same environment may have different effects on children with different characteristics.* An excellent example of these forces at play is that of the vulnerability or the resilience of the child being cared for in facilitative or poor environments with respect to developmental outcomes. Consider these scenarios and attempt to predict the outcome:

- Baby Rose is born six weeks prematurely. She is irritable, unsettled, and has a difficult temperament. She does not feed or sleep easily.
- Baby Joe is a happy, healthy infant. He sleeps well and eats regularly without much trouble.

These infants may be cared for in widely different environments:

- The parents are unemployed, there is a history of violence in the family and there are limited support structures around this young couple living in poverty.

■ The parents have been planning for this baby. They have a good income and plenty of family and community support around them.

Obviously, these babies start life and the developmental challenges ahead of them with unequal advantage. Rose has certain disadvantages, which mark her as being more *vulnerable*, while Joe, with his sunny disposition, is advantaged by an easy temperament: he is more *resilient*. One environment is likely to be poor, much *less facilitative* than the second *more facilitative* one. According to Horowitz (1990), a resilient child in a poor environment may still do quite well, capitalising on all that is made available to her, whereas a vulnerable child in the same non-facilitative environment will not be able to cope with the stresses so well, putting her at high risk for poor outcomes in such areas as IQ or skill in social relationships.

Nature after birth

The genetic programming is inherited from the parents, but its unfolding occurs in the years to come in sequential patterns of development. *Maturation* is the process whereby predictable changes occur in a particular order over time across all members of a species. It is usually resistant to environmental influence or training. All children share these forces: they learn to walk, to run; they grow teeth, and they go through puberty. We attribute these qualitative changes to maturation. Children also increase in quantitative measures such as weight and height; these physical changes are attributed to *growth*.

Influence of environment on maturation

What are the ways in which the unfolding pattern is affected by nurture? Aslin (1981) makes some suggestions:

■ The environment can have a *maintenance* function for a skill that has developed maturationally so that it doesn't deteriorate: keep a leg in a cast too long and the muscles will atrophy, interfering with walking.
■ A skill may develop somewhat earlier (*facilitation effect*) if the environment provides extra stimulation, although that effect will *not* be sustained in the long run: training an infant to climb stairs at ten months will have no appreciable effect on her walking skills by two years.
■ *Attunement*, in which experience speeds up the development of some skill to a level *beyond* normal maturation: enriched preschool experiences for disadvantaged children seem to raise their IQ scores.
■ The environment may also make possible a particular behaviour which could occur only with experience—*induction*: piano lessons and second-language-learning opportunities are good examples.

There are at least two other effects we need to acknowledge in exploring the ways in which environment can shape innate characteristics.

- *Timing* can be a crucial determinant in whether or not the environmental effects will take hold. *When* stimulation or enrichment is provided may be as crucial as *how much* or *what type* of interventions are made available to a young child (we review the concept of critical periods in Chapter 2).
- We are only beginning to appreciate the strength of the *contextual and cultural influences* acting on families and children. Such internalised systems of meanings, which span generations, have particular significance for multicultural societies like Australia. Without understanding these influences, our conclusions are bound to be flawed.

Environmental effects on at-risk children

For children born with biological vulnerabilities, such as various genetic abnormalities, prenatal trauma or preterm birth, the effects of the environment become even more pronounced. Consider these findings:

- Infants born with low birthweight are likely to have normal IQs if they are reared in middle-class homes, but risk substantial mental retardation if they are reared in improvished homes (Bradley, Whiteside, Mundfrom, Casey, Kelleher & Pope, 1994).
- Infants malnourished prenatally, or those with complications during pregnancy or delivery, do not show developmental delay if they are placed in special enriched preschools, but have significantly lower IQs if reared at home by ill-educated mothers (Breitmayer & Ramey, 1986).
- Children born with cytomegalovirus (CMV) are much more likely to develop learning disabilities if they are reared in improvished environments than if they are brought up in middle-class homes (Hanshaw, Schneider, Moxley, Gaev, Abel & Schneiner, 1976).

The nature of development: quantitative or qualitative?

The way we look at children is heavily influenced by the way in which we conceptualise developmental change. The two main filters through which we may look are as follows.

Children develop in additive, *quantitative* ways. An older child does what she did as a toddler, only better, more smoothly, more efficiently. In this approach we are not interested in the underlying processes, but focus on the number (more friends), the size (more words in the vocabulary) or the speed (can string beads more quickly). *Growth*, a quantitative measure, usually implies increase over time in physical characteristics like height and weight, but not necessarily in complexity.

Children essentially engage in *qualitatively* different processes during the course of development. Older children use different *structures*, *strategies* or *processes* than their younger peers: the fact that they can use longer sentences as they get older, for example, is because of the way they have been able to express the meaning of relations between events, and thus reflects a *kind* of change rather than just a change in the number of words used. We will refer to this orientation extensively as we review cognitive development. *Development* is a qualitative concept and implies increased complexity, differentiation and specialisation of a function over time.

Ages, stages or sequences?

When we accept that there are some fundamental qualitative changes in the strategies children employ in different periods in their lives, the term *stages* is appropriate. If change was an increase in size or quantity of an attribute only—a quantitative orientation—the concept of stages would not be necessary. The stage orientation is quite common in developmental psychology. More recently, this concept has been modified to *sequences of development in content areas* (Flavell, 1992).

These sequences are applied to broad areas in development—acquisition of language skills, construction of gender identity, utilisation of memory strategies, and others. The advantage to this orientation is that it can account for both qualitative as well as quantitative changes; it also allows for individual differences in children's developmental profiles, as one sequence may be slow to develop while many others are within the expected age levels.

MAJOR THEORETICAL FRAMEWORKS IN CHILD DEVELOPMENT

For our purposes, we will visit five major frameworks often used in the study of the child.

- *Psychodynamic–psychoanalytical theories* have their roots in the 19th century and Freud.
- *Behaviourist/learning theories*, which enjoyed huge popularity in the 1960s, have lost their prominence as an all-encompassing explanation of development.
- *Cognitive–developmental models* came about in part as a reaction to the reductionist views of the behaviourists.

Towards 2000, the field seems to have moved in two basic directions:

- *Contextual–cultural theories* acknowledge the significance of the mutual influences in development between the child, family, society and the culture within which all is embedded.
- *Neurobiological models* investigate the marvels of the human brain and other organic structures to provide some fascinating answers.

Interestingly, such macro- (looking at more global influences) and micro- (investigating fine-grained variables) analyses seem to complement each other, each making indispensable contributions to our understanding and work with children.

Often there are choices between the theoretical orientation needed (and vigilantly maintained) in academic research in child development and the applied concerns, where people working with children may find themselves utilising the best that each framework affords to suit the needs of particular children. Such an *eclectic* approach is most fruitful after a good understanding of all existing models and sufficient reflection to allow for individual syntheses.

Psychodynamic–psychoanalytical framework

Freud, the founder of psychoanalysis, postulated that behaviour was governed not only by conscious but also, and more significantly, by *unconscious* processes. He conceptualised personality development from childhood as a series of conflicts between the primitive desires, the *libido* or unconscious sexual drive, and society's attempt to harness them (Freud, 1920). Three parts of the personality interplay in personality development:

- The *id* seeks gratification of pleasurable impulses unconsciously, and is the hothouse for all instincts and desires. It is impatient and impetuous.
- The *ego* represents reality and guides the id to gratification by socially acceptable means. It is the problem-solver, the negotiator of optimal solutions.
- The *superego* represents the internalised models of societal expectations and morality, and acts to inhibit the id's impulses from adversely affecting the society. It is our conscience, and the guilt we feel when we transgress.

Freud claimed that there are five *psychosexual* stages of development from birth onwards, and sensitive parts of the body in each where conflict is centred. Before moving to the next stage, the conflict needs to be resolved; if not, fixation on that stage occurs.

- In the *oral* stage (first year of life), the conflict is centred around the mouth. The infant wants immediate gratification of her feeding needs. Weaning is seen as a crucial event: too abrupt weaning will lead to frustration and excessive preoccupation with the mouth (characterised by eating disorders, excessive smoking and drinking).
- In the *anal* stage (one to three years), the conflict is between the parents' attempts to toilet-train the infant and her desire to perform this function at will. Fixation at this stage potentially leads to 'anal retentive' personality, with such characteristics as stinginess, stubbornness and greed.
- In the *phallic* stage (four to six years), the genital region is the pleasure centre. The basic conflict is between the unconscious love and jealousy felt for the opposite-sex parent (Oedipal conflict) and the societal incest taboos mixed with feelings of love for the same-sex parent. The superego

develops at this stage, and successful resolution of the conflict leads to the identification with the same-sex parent.

■ *Latency* and *genital* stages (late childhood and adolescence) follow, where sexual desire can be transformed into mature sexual love on the successful resolution of the conflict, which stems from having developed coping mechanisms in the earlier stages inhibiting such expression.

Now let us look briefly at some of these coping or *defence mechanisms*, which serve the purpose of protecting the self from excessive anxiety according to this framework. Please bear in mind that these are unconscious mechanisms shared by *all* people; it is the degree to which these mechanisms distort reality (and they all do), and the intensity of their use, which may mark psychopathology or maladaptive behaviour. Some are quite common in children, especially in times requiring new adaptation strategies or of stress.

■ *Repression.* Pushing a memory or feeling below conscious awareness because it is too painful to deal with. Many victims of child abuse may have used this mechanism.

■ *Denial.* Acting as if the painful event never took place. Many families of children with special needs may find themselves in denial.

■ *Projection.* Putting the blame onto another person or event. Students are known to complain about how difficult the exam was if they've been partying the night before!

■ *Regression.* Reverting to earlier, less mature forms of behaviour to seek security and comfort. A classic example is that of a trained young child starting to bedwet after the arrival of her sibling.

■ *Rationalisation.* Attributing outcomes to reasons other than the real desires. A child not invited to the birthday party of a friend states (dejectedly) that she hates her and would not have gone anyway.

■ *Compensation.* Making an effort to overcome or overshadow an area of less strength by another deed or achievement. A child with reading difficulties may excel in dance.

■ *Sublimation.* Repackaging unacceptable or unfulfilled sexual desire in a socially acceptable form. If Romeo could write love songs to Juliet and keep it at that . . .

A newer generation of *humanist* psychoanalysts have promoted cultural influences and the individual's inner strengths, and have thus perhaps softened the pathology-oriented approach of Freud and his followers. Of these, Erik Erikson (1950) has formulated a *psychosocial* stage approach to human development that occurs within the social matrix and cultural demands put on the child. Erikson sees the child as moving through invariant progressive stages, each with a task that needs a successful resolution before moving on to the next one. The psychosocial stages of development and their tasks are as follows:

- *Trust vs mistrust.* In the first year of life, the infant's nourishment, comfort, attention and love needs are met by the mother/caregiver. If all goes well, the infant learns to have confidence in the orderliness and predictability of her environment; if not, she learns mistrust and is likely to become fearful and apprehensive.
- *Autonomy vs shame, doubt.* During toddlerhood, toileting and relations with parents become significant. If all goes well, the child will achieve a degree of self-control, willpower, independence and self-confidence; if not, she develops a sense of shame, embarrassment and self-rejection.
- *Initiative vs guilt.* In the preschool years, sexual exploration and play are prevalent. If all goes well, the child will gain direction and purpose; if not, she is likely to be unduly dependent on and fearful of others, and to be restricted in imagination and play skills.
- *Industry vs inferiority.* During early school years, making and doing things in a group setting and obtaining feedback becomes increasingly important. If all goes well, the child develops social competence and a sense of achievement; if not, she is likely to develop a sense of personal and social inadequacy.
- *Identity vs role confusion.* The task in the adolescent years is to resolve a sense of self and the directions to be pursued.

The last three stages, intimacy vs isolation, generativity vs stagnation and integrity vs despair, pertain to adulthood and are beyond the scope of this discussion.

The contribution of these *psychodynamic* (centring on conflict resolution) models to child development has been substantial, although they have been backed up mainly by clinical research. Other important thinkers, like John Bowlby, have been influenced by it. The fact that the interactivity of the caregiver/child relationship is so heavily focused on in the first years of life has been catalytic to the development of *attachment theory* (see Chapter 5).

Behaviourist/learning theories

Behaviourist theories have taken the 'nurture', or the influence of environmental factors, as the driving force behind development. Human behaviour is seen as being highly susceptible to experience and learning. Learning is achieved by the rewards or the punishments associated with certain events. Two major figures have become eminent, each with a learning or *conditioning* paradigm—Pavlov and Skinner. Let us review these paradigms before we consider Bandura's social learning theory.

Pavlov's *classical conditioning* was made famous by his experiments with the salivating dogs (Pavlov, 1927): the hungry dog would salivate (*un*conditioned response; no learning is necessary) at the sight of food (*un*conditioned stimulus; normally brings about the response). A bell (conditioned stimulus; needs to be learned) comes on each time the food morsel appears. Before we know it, the dog salivates at the sound of the bell (now a conditioned or learned response) even without the food. In other words, a neutral stimulus can evoke the natural response if the two have been paired.

The first year of life is quite dependent on such conditioned learning, particularly in emotional responses. The infant learns to associate food preparation rituals with feeding and is excited before the bottle or the nipple appears; feelings of warmth, comfort, security, pleasure and love are associated with the parents' presence. (When such associations are predictable and consistent, the stage is set for Erikson's basic trust.) No wonder a place, a sound, a perfume—even the whiff of freshly baked bread—evokes pleasant memories and pleasurable experiences for most of us. On the other hand, imagine the anticipation and the emotional state of an infant who has been hospitalised many times in her few years when she sees people in white uniforms, or those of a child who has to endure erratic, violent behaviour in the family. How these experiences set the emotional tone in our lives becomes apparent.

In Skinner's *operant* (or *instrumental*) conditioning, the organism is not a passive recipient—rather, it has to *do* something to obtain a result (Skinner, 1957). Scientific study of both these paradigms seems to have originated with animals as the subjects: with Skinner's pigeons, the bird has to peck a certain lever in order to obtain the food. The principle is that any behaviour that is *reinforced* will have a higher likelihood of being learned and repeated in similar circumstances. Here are some terms often used in this framework.

- *Positive reinforcement.* A reward or a pleasant consequence which strengthens the response. For example, the child repeats the word instead of pointing to or whining for milk, the mother praises her effort and gives her a glass of milk. She has positively reinforced the use of the word milk by making the child's desire for milk be satisfied when the word for it is uttered. Note that she has also praised her in the process, a *social* positive reinforcement. The child is more likely to say milk next time.

- *Negative reinforcement.* The removal or cessation of an unpleasant event, which strengthens that response. The infant is teething and crying in distress; the father gives her the cold teething ring; she is relieved. The likelihood of her wanting the ring is increased, as is the likelihood of the father giving the ring to the child, as it stopped her crying—a consequence most parents love to achieve.

- *Punishment.* An undesirable consequence following a behaviour that decreases the likelihood of that response. The toddler touches the hot stove and burns her fingers, an event she is not likely to repeat. Time out, grounding and spanking are in this category. However, caution is needed in administering punishment to 'teach' children, for often it does not produce the desired outcome. Physical punishment given for hitting another child has neither modelled the correct behaviour nor decreased the child's feelings of frustration.

■ *Intermittent reinforcement.* Reinforcement is received at unpredictable intervals after learning, sustaining that behaviour for longer periods of time. One small win at Lotto and we tend to buy a ticket for weeks on end. The issue of consistency becomes an important consideration in efforts to curb undesirable behaviour, based on this notion: for example, if swearing, the undesirable behaviour, elicits only an occasional parental punishment, the likelihood of swearing to extinguish or disappear is low.

In its pure form, behaviourist theory claims that only observable phenomena such as stimuli and responses can be properly studied scientifically: as we have no direct way of studying the human mind, the mind is the 'black box', and is not relevant to understanding behaviour. The influence of social and cultural context on the developing individual was similarly ignored. However, *Bandura's social learning theory* has had significant influence in developmental psychology. More recently, Bandura (1989) has incorporated mental dimensions in his theory, bridging the gap between the behaviourist and cognitive–developmental frameworks. Some of its highlights are:

■ learning does not always require direct reinforcement, and can occur also through modelling and observational learning;
■ intrinsic rewards/reinforcements such as pride or discovery can be just as powerful as external reinforcers;
■ the child may extract the *rules* underlying the behaviour in the process of learning by modelling, thereby acquiring attitudes, values, problem-solving strategies—even self-evaluation skills.

Behaviourism has had an impact on child-rearing practices in Western countries in the earlier decades, and not always a positive one. Because it focuses so stringently on behaviour, the affective and emotional states of the infant are not well accounted for. The typical example of 'not reinforcing the crying behaviour by picking the baby up' would be interpreted as not being responsive to the infant in more contemporary views. It has also left its mark on our educational systems, particularly in behaviour management. In special education, it has given us the tools by which small bits of behaviour are systematically analysed, shaped and modified towards better-developed outcomes, a significant contribution.

Cognitive–developmental theories

The cognitive–developmental framework, unlike behaviourism, sees the role of the mind—and therefore cognitive development—as being central. Like the psychodynamic approach, it accepts the significance of the relationships of the developing child with a few key people in forming *internal representations*, but sees interactions of the child with people and inanimate objects as crucial to development. The child is seen as an *active participant* in the process of development, *constructing* her knowledge about the world through interactions with events and relations, as well as with toys and objects.

Most frameworks have a 'grand theorist'; Jean Piaget has been most influential in this cognitive–developmental approach. Perhaps his framework has been put to the test more than any other. The Swiss biologist-turned-psychologist initially studied his three children in amazing detail, and noticed that there were great regularities in the sequence of their discoveries about the world and misconceptions they had in solving the problems in it. Indeed, his stages of cognitive development have been replicated in experimental studies almost universally and, with minor modifications, remain the cornerstone in cognitive development in children to date (Piaget, 1952).

■ *Sensorimotor stage* (birth to age two). The infant learns to deal effectively with the physical and social world, and moves from being a reflexive neonate to a toddler who can represent knowledge of the world with emerging language.
■ *Preoperational stage* (two to seven years). The ability to think about objects and events is prelogical, often magical. Areas of play, moral awareness and social functioning reflect the manipulation of symbolic or representational functioning.
■ *Concrete operational stage* (seven to 11 years). Thoughts are now organised into an integrated system of logical operations. Thinking is still limited to the rational understanding of tangible objects.
■ *Formal operational stage* (over 11 years). Abstract, hypothetical–deductive tools of thought are established for lifelong problem-solving. Knowledge now grows as further information is gathered and assimilated.

We examine these stages and their substages in detail in Chapters 5–8. What is readily apparent, however, is the *qualitative* nature of change in each of these sequential and invariant stages.

Piaget (1970) assumed that all organisms *adapt* to their environment, by actively seeking to understand it through active *exploration*. Three basic processes are used while children test their theories about how their world works, and construct knowledge (the term *constructivism* reflects this orientation):

■ *assimilation,* where a new object is incorporated into an existing *schema,* which is an integrated system of behaviour patterns;
■ *accommodation,* where the new object does not fit the existing schema. The schema needs to be altered to make the adaptation;
■ *equilibration,* where these two dynamic forces interplay, producing more and more sophisticated conceptual structures and thought patterns.

You will note from this brief description that Piaget has not paid a lot of attention to the social context in which cognitive development occurs. Lev

Vygotsky (1934/1962), the long-forgotten, now eminent, Russian psychologist addressed this concern. His concept of the *zone of proximal development* is based on the notion that cognitive growth occurs when the child, in the process of exploration and discovery, is scaffolded by a more competent person (an older child or adult). Through that interaction, if the new information presented by the more competent person fits the schema of the younger child's understanding of the world, growth occurs. The language used in such interactive experiences and the self-talk children engage in during problem-solving are also given prominence in Vygotsky's view. Being a product of a culture that valued the collective rather than the individual, Vygotsky's emphasis on contextual and societal influences continue to shape our thinking in child development and education. You will find a fuller discussion of these theorists in Chapter 7.

Contextual–cultural frameworks

While the influence of the family, and the mother in particular, has been acknowledged in child development theories in general, there is a growing awareness that the influence of the larger social context also plays a significant role in forces shaping the developing child. *Bronfenbrenner's ecological theory* is one such contextual orientation.

Urie Bronfenbrenner (1989) describes social ecology as the complex system of social influences surrounding the child and her environment. If you think of these influences as concentric circles with the child in the middle, they proceed as follows:

- *microsystem*: made up of all relationships and transactions in a particular setting; the social and physical environment of the family;
- *mesosystem*: includes the interrelationships between the major settings in which we find children, such as family and school;
- *exosystem*: extends to include the employment status of the parents, neighbourhood support and organisation, social policies, the economy and even transportation, which have an effect on the systems affecting the child;
- *macrosystem*: contains all the general tenets, beliefs and values of the culture or subculture, which reflect the meaning and value of life and control the nature of the interactions between the various levels of the social system.

You can see how the continuous and mutual transactions between these levels would contribute to an understanding of the child and the family within the larger social-cultural context. Children brought up in homes in which the parents share one cultural heritage and have themselves been reared in it, say, the Anglo-Australian tradition, will not be surrounded by the same mores, values, attitudes or beliefs as a set of parents who have been raised in an entirely different tradition, say, a native Australian or a migrant Egyptian family.

We will keep on underlining the mutuality of influences and the effects of the social context on development in the chapters to come.

Neurobiological frameworks

Biological explanations of development have been progressing substantially over the past decades. The field of *neuroscience* has now become part of the cognitive science which aims to explore the human mind through the interdisciplinary studies of not only psychology and neurology but philosophy, anthropology, computer modelling of human behaviour and linguistics. You will have an opportunity to explore the influence of neuroscience on early childhood in Chapter 3, as it is crucial to understand the developing brain and the many frontiers it opens up in critical years of early development.

Another field of study that has enhanced our understanding is that of *behaviour genetics*, which involves the mapping of the human genes with particular behavioural characteristics. This field has provided important information on the pathological conditions that interfere with normal development, as well as offering explanations for physical and psychological attributes. The interaction of the biological potential with the environmental influences encountered in development is a theme we will revisit continually. Neurobiological models are promising predictors of both general and individual patterns of development.

RESEARCH METHODS: TOOLS IN UNDERSTANDING CHILD DEVELOPMENT

Theories and frameworks in any discipline are as good as the universal predictability of behaviour they offer. After all, they are formulas or templates that discern the underlying patterns of behaviour. They allow us to make predictions about outcomes when we have taken into account the variables that the theory claims are important elements. We can either take a framework at face value, or collect and systematically analyse the data to see whether its predictions hold. Often, only by the addition of such new information are we able to make revisions or modifications to a theory. No wonder theories take on a life of their own—growing, changing, expanding with time and added information. In that sense, they are somewhat like developing children!

There are methods and techniques available to us in gathering descriptive information to test theories or to understand the effect of particular interventions and treatments.

Observational methods

Of these, *naturalistic observation* is probably the least intrusive, and involves the silent observation of children in their natural environment. The objectivity of the conclusions drawn often needs to be carefully guarded, and it does not answer all developmental questions. For example, the nature of friendships with four-year-olds may suit this method, while children's conceptions of death at that age may not.

Probably the most extensive technique is *ethnographic observation*, a method commonly used by anthropologists. Particularly when understanding cross-cultural differences, being immersed in one culture for long periods of time to study certain patterns yields invaluable information.

Systematic observation provides a more structured approach: the researcher has a systematic tool such as a questionnaire, survey or a checklist, to collect the information necessary to answer a question. Such self-reports may contain a bias (untruthful or distorted responses) and, in the study of young children, rely on people other than those being studied to provide the information.

Experimental method

This is the most controlled method, and strives to isolate the variables under investigation. The *independent variable* is the one being manipulated (e.g. numbers of hours of training in phonetic awareness), and the *dependent variable* is the outcome, or the result, attributed to the training (e.g. improvement in speed of reading). In this instance, we like to call the group that has received the training the *experimental* group, and compare its members with a matched *control* group to see the differences in the results.

Laboratory experiments may also be used in the study of children: here, certain responses are carefully documented under certain conditions. The 'strange situation test' in determining attachment behaviour in infants (see Chapter 5) is an example of the use of laboratory conditions in studying children.

There are many instances of each one of these methods referred to in the chapters to come. Another crucial dimension in developmental research is the *design* employed in the study. As different designs may appear to suggest different conclusions on similar phenomena, we need to be aware of each to be able to make an informed and critical evaluation of their claims.

Cross-sectional design compares different age groups at a single point in time with respect to a variable; for example, three groups of three-, five-, and seven-year-olds are given the same shape- and colour-sorting task to investigate the nature of this skill over age. This design makes it possible to get information from large numbers in a relatively short period of time, but has some serious *confounds* which may affect the obtained results adversely. For example, it does not control the *cohort effect*, which is the variation between subjects (in this case, children) born in different years. To illustrate, do you think there would be differences between children of an earlier era, where preschool experience was the exception rather than the rule, and today's *Playschool* and computer-savvy toddlers? Also, it does not separate *cultural and historical (time) effects* unique to each child's experience from age-related effects.

Longitudinal design follows up the same participants over a period of time, evaluating the attribute under investigation at their different ages. For example, the ability to sort by colour and shape is studied on the same group of children from 18 months to six years in six-month intervals. You can see how this would control the above confounds, but we still have to pay a price:

■ It is expensive to carry out a project over an extended period of time. Also, original participants may move away or become inaccessible.
■ Selective attrition—that is, the dropping out of participants such that only the most capable or interested remain in the group—may confound the findings.

Sequential designs combine these two, so that the participants tested in a cross-sectional design are retested at a later time.

Research in child development, with its many methods, designs and potential problems, enables us to answer questions systematically. Since we cannot study *all* subjects (i.e. children and their families, teachers and others), we select a small group, a *sample,* to represent the entire group we are interested in understanding. We increase our chances of good representation if the group is sampled *randomly,* so that *biases* are controlled. The goal is to achieve at least a degree of *true representation* so that the findings can be generalised to all children within those parameters. We can present the data *descriptively,* or we can give it some probability power: *statistical* methods such as correlations or tests of significance allow us to have a degree of confidence in the representativeness of the results of our study.

CONCLUSIONS

We have highlighted only some significant issues in child development research such as the nature–nurture debate and the nature of developmental change. Our brief review of the major theoretical orientations seems to indicate the advances made in our appreciation of the multitude of influences on developing children. Finally, research is seen as a tool of understanding development—one that is vital if we are to remain reflective and inquisitive in this field.

All students of child development, sooner or later, agree that its study is a very exciting venture indeed!

2

Biological roots: genetics, heredity and prenatal development

From the two cells uniting to form the beginnings of human life (the egg and the sperm) to the birth of the human infant about 265 days later, some pretty amazing things happen. At birth, the particular combination of the baby's genes and chromosomes will be unlike any other before him: a totally unique person-in-the-making, with all his genetic blueprint already sealed. In fact, so complex is this process, with so many possibilities of so many events taking the wrong turn, that it is indeed a miracle to have such a relatively low incidence of birth defects. Let's start with some of the building blocks (the cells and chromosomes), examine how their defects can be passed on to the infant, what some of these disorders are, and how they can be diagnosed during pregnancy.

CELLS AND CHROMOSOMES

All the cells in the human body (except the egg and the sperm) have a *nucleus*. Within the nucleus of every cell are 23 *pairs of chromosomes,* half of each pair having passed on from the mother and the other half from the father, a total of 46 in all. The sperm and the egg, however, are special cells: each contains only *half* the number, or 23 chromosomes, and at fertilisation they complement each other to form the 23 pairs.

Pairs 1–22 of the chromosomes, called *autosomes,* look similar, and are collectively responsible for all our biological and physical heritage. The 23rd pair comprises the *sex chromosomes*: if it contains two X chromosomes it marks the female, if it has an X and a Y it marks the male. The chromosome contains *deoxyribonucleic acid (DNA),* which looks like a double helix. The unfolding of the mysteries of DNA continues to be one of the major revelations in science.

Karyotyping is a procedure whereby chromosomes are counted and laid out, with the band patterns on each quite visible. As all cells in the body carry the same 23 pairs of chromosomes, this procedure can be done on any cell in the body.

Each chromosome consists of thousands of genes. Abnormalities in the process of formation of the genetic code may lead to *mutation*, which can occur by chance or as a result of external factors such as drugs, viruses or radiation. Since such errors affect the egg and the sperm cells as well, genetic mutations can pass on from one generation to the next. Some mutations are considered to be a part of the natural evolution process and are seen as being helpful in adapting to the environment. Others are harmful and can predispose the carrier to various disease processes, such as cancer or diabetes.

The inheritance of such physical features as eye colour is determined by a single pair of genes, one from each parent. As Mendel, the founder of modern genetics, discovered, some are more powerful than others in this union and will exert their *dominance*, so that the other member of the pair is *recessive*. Using the example of eye colour, brown eyes are coded on a dominant gene, while blue eyes are carried by a recessive one. So how do blue eyes survive as a trait in the face of such strong dominance? The answer lies in the fact that the brown-eyed parent may also contain a gene for blue eyes, recessive though it may be, inherited somewhere in his lineage. If, at the time of conception, the sperm cell that penetrates the egg happens to have the gene for blue eyes, the offspring, having received the other gene for blue eyes from his mother, will indeed have blue eyes.

Genotype refers to the entire genetic inheritance of an individual. *Phenotype* is the *visible* pattern of inherited characteristics.

A phenotype may be the product of the genotype, the impact of environmental influences on it during intrauterine development, and the interaction of nature and nurture forces after birth. A child with a genotype for superior intelligence may have mild retardation if the mother has been subjected to harmful effects during pregnancy. Similarly, a child with a genotype for high activity and distractability may be raised in an environment of high support, resulting in successful self-regulation and adaptation.

GENETIC TRANSMISSION PATTERNS

Now let us examine how some mutant recessive and dominant genes interplay in inheritance patterns when parents are carriers, with resultant inherited disorders. We will look at autosomal recessive, autosomal dominant and X-linked transmissions of genetic disorders.

Autosomal recessive disorders

These can occur in the offspring (i.e. become a phenotype) only if *both* parents are carriers of the defective recessive gene, as the recessive gene from one parent only will remain a 'silent' genotype. Look at the possible combinations with *one carrier* parent (N = normal; D = defective):

	Mother's genes: N	D
Father's genes: N	NN (normal)	ND (carrier, no symptoms)
N	NN (normal)	ND (carrier, no symptoms)

This means that there is a 50% *probability* of having children who are carriers and a 50% probability of having children who will not be affected by the disorder at all.

Where *both parents* are the carriers of the defective recessive gene:

	Mother's genes: N	
Father's genes: N	NN (normal)	ND (carrier, no symptoms)
D	DN (carrier, no symptoms)	DD (affected)

This means that the probability of having normal children is reduced to 25%, that of having children who are carriers 50%, while there is a one-in-four chance, or a 25% probability, of having an affected child (i.e. symptomatic), and of course a carrier of the defective gene as well.

Autosomal dominant disorders

The carrier of the defective gene here is also the affected. Consider if only *one* parent has the defective gene:

	Mother's genes: N	N
Father's genes: N	NN (normal)	NN (normal)
D	DN (carrier and affected)	DN (carrier and affected)

This shows the probability of having an affected or unaffected child to be 50/50.

Now consider the case where *both parents* are carriers (as well as being affected):

	Mother's genes: N	D
Father's genes: N	NN (Normal)	ND (affected)
D	DN (affected)	DD (lethal dose)

This distribution shows that the probability of having a normal child is 25%, with a 50% probability of having an affected child. There is a 25% probability of losing the fetus (usually by spontaneous abortion), as a double dose of the defective gene is lethal.

X-linked disorders

In this category, the disordered gene is carried only by the X chromosome of the 23rd pair, the sex chromosomes. Since females have two X chromosomes, the defective X acts like a recessive gene in the female but a dominant one in the male. Therefore, there is a much higher probability of the disorder to be passed from mother to son.

Where the *mother only* carries the gene, she will not be affected. With a non-carrier father, the transmission distribution will be:

	Mother's genes: Nx	Dx
Father's genes: Nx	NxNx (unaffected girl)	NxDx (carrier girl)
Ny	NyNx (unaffected boy)	NyDx (affected/carrier boy)

This indicates that, in all probability, of the female children half will be normal, and half will be carriers without the symptoms. Of the male children, half will be unaffected, half will be affected.

Finally the scenario where *both parents* have the defective gene, with the female as the carrier only and the affected male:

	Mother's genes: Nx	Dx
Father's genes: Ny	NyNx (unaffected boy)	NyDx (affected boy)
Dx	DxNx (unaffected carrier girl)	DxDx (affected carrier girl

The probability is 50% for a male child to inherit the disorder. Half the time the female child may be affected by the disorder, and half the time she is likely to be a carrier only. You can see that it is possible to have female children affected by X-linked disorders but the incidence of this is very low, possibly because of genetic counselling or the overtness of the symptom in the father. Haemophilia, an absence of the blood-clotting substance, is one such disorder and may lie dormant across generations before it appears in a son, much to the shock of the parents.

GENETIC AND CHROMOSOMAL DISORDERS

Recessive gene disorders

These usually imply *an enzyme deficiency* which leads to some abnormal biochemical event, such as accumulation of toxins in the nervous system or inability to process certain nutrients. Intermarriage is a common factor propagating recessive genetic disorders, since the parents have a shared gene pool and usually no overt symptoms of the disease to alert them.

Tay–Sachs disease

Characterised by a progressive degeneration of the nervous system, because the gene responsible for breaking down a toxic product into an non-toxic one in the neurons is missing. When the toxic substance accumulates in the brain, it causes brain damage and eventual death. This disease is linked to Jewish families who had a chance mutation less than 200 years ago that has since been passed on. Affected children develop normally for the first six months and then deteriorate rapidly, progressively losing all motor and cognitive skills. Their life-expectancy is about five years.

Phenylketonuria (PKU)

Characterised by the newborn's inability to process the amino acid phenylalanine, which is found in meat protein and milk. Food-processing technology has made this substance appear even in diet cola! When it accumulates in the body it is toxic to the nervous system, causing mental retardation. With a phenylalanine-free diet the physical effects can be controlled, although Australian parents of these children report a high level of anxiety and stress (Cole, 1987).

Cystic fibrosis

Characterised by the incorrect functioning of the glands controlling the production of mucus, sweat, tears and saliva, where the sweat tastes salty and thick mucus in the lungs makes breathing difficult. The amounts of nutrients, particularly the fat content, required by these children are considerably higher, due to an impaired fatty acid absorption mechanism. Symptoms include cough, recurring pneumonia, small size and enlarged fingertips. Early diagnosis, and antibiotic and other treatment, has improved the quality and span of life.

Sickle cell anaemia

Characterised by the sickle shape of the red blood cells, which lack the full capacity to carry oxygen. This results in poor physical growth and secondary infections, such as pneumonia. People of African origin seem most vulnerable to this disease.

Dominant gene disorders

These usually involve *structural and physical* abnormalities. Although a family history of the disease is common, individuals may carry a *new* mutation (one that took place in the cell-division phase after conception) without such lineage.

Huntington chorea

Symptoms include jerky movements and progressive mental deterioration. These usually appear in middle age, so the defect can unknowingly be passed on to the offspring. It is traced to a family of British immigrants who lived in New York in the 18th century.

Marfan syndrome

Characterised by tall, thin stature with long, skinny limbs, hypermobility (overextended range of motion) of joints, visual abnormalities, and normal intelligence.

Neurofibromatosis (von Recklinghausen disease)

Characterised by multiple 'café-au-lait' (coffee with milk) spots on the body, as well as nerve tumours (*neurofibromas*), which can cause serious damage if the growth is on critical areas such as the auditory nerve. The disease shows a wide variability, from spots only to serious disfigurement, although intelligence is usually not affected.

X-linked disorders

These are usually transmitted from mother to son. Besides causing physical disabilities, approximately 25% of the intellectual deficits in males, as well as 10% of the learning disabilities in females are attributed to X-linked disorders (Uchida, Freeman, Jamro et al., 1983).

Muscular dystrophy, Duchenne type

Characterised by muscular weakness which appears by middle childhood, progressing to total debilitation necessitating the use of a wheelchair usually in adolescence. The disease affects all muscles, and becomes fatal when the heart and the diaphragm muscles (needed for breathing) become involved.

Haemophilia

Characterised by the missing blood-clotting agent Factor VIII, where a minor injury or accident can precipitate uncontrolled bleeding. Bruising is severe and frequent injection of the missing factor is required. It can also cause muscle contractures, bone deformities, and is often accompanied by chronic illnesses.

Fragile X syndrome

Characterised by mental retardation, and thought to be the most common form of hereditary retardation (see Chapter 11). Physical features associated with the disorder are a prominent jaw, large ears and large testes. Behaviour problems, hyperactivity and autistic features are also associated with the condition; it accounts for 10% of mental retardation in Australia and New Zealand (Hay, 1986).

Colour blindness

Characterised by an inability to distinguish red and green, this is also transmitted by the X chromosome.

Chromosomal abnormalities

These are usually sporadic malformations and take place after conception, and are not dependent on the above-stated inheritance patterns. That is to say, although some of these 'mishaps' are related to some variables (e.g. Down syndrome and maternal age), they are basically random errors. They occur in 3%–8% of all fertilised eggs because of faulty cell division, leaving the egg with too many or too few chromosomes. Of such abnormalities 90% are spontaneously aborted soon after conception, with only about 1% of live births being affected.

At this point, let us make a distinction between two terms: *inherited* refers to characteristics that a child is born with which have the genetic inheritance from one or both parents; *congenital* refers to characteristics the child is born with which are not necessarily inherited but have occurred during intrauterine life.

The following are some chromosomal abnormalities resulting in birth defects (Buyse, 1990).

Down syndrome

Perhaps the best known of the (congenital) chromosomal aberrations. It is characterised by mental retardation, small head size, low muscle tone, slanted eyes, fine skin and hair, and heart defects. The most frequent aberration occurs on the 21st pair of chromosomes, which has an extra one (trisomy 21). I have more to say on this disorder in Chapter 11. Other extra chromosome disorders, like those on pair numbers 13 and 18, tend to show much more severe abnormalities and a very short life span.

Cri du chat (cry of the cat)

Characterised by the deletion of the one arm of the chromosome pair five. The newborn's cry is shrill and cat-like. Effects include abnormal heart development, as well as retarded physical and cognitive development. Medical advances have lengthened the life-expectancy of afflicted children.

Other chromosomal aberrations occur on the *sex chromosomes* (23rd pair), and are reflected as dysfunctions, primarily in sexual characteristics:

Kleinefelter syndrome

Characterised by an extra X chromosome in the male (XXY). Infertility, small testes, lanky limbs and feminine appearance are typical, with possibly mild mental retardation. Many such children are not recognised until adolescence. Administering of male hormones masculinises body characteristics.

Turner syndrome

The only known disorder where survival is possible with a missing chromosome. It is characterised by a single X chromosome in the female (XO instead of XX), with sterility, underdeveloped reproductive organs and breasts, and short height. Treatment with hormones at adolescence leads to normalised sexual appearance, but does not alter sterility.

XYY syndrome (super male)

Characterised by taller than average male, with normal sex organs but abnormal brain patterns, causing seizures and mild retardation. Although such males tend to be more impulsive and have more acne, the initial speculation about the extra Y chromosome being the 'criminal' chromosome (as the disorder was first recognised in inmate populations) is not substantiated.

Prenatal diagnosis

Most pregnancies will not need measures to assess the prenatal risk of genetic or chromosomal abnormalities. Where there is some risk, the genetic counsellor and attending specialist may recommend a variety of prenatal screening procedures, a decision that needs to be made prudently since there is minor risk associated with most procedures. One of the most significant factors making such an evaluation necessary is the mother's age, as this bears a significant relationship to the birth of an infant with Down syndrome.

Down syndrome: nature or nurture?

- The incidence is about 1 in 2000 in 25-year-old mothers, 1 in 400 by the age of 35, 1 in 90 by 40, and 1 in 32 by 45 (Hook & Fabia, 1978).
- The defect originates in the egg 85% of the time, in the sperm 15% of the time (Dagna-Bricarelli, Pierluigi, Grasso, et al., 1990).
- Fathers exposed to various pesticides and toxins are at a significantly higher risk of having babies with Down syndrome (Olshan, Baird & Teschke, 1989).

Screening procedures

Below are some of the prenatal screening and diagnostic procedures (Bathshaw & Perret, 1992):

Amniocentesis. This is the procedure where a small quantity of *amniotic fluid* is drawn from the abdomen of a pregnant woman between 14 and 17 weeks of gestation; the needle is often monitored by ultrasound to avoid puncturing the fetus. The amniotic fluid, which bathes the fetus, has some fetal cells in it, which are removed and cultured for about two weeks preparatory to *karyotyping* for chromosomal analysis. Some metabolic disorders in which enzymes are missing can be identified through analysis of the fluid, by examining the levels of *hexosaminidase* for Tay–Sachs disease, and *alpha-fetoprotein (AFP)* for spina bifida, a disorder where the spinal column fails to enclose properly.

Serum AFP.   Also used as a screening tool for Down syndrome and spina bifida (between 14 and 18 weeks of gestation) this test is prone to error and needs to be followed up by more definitive procedures.

Chorionic villus sampling.   Performed between eight and ten weeks of pregnancy, this newer method can reveal as much as amniocentesis, except for spina bifida. A minute amount of *placental* tissue is removed through the vagina by suction and is analysed directly under the microscope. The shorter period before obtaining results and earlier detection (prior to the movement of the fetus) are advantages, although the procedure is slightly more risky than amniocentesis (0.5% vs 1% risk of miscarriage).

Ultrasound (ultrasonography).   This uses sound waves to create an image of the fetus by different refractions from bone and soft tissue. It can produce an amazingly detailed representation. Some conditions that can be revealed are spina bifida, various anomalies associated with the skull (such as *hydrocephalus*), Down syndrome, and congenital heart abnormalities. The size and gender of the fetus can also be determined. This quite safe procedure can be supplemented with *magnetic resonance imaging (MRI)* if clearer pictures are required to investigate a possible abnormality.

DNA studies.   These can be performed, with varying degrees of certainty, on most of the 2000 or so genetic mutations that have now been established (and whose identification is rapidly increasing, thanks to the advances in genetic biology). The specific location of the gene responsible for the mutation needs to be known; among the diseases that can be identified by DNA testing are PKU, muscular dystrophy and cystic fibrosis.

Fetal therapy.   With the aim of treating the affected fetus in utero by providing it with the missing enzyme or replacing the defective gene, this procedure enjoys limited success at present—it is very promising, however, in averting serious disabilities. Already, successful in-utero surgical interventions are possible with hydrocephalus (where a shunt is placed for drainage of the excess fluid produced in the brain) and bladder obstructions.

PRENATAL DEVELOPMENT

Conception occurs when a mature female egg (*ovum*) in the fallopian tubes is penetrated by one of the many millions of male sperm. The fertilised egg then travels to attach itself to the walls of the uterus. If there are two ova, and they are both fertilised, *dizygotic* or fraternal twins result, each with a distinct genetic blueprint. If, on the other hand, the one fertilised ovum divides such that two organisms are sustained, the twins are *monozygotic,* or identical. After 38 weeks, or about 265 days of the normal intrauterine gestation period, the baby is born. Equal thirds of pregnancy are known as *trimesters.* In terms of developmental characteristics, however, pregnancy has three distinct stages.

The germinal stage

This is the first ten to 14 days after conception. The cells start replicating themselves in the first four days, and cell differentiation occurs before the *zygote* implants itself on the uterine wall. Of its three layers, the *ectoderm* develops into skin, spinal cord and the teeth; the *mesoderm* develops into the blood vessels, muscle and bone tissue; and the *endoderm* becomes the internal organs.

The embryonic stage

The first task in this stage, which usually takes about two months, is the production of the *chorionic gonadotrophin* hormone, which stops the tiny embryo being washed away by menstruation. The support structures for the embryo, the *amniotic sac* and fluid, the *placenta* and the *umbilical cord,* are formed. The placenta lies between the mother's and embryo's circulation systems, thus providing the nutrients through the mother's blood and acting like a filter for many larger (but not all) harmful substances for the embryo. *The embryonic stage or the first trimester is the most vulnerable stage for the developing organism, because all organ systems are basically differentiated at this time.* Here is a glimpse of what has happened by the time this *organogenesis* is complete:

- By day 20, when it is less than half-a-centimetre long, the neural tube folds to form the spinal cord;
- By day 28, the structures for the eyes, the ears and the jaw are formed;
- By day 35, the heart begins to form, and the arm and leg buds are visible;
- By day 56, the embryo is about 4 cm, the heart is beating 60 times per minute, the toes and fingers are formed, and the brain is half the size of its (recognisably human) body.

The fetal stage

This lasts for the next seven months, during which the body parts and organ systems are enlarged and refined. Some milestones in fetal development are:

- By 12 weeks, sex can be determined; eyelids and lips are formed;
- By 16 weeks, the mother feels the fetus kicking; he is about 20 cm in height and 170 g in weight by now.
- By 20 weeks, hair growth begins and he can suck his thumb; half the birth height is achieved.
- By 24 weeks, he is able to breathe, and has a chance of survival if born prematurely.

The final three months of the fetal period are primarily devoted to weight (half the birthweight is achieved by 32 weeks) and length gain, and to the establishment of connections between the brain cells. By the time a full-term infant is born, he weighs about 3200 g and is about 50 cm in length.

Effects of the environment on prenatal development

So far, we have mostly explored the maturational factors that propel development—that is, the forces of *nature* which unfold because of species-specific developmental organisation, timing and predictability. These forces thrive in their natural setting, in the absence of environmental prompts; *nurture* can provide the optimal conditions for this unfolding to occur, although it can neither speed it along nor contribute to its characteristics. However, similar to a number of 'nature' mutations or accidents we have discussed, nurture can adversely affect prenatal development, particularly in the first trimester. These factors are collectively known as *teratogens*. They can be due to diseases contracted by the mother during pregnancy, or to the substances she ingested or smoked; they can also be the result of an exposure of the mother to a variety of toxic substances. Here are some of the better-known ones.

Rubella.   Also known as German measles, Rubella is most dangerous when contracted by the mother in the first few weeks of pregnancy. Hearing impairment, cataracts and heart defects are the most common abnormalities. If contracted in the latter six months of pregnancy, the probability of the fetus suffering an adverse effect is only around 10% (Moore & Persaud, 1993). If the woman has not been immunised for rubella in childhood, she can be vaccinated safely provided this precedes the pregnancy by three months.

AIDS.   According to US statistics, AIDS is the seventh leading cause of death in children from birth to four years of age. Transmission rate from infected mother to infant is about 20%–25%; mothers who are treated with AZT show a significantly lower transmission rate (Centers for Disease Control, 1994).

Cytomegalovirus (CMV) and genital herpes.   These can both be transmitted to the infant at birth if the mother is in the active phase of the illness. Mental retardation and deafness are common symptoms.

Other maternal infections causing fetal malformations.   Chickenpox, toxoplasmosis and syphilis are included in this category.

Smoking tobacco and marijuana. Both forms of smoking seem to have a similar effect, of constricting the blood flow to the placenta from which the fetus derives its nutrients, which results in low birthweight. Higher rates of behaviour problems and learning difficulties have also been reported in children whose mothers smoked heavily during pregnancy (Fergusson, Horwood, & Lynskey, 1993).

Alcohol ingestion. This has a serious negative effect on the developing fetus. *Fetal alcohol syndrome (FAS)* is the leading cause of mental retardation in the USA (Streissguth, Aase, Clarren, Randells, LaDue & Smith, 1991). These children have small heads and facial deformities, mild to severe cognitive impairment, and attention-related problems (see Chapter 11).

Cocaine. While this drug appears to produce no recognisable deformities, cocaine is associated with prematurity, low birthweight, and 'withdrawal symptoms' after birth.

Radiation. A well-established teratogen, the effect of radiation on the fetus is dependent on the amount as well as the time of exposure in gestation. Exposure of less than 5 rads, typically prescribed for diagnostic X-rays, has not been observed to cause malformations or growth retardation; nevertheless, caution and use of alternative procedures such as ultrasound are advised (Bathshaw & Perret, 1992).

Thalidomide. The crippling effects of this drug remain the most salient in teratogenic medications. When taken between days 21 and 35 of pregnancy, it arrested normal growth of the arms and legs (Newman, 1985).

Most anticonvulsant medications. These may result in craniofacial defects and developmental delays in children (Holmes, 1988).

Chemotherapeutic agents. Used in cancer treatment, they are also thought to cause fetal malformations.

DES (diethylstilboestrol). A synthetic oestrogen given to pregnant women to avoid miscarriages, it seems to have an adverse effect as well. Daughters of these women have been found to have higher incidence of some cancers, and 30% of their sons have been reported as being infertile (Rosenblith, 1992).

Lead. Mainly obtained from base paint and petrol, it is also associated with mild developmental delays.

Severe malnutrition. Very early in pregnancy, it is associated with higher risk of miscarriage as well as higher incidence of spina bifida, hydrocephalus and prematurity (Brent, 1986). Malnourishment later in the pregnancy results in low birthweight.

Principles of development

The following principles are evident from our brief review of prenatal development and the forces shaping it.

- Development is an orderly and *sequential* process, which progresses from the simple to the complex.
- Development is characterised by *differentiation* (increased specificity of function) towards its integration with a whole.
- The direction of development is *cephalocaudal* (from top to bottom; brain forms before the legs), and *proximodistal* (from the centre to the periphery; spinal cord develops before the arms).
- Development is particularly sensitive to influences during *critical periods*.
- Both *heredity* and *environment*, as well as their *interaction*, influence the process of development.

CONCLUSIONS

We have reviewed the building blocks of our genetic constitution, the cells and chromosomes, and looked at some patterns of transmission of genetic disorders from one generation to the next. Prenatal development and environmental influences seem crucial in the health and wellbeing of the infant, and medical science is rapidly advancing in prenatal screening and diagnosis of various disorders. In Chapter 4, we take a closer look at early brain development as it relates to all functions in development; the mutuality of the influences of heredity and environment will become even more intriguing.

3

Birth and the newborn child

Cultural variations in childbirth poignantly remind us of the nature–nurture interaction. We will review the birthing process from a Western cultural perspective, keeping in mind the diversity that is likely to occur in an experience so universally human.

Birth had no pangs for the young mother. She knelt down, rested her buttocks on her heels, pressed her breath, and the baby was born, so easily, so free from pain and obstruction, that there was rarely a cry. The operation performed on the young girls and their initiation to womanhood at an early age tends to this painless birth. The baby is left on the ground, a mother or elder sister will snip the umbilical cord with her strong and long nails, leaving two or three inches on the navel. This is tied in a loose knot and flattened down, and later, when it dries and falls off, hair is netted about it in a little ring, to be hung around the baby's neck and left there for weeks and months. It is supposed to contain the child's spirit existence, and when it withers off the baby has absorbed the spirit. The baby is massaged tenderly with soft ashes and charcoal.

Daisy M. Bates (1966). *The passing of the Aborigines: A lifetime spent among the natives of Australia* (p.235). London: J. Murray.

LABOUR AND DELIVERY

By the sixth month of pregnancy, the fetus establishes a head-down position in the mother's pelvis (referred to as *vertex presentation*), after which the prospects of turning around in the womb will be progressively more difficult, given the fetus' growing size. If the presentation is not so, birth complications may occur. The time surrounding the final stages of pregnancy and delivery is known as the *perinatal period*.

Normal labour generally proceeds in three stages (Biswas & Craigo, 1994). In the *first stage of labour,* two important processes prepare the mother for delivery. The opening at the bottom of the uterus or the *cervix* must widen (*dilation*), allowing for the moulding of the baby's head to the birth canal. Also, the pelvic bones must spread out (*effacement*), which usually starts some weeks before delivery. Commonly, there are three phases within this stage, although their length and intensity may vary.

- In the *early* phase, the contractions are relatively far apart; discomfort is moderate.
- The *active* phase begins when the cervical dilation is 3–4 cm and lasts until 8 cm; contractions are more frequent and intense.
- In the *transition* phase, the cervix dilates a further 2–3 cm; contractions are strong and discomfort intense.

During the *second stage*, which takes about an hour, the baby's head pushes through the birth canal and becomes visible at the vaginal opening; the mother usually has an urge to push, to ease the baby out. The baby arrives.

In the *third stage,* the placenta or afterbirth is expelled.

A great majority of all babies are born through such uncomplicated vaginal delivery. The infant's nose and mouth are suctioned and the mother has the baby in her arms, counting fingers and toes usually with joy and relief. There is unfortunately a small percentage of parents and babies for whom problems arise, which may be due to factors intrinsic to the mother or the infant.

HIGH-RISK PREGNANCIES

The first group of women at risk of perinatal complications may also be those who are at environmental risk: they themselves may have received little prenatal care, inadequate nutrition, and suffer the chronic ills of society in general, and poverty in particular, such as drug and alcohol abuse. The probability of complications also rises for women at the two ends of the fertility spectrum—that is, teenage mothers as well as those over 40 years of age. Various illnesses and conditions may also predispose women to birth complications or premature delivery:

Diabetes.   If not controlled carefully, this may have harmful effects. The fetus' pancreas produces excess insulin for the condition, which results in abnormally low levels of blood sugar levels or *hypoglycaemia* which, if not treated, results in brain damage in the infant.

Herpes virus infection.   An active infection can be transmitted from the mother to the relatively immune-deficient infant during delivery, where it causes death in 60% of infected infants and significant neurological damage in half of the survivors (Kibrick, 1980).

Alcohol consumption.   This and substances such as *cocaine* constrict the blood vessels and therefore starve the placenta, resulting in prematurity, placental separation and fetal distress in delivery (Rosenak, Diamant, Yaffe, et al., 1990).

Hyptertension.   Pregnant women sometimes have elevated blood pressure in the second half of pregnancy which, if combined with *oedema* (accumulation of fluid in tissue) and/or protein in the urine, results in a condition known as *toxaemia of pregnancy* or *pre-eclampsia*. The condition will persist until after delivery, and carries a significant risk of prematurity and intrauterine growth retardation (Gilstrap, 1990).

Placental abnormalities.   In *placenta praevia*, the placenta is abnormally located over the cervical opening instead of lying in the top portion of the uterus, and requires careful monitoring and bedrest ('Sophia Loren's illness'). In *placenta abruptio*, the normal placenta is detached or torn, a condition associated with hypertension or accidents. Profuse vaginal bleeding may place the mother's and fetus' life at risk.

Premature rupture of the amniotic sac.   This condition may precipitate premature labour or lead to infection or fetal deformities.

Structural abnormalities.   The mother's pelvis may put her at risk as well. It may be too small to allow the passage of the baby's head (*cephalopelvic disproportion*) or it may dilate too early (*incompetent cervix*), which can result in premature delivery or miscarriage.

Uterine contractions.   The strength and frequency may also have adverse effects. If the uterus contracts too forcefully, it can interfere with fetal circulation, causing oxygen deprivation or bleeding in the brain. With too weak contractions, labour will not progress normally.

Breech delivery.   When the baby's head is not positioned on the cervix, there are some potential problems—mainly, prolonged labour and decreased oxygen supply (*hypoxia* or *anoxia*[1]). Since the brain can tolerate only a few minutes of such oxygen deprivation before sustaining degrees of damage, the delivery may be by caesarean section.

Birth defects.   Defects such as hydrocephalus can lead to complications in delivery: 5% of stillborn infants have been reported to have major chromosomal abnormalities and malformations (Valdes-Dapena & Arey, 1970).

Multiple pregnancies.   Twins also pose some risk. The first baby may be delivered uneventfully, but the second, whose head is usually placed in the

1   Remember the prefixes that determine the AMOUNT and QUALITY of something.
  • *Hypo* is under (too little), as in hypoxia, or hypoactivity.
  • *Hyper* is over (too much) as in hyperventilation, or hyperactivity.
  • *A* is none (lack of) as in anoxia, or atrophy (total wasting away of e.g. muscles).
  • *Dys* is malfunctioning, as in muscular dystrophy.

incorrect breech position, may be vulnerable to complications via a *prolapsed umbilical cord*, where the cord may choke the baby.

Apgar score

A *neonatal* (newborn) evaluation measure which reflects the health and status of the baby, an Apgar score is given at one minute and five to ten minutes after birth. It is a routine measure, particularly for babies who have undergone some distress during delivery. Each of the five attributes is given a score of 0, 1 or 2, indicating the level of function. Table 3.1 shows the measures (Francis, Self & Horowitz, 1987, pp. 731–732).

	0	1	2
Heart rate	Absent	Less than 100/min	More than 100/min
Respiratory effort	Absent	Slow, irregular	Normal; crying
Muscle tone	Flabby	Limited flexion	Active motion
Stimulation of feet	No response	Grimace	Cry
Colour of skin	Blue/pale all over	Blue arms and legs	Pink all over[a]

TABLE 3.1

Apgar scoring for neonates

[a]   What happens on this measure with dark-pigmented babies? 'Check their palms and soles' (Dr Wittekind, 1997; personal communication).

As you can see, 10 is the maximum score obtainable. It is quite common to have scores lower than 10 in the first round, since babies usually have blue fingers and toes on arrival. At the five-minute evaluation, the majority of babies score 9 and 10; 7 or better indicates that the infant is not in danger. A score of 4–6 indicates that the infant requires assistance in establishing normal breathing patterns. Scores lower than 3 indicate that the baby is in a critical condition and requires active intervention.

A low Apgar score usually signals that the baby is more likely to have a developmental disability, although such children may proceed to normal development. Nelson (1989) reports that 12% of a group of babies with Apgars lower than 4 at five minutes developed disabling conditions such as cerebral palsy, mental retardation and seizures.

PHYSIOLOGICAL CHANGES AT BIRTH

Birth signifies the transition from an aquatic life, with (an umbilical) life-support system, to an air-breathing, independent one. Thus, the most important changes the infant will adjust to immediately in her new existence will be in her respiratory and circulatory systems. Others, of course, will be in her ability to regulate temperature and to absorb nutrients in this new and challenging medium.

At birth, the lungs are collapsed and need the pressure of a good, strong cry to open up the *alveoli* (the tiny air sacs) so that the air can get in and exchange of oxygen can take place. For the lungs not to collapse at exhalation, the alveoli are coated with the substance *surfactant*, which allows the alveoli to adhere to the outer lining of the lungs; inadequacy of this substance causes the common respiratory problems in prematurely born babies.

In the fetus, the blood bypasses the lungs. Two flaps need to close these openings in the first few days of postnatal life for proper circulation to occur. Also, there is a detour around the liver allowing the fetus to process the waste in the placenta through the umbilical arteries and veins. These structures should close to allow the liver to cleanse the toxic products.

A strong *rooting* (orienting to the nipple when the side of the mouth is stimulated) and *sucking reflex* needs to be active to enable the infant to obtain nourishment from the breast or the bottle.

Most babies born prematurely are not yet ready to go through these physiological transformations, and require technological and medical support as they mature towards an independent sustenance of life. Before we take a closer look at them, let us investigate some of the causes of illness and death in newborns.

Illness and death in the newborn

Unquestionably, the most vulnerable time in our life span is the first month of life after birth. The cited incidence of severe illness for this period is 1 in 100, and of death, 1 in 1000. Below are some of the causes (Dollfus, Patetta, Siegel, et al., 1990).

Asphyxia (suffocation resulting in anoxia; oxygen deprivation). Resulting from many of the factors cited above, the incidence of asphyxia may fall because of fetal monitoring, which allows for preventive measures. Diffuse brain damage can occur if the deprivation is prolonged. Mental retardation, seizures, spastic quadriplegia (where all limbs are affected) are other potential outcomes.

Intracranial haemorrhage (bleeding inside the skull). Resulting from direct trauma and tearing of a blood vessel during delivery, the immature capillary blood vessels of the prematurely born baby make such bleeding more probable.

Generalised bacterial infections (sepsis or blood poisoning). The newborn is very susceptible to these because her immune system is not yet able to defend against bacteria that are harmless in the mother's system or against her environment. If not diagnosed early enough, the infection can spread rapidly throughout the infant's body and cause *meningitis*, where the brain membranes are affected. Antibiotic treatment has drastically improved survival rates, although infections remain a significant threat, accounting for about 3% of infant deaths.

Rh factor incompatibility. Incompatability between the blood groups of the infant who is Rh+ and the mother who is Rh–, it is not a threat to the baby if the mother was injected with an antibody (RhoGAM) after her first child, which prevents the formation of severe *anaemia* (depletion of red blood cells) and the accumulation of *bilirubin* (a byproduct when red blood cells die) in the liver of the infant. Jaundice or *hyperbilirubinaemia* occurs when, in utero, an occasional fetal blood cell gets into the mother's circulation system. The mother's immune system treats the Rh+ cell of the fetus as a foreign body and forms antibodies to fight it, which then cross the placenta to the fetus and proceed to destroy the fetus' blood cells. This high drama results in a severely anaemic newborn and a condition known as *kernicterus*.

In addition to the genetic and chromosomal abnormalities (discussed in Chapter 2) that may cause the death of newborns, there are structural abnormalities of the brain, the aetiology of which is unclear. The brains of these infants may be too small, malformed, or missing.

PREMATURITY

Infants born at least one month before the estimated date of birth, or 36 weeks' gestation, are defined as *premature*. In our discussions so far we have already mentioned that this group of infants would be at higher risk of factors interfering with normal growth and development. Obviously, the longer the gestational period, the less important such risk factors become; nevertheless, medical science has made some remarkable progress not only in keeping some tiny babies alive but also in improving their developmental outcomes. The limit for *viability* or survival of preterm infants is about 500–600 g birthweight, or about 23 weeks' gestation (Allen, Donohue & Dusman, 1993).

Another vulnerable group is the *small for gestational age (SGA)* or *low-birthweight* babies, defined as newborns whose weight is below the 10th percentile (that is, 90% of babies born at that gestational age will weigh more than the SGA infant). The SGA infant born at term may be as small as a premature infant born considerably earlier, but the physiological changes preparing the infant for extrauterine survival have been much better accomplished due to the advantage prenatal life provides.

Causes

Premature births account for 5% of all births; 20% of all premature babies are born to teenagers (Goldberg & Craig, 1983). Among the *causes* that contribute to the birth of preterm babies are inadequate prenatal care, poor nutrition, drug abuse, weak cervical muscles associated with multiple previous pregnancies, carrying twins or multiple fetuses, maternal infections in the third trimester, premature rupture of the amniotic sac, chronic maternal illness such as diabetes, and certain congenital malformations (Usher, 1987).

Characteristics

The physical and neurodevelopmental *characteristics* of the preterm infant are often evaluated on a clinical scale. Some of the salient features include the following (Ballard, Khoury, Wedig, et al., 1991):

- lack of *muscle tone*, as growth in muscle tone and decrease in joint mobility are achieved by the neurological development that takes place in the third trimester. The muscle tone gradually improves after 28 weeks and the 'rag doll' appearance of the arms and the legs decreases, together with the double-jointedness;
- *lanugo*, or fine hair all over the body, which is usually lost by 38 weeks of gestation;
- lack of skin *creases at the soles* of the feet, which develop after 32 weeks;
- *reddish skin* colour and wrinkled skin, attributed to underdeveloped fat tissue and the vessels being closer to the skin surface;
- lack of *breast buds* and *ear lobe cartilage*, which develops after 34 weeks; Underdeveloped *genital organs*, as testes in the male fully descend and labia in the female fully develop towards the end of the gestation period.

Complications

As we mentioned, a number of *complications* may be encountered with prematurely born infants, their severity being proportional to the extent of prematurity. Some common problems are listed below.

Respiratory distress syndrome (RDS). Experienced by 60% of babies born at 32 weeks or sooner, RDS develops within a few days of birth since the baby is unable yet to produce the chemical *surfactant* to keep the alveoli open. The survival rate of babies has improved from 50% in 1970 to over 90%, primarily due to treatment methods that keep a constant pressure on the alveoli and ease the baby's breathing efforts by a ventilator under positive end-expiration pressure (Usher, 1987). Other methods include surfactant sprayed directly into the lungs of the infant, and medication given to the mother shortly before delivery, which promotes the production of the substance in the fetus.

Retinopathy of prematurity (retrolental fibroplasia). A detachment of the retina that can lead to blindness, this condition is usually associated with high concentrations of oxygen given to babies with RDS. Heightened awareness of this association has reduced its incidence although careful monitoring is advised, as such tears can be treated with laser therapy if identified early (Bathshaw & Perret, 1992).

Bronchopulmonary dysplasia. Following RDS, some babies develop a chronic lung disease where the walls of the lungs thicken, making breathing a very laboured process. These children may require years of oxygen therapy, ventilators and medication to keep the air passages open.

Sudden Infant Death Syndrome (SIDS).   The premature baby's central nervous system may also not be mature enough to sustain continual breathing. Periods of non-breathing lasting for 20 seconds or more are known as *apnoea*; this is often accompanied by *brachycardia*, or a reduction in the heart rate, and is associated with SIDS (cot death): 20% of SIDS cases occur among premature infants (Goyco & Beckerman, 1990).

Intracerebral haemorrhage.   Breathing difficulties may also pave the way to bursting of blood vessels in the brain. Such bleeds occur because of the fragility of the network of blood vessels nourishing the brain, which cannot resist the lowered blood flow and raised pressure RDS produces. The areas around the *ventricles* deep within the brain seem particularly vulnerable, and as this area often contains nerve fibres controlling movement in the legs, such damage is associated with a high incidence of *spastic diplegia* in prematurely born children (Graziani, Past, Stanley et al., 1986).

Other concerns.   These include jaundice, low blood sugar levels (*hypoglycemia*), and *hypothermia* (body heat loss due to inadequate fatty tissue). Because the feeding reflexes are often absent, the babies need to be fed intravenously or through a gastric tube. The protected and highly regulated environment of the incubator is essential to the survival of these babies within neonatal intensive care units (NICU) until they have stabilised (Bathshaw & Perret, 1992).

Developmental outcomes

Improvements in developmental outcomes of premature babies are a testament to the success of medical breakthroughs in the field of neonatology. As a matter of fact, the closer to recent times such a baby is born, the better the long-term prognosis and developmental outcome seems to be (Perlman, Claris, Hao, et al., 1995). The long-term outcomes depend not only on the quality of hospital care available to the infant, but also on how small the baby was and what kind of family she grows up in (Bendersky & Lewis, 1994). Most preterm infants born more than 1500 g who were not SGA seem to catch up to their peers within a couple of years. Smaller ones, particularly those below 1000 g, have significantly higher rates of long-term problems, such as neurological impairments, lower IQ, smaller size, and difficulty in school.

The results of two longitudinal studies, Australian (Victorian Infant Collaborative Study Group, 1991) and American (Hack, Taylor, Klein, Eiben, Schatschneider & Mercuri-Minich, 1994), which have followed up low-birthweight premature infants, are summarised in Table 3.2. Please note that the Australian study had a larger sample size than the American study (351 vs 243), but both included the *micro* premature infants (500–750 g) with a survival rate of only 25% (89 out of 351) and 28% (68 out of 243), respectively. It would be a fair estimate to say that many more of those babies might well have survived today, had they had the benefit of current medical technology.

	Australian study: 351 infants born in 1979–1980	US study: 243 infants born in 1982–1986	US study comparison group
Criteria	500–999 g	Less than 750 g	750–1500 g
No. of survivors (all followed up)	89	68	65
Assessment age	8 years	7 years	7 years
With severe/multiple disabilities[a]	21%	38%	18%
With moderate disabilities[b]	19%	29%	20%

[a] IQ below 70, deafness, blindness, cerebral palsy.
[b] IQ between 70 and 85, significant learning problems.

ADAPTING TO THE NEWBORN

The arrival of a baby into a family is a major transition, and requires a considerable adjustment at the best of times. For most adults, the role of parent brings with it intense feelings of satisfaction and a greater sense of purpose, as well as self-worth. But such joy is not without strain: in particular, marital satisfaction is reported to decline in the first months after the birth of the first child (Glenn, 1990), with a strong sense of loss of time and intimacy in the marriage relationship itself (Feldman, 1987).

Families who have the responsibility of care for a premature baby face additional challenges in the psychological adjustment to the process: premature infants tend to be irritable and cry a lot; their poor sleep–wake cycles can be exhausting for the sleep-deprived parents. Feeding is difficult due to immature suckling patterns and a tendency to vomit afterwards. Then there are the health concerns and fears, often laced with guilt and anxiety, even estrangement. There are medications to be given, respiration monitors to be set up; and sometimes all this responsibility falls on the shoulders of a teenage mother, with the minimum of social, emotional and economic support systems for sanity, survival and resourcefulness demanded by this role.

Silcock (1984) made a longitudinal investigation of 24 Australian mothers and fathers over a period of time, from the birth of a baby who weighed less than 1500 g, through to several months of age in which the infant returned to a normal home life. She identified four stages and tasks in this arduous process.

1. *Coping with grief.* All parents had to cope with the possibility of their infant not surviving. Many also experienced a reactive grief for not having had a normal, full-term infant. Another important aspect of the grief

reaction was the surrendering of the fantasy of the 'perfect baby' and acceptance of the preterm baby as theirs. Mothers who were not able to come to terms with acceptance disparaged their infant by two years of age, when development had objectively reached normal.

2. *Dealing with a sense of failure.* Mothers, and some fathers, were inclined to feel that they had failed in the task of normal child-bearing. The support extended by the spouse, friends and extended family reduced the feelings of loss of self-confidence and self-esteem, while their response to fear, avoidance and unhappiness exacerbated the feelings of failure and inadequacy.

3. *Resumption of normal parenting.* In addition to the successful resolution of the first two tasks, the frequency of the mother's visits to the baby during the hospital stay was the best predictor of the mother–infant relationship once the baby came home.

4. *Understanding the needs of the preterm babies.* Despite the support provided by the hospital staff in educating the parents on the special needs of premature babies, ten mothers proved either unable or unwilling to come to terms with the special style of care their infants required at home. Five of these mothers were teenagers.

The needs, particularly of the young mothers without adequate support structures, and their ambivalence, is well highlighted in these findings. Both the children's and the parents' wellbeing may be at stake in the absence of adequate supports. Adults have been found to react with more physiological stress and aversion to the cries of the premature infant than the full-term infant (Frodi & Lamb, 1980), which may explain why premature infants incur a higher risk of child abuse.

NEWBORN CHARACTERISTICS AND COMPETENCIES

One of the most exciting developments in psychology over the past decades is in the way we have changed our conception of the newborn infant from a purely reflexive creature, who existed quite helplessly in a 'booming buzzing confusion', to one who is already wired to interact with the parents and affect the nature of the interaction, one whose perceptual systems have already been tuned to the significant sensory experiences around her, and one who is much more competent that we thought possible. We will review the first year of life and its crowning achievements in Chapter 5. Here we present a brief review of typical patterns and behaviours of the neonate, before we look at that momentous first year of life in more detail.

■   In terms of *physical growth*, she will go through the fastest growth period in her entire life, where the average birth weight of 3 kg will have doubled by the fourth month, and nearly doubled again over the next eight months, with an average weight of 10–12 kg by the first birthday. Her height also increases steadily at a rate of about 2.5 cm a month each month in the first 12 months.

- From birth to adulthood, the head (housing the brain that already contains all the neurons the baby will ever have) will only double in size, whereas the trunk will triple, the arms quadruple, and the legs and feet grow fivefold in size.

- The first month of life is governed by the survival activities of sleeping, crying and feeding. These basic aspects of the baby's life will demand as much flexibility and change of habits from the parents as it does from the baby's transition, until the baby and the household fall into rather predictable, harmonious patterns.

- Infants and toddlers sleep longer than adolescents, but newborns sleep the longest. Much to the dismay of the parents, however, the 16 hours of necessary sleep are not taken as an uninterrupted night sleep but as a series of naps.

- Newborns spend at least half of their sleep in *Rapid Eye Movement (REM)* sleep, while adults spend about 25%. REM sleep is typically associated with dreaming, and is accompanied by fluttering of the eyelids. The EEG pattern, which reveals the electrical activity of the brain, indicates that REM sleep closely resembles wakeful attentiveness. It is thought that REM sleep provides the newborn with some mental stimulation, and activates the brain centres and neural pathways; this will be needed to process information from the environment at later stages.

- The remaining 50% of neonate sleep is non-REM sleep, which is a period of quiet relaxation during which brain activity switches to a slow, synchronised pattern, bodily muscles relax, breathing slows down, and the body's temperature is reduced.

- Newborns—in the absence of colic, which distresses them for hours, particularly in the evening—have different *cries* for hunger, pain and anger, and engage in crying from 2% to 11% of the time (Korner, Hutchinson, Koperski, Kramer, & Schneider, 1981).

- The reflexes exhibited by the newborn can be thought of in two categories: the *adaptive reflexes* help the baby survive. The rooting reflex mentioned above, as well as sucking, swallowing, coughing, sneezing and withdrawing from a painful stimulus all have clear utility for the infant in sustaining and preserving life.

- *Primitive reflexes*, on the other hand, are reactions mediated by lower centres of the brain, and will become extinct as more complex patterns of reflexes replace them (see Chapter 5). *Moro reflex*, where the baby startles by throwing her arms out and arching her back, and *Babinski reflex*, where the stimulation of the soles of the feet yields a spreading of the toes, are among the primitive reflexes.

- By one month of age, the baby is usually able to hold her chin up lying on her stomach, although the perceptual abilities are considerably ahead of the motor skills at this age. While the repetitiveness of movement in their limited motor skills repertoire appears random, it does seem to serve a rehearsal function: for example, babies are observed to peak their kicking movements immediately before crawling (Thelen, 1981).

We review the perceptual skills of infants at some length in Chapter 5; nevertheless, the following points are a helpful summary.

- Newborns can *visually focus* their eyes to a distance of 20 cm, an ideal distance to engage in eye contact with the mother from the very onset of the feeding experience, the crucible of the social exchange.
- At about one month, the baby shows a preference for the human face and focuses on its perimeter, i.e. the hairline and the chin (Cohen, DeLoache & Strauss, 1979).
- She can hear sounds in the pitch and loudness ranges of human voice, and can discriminate the mother's voice, with which she is soothed.
- She can discriminate all four tastes, with a distinct preference for the sweet, and can discriminate her mother's milk odour from others (MacFarlane, 1977).

CONCLUSIONS

The neonate faces a significant challenge in adaptation to the new environment of extrauterine life. Perhaps the most important attribute the infant is born with is the ability to engage the carer(s) in a mutual social interaction. Despite her limited motor skills, the perceptual apparatus of the neonate already appears primed to promote and regulate this social dance. She responds to caring, and very quickly tantalises the parents with smiles and preverbal communications, moulds to their body when held; she can even take turns (Kaye, 1982) with the mother in feeding routines. All of this transaction and interactivity is the very crucible of affective, communicative and, in a substantial sense, cognitive development, as we will discover in the next chapter on infancy. If it takes two to tango, the baby knows the steps already!

We also need to be aware of the difficulties involved in knowing or learning these steps when it comes to the social dance between an infant with a biological vulnerability and her carers.

4

The developing brain: neuroscience and early childhood

All aspects of our adaptive life, including thought, perception, language, emotion, as well as fine and gross motor skills, are mediated by the brain. A vast majority of the developmental disorders of childhood are attributable to some brain-related event. The human brain holds amazing mysteries, especially during the early childhood years. As neuroscience unfolds to inform us of some of its wonders, we come to realise how necessary it is to understand and apply this knowledge to our practice with young children.

At birth, the infant's brain already possesses all the *neurones* (the nerve cells) it will ever have! Unlike the other organ systems, which grow and regenerate their cells, the brain does not grow in the numbers of the neural cells that it has. What contributes to neural development and gain in brain weight is growth in the *connections* between the cells via their fibres, which literally sprout and reach out and touch each other. They establish links and networks that will expand and strengthen as the experiential repertoire of the baby expands.

Some neural connections are already 'hard-wired', probably by the genes in the fertilised egg, allowing the newborn to regulate his breathing, heart rate and body temperature, and to manifest reflexes, all of which are necessary for survival. Other neural connections are awaiting the experience that will trigger the circuitry. The analogy between computers and the brain is quite well justified (although the most powerful computer known to man cannot come close to simulating the complexity of even a single nerve cell): at birth, the brain is like state-of-the-art hardware (nature); experience (nurture) is like the software that will bring about its functions, with nearly infinite potential.

The human brain, the organ of the mind, is a dynamic and responsive structure, which is deeply affected by experience and shaped by stimulation. In the newborn, different areas of the brain establish connections with each other as the environmental input allows for discovery and exploration, thus making sense of the world. In no other period in development is the brain as responsive to environmental input as in early childhood.

The period of early childhood is also *qualitatively* different with respect to how the brain functions. The young child's nervous system has some stunning capabilities that are unique to this early phase of development in human life. We begin our discovery by reviewing some of the structural and functional components of the human nervous system.

BASIC ROAD MAP: THE HUMAN NERVOUS SYSTEM

Let us begin with the structural and functional properties of the human brain. The human nervous system is divided into two basic parts: the *central nervous system (CNS)* consists of the brain and the spinal cord; the *peripheral nervous system* consists of the collection of nuclei that regulate our bodily functions (autonomic nervous system), and the extensive network of nerve fibre bundles which carry sensory (incoming) and motor (outgoing) information between the brain and the entire body.

The unit of the human nervous system is a *neurone*, and each nerve cell has two types of projections, an *axon*, a single long projection, which carries information *away* from the cell; and many branching *dendrites*, which carry information *towards* it. There are estimated to be in excess of 100 billion neurones, and 100 trillion connections—a mind-boggling complexity of networks, especially when we realise the physical size of the brain, which is around 1400 g in the adult.

- *Dendrites* usually carry *sensory* information from the sensory receptors towards the CNS. They have many spines along their many branches, which increase their surface area so they can interconnect more effectively. Children with Down syndrome have dendritic spines that are quite sparse and small (Purpura, 1974).
- *Axons* usually carry *motor* impulses from the CNS towards the muscles. After birth, axons begin developing a fatty coating, known as *myelin*, which aids in the faster conduction of impulses.
- Collections of these two projection fibres make up the *white matter* in CNS.
- The cell bodies in the CNS make up the *grey matter*, the outer layer of the brain.

Nervous impulse is the transmission of the electrical energy generated in the neurone. The point of transmission is known as a *synapse*. The current travels

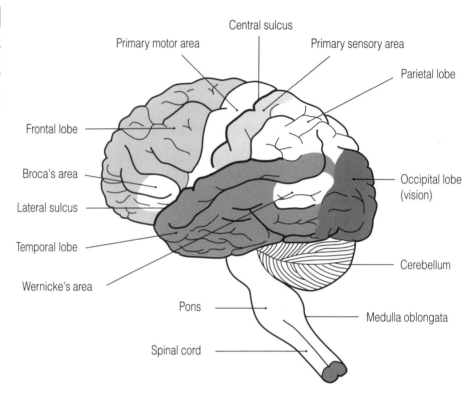

FIGURE 4.1

Schematic
organisation of
structures and
functions of
the brain
(side view)

along an axon and, with the aid of chemical substances known as *neuro-transmitters,* jumps along towards its destination.

CNS: brain and spinal cord

The fact that both these structures are encased in a bony vault (the *cranium* houses the brain; the *vertebral column* protects the spinal cord) shows their importance; nature has gone to some lengths to protect the precious cargo. Three membranes provide further protection and nourishment to the brain and the spinal cord: the *dura* is the tough, cartilaginous membrane closest to the cranium; the *arachnoid,* so called because of its spidery appearance with its rich vascular supply, is the middle one; the delicate, flimsy *pia* adheres to the brain surface like a fine veil. The brain itself is a gelatinous substance, which would crush under its own weight. The *cerebrospinal fluid,* which circulates around the brain in the *subarachnoid space,* protects it from shock, bathing it and floating it.

The *cerebrum,* or the roof brain, has a right and a left *hemisphere,* each hemisphere with different functional properties, particularly in interpreting verbal and non-verbal messages. They are connected by a broad band of

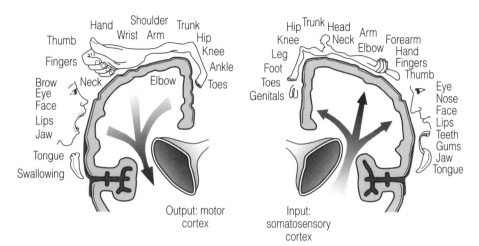

FIGURE 4.2

Cross-section of the primary motor and sensory cortical areas and the unequal distribution of neural innervation to different body parts.

Output: motor cortex

Input: somatosensory cortex

connecting fibres known as the *corpus collosum,* which allows for synchronous sharing of information by both hemispheres. The surface of the cerebrum (*cortex*) is highly *convoluted* and compacted, a process that takes place developmentally: although a smooth surface in the fetal stage, if all the grey matter were spread out in a fully grown brain it would cover about 1.5 m². There are four *cortical lobes* (regions) we need to be aware of, as each has at least one distinct and important function.

- *The frontal lobes.* Located in the front part of the brain, these have structures that regulate three important known functions.
  - The frontmost portion, or the *prefrontal lobes,* are responsible for mediating such functions as motivation, attention, initiative, intentionality, as well as organisation and planning. These are collectively known as the *executive function,* since they assist in decision-making and planning for purposeful activity.
  - Further back, the *primary motor area* is the seat of all *voluntary* movements, where each hemisphere has the responsibility of governing the opposite side of the body. This precise and voluntary system is known as the *pyramidal* motor system. The cortical surface represents the body *topographically* in a disproportionate map of neural-to-body area, in which the hands, for example, get more representation than the entire trunk (see Figure 4.2). Obviously, the more cortical motor cells allocated to a part of the body, the more motorically able and diversified it is.
  - *Broca's area,* located in the *left* hemisphere (for most people), regulates the motor planning and production of speech.
- *The parietal lobes.* Next to the frontal lobes going towards the back of the head, these contain the *primary sensory area,* organised in a point-by-point

representation of the entire body, similar to the motor system. This area processes all bodily sensations, such as the *tactile* (touch, pain, temperature) and *kinaesthetic/proprioceptive* (joint and muscle position) senses. Furthermore, this lobe contributes in integrating the input received from all senses, giving it meaning.

■ *The occipital lobes.* Located at the back of the cortical hemispheres, these are primarily concerned with *vision.* The visual nerve relays the messages from the retina to the visual cortex, where they are analysed, reconstructed and made sense of, before travelling to the parietal lobe to be integrated with more perceptual information.

■ *The temporal lobes.* Located below the frontal and parietal lobes, these are responsible for receiving, analysing and interpreting *auditory* stimuli. *Wernicke's area,* located in the *left* temporal lobe (for most people), regulates the comprehension and formulation of language.

Deep within the cortex is another structure known as the *limbic lobe,* whose function it is to determine and regulate the *emotional* tenor of our lives. As basic emotions such as anger or fear have survival value, limbic structures form a network with some deep brain nuclei, common to all mammals.

Within the white matter underlying the cortex, there are cave-like structures, called *ventricles,* in which the cerebrospinal fluid is generated. This fluid then passes through tiny openings to the meninges surrounding the CNS. When there is an obstruction of the circulation of this fluid, *hydrocephalus* may occur, which raises intracranial pressure and presses the soft neural tissue against the hard bony surface.

The *thalamus* is an egg-shaped core brain structure which is made up of many nuclei. It serves as a relay station for all sensory information before it is received and interpreted at the cortical level. The nuclei surrounding the thalamus are known as the *basal nuclei,* and their function is to contribute to the *extrapyramidal motor system,* which regulates involuntary movement patterns, posture and muscle tone.

Further down, the *midbrain, pons* and *medulla* form the *brain stem,* which is the portion of the brain that narrows down before it becomes the spinal cord. In addition to *tracts* (bundles) of fibres that go up to as well as come down from the cortex, the brain stem contains the nuclei of the *cranial nerves,* which regulate such special functions as breathing, regulation of heart rate, swallowing, hearing and seeing.

The *cerebellum,* with its multifolds, rests below the occipital lobe and over the brain stem. It is primarily responsible for contributing to the extrapyramidal motor system by regulating balance, as well as precision and fluidity of movement.

The *spinal cord,* which is approximately as thick as a pencil, runs down about two-thirds of the vertebral column. The bottom third contains the spinal nerves, which float in the cerebrospinal fluid, each pair of nerves progressively exiting at each side of the appropriate vertebral level. *Lumbar puncture,* the process by which cerebrospinal fluid is drawn, is performed in this site with minimal damage potential to the spinal cord itself, as the inserted needle can gently part the nerves without puncturing them.

There are 31 pairs of spinal nerves, each pair corresponding to, and exiting from, each of the 31 vertebrae: these are, from the top, eight cervical, 12 thoracic, five lumbar, five sacral and one coccygeal. Each pair (right and left) contains half motor and half sensory tract fibres, going to (motor; from the cortex to the muscles) and coming from (sensory; from the sensory receptors on the body surface to the cortex) predetermined areas of the body. The term *segmental innervation* refers to this organisation, where successive segments of the body are supplied by spinal nerves.

COMMON DISORDERS ASSOCIATED WITH CNS STRUCTURES

The disruption of or damage to a structure often illuminates its function, although the complexity of the networks within the brain may make such conclusions tentative. The common disorders of the CNS given below may assist you in bringing together some structures and their functions.

Spastic paralysis or spasticity. Associated with damage to the pyramidal motor system (primary motor area in the frontal lobe) or its tract, resulting in abnormal muscle contractions and inability to perform voluntary movements freely and smoothly.

Athetosis. Associated with damage to basal ganglia and other extrapyramidal structures, resulting in uncontrollable writhing head, arm and hand movements, particularly with volitional activity.

Ataxia. Associated with damage to the cerebellum, resulting in easily lost balance and wide gait of the legs, or inability to perform finely tuned motor acts such as reaching out to hold an object (see cerebral palsy, Chapter 16).

Extrapyramidal disorders. Associated with disorders of the extrapyramidal motor system, resulting in abnormal movement patterns, such as Parkinson's disease (involuntary tremor and rigidity) or Huntington chorea.

Multiple sclerosis. Associated with gradual disappearance of the myelin sheath coating the axons, making efficient movements difficult and often resulting in confinement to a wheelchair.

Cardiovascular accident (CVA, or stroke). Associated with bursting of a blood vessel and deprivation of oxygen to the brain tissue, resulting in varying degrees of brain damage, from paralysis (usually on one side only), to loss of speech and language; effects can be transient or long-lasting.

Expressive aphasia. Associated with damage to Broca's area in the frontal lobe, resulting in difficulty planning and executing sequential speech movements; in severe cases, inability to talk.

Receptive aphasia. Associated with damage to Wernicke's area in the temporal lobe, resulting in difficulty comprehending verbal language and responding appropriately.

Cortical blindness. Associated with damage to the occipital lobes, resulting in inability to see or to interpret visual images, despite normal vision and intact visual nerves.

Polio. Associated with a virus that destroys the motor cells in the spinal cord, resulting in flaccid (hypotonic; no muscle tone) paralysis below the level of the *lesion* (insult; cut; damage).

Spinal injury. Associated with accidents, bullet wounds or sports injuries. The resulting damage depends on the level of the disruption to the cord: the higher up towards the head it is, the more extensive the damage, as no sensory information coming from the neck down can reach the cortex, and no motor impulses directed to areas below the neck can reach the muscles.

Spina bifida. Associated with that birth defect where the spinal cord has failed to close properly; in the most severe cases, spinal nerves will be outside the spinal column in a sac, usually in lower spinal levels. Youngsters with the disorder may exhibit flaccid paralysis and no sensation from the body, from the level of the lesion, down (see Chapter 16). Muscles that do not receive any innervation gradually waste away or *atrophy.*

Hydrocephalus. May be associated with spina bifida, which disrupts the circulation of the cerebrospinal fluid; it may also be caused by congenital abnormalities, or *meningitis,* an infection of the protective membranes of the CNS (see Chapter 16).

At this point, it is important to state that disruptions of the infinite cortical and subcortical *networks* are just as likely to contribute to atypical behavioural outcomes as are localised lesions. Many developmental disorders are not necessarily associated with a clearcut site on the brain that is responsible for the dysfunction, although they may have neurological bases.

Attention deficit hyperactivity disorder (ADHD). Has been associated with abnormalities in the *reticular activating system* (which regulates attention and arousal of the cortex by selectively screening perceptual input), and prefrontal lobe lesions (Lou, Henriksen & Bruhn, 1984; see Chapter 12).

Dyslexia. Reading difficulties may involve both auditory and visual processing mechanisms (Duffy, Dencla, McAnulty & Holmes, 1988):

- *Auditory processing disorder.* Associated with parietal/temporal dysfunction, resulting in difficulty comprehending oral language, it may be reflected by measures such as difficulty following directions or learning new vocabulary items;
- *Visual processing disorder.* Associated with parietal/occipital dysfunction, it may result in difficulty deriving meaning from visual stimuli, making visual interpretations, or reproducing visual forms.

Autism. There is near-consensus that this autism is caused by neural aberrations; among the findings are cerebellar and prefrontal and temporal lobe abnormalities, and various neurotransmitter disturbances (Nelson, 1991) (see Chapter 15).

New investigation methods

The present-day advances and refinements in technology used to investigate the brain are being applied to the diagnosis of learning problems of suspected neurogenic origin, as well as other developmental disabilities. Although the results can be both misleading and imprecise, such technology holds promise in contributing to our understanding of many conditions. In the future, knowledge gained from actual functioning modes of the CNS may be essential in the identification of, and even treatment methods for, early atypical development.

Magnetic resonance imaging (MRI).   Obtained from the resonance of hydrogen atoms occurring in different densities in the brain, it yields a high-resolution computer-constructed image of neural tissues.

PET scan (positron emission tomography).   This technique uses radiation that is generated as glucose is metabolised by the brain to map out the different areas of brain activity. Differences have been reported between dyslexic and control subjects using this technique (Duffy et al., 1988).

BEAM (brain electrical activity mapping).   Related to *EEG (electroencephalogram)*, this technique records different electrical waves generated by the brain. Selective effects of medication for children with dyslexia is reported by this method (Conners, 1989).

ERP (event-related potentials).   Another technique that records electrical potentials from the scalp in association with external stimuli and behavioural responses has been useful in the study of disorders of attention and hyperactivity (Loiselle, Stamm, Matinsky & Whipple, 1980).

BRAIN FUNCTIONS UNIQUE TO EARLY CHILDHOOD

There are some neural phenomena that seem to occur only in the early years of life. As we see below, their effects are significant and their implications are powerful, particularly in recovery from *acquired* (postnatal) CNS damage, and the benefits derived from early facilitation and intervention.

Critical (sensitive) periods

In the course of early development, specific (critical) periods of time seem to mark most receptivity and sensitivity to certain environmental stimulation. If these windows of opportunity are not properly provided for in the most impressionable times, the young brain seems to have difficulty achieving that function. The critical periods seem to be in evidence for most domains of development.

Early evidence for the existence of critical periods came from animal experiments. When one eye of a kitten was patched for as short a time as a single day in its fourth week of life, the result was a major impairment to the visual cortex, with no such impairments before or after that time (Blakemore, 1982). This suggests that, in that short period, visual input is essential for the cortex to establish its visual circuitry. Some evidence from young children and such sensitive periods is summarised below.

- In infants, neuronal growth spurts in the visual cortex seem to occur between four to eight months of age. If a baby is born with cataracts that are not removed by two years of age, he may become cortically blind.
- Prolonged periods of reduced linguistic input in early childhood affects the development of language. The most poignant example is that of Genie (Curtis, 1977), a child kept in severe isolation until she was discovered at age 13. She subsequently failed to develop but a rudimentary language system despite intensive remediation efforts.
- Links between a conductive hearing loss associated with chronic middle ear infection, and language delay are clinically well established.
- Intermittent conductive hearing loss and attentional deficits and learning disabilities seem associated (Adesman, Altshuler, Lipkin & Walce, 1990).
- Attachment, where the infant forms mental representations for his affections towards his mother or other primary carers in the first year of life, also seems such a time-dependent construct (Myers, 1987).
- Parental neglect, abuse, indifference or severe discipline seems to alter the circuitry in the prefrontal lobes in young children, affecting their emotional response style (Davidson, 1994).
- Restriction of movement in the early years seems to prohibit the synaptic connections in the cerebellum. A child immobilised in a body cast until four years of age would learn to walk eventually, but never smoothly (Greenbough, 1996).

Plasticity

Plasticity refers to the fact that the brain organisation is quite *fluid*, and that it can *recover from injury* in early development, whereas such recovery would not ordinarily be possible in the later years. Indeed, the adaptive powers of the young brain and its ability to utilise functional compensation in the face of acquired damage are amazing. In fact, one hemisphere can do the job for two.

Infants whose left cortical hemisphere has been removed are shown to develop close to normal language capacities (Mehler, Morton & Jusczyk, 1984). A severe CVA to the left hemisphere in adults would easily result in enduring loss of speech and language function (see *Hemispheric specialisation* below). Over time, these infants would develop a slight paralysis of the opposite side of their bodies, but they would not be disabled enough to need a wheelchair; in fact, the condition improves with activity.

Another area of interest is that of the effects of *enriched environments* on cognitive growth. Early evidence from animal studies showed that mice reared in rich and stimulating environments with objects to manipulate, varied pathways to explore and problems to solve, developed thicker and heavier cortices than control animals reared in impoverished environments (Bennett, Diamond, Krech & Rosenzweig, 1964). There have been many studies demonstrating the effects of environment on improved learning behaviour; however, extrapolations from animal studies to young children are arguably incorrect or unsound. Nevertheless, pioneers in early childhood education such as Maria Montessori have based their applications on similar (veritable) assumptions. Early enrichment programs, like Head Start (see below), hold a similar premise of the effects of enriched environments on young children.

In his classic study on institutionalised children with significant cognitive handicaps, Kirk (1958) was able to demonstrate a 20-point rise in the IQ scores of those children educated in an enriched preschool environment, when compared with their institutionalised peers. Better integrated brain activity and higher IQ scores are reported in prematurely born infants raised in responsive homes, suggesting an environmental facilitation effect (Beckwith & Parmalee, 1986).

The malleability and responsiveness of the young brain to the environment can also be seen in the activation of its circuitry.

Brain circuitry

The circuitry in the brain may have fixed pathways, which are thought to be modified by enriched environmental influences as children mature. The circuitry for word knowledge may be dependent on the amount of input the baby receives. The vocabulary size of babies with highly conversant mothers is reported to be considerably larger than of those with taciturn mothers, the gap being wider at 24 months than at 20 months (Huttenlocher, 1991).

Although infants seem to have an innate circuitry to enable them to make discriminations on all speech sounds before they are six months of age, early experience with specific speech sounds of the input language determines the perceptual map on the auditory cortex (Kuhl, 1993). Unless other speech sounds are used by middle childhood, the ability to learn them with ease is minimised, suggesting that second language learning should not be delayed until later years.

Pruning

Neurophysiologists have identified an initial burst of synapse formation in the first month after birth, followed by a pruning of synapses in all areas of the brain. This process seems essential because initially there are many more connections than necessary, and this abundance creates many redundant pathways. Experience seems to erase some of these connections and strengthen the necessary ones in the wiring diagram. Interestingly, pruning appears to occur in tandem with the developmental process. The maximum density of synapses in the areas of the brain responsible for language comprehension and production occurs at about three years, while the cortical cells responsible for vision are maximally dense at four months of age (see Chapter 5 on visual development), with rapid pruning thereafter (Huttenlocher, 1994).

It is intriguing to note that the combination of an early surge of synaptic growth followed by pruning, or *canalisation*, means that the one-year-old actually has denser synapses and dendrites than the adult. Pruning continues throughout early childhood, into adolescence.

EARLY INTERVENTION: NURTURE LEADING NATURE

The insights gleaned from neuroscience reaffirm the efficacy of early intervention in children with obstacles to accomplishing age-appropriate adaptive behaviours. However, lasting benefits of early intervention seem to depend on the *time* in development in which enrichment is introduced.

Follow-up studies on Head Start, a major *preschool* early intervention project in the USA, indicate that the initial IQ gains made by participating disadvantaged children do not seem to last, although they tend to show better school adjustment than their peers (Zigler & Styfco, 1993).

In a tightly controlled investigation of another early intervention and enrichment program (Abecedarian Project), however, the group that participated in the enrichment program from *infancy* (six to 12 weeks of age) did not show an erosion of the IQ gains made after the intervention, *maintaining the benefits* (Campbell & Ramey, 1994). In this investigation, the children who were provided with enriched experiences *after five years of age* did *not* sustain any benefits compared with their controls.

The *timing* of the facilitative experience provided seems more crucial than the amount of stimulation provided. Perhaps the safest maxim for early intervention is 'from birth on is not too soon'.

OTHER EARLY NEURAL MECHANISMS

Hemispheric specialisation

In the fully grown brain, the two cortical hemispheres have specialised functions.

- The *left* hemisphere typically processes and responds to *verbal* information, attends to logical-mathematical, analytical tasks, and is credited with the ability to organise and process sequential material.
- The *right* hemisphere, on the other hand, is typically said to process stimuli in a holistic, gestalt-like manner, to analyse and decipher *spatial* visual clues, and to be sensitive to the melody and other musical, rhythmical aspects of the information received, analysing it simultaneously (Springer & Deutsch, 1984).

Folk psychology tends to attribute the more logical, analytical qualities of the left hemisphere to masculine, and the more visual, melodic, intuitive qualities of the right brain to feminine characteristics. But, as in life, these characteristics cannot survive on their own merits; indeed they are *complementary*, and need each other to be able to make the best sense of the world.

You will recall, from our review of cortical lobes, that the two areas responsible for speech and language processing are typically located in the left hemisphere. The hard-wiring for this specialisation may be present from the very early months of infancy. However, the *functional* specialisation for language processing in one hemisphere shows a developmental progression. No hemispheric preference was found in visual and auditory language processing in three-year-old children, although a preference became progressively stronger in six- and nine-year-olds. By 12 years of age, hemispheric asymmetry (*lateralisation*) was found to be strongly established (Talay, 1978).

The fact that young children can recover speech and language after an injury to the left hemisphere reflects such plasticity and a progressive stabilisation of this function. As this organisation becomes irreversibly established by puberty the extent of recovery from injury diminishes.

Hemispheric dominance and hand preference

Hand preference in young children is usually evident by school age. Traditionally, there has been an association between right-handedness and left-hemisphere dominance.

Hand preference does not seem to have any bearing at all on the adaptive and learning styles of young children, except in cases where mixed (unclear) laterality is observed. Mixed dominance, where a child may exhibit right-hand but left-foot preference, no preference between hands (*ambidextrality*), and difficulties in crossing of the midline with either hand or foot, are often reported in clinical investigations of children with learning difficulties (see Chapter 12).

Hemispheric preference vs cooperation

Learning or cognitive styles observed in children perhaps reflect their preference for neural circuits that are better established or the hemisphere that tends to exert a stronger influence. However, cooperation between structures with different processing styles results in optimal efficiency. Furthermore, stimulating one hemisphere may result in a facilitated processing ability in the other.

Preschoolers given piano and singing lessons were found significantly to improve in maths and in complex spatial reasoning tasks, such as working mazes, drawing geometric figures and copying patterns, compared with their controls (Rauscher, 1994).

Two styles of *maths* learning has been identified: one that is more verbal, and sequential; the other more spatial, and holistic. Davidson (1983) has developed strategies that benefit children for both (hemispheric processing) styles by varying regular classroom instruction.

The right hemisphere is the one in which visual imagery is generated, while comprehension of language occurs in the left. However, comprehension of verbal material is enhanced when it is accompanied by visualisation, which is presumably achieved by the simultaneous collaboration of the left and right hemispheres. With school-aged children, the reading comprehension ability of a group of low-achieving students was significantly improved by teaching them to *visualise* the material read (Wittrock, 1978).

Brain growth and growth spurts

The brain reaches 70% of its adult weight by two years of age, nearly 90% by age six, and its full weight by puberty. It consumes twice as much glucose, the brain's source of energy, as the adult brain from age four until about puberty. Researchers think that young brains are as primed as they will ever be to process new information.

There appears to be a relationship between the rate of brain growth and children's ability to learn. Epstein (1980) suggests that brain growth spurts occur from the ages of three to ten months, two to four years, six to eight years, ten to 12 years and 14 to 16 years. Interestingly, these periods roughly correspond to the Piagetian stages of cognitive development. Since these periods are claimed to be most opportune for learning, the theory has some educational implications, which are being trialled in some schools in the USA.

NEUROSCIENCE AND EARLY CHILDHOOD EDUCATION

Recent developments in the field of neuroscience have helped us sharpen our appreciation of the windows of opportunity presented in the early years.

- Second-language learning is easiest in early childhood, a common observation not often followed in educational practice.
- Right and left hemispheres can be prompted to work in tandem: music seems to excite the innate circuits, enhancing complex reasoning and maths skills.
- Emotional tonality set in infancy may assist in or hinder a child from self-regulating at later stages. It also seems to effect the ease with which the child adapts and interacts in a learning environment.
- Teaching young children to visualise as they listen to verbal material may enhance their comprehension of language and serve as a safety net in language-related learning disabilities.
- Better understanding of hemispheric preference and learning styles may have a significant impact on facilitating young children's cognition.
- The role of early intervention, or environmental enrichment and stimulation in the growth and development of the at-risk child, from the first few weeks of life, seems central to sustained positive results.
- Interdisciplinary collaboration between neuroscientists, child development specialists and educators is an essential step towards uniting theory and practice with young children.

CONCLUSIONS

We have taken a bird's-eye view of a complex and often underscored field of study in early childhood—the human brain and its developmental properties. The implications we draw from it make it imperative that we incorporate this knowledge in our understanding of and practice with young children. The field of neuroscience and child development (*developmental neuroscience*) will probably continue to challenge our thinking and expand our horizons in the years to come. Theirs is a promising partnership!

PART II

Normal development

5

Infancy: from reflex to representation

Comprising only about 2% of the human life span, infancy is probably the most crucial and rapid stage of development. It spans the period from birth to early language use at about 18 months. We have reconceptualised our understanding of the infant as a competent being, well equipped to interact with the physical and the social world and displaying many complex capabilities from the onset. Indeed, from birth the neonate is innately wired to adapt to her environment, exhibiting such behaviours as an organised sleep–wake cycle, an ability to seek assistance via crying patterns, and a capacity to learn.

EARLY REFLEXES AND STATES

Reflexes refer to the neonate's ability to respond motorically to some sensory stimulation in predetermined ways. Some reflexes, such as sucking, are *adaptive*, and help survival. Others, like the Moro reflex, are *primitive*, and are integrated into more complex patterns as the baby's nervous system matures and more voluntary, purposeful patterns evolve. Early primitive reflexive behaviour usually disappears by six months of age; some are thought to play a facilitating role in organising voluntary motor abilities in later life (Sheppard & Mysak, 1984). Here are some of the prominent ones.

- *Rooting*. Head-turn as a response to the stimulation of the corner of the mouth in preparation for sucking.
- *Sucking*. Precipitated by having a nipple in the mouth, it allows for regular and rhythmical feeding behaviour. Both of these reflexes may be absent in babies deprived of oxygen during birth.

- *Palmar grasp.* Simultaneous grasp precipitated by pressing the baby's palm by a finger, which disappears by three to four months as the baby moves to voluntary grasping.
- *Moro.* As a response to a sudden loud noise, the infant arches her back, extends her legs and throws her arms outward. The reflex disappears by six months of age.
- *Babinski.* As a response to stroking the sole of the foot from the toes towards the heel, the big toe extends and the smaller toes spread. Disappearing by the first year, this reflex may be absent in neonates with lower spinal cord damage.
- *Tonic neck.* As the baby is lying on her back, turning the head to one side results in the fencing position (arm extended on the side of the head-turn, with the arm on the other side flexed). This reflex tends to disappear after four months.
- *Walking.* When held under the arms with feet touching the surface, the infant lifts one foot after the other in a walk-like position. This reflex tends to disappear by two months of age.
- *Blinking, sneezing, coughing, swallowing.* These adaptive reflexes are retained for life.

Early reflexive behaviour and its developmental course allow for neurological assessment of the infant. Retention of reflexes after their anticipated time of disappearance, weak or absent reflexes, or exaggerated reflexes, may signal varying degrees of brain dysmaturity or damage (Touwen, 1984).

Newborns spend their time in various *states* of sleep and wakefulness. Wolff (1987) has described gradations of these states in seven stages, as follows (starting with least arousal):

1. *Regular sleep* occurs when the infant's eyes are closed with no movement, accompanied by deep and regular breathing.
2. *Periodic sleep* is slightly more active; the respiratory movements can alternate between bouts of rapid and shallow breathing.
3. *Irregular sleep* contains more motor activity, such as gentle arm movements and stirring. It also shows occasional rapid eye movements and facial grimacing, with somewhat faster breathing.
4. *Drowsiness* precedes falling asleep, or follows waking up. Eyes are open part of the time, with a glazed look and poor focusing.
5. *Alert inactivity* is with open, attentive and focused eyes, and steady breathing, although the infant is not active.
6. *Waking activity* is characterised by frequent and diffuse activity. The breathing pattern is irregular and the facial expression is highly variable, from relaxed to ready to cry.
7. *Crying,* in which vocalisations are accompanied by vigorous and diffuse motor activity.

It has been estimated that the 16–17 hours a neonate sleeps are fairly equally divided into periods of *sleep* and wakefulness throughout the day and night.

- Babies are able to have longer periods of night sleep by five to six weeks of age and eight hours of night sleep by four months of age (Berg & Berg, 1987), although this seems to be a Western-pattern imposed on the infant.
- In cultures like rural Kenya, where infants feed on demand and sleep with their mother, the three-hour sleep cycle remains until the infant is about one year old, suggesting that the Western culture may be pushing the infant to the limits of her neurological maturity for the sake of the parents' convenience (Super & Harkness, 1982).
- Because the neonate's sleep comprises 50% REM (rapid eye movement) sleep in which the brain is intensely active, her great requirement seems to be for this type of sleep. REM sleep seems to be a way of compensating for the relative paucity of activity in early infancy and, as such stimulation is vital to the maturation of the brain, the absence of REM sleep may impair brain structures (Roffwarg, Muzio & Dement, 1966).
- Between infancy and adolescence, REM sleep decreases from eight hours a day to under two hours, while non-REM sleep decreases from eight to six hours. Whereas neonates begin their sleep with REM sleep, adults enter this state for at least an hour after non-REM sleep. Infants begin their sleep cycle with non-REM sleep at about 18 months of age (Berg & Berg, 1987).
- Disturbances in REM and non-REM sleep patterns are commonly observed in infants with brain damage, prematurity and other birth complications (Theorell, Prechtl & Vos, 1974).

The *cry* of the newborn is a complex expressive behaviour, summoning the attention and proximity of carers. From *discomfort* and *pain* to *hunger* and *boredom*, the infant has a powerful mechanism with which to signal her state. The basic cry seems to have a fundamental rhythmic pattern, the anger cry is typically louder and more intense, and the pain cry has an abrupt and loud onset. It seems that the *intensity* of the cry, rather than its acoustic characteristics, guides the carer to the state that is being signalled (Gustafson & Harris, 1990).

- Mothers (but not fathers) of five-month-olds can discriminate between taped episodes of anger and pain cries in their *own* babies (Weisenfield, Malatesta & DeLoach, 1981).
- The newborn seems to be able to *discriminate* between the sound of another infant's cry and her own. Tape recordings of another infant's cry induces her to cry, while the sound of her own cry calms the newborn (Martin & Clark, 1982).

■

- Picking up the baby to shoulder level seems to regulate the crying behaviour 80% of the time (Reisman, 1987).

- *Responding* to the infant's cries may not promote spoiling and dependency. Mothers who delayed responding to their babies' cries had infants with more persistent crying in the latter part of the first year, as well as less mature communicative behaviours. Since the infants' proximity-signalling needs were not properly met, they appeared to be left with crying as the most viable communication strategy (Bell & Ainsworth, 1972).

- However, the parent's response should perhaps depend on the *type* of crying. Non-response to intense distress cries may well be damaging to the security and attachment of the child, whereas an immediate response to milder cries and whimpers seems to increase the frequency of these behaviours (Hubbard & van IJzendoorn, 1987).

- Outstanding acoustic characteristics of the newborn cry seem to be related to the integrity of the nervous system. Among a group of high-risk infants, those with more shrill and *high-pitched* cries had significantly lower IQ scores at five years of age (Lester, 1987).

MOTOR DEVELOPMENT

Motor development is the most readily observable domain in the first year. Early assessments of infants relied heavily on motor achievements, although there is considerable individual variability in the emergence of motor milestones, as well as some cultural differences which affect their development. Furthermore, many milestones are achieved earlier today, compared to the turn of the century, probably because of such factors as better health care and nutrition, and changing views on child-rearing practices. One normative tool that looks at motor development closely, the *Bayley Scales of Infant Development* (Bayley, 1969), is helpful in giving us the sequence and nature of early motor milestones (Table 5.1). Note that the average age of reaching the skill is not sufficient: the age *range* within which the milestone is achieved accounts for more infants in the normal distribution.

As babies achieve progressively more complex motor skills, a whole new world opens up to them. Not only does their perspective of the world change from a lying to a sitting position, but their mastery of the environment is strengthened by their ability to point, grasp, explore and socially engage the carer in the exchange. The carer can now spend more time in social play and verbal exchange, thereby scaffolding the infant's acquisition of language. You can readily see the effect of one domain of development on *all* domains.

For a long time, Gesell's strong maturational views were accepted with reference to the environmental stimulation not accelerating motor development. Gesell (1929) believed that voluntary motor behaviours such as walking emerged when the infant's nervous system was ready; maturation of the cortex

Motor skill	Average age achieved	Age range for most infants
Holds head steady when held upright	7 weeks	3 weeks–4 months
Lying on tummy, lifts self up by arms	2 months	3 weeks–5 months
Rolls from side to back	2 months	3 weeks–5 months
Rolls from back to side	4.5 months	2–7 months
Grasps cube	3 months, 3 weeks	2–7 months
Sits alone with coordination	7 months	5–9 months
Crawls	7 months	5–11 months
Pulls to a stand	8 months	5–12 months
Uses clear pincer grasp	9 months	7–10 months
Plays pat-a-cake	9 months, 3 weeks	7—15 months
Stands independently	11 months	9–16 months
Walks alone	11 months, 3 weeks	9–17 months

TABLE 5.1

Motor milestones

Source: Bayley, 1969.

would replace reflexive control over movement, with cortical and voluntary control, as motor behaviours such as reaching, grasping, crawling, and walking are genetically programmed.

Nature or nurture?

Six-month-old Anbarra Aboriginal infants in Arnhem Land are capable of sitting unsupported on their mothers' shoulders, clutching their mother's hair for a five kilometre walk, a postural control not expected of European-Australian infants before 12 months of age (Hamilton 1981). Since a mother carrying an infant would be hindered in her traditional food gathering, infants are encouraged for early motor development by often being propped into a sitting position as early as eight weeks of age. Caregiving practices affect even motor development.

It is now held that infants' motor milestones are far from being isolated, discrete achievements; rather, they are woven into a complex web of *dynamic systems* of action, which are gradually organised, modified, and integrated into more intricate and effective modes of exploring, controlling and gaining mastery over the environment (Thelen, 1989). Visually guided reaching is a case in point.

Visually guided reaching is a crucial skill in the manipulation of the environment, which is seen as having a central role in the Piagetian framework of cognitive development in infancy. It also exemplifies the progression and differentiation process from gross, diffuse patterns into skilled and fine motor activity.

■ Neonates exhibit primitive reaching behaviour, resembling swipes at an object in front of them, without coordination or accuracy.

■ By three months of age they begin to use their eyes in guiding their arms and hands, often being able to correct their near-misses (Bushnell, 1985).

■ Before five months of age they are able to reach to objects on the opposite side of the body as well as the midline, and they are able to use both hands in coordinated exploration and to transfer objects with *ulnar grasp,* where the fingers close against the palms (Rochat, 1989).

■ By eight to 11 months of age reaching and grasping are executed almost to perfection; further, babies no longer need the active participation of their eyes, which frees up their resources so they can absorb and integrate the other significant events around them. Infants' ability to reach for hidden objects is thought to be related to such advances (Bushnell, 1985).

PERCEPTUAL DEVELOPMENT

Sensory systems channel the information from the body as well as the environment to the brain. Experience allows these sensations to become integrated with meaning; thus, *perception* is our *interpretation* of our sensations, which fit into our knowledge of the world. Perception (together with motor exploration) is the foundation of cognitive development in infancy, as perceptual sets are integrated into larger wholes as well as being used to consolidate other developmental domains: hearing is crucial in language, and vision is crucial in social interactions. Impaired perceptual mechanisms will necessitate compensatory modalities to achieve similar ends.

Developmental psychologists have outwitted infants in designing experimental paradigms to study infant perception—a necessary challenge, as babies are not able to tell us about the nature of their perceptual experiences. Babies hate boredom, and seek interesting and novel stimuli to engage their attention, often manifesting their interest by a bodily response which, in turn, can be used as an indicator of their perceptual experiences. Here are some methods.

Non-nutritive sucking.   As the baby's attention peaks, so does her sucking rate on a dummy nipple. As the baby *habituates*, or gets used to the novel qualities of the stimulus, her sucking rate slows down. Sucking rate can be monitored to study infant perception.

Respiration and heart rate.   Both tend to rise when a new stimulus is processed by the infant—not unlike being excited at the sight of a favoured person!

Visually reinforced discrimination.   As the infant makes a head-turn response to a (usually auditory) stimulus, she is presented with a visually pleasant reward, like a puppet show. She soon learns to respond selectively. Many paediatric audiologists also use this technique in assessing infant hearing.

Other techniques.   These involve tracking the infant's *eye movements,* and monitoring facial expressions and reflexes.

Vision

This modality has been investigated more than any other, as exploration of the environment relies so heavily on it, yet it is the least developed of all senses *at birth*.

The *fovea,* centrally located cells on the *retina* (the inner lining of the eye ball comprised of nerve endings), which are responsible for receiving the sharpest and clearest images, do not contain such densely packed cells in the neonate as in adults. Also, the muscles that allow the *lens* of the eye to change shape so that images can focus properly on the retina (*visual accommodation)* are not yet fully functional. However, by three months of age, infants can *focus* on objects of varying distances as well as their parents can.

The neonate has very poor *visual acuity;* in fact her vision is so blurred that, whereas normal vision is 20/20, the neonate's is about 20/400; that is, the newborn can see objects at about 7 metres as clearly as individuals with normal vision would if they were about 135 metres away. Thus, the effective distance of clear focus is about 20 to 30 cm, which is the approximate distance between baby and mother in the *feeding position.*

By 6 months, the infant's visual acuity has improved to 20/100. The fovea becomes fully functional before the first birthday, with 20/20 vision (Haith, 1990). The *optic nerve* and the *visual cortex* also develop substantially, to contribute to the greatly improved visual capabilities of the infant by the end of the first year (Banks & Salatapek, 1983) (see Chapter 14 for a fuller discussion of the visual system and its impairments).

Acuity and focusing alone are not sufficient to gather and interpret visual information. The development of *functional* visual skills is also necessary. Some of these skills are as follows:

- The eye movements necessary to *scan and track* in the newborn reveal an active and organised manner of visual exploration. The baby moves from a restricted, single-feature selection to a broad and thorough examination of complex visual stimuli such as a human face in the first two months of life. Fixation on a visual stimulus also improves rapidly, from *saccadic* (shifting) eye movements to the smoother pursuit of moving objects by six months of age (Hainline, 1985).
- *Depth perception* seems to develop in stages. By three weeks of age, infants can react to what looks like the object coming towards them (based on increasing size cues) by blinking.
- Depth is perceived because each eye sends an image from a slightly different perspective to the brain, which then resolves these *binocular depth cues.* Infants over three months of age seem to perceive and respond to these cues, interpreting them correctly (Yonas & Owsley, 1987).

- As infants begin crawling, depth cues become more important. In the classical experiment with the *visual cliff*—the chequered box with a transparent surface for the baby to crawl on to cross towards her mother—most infants over six months of age required extensive coaxing from their mothers to take the dare, whereas younger infants moved on it freely (Gibson & Walk, 1960).
- By two months, *face recognition* allows the infant to select the mother's face; the infant also shows a clear preference for a human face over scrambled arrangements (Maurer, 1985). After three months, the infant's *social smile* is selective, mostly directed to familiar people.
- While *shape constancy* (stability of a shape despite different retinal images) is evident in newborns, *size constancy* (unfluctuating size of objects despite varying retinal images) emerges between six and eight months (McKenzie, Tootell & Day, 1980).
- Although neonates prefer to look at coloured rather than grey stimuli, a preference for particular colours does not appear until three months of age (Adams, 1987).
- By five months of age, babies respond differently to faces displaying different emotions, such as surprise, anger, happiness and sadness (Balaban, 1995).
- Before the first birthday, when they face an unfamiliar object or situation to which they cannot decide how to respond, infants check the facial expressions of the mother or father and match their facial expression to theirs (*social referencing*) (Walden, 1991).

Most researchers agree that the maturation of the visual system is largely accountable for the infant's growing preference for complex, dynamic and integrated patterns, which scaffolds her exploration of the environment. The infant's early visual capabilities seem primed for social interaction and reciprocity of affect. Neural receptors appear to be prewired to respond to particular visual stimulus patterns, such as angles, and curved or straight lines, which eventually get integrated into a recognition of *invariant patterns* (stable characteristics in an object or a pattern), allowing the infant to make preferences, discriminations and generalisations.

In Chapter 14, we review how a visual handicap can interrupt and delay the developmental processes. How can the affectional bond be strengthened between infant and carer in the absence of sharing a smile, that very potent social and uniquely human currency of love, mutuality, acceptance and regard? How does visual perception guide motor development? We will tackle these and other issues.

Hearing

Hearing or auditory perception is crucial in the acquisition of speech and language. At birth, infants are much better equipped with audition than they are with vision. Research indicates that the human infant is prewired and predisposed to the human voice.

- Within the general range of pitch and loudness of the human voice, infants have an auditory acuity comparable to adults, although high-pitched sounds are better heard at slightly louder levels (Werner & Gillenwater, 1990).
- Newborns can discriminate between their mother's voice and another female voice, but not between their father's voice and another male voice, and prefer their mother's, possibly because such learning occurs in utero (DeCasper & Fifer, 1980).
- When mothers were instructed to read a story, such as Dr Seuss' *Cat in the Hat*, in the last six weeks of pregnancy, their infants showed a clear preference for that story over one that they had not heard (DeCasper & Spence, 1986).
- By six months of age infants have mastered the skill of associating a parental voice with its owner (Spelke & Owsley, 1979).
- Speech perception and discrimination skills of infants under controlled laboratory conditions have been impressive. Using a visually reinforced habituation paradigm, infants as young as one month have been shown to discriminate speech sounds like *pa* and *ba* (Trehub & Rabinovitch, 1972).
- Babies can discriminate speech sounds in *all* human languages by three months, but lose this sensitivity and can only make successful distinctions in the input language after six months of age (Polka & Werker, 1994). It seems that the innate ability to distinguish speech sounds becomes a specialised one, where the infant, now busy absorbing the sounds of the native/input language in which she will soon be communicating, has to pay closer attention to that language system alone.
- Infant speech discrimination skills have been shown to be related to later competencies in receptive language. Between two groups of infants, one performing a speech discrimination task successfully and the other not reaching the target performance, the failing group had significantly lower receptive vocabulary scores at three and five years of age (Talay-Ongan, 1996).

Olfaction and gustatory senses

The smelling and tasting senses have not been studied so extensively as the other senses.

- Newborn infants who had never been fed reacted differently to sweet, sour and bitter flavours, indicating a preference for the sweet-tasting stimulus (Steiner, 1979).
- One-week-old babies who were being breastfed could discriminate between their mother's smells and other women's smells (Cernoch & Porter, 1985).

Tactile sensitivities

These appear to be well developed in the neonate. Babies seem especially sensitive to touches on the mouth, the face, the hands, the soles of the feet and the abdomen, with less sensitivity in other parts of the body (Reisman, 1987).

Intermodal association (or cross-modal transfer)

Intermodal association refers to the ability to connect the information received by separate senses, so that associations between different perceptual characteristics of an object can be made. For example, when an infant is able to identify by touch a toy she has only seen before, she is transferring her knowledge of the visual properties of the object to her understanding of what it may feel like. It is an important attribute, because it allows for the ability to extract representations and abstractions as the infant becomes increasingly competent in interacting with the physical and social world around her.

Piaget believed that intermodal association was not present until later in the first year, by which time the infant had collected a sufficiently wide range of sensory experiences to know how objects simultaneously felt, sounded and looked. Empirical findings, however, indicate that infants are quite capable of this skill by six months (Rose & Ruff, 1987).

COGNITIVE DEVELOPMENT

The prevailing thought in infant cognitive development is that infants 'construct' their knowledge about the world through their interactions with their caregivers and others, as well as by exploring the environment and discovering the properties of the objects in it. In Piagetian terms, it is a process of building up (constructing) mental concepts, images and schemata through *assimilation*, or changing and modifying existing ideas to make them consistent with the newly acquired information through *accommodation*. The competent infant strives for knowledge, and is attentive to problems and their solutions in her explorations of, and interactions with, the physical and the social world. Piaget is the force behind this *constructivist* view of mental development, in which development is seen in invariant sequential stages, with *qualitative* differences between each stage.

In the stage of *sensorimotor* development during the infant's first two years, Piaget describes six substages, which are summarised below (Piaget, 1952):

1. *Reflexes (0–1 month).* The infant exercises innate reflexive patterns, such as crying and sucking. Although she possesses innate reflexes, she has no understanding of the world of objects as separate from the self, and is thus said to be completely egocentric.

2. *Primary circular reactions (1–4 months)*. The infant *accidentally* forms associations between behaviour patterns that result in interesting results on her own body, and repeats them. Repetition of chance behaviours that have a positive outcome soon leads to a more varied repertoire. The infant can anticipate some events and engage in rudimentary repetitions. Visually guided reaching and smiling appear.

3. *Secondary circular reactions (4–8 months)*. The infant is beginning the separation of means (processes) from ends (results). Attention is shifting from the infant's body to the world of objects, with evidence of purposeful actions and brief search behaviours, aided by the connections between sensory modalities. Manual activities involve pulling, stroking, swinging and striking. The infant still repeats newly acquired actions, with little understanding of objects existing independently of her actions.

4. *Coordination of secondary circular reactions (8–12 months)*. Intentional behaviour emerges, which indicates further separation of means from ends. The infant is interested in the qualities of objects, exploration, search for hidden objects, anticipation of events and tool use. When an object is hidden from her view, she can remove the cover (means) and grasp the object (end). Such purposeful means–goal-related behaviour is seen as truly intelligent behaviour and as the foundation of the problem-solving skills to come.

5. *Tertiary circular reactions (12–18 months)*. The infant is engaged in reciprocal exchanges with the environment, using variations of means to achieve desired ends. She enjoys active experimentation to produce novel effects, searches systematically for hidden objects, and is able to produce complex imitations. The infant can now search for the hidden object in various locations, and acts on familiar objects in different ways. Because the infant can now vary her actions on the objects, it is said that she can separate herself, and her actions, from the world of things. This marks the end of the sensorimotor egocentricism.

6. *Invention of new means (18–24 months)*. The infant is able to have internalised thought, and mental problem-solving strategies. Trial and error is replaced by insight. With the ability to represent reality internally, she understands that objects can be moved even when they are out of sight. She uses symbolic representation evidenced in language, as well as symbolic (make-believe) play and deferred imitation, where mental representations can be acted out in the absence of the original stimulus.

Infant research continually demonstrates babies' active constructing of knowledge at work.

Competence + control = delight

Infants learn active modes of controlling the environment by repeating behaviours that lead to interesting outcomes in *action–consequence* paradigms.

- Two-month-old infants can learn to activate the spinning and shaking of a colourful mobile hung over their cribs by kicking (Rovee-Collier, 1984).
- Four-month-old babies can turn their head to the right or the left to activate a light switch. They became alert and fussy, and frowned if they could not; when they achieved the correct solution, however, they showed signs of relaxation and pleasure (Papusek, 1974).
- When infants are deprived of explorations and control of their environment, and when the environment is disorganised or unpredictable so that their efforts do not produce a contingent positive outcome, various developmental problems, from delay to depression, can occur (Cicchetti & Aber, 1986). Such ineffectual patterns later lead to *learned helplessness.*

Let us take a minute to look at infants' developing confidence and control: Sroufe (1983) points out that infants are emotionally invested in being able to trust and predict events. They are *delighted* when an occurrence matches their mental anticipation. Developing infants also have the ability to fit novel but not totally unfamiliar events into their cognitive slots, or schemas. When they figure out a problem, delight takes the form of smiles; the cognitive tension is resolved, the baby is in control.

What happens when a baby is not able to make sense of events while others in her age group generally can? Cicchetti and Sroufe (1976) were able to *predict* the IQ scores of a group of infants with Down syndrome at 16 months with near-perfect accuracy, based on the infants' ability to *laugh* at some situations at nine months. These situations included the mother going towards the baby in a penguin walk with her arms extended open, 'I'm gonna get you!' games, and gently blowing at the baby's hair.

> Laughter in predictable but tension arousing situations serves as a strong predictor of mental development, as it is indicative of the infant's emotional, attentional and cognitive development.

Memory and imitation ability

The fact that infants come equipped with perceptual processes much more sophisticated than was earlier thought is also demonstrated in their ability to imitate. Infants between 12 and 21 days of age were able to show a rudimentary visual imitation ability when they replicated the facial expressions and tongue protrusion of the adult facing them (Meltzoff & Moore, 1977). Although more advanced strategies such as *deferred imitation* do not emerge until the second year, this early ability has significant repercussions in infant and carer *attachment.*

Recognition memory is based on a comparison of old information with the new information. *Recall*, or *productive memory*, on the other hand, requires old information to be brought up without such a comparison. Infants exhibit some remarkable memory skills as well:

- Using a habituation paradigm, five- and six-month-old babies were found to discriminate human faces. When exposed to a baby's face for a short time, the infant habituated to it by scanning it. Then, when the same picture was shown together with a bald man's face, the infant spent more time and attention looking at the new stimulus, indicating that she had recognised the baby's face as the old information and was busy assimilating something different (Fagan & Singer, 1979).
- The manner in which babies habituate and dishabituate to new and old stimuli correlates moderately with later intelligence, and is considered a good predictor of cognitive ability. Babies with Down syndrome, for example, take considerably longer to habituate (Bornstein & Sigman, 1986).
- By 12 months of age, infants demonstrate productive memory capacity, as they spontaneously imitate ritualistic games and remember the location of objects. This skill plays a fundamental role in the emergence of representational and language skills.

Object permanence is a central concept in the first year and probably forms a cornerstone of most facets of infant development. It refers to the idea that objects do not cease to exist when they are no longer visible. As basic as it sounds, infants develop this idea at about six to eight months, at which time they are able to retrieve a toy half-covered by a blanket, indicating that they can recognise a part of an object they are familiar with. Before that time, babies operate on an 'out of sight, out of mind' principle: even as they watch a toy being covered, they do not make an effort to search for or retrieve it, probably thinking that it has ceased to exist. By eight to 12 months, infants will make an active effort to remove the cloth covering the object, or actively seek it when it is obstructed from view.

The necessity of *object permanence* to cognitive development is well recognised by Piaget, and this concept contributes to our understanding of *infant intelligence* within the constructivist framework. It is also an essential skill in *language acquisition*: it is hard to conjecture how the infant could use symbols to represent something unless it had an enduring presence. It is also thought that *attachment behaviour* is predicated on object permanence, since the infant's yearning for the mother would be dependent on her mentally representing that figure in the mother's absence (Flavell, 1985).

PREVERBAL (PRELINGUISTIC) COMMUNICATION

Before we start talking about language or prelinguistic development, we need to frame the concept of language. Language is a *systematic* (rule-governed) use of *symbols* (words) which stand for objects, events, relations and ideas, to generate and convey *meaning* through potentially *infinite* combination of the symbols. It usually involves verbal symbols with words, sentences and narrative—verbal language. Its essence is *communication*; therefore it does not necessarily depend on verbal symbols; gestural or manual languages such as those used in hearing impairment are equally legitimate languages. Furthermore, the use of verbal language is often augmented by non-verbal communication, such as gestures and facial expressions. We review speech and language development, and their deficits, in Chapter 10. Our purpose here is to appreciate: that this uniquely human attribute starts virtually from the first day of life; what the infant brings to the task, and that the substrates of language are entrenched in a prelinguistic social interaction between the infant and her carers.

Infancy is the period in the life span that perhaps best exemplifies the *interdependence and interrelatedness of developmental domains*. The infant's developing of linguistic skills are predicated on her cognitive skills, which are dependent on her sensorimotor exploration and discovery as well as her skills in social interactivity. Language acquisition is a formidable *cognitive* task, where the infant must figure out the rule systems of the input language and, gradually and with communicative intentions, *map* her knowledge of the world onto linguistic structures. She will achieve this without direct 'teaching' from the mature language-users; however, both infant and caregiver bring into play *strategies* that facilitate this process. Thus, three major determinants of language acquisition in infancy need to be considered:

- the *infant's innate readiness* or prewiring for communication and problem-solving;
- the *learning strategies employed by the infant* in decoding and encoding oral language;
- the *teaching/scaffolding strategies employed by the caregiver* in communicating with the infant.

Innate readiness

In reviewing the perceptual capabilities of the newborn, the following findings make it clear that the human infant is ready, willing and able to establish the basics of communication (clearly, a handicapping condition may form an immediate barrier):

- Auditorily, the infant demonstrates the ability to recognise and discriminate speech sounds.
- Visually, she shows a preference for the human face, and has the ability to focus at a distance perfectly suited to engaging in eye contact with the mother during feeding and other close-range activities.
- As early as the first day after birth, the infant seems to engage in a

turn-taking routine during feeding, which is amazingly similar to the structure of a conversation and is organised like suck–pause–mother's jiggle–suck. The conversational counterpart would be talk–listen–prompt–talk.

■ The cognitive attainments allow the infant to have mental images and representational thought–crucial in acquiring language, which itself is a set of symbols.

Infant learning strategies

The language surrounding the infant in the home, with its fast-paced, noisy conversations between family members, is probably less than optimal for ease of language learning. Indeed the speech directed to the infant is greatly modified. The infant must still decide which utterances are good examples of the language, and hypothesise about the underlying meanings and structures. Some strategies for this process include the following.

Interrogative (questioning) utterances.   Questions are a direct way of testing hypotheses for the meaning of words. When seeking information or verification, the baby uses a rising intonation pattern (i.e. 'doggie?' or 'that?'), to which the adult responds with appropriate feedback. Infants can seek information with vocalisations and gestures by nine months of age (Halliday, 1975).

Selective imitation.   Imitation can be employed by some children. The usefulness of imitation decreases with age and as language becomes more complex. In the early phases, the infant's ability to imitate words depends on her understanding of their meanings (Ricks, 1979). Interestingly, children with delays may maintain this strategy long after it has stopped being a viable learning tool (Owens & MacDonald, 1982).

Early processing strategies.   Some operating principles may assist the infant in the task of language learning (Slobin, 1973). These include:

■ looking for systematic modification in word forms: the root word *walk* may be gleaned from analysing *walked* and *walking*;
■ looking for grammatical markers that clearly indicate the underlying meaning. Once *-ed* is discovered as marking past tense, for example, the *overextension* (overgeneralisation of one attribute to others with similar features) is seen in *breaked,* or *goed*;
■ avoiding exceptions and paying attention to the *ends* of words aid in learning the grammar of the language, accounting for the overextensions in tense as well as plurals (*book–books; foot–foots*).

These and other strategies must be quite effective, as children approximate adult grammar and have around 15 000 words in their vocabulary by six years of age, adding about nine words a day between 18 months and six years (Clark, 1983).

Caregiver teaching strategies

Adults engage in minimal direct language teaching, but *unconsciously* facilitate language acquisition by their behaviours. In the first two years of life, parents are talking with the child, labelling objects and events, and responding to the child's communication bids, by engaging in modelling, cuing and prompting. The parent (although most research is focused on the mother's patterns) modifies his/her own behaviour as the child's communication behaviours develop in an 'exquisitely tuned' manner (Bruner, 1978, p.9). When the child follows her pointing, the mother immediately asks a question. Whether the child responds with a gesture or a smile, she will supply a label. After the child is able to vocalise, the mother 'ups the ante' and withholds the label, or repeats the question until the child vocalises; then she gives the label. The mother may not accept babbled responses once her child is able to use single words; instead she responds with 'what's that?', requesting a restatement (Ninio & Bruner, 1978).

In addition, the mother makes modifications in the way she addresses and holds conversations with the infant, collectively called *motherese* or *parentese*, which is different from adult to adult speech in the following ways (Newport, Gleitman & Gleitman, 1977; Snow, 1977):

- slower speech with longer pauses between utterances and content[1] words;
- higher overall pitch, greater pitch range, and exaggerated intonation and stress;
- fewer words per minute, spoken fluently with a restricted vocabulary;
- more concrete reference to here and now, and three times as much repetition;
- fewer ungrammatical sentences, which are shorter and less complex;
- more imperatives (sentences that request and demand).

The infant is able to exhibit turn-taking ability very early on, and engages in *protoconversations* with her caregiver. The mother does not use turn-keeping behaviours, but enables the child to participate by turn-passing devices, maintaining the interaction (Wilkinson & Rembold, 1982) through:

- second-guessing the child's communication intentions;
- compensating for the child's communication failures; and
- providing feedback for those failures.

Such mechanisms are adult *scaffolds* to the development of language in infants.

---

1   *Content* words refer to words that have a tangible meaning, such as names of things, their attributes, and actions. *Function* words are smaller words which add grammatical elements, such as prepositions and articles. Children's first utterances are composed overwhelmingly of *content* words (Nelson, 1973).

Contraints

The baby comes equipped with the attributes necessary to elicit nurturing behaviours from the carers, from her physical features to her responsiveness to nurturing. Her perceptual and cognitive apparatus is prepared to form and test hypotheses in extracting meaning, and in gradually finding linguistic symbols and structures to map them onto. The stage is set: the social dance—genesis of communicative development, scaffolded by the carers towards linguistic competence and propped up by the infant's learning strategies—has begun. At this point, you may wish to consider how this natural interactivity and mutual responsivity may be disrupted if the mother or baby experience *constraints*, which inhibit or impede the process. A premature infant who is colicky and is hard to settle down, or a baby with a birth defect, and a mother with (postnatal) depression, for example, may battle such constraints that hinder their natural and spontaneous flow of communication.

Developmental stages

The following are some *developmental stages* towards emerging language in infancy.

- From birth to one month of age, the infant is primarily engaged in crying, although gurgles of contentment and fussing sounds are also common.
- From the second month, the sound repertoire expands to *cooing* of vowels and frequent sounds of laughter, with modulated pitch and intonation.
- At about six months, *babbling* begins in the form of vocal play, in which the infant begins to use consonants and vowels in repeated syllable sequences. From six to 12 months, about half of the baby's sounds are made up of such duplicated syllables (Mitchell & Kent, 1990). These strings often reflect the intonational patterns of the sentences the infant hears, suggesting that the melody of the input language is being practised.
- By nine to ten months, the infant has developed a set of *gestures* coupled with *vocalisations*, which clearly mark her intentions, and various functions, such as requesting and regulating the listener's actions (Halliday, 1975).
- Children understand before they can speak. Mothers report that, on average, their ten-month-old understands (*receptive language*) about 30 words, while their 13-month-old understands 100 words (Fenson, Dale, Reznick, Bates, Thal & Pethick, 1994).
- First words (*expressive language*), which are used consistently to refer to some object, action or attribute, *regardless* of how far removed they may be from the adult use, appear around 12 to 13 months. This is a rather slow stage, and infants usually use a limited repertoire of a few dozen words for about four months.

- From about 50 words at 16 months, the acquisition of new words tends to go through a 'vocabulary explosion', such that by 24 months, the average word number has reached 320, made up mostly of nouns (Fenson et al., 1994).

We examine the *semantic* (meaning), *pragmatic* (social use), *syntactic* (grammatical) and *phonological* properties of language development and their disabilities in Chapter 10.

PERSONALITY AND SOCIAL DEVELOPMENT

The individual differences manifested by babies are sometimes apparent by their activity levels in the womb. From their first day, some babies will sleep more, some will cry more, and others will watch the world in a calm and alert state. Such personality and *temperamental* differences will interact with the environmental and cultural variables, and contribute to the unique constellation of characteristics of that individual. It will also have a significant effect on the formation of *attachment*, which is thought to have a lasting imprint on social, emotional and cognitive behaviour.

Temperament

Temperament describes a collection of characteristics exhibited by an infant, and has been studied systematically in a pioneering longitudinal study (Thomas, Chess & Birch, 1963; Thomas & Chess, 1977). Accordingly, the ease or difficulty of caregiving to an infant is determined by her perceived temperamental characteristics. Certain groupings of temperamental characteristics such as cheerfulness, regularity of rhythms, and placidity mark the infant most parents wish for. Other infants may present challenges to the caregivers, particularly if they are easily irritated and hard to console. The infant temperamental *dimensions* and the *types* based on such assessment are summarised below.

temperamental dimensions / '*Types*'

- *Activity level:* the level and extent of motor activity, including reflexes.
- *Rhythmicity:* the regularity with which behaviours such as sleeping and feeding occur.
- *Distractability:* the degree to which child behaviour such as crying can be changed by intervention and diversion.
- *Approach/withdrawal:* the child's typical response to a novel stimulus or an unfamiliar person.
- *Adaptability:* the ease with which the child adapts to the changes in the environment.
- *Attention span and persistence:* the degree of task engagement; time devoted to an activity and the effect of distraction on that task.

- *Intensity:* the level of energy displayed in a reaction or a response.
- *Threshold of responsiveness:* the strength of the stimulus required before eliciting a visible response.
- *Quality of mood:* the preponderance of positive, happy and friendly behaviours, as opposed to negative, unhappy and unfriendly behaviours.

Of these dimensions and their ratings, *rhythmicity* (irregular), *approach/withdrawal* (withdrawal), *adaptability* (slowly adaptable), *intensity* (intense), and *quality of mood* (negative) mark a *difficult* temperament. Such knowledge can be helpful to a parent, who might then cater to the infant's temperament by introducing change gradually and maintaining a predictable environment with its daily routines to ease the infant's adjustment in the process of socialisation.

In one Australian study, a large representative sample of 2443 families were surveyed with respect to the temperamental characteristics of their four- to eight-month-old infants (Sanson, Prior & Oberklaid, 1985). Some of the findings are given below.

- In all, 39% of the infants were rated as being easy, 40% as being average, 8% as being slow to warm up, and 12% as being difficult. This distribution dovetailed with the US study results, which nevertheless indicated a slightly higher incidence of slow-to-warm-up (10%) and difficult (15%) infants.
- No gender differences were found in the classification of temperament.
- Birth variables, such as prematurity, low birthweight, complications of delivery and perinatal stress, were taken into account; no association was found between these variables and temperament.
- Birth order (first- or last-born status) or urban vs rural habitation did not relate to temperament.
- A physiological variable, mainly colic, *did* exhibit a significant relationship to temperament: only 20% of the babies with easy temperaments experienced moderate to severe colic, while more than 50% of the babies with difficult temperament did so.
- Cultural background also yielded some differences: about 20% of the mothers and 27% of the fathers born outside Australia were found to have significantly more slow-to-warm-up and difficult temperaments in their infants.

Thomas and Chess (1977) coined the term *'goodness of fit'* to describe the amount of concordance between the temperamental characteristics of the child and the parents' desires of the child, which in turn reflect their own personality attributes. To the extent that there is a good fit, the child's temperament will probably continue. A poor fit may result in more discontinuous patterns, as well as being a potential source of conflict. To illustrate, a cuddly baby and a parent who seeks and rewards bodily contact have a good fit; the attribute is likely to remain throughout the socialisation process. A non-cuddly baby and a reserved parent who may express his or her affection through visual gaze or verbal means would also indicate a good fit; where one is different from the other in terms of needs for physical closeness, experiences of some frustration are inevitable.

A longitudinal investigation from infancy to adulthood of 133 infants classified as either having easy or difficult temperament indicated that the ratings at three years were considerably more indicative of the adult temperament of the participants, particularly in boys with difficult temperament (Korn, 1984).

The directionality of change in temperament between infants and parents may be *reciprocal*: children also effect change in their parents. Mothers of the boys with difficult temperament reported at 18 months that they exerted much less effort to change them now than they did when they were 12 months of age (Maccoby, Snow & Jacklin, 1984). Such gender effects may be consistent with the goodness of fit hypothesis, since attributes such as high activity level, stubbornness and intense negative reactions may be more acceptable in boys than in girls. The socialisation influences exerted by parents, teachers or peers are likely to be less vigorous to modify difficult temperament in boys than in girls.

> Parent–child relations can be viewed in a context of reciprocal determinism . . . Mothers' child-rearing practices alter children's behaviour, and children's behaviour alters mothers' child-rearing practices (Siegal, 1985, p.70).

Attachment

Attachment is another *central* construct which will have lifelong effects on the developing infant. Secure attachment in early childhood will affect feelings of emotional wellbeing, social development and cognitive growth; in later life, dividends are likely to be contentment with self, reciprocity in love relations, and good adjustment and mental health. To better understand this construct, let us recall the infant's reactions to adults.

1. From birth, most infants prefer people to inanimate objects.
2. Until about three months, they exhibit totally indiscriminate affection towards humans in receiving care, nurturing and attention. The social smile is dispensed freely, and separation from *any* caring human is protested.
3. By four months, *differential sociability* emerges, where the infant begins to single out the familiar few people she takes delight in interacting with, although a competent carer can replace the leaving parents without much fuss.
4. From six to eight months until about 18 months, however, some dramatic

changes take place: out goes the friendly, spontaneous sociability, and in comes the fear of strangers, crying, and clinging to the departing parent. The infant has fallen in love with her primary caregiver, and no-one else will do as well. The fact that the baby has achieved object permanence has a lot to do with her searching for the mother and the accompanying *separation anxiety* from her.

5. From 18 months to two years and on, factors like rapid growth in language and representational skills will permit the infant to predict the departures and arrivals of the mother, with a considerable lessening of the separation anxiety by three years.

Bowlby (1969) suggested three phases in the development of an infant's attachment.

Non-focused orienting and signalling.   Through innate mechanisms, the newborn is building expectancies, schemas, and the ability to discriminate mother and father from others by crying, eye contact, clinging, cuddling and responding to parents' efforts to soothe. However, these early *proximity-seeking* behaviours are simply emitted, rather than being directed to a particular person (Ainsworth, 1989).

Focus on one or more figure(s).   From three months, the baby starts to smile discriminately to her caregivers, although no-one in particular has yet become the safe base, nor is *separation anxiety* and fear of strangers evidenced at separation from the parents.

Secure base behaviour.   By six months of age the now sitting baby is able to signal the caregiver, as well as proceeding to approach her in *proximity-seeking* behaviours. A caregiver has been chosen (usually the mother) as the safe base/most important person, although the infant may exhibit attachment behaviours with a number of caregivers, such as the father, older siblings, grandparents or baby-sitters. By ten months, *social referencing* has begun to occur: she checks the facial expression of the parent before venturing on a novel experience. Fear of strangers and separation anxiety are present.

Some behaviours that indicate the baby's attachment to a particular carer include (Ainsworth, 1973):

- crying to attract the carer's attention; smiling at her more than other people;
- crying when she leaves or puts her down; following her;
- looking at the direction of the carer's voice;
- after a separation, greeting the carer with joy and excitement; lifting arms towards her, clapping hands, embracing, hugging, kissing;
- exploring the environment in the carer's presence, which serves as a secure 'home' base;
- Running to the carer in perceived danger.

Using these behaviours as indicators, Ainsworth and her colleagues designed a laboratory procedure known as the *strange situation,* in which attachment behaviour could be carefully and precisely evaluated. In this paradigm, the following steps are performed (Ainsworth, Blehar, Waters & Wall, 1978):

1. Infant and mother enter the empty room (which has a one-way mirror for recording).
2. Infant plays with toys while mother is seated in the room for a few minutes.
3. An experimenter (the stranger) enters, sits down and talks to the mother.
4. After a few minutes, the mother leaves, and the infant is alone with the stranger, who comforts her if she is upset.
5. Mother returns, greets the baby and comforts her (as necessary) for three minutes.
6. Mother leaves the room, leaving the baby alone for a few minutes.
7. Stranger re-enters the room, and offers comfort.
8. Mother returns, greets the baby and comforts her; tries to divert her to toy play.

Although the reunion episodes are the most significant ones, all of the episodes are measured with respect to infant's ways of establishing contact, exploratory play behaviour, and crying. The expectation was that, if the attachment had taken place as it should, the baby should show feelings of security with the mother. Infants are classified with respect to the nature of their attachment, based on the observed patterns. One secure attachment and two patterns of insecure attachment are identified by the Ainsworth team (1978); a fourth one (disorganised attachment) has since been described (Main, Kaplan & Cassidy, 1985). The incidences cited are in middle-class American children.

Type A: Avoidant attachment.   Infants are not usually stressed during separation; they react to the stranger in much the same ways as they do to their mother. When picked up by the mother they do not resist physical contact, but neither do they cling (20%).

Type B: Secure attachment.   Infants, if they cry, do so in the mother's absence, indicating a preference for her over the stranger. On her return, infants actively seek contact and their crying diminishes immediately (about 65%).

Type C: Anxious/resistant attachment.   Infants seek closeness before the mother's departure, but after she returns they exhibit visibly angry and resistive behaviour, which may include hitting or pushing away. They continue to cry after being picked up, and cannot easily be soothed by the mother (10%–12%).

Type D: Disorganised/disoriented attachment.   Reflecting the greatest insecurity, babies display an array of confused and contradictory behaviours in the reunion episodes, such as looking away when being held. They seem to have a glazed look, odd postures, and unpredictable crying episodes (less than 5%).

The following mothering variables are found to be related to secure attachment (Bretherton & Waters, 1985):

- the mother's frequency of affectionate verbal and physical contact with the baby;
- the speed with which she responds to the baby's distress calls;
- the appropriateness of her distress-relieving strategies;
- the mother's contingent responsiveness to the baby's vocalisations;
- the frequency of her play with the baby, which is cognitively stimulating.

Obviously, the mother's sensitivity to the infant's cues is the key to secure attachment. Accurate interpretation of the infant's signals by a sensitive parent is also foundational to the early communicative exchange on which competent communication is built (Bruner, 1983). Below are some outcomes in securely attached children. In comparison with their insecurely attached peers, they score higher on (Sroufe, 1985):

- self-esteem and popularity with peers;
- skills for coping with difficult cognitive or social challenges;
- skills for dealing effectively with failure;
- curiosity, enthusiasm and persistence in learning;
- mature independence and autonomy from their parents;
- lack of problem behaviours such as aggression, anxiety and antisocial conduct.

Attachment is a *mental representation* of how the world and the interpersonal relations in it are viewed by the growing child, and it spans a lifetime. We carry it with us, unless a wilful attempt is made (self-discovery, counselling or psychotherapy) to change our belief, understanding and representation of this *cognitive* notion. Attachment research is a cornerstone of developmental psychology.

CONCLUSIONS

In our review, we have underlined the notion of the 'competent infant' who, in a very short span of time after birth, proceeds to influence her environment and the agents in it quite skilfully. The interrelated nature of *all* developmental domains also become quite evident in our study of infancy, where no one domain can be examined irrespective of the influences exerted on it by others: language is dependent on cognition, which is dependent on motor exploration, which is guided by perceptual processes, all of which have a role in affecting the socioemotional connectedness between the infant and the caregivers. We revisit attachment in the growing child in the following chapters and examine a hot debate: attachment and daycare.

Now on to the wondrously terrible twos!

6

Toddlerhood: becoming one's own person

After infancy, *toddlerhood* is the next phase of development; it roughly covers the period from 18 months to three years of age. It is a fascinating period of development, during which the infant increasingly assumes the characteristics of a little person, with a mind of his own, communication skills that are quite powerful and an emerging awareness of social interrelatedness and play. As the toddler realises that he is a separate entity from his caregivers, he often utilises the infamous tool of protest against parental requests; thus the 'terrible twos', which in fact is a significant step towards achieving personhood. As we discuss self- and gender concept, language, play and social, and cognitive domains, we again realise how interwoven the domains of development are in the young child.

DEVELOPMENT OF SELF-CONCEPT

The traditions that have left the most indelible mark on child development, those of Freud and Piaget, both conceptualise the newborn as not having a sense of separateness. Freud thought of the unity of the infant and the mother as a *symbiotic relationship*, while Piaget claimed that until the infant had achieved object permanence he would not be able to achieve *self-permanence,* where the self is seen as a separate and continuous entity.

Current views seem to support an emerging sense of self from an *existential understanding* of 'I exist', which emerges in the second to third month, to one of 'I exist separately from mum and dad' by the time object permanence is established. This is the emergence of the *subjective* self.

The second task for the toddler is for him to realise that he has *objective* properties, qualities and descriptors. This awareness of self as an agent in the environment initially presents as *concrete categorical self*, since the toddler would define himself according to physical categories and attributes. The child will move towards more *abstract categorical self* in later childhood and adolescence as the determining descriptors of self are centred more on psychological attributes (Lewis, 1991).

One ingenious method of ascertaining self-awareness in babies is the lipstick-on-the-nose paradigm (Lewis & Brooks, 1978). In this procedure, the baby is allowed to look at himself in the mirror. After a period of free exploration, the experimenter puts a spot of lipstick on the baby's nose while pretending to wipe his face with a cloth, and then the baby resumes looking at the mirror.

- None of the nine to 12-month-old babies made an attempt to touch their own noses, but continued to interact with the mirror image of themselves without any sign of recognition that it was their *own* image they were looking at.
- By 21 months, nearly three-quarters of the toddlers touched their own noses when they saw their mirror image, indicating that they had recognised themselves, and were aware of the red dot that they did not expect from their earlier experiences with the mirror.
- Another test of self-awareness is that of children's ability to name themselves when they are presented with a photo of themselves. This self-naming occurs at the same time and rate as mirror recognition: it emerges by 15 months, and stabilises before the second year (Bullock & Lutkenhaus, 1990).
- Expressions of *self-conscious* or self-evaluative emotions, such as pride, shame or embarrassment, occur at about the same time (Lewis, Allesandri & Sullivan, 1992).

This awareness of self is reflected in the toddler's quest for independence and autonomy. He knows and claims passionately the toys that are his; he tests the boundaries of parental expectations to their limit. The terrible twos are actually the wondrous twos of self-awareness and increased freedom, and mark the toddler's becoming his own person. The two-year-old knows who he is: he can tell his name, probably even his gender, and certainly how big or little he is! The toddler has now acquired a repertoire of social *scripts*, or routines of play, that he uses in interacting with others. He is some years away from defining himself in terms of more global attributes (i.e. 'I'm good at swimming'), and capitalises on concrete ones like 'I'm strong'; nevertheless, the journey towards the consolidation of the sense of self and, later, self-esteem has begun.

Development of gender concept

A young child's ability to figure out gender proceeds by incorporating a number of concepts. This includes *gender identity*, which refers to the ability of the child to label his own sex, as well as to identify others as boys or girls, men or women.

- Babies as young as nine to 12 months of age seem to respond differentially to male and female faces, indicating an understanding that they are different (Fagot & Leinbach, 1993).
- Within the second year, the labels of boy and girl are acquired. Most two-year-olds are able to pick out the picture that represents their gender from a set containing one same-sex picture, with several opposite-sex ones (Thomson, 1975).
- By 30 months to three years of age, most toddlers can correctly identify pictures of boys from girls by labelling them appropriately, although cues of hair length and clothing seem to drive their decisions.

Gender stability is not sufficiently indicative of a true understanding that one's gender remains so for life. Indeed, it is only by four years of age that questions like 'When you grow up, will you be a mummy or a daddy?' or 'When you were a baby, were you a boy or a girl?' are answered correctly (Slaby & Frey, 1975).

Gender constancy is the understanding that person's gender will not be altered by changes in such physical attributes as clothing or hair length. This skill appears to be related to solving the *conservation* problems towards the end of the preoperational stage (we discuss these cognitive accomplishments in Chapter 7).

Development of *sex-role* concepts and stereotypes seems to begin as soon as toddlers recognise and discriminate between genders. Interestingly, children's *own* behaviour appears to be *sex-typed* earlier than their notions regarding sex stereotypes. Toddlers show a preference for sex-stereotyped toys (i.e. dolls for girls and guns for boys) before they can identify their own gender (O'Brien, 1992). By three years of age, before they have mastered the concept of gender stability, children begin to show a preference for same-sex playmates (Maccoby, 1990).

These notions will become much more entrenched in the preschool and later years. How do sex-role and gender-specific concepts develop? A likely explanation is provided within the Piagetian framework (Martin, 1991): self-concept necessitates the formation of a *'self schema'*, as gender concept requires a *'gender schema'*. Children as young as two years can form a gender schema and, because gender is clearly categorical, information derived from experiences is easily assimilated into it. Thus, gender preferences and *stereotyping* begin very early in life (and undoing them is probably considerably more difficult than acquiring them).

SYMBOLIC DEVELOPMENT AND LANGUAGE

You will recall that one of the greatest discoveries the infant made was that of the association between distinct clusters of sounds and a matching set of meanings. Genuine comprehension of word meanings requires a number of skills (Lenneberg, 1969):

- The child needs to conduct a *phonetic* analysis which dissects complete words into its constituent sounds, as well as understanding the boundaries of words.
- He will need the *semantic* ability to recognise that all things can have names, even those objects whose names he has not heard before.
- He will also need the *syntactic* ability to analyse the utterances, so that he can extract the rules underlying their organisation and the knowledge of how individual words relate to the utterance.

Children acquire the concepts before they use words; they map words onto meanings they know. Typically, the range of things they want to talk about exceeds the words they have available to them. That is to say, their *comprehension* is far greater than their *production.* Some early word use may have the following characteristics:

- Early phonological development and a semantic understanding of the world are interdependent. The first words produced by a child are likely to be those that contain familiar and phonologically producible sounds (Schwartz & Leonard, 1982).
- Children apply systematic rules to fit their phonological capabilities (see Chapter 10). Toddlers can correctly identify pictures by pointing when they are presented by the adult pronunciation, although they cannot produce the sounds themselves (Barton, 1980).
- The attainments of the sensorimotor period are reflected in the choice of the first words acquired. The mastery of *object permanence*, for example, allows for words connoting *disappearance* (i.e. 'allgone') to emerge. When the child is able to use insight and not just trial and error in problem-solving, as he does in stage 6 (*invention of new means),* terms like 'there . . .' or 'oh–oh' appear (Gopnik & Meltzoff, 1987).
- *Fast mapping* refers to the ability of the young child to build a large vocabulary amazingly fast. This cognitive process provides support for vocabulary growth, by the availability of the memory traces of the new words for several days. Young children can fast map new words even from television programs (Rice & Woodsmall, 1988).

During this fast-paced vocabulary expansion period, toddlers are bound to make some errors, particularly because their comprehension trails ahead of their production. Common errors, which basically reflect the child's experimentation and problem-solving with language, include the following (Clark, 1983):

- *underextension,* where the child uses a very restricted use of the word to represent a class of words. It is difficult to spot this unless contextual cues are being utilised, because the child appears to use the word correctly. For example, the word 'cat' may be used to label only the family pet; all other cats are yet nameless;

- *overextension,* where the child uses a word to denote a larger collection of attributes. For example, the word cat may be used for all four-legged creatures, including dogs, horses, monkeys and bears. These are not random errors, and only objects in the same class, with similar referents, are overgeneralised by the use of one word;

- *invented descriptors,* another fascinating example of the young mind at work. When the child does not know the word for an object or a function, he invents one based on its properties. For example, my daughter's words for the bath sponge was 'sweeze wada' (squeeze water), our veterinarian was 'dog man'.

A possible explanation for how children acquire word meanings (Clark, 1983) is that they are constantly highlighting new information against the known labels in their repertoire. Use of words facilitates cognitive development, as cognitive development promotes linguistic competence. This reciprocal influence will probably continue: the acquisition and use of new words and verbal expressions facilitates cognitive development by allowing their meanings to be clear and explicit, by permitting their use to go beyond the 'here and now' as well as contributing to the efficiency and flexibility of human thought.

Individual differences

Children acquire language at different *rates* within the developmental continuum. Furthermore, individual differences in the *form* of language development may be evident in the use of the first words. In her classic study, Nelson (1973) investigated a group of 12–30-month-olds, and reported on the differences in the words the children produced.

- *Referential style* children used many familiar object names and nouns, with fewer verbs, proper names and modifiers. This group thought language served the purpose of talking about *things.* They used clearer articulation in their early sentences, and showed quicker growth in their vocabulary and grammar.

- *Expressive style* children used more pronouns and social formulas, which were often compressed into a single utterance (i.e. I want it; stop it), and fewer nouns, verbs and modifiers. This group thought language served the purpose of talking about expressions of feelings and needs, the self, and other people. They used more pronouns and verb phrases in their early sentences.

Some of these early differences persist into preschool years. They also highlight the interdependence of the child's temperamental characteristics and the social interactional environment that sustains them (Goldfield, 1987). The *referential* child seems to have a keen interest in exploring objects, with a rich array of play materials to manipulate and parents who respond with words to the child's early attempts to communicate. The *expressive* child seems to have a more socially oriented temperament, and is raised in an environment where language is often used to mediate social relationships.

Grammatical development

Young children's early two-word combinations are sometimes described as *telegraphic speech*, because they seem to compact the most important information into the fewest possible utterances. Although this clever strategy may contain conventional grammatical structures (such as word order in English), the mature use of grammar is not the organising principle behind these early sentences. Rather, children use *semantic relations* to express meaning. For example, the sentence 'daddy car' may mean 'daddy is driving the car' or 'the car belonging to daddy' or 'daddy is over there by the car', depending on the context (see Chapter 10).

Between 18 months and three-and-a-half years, children also begin acquiring grammatical *morphology*, such as prepositions (in, on) and verb tenses and endings (-ing, -ed), which gradually gives cohesion and clarity to their utterances. *Mean length of utterance* is a commonly used method for examining grammatical development of early sentences. These concepts are more fully reviewed in Chapter 10.

The interdependence of all domains of language is vividly evident in the early stages of language acquisition. The child uses meaning to scaffold grammatical development, and uses grammar to infer meaning. Here is an interesting study with two-year-olds to demonstrate this point (Heibeck & Markman, 1987):

> Children were given words which had attributes like colour, texture or shape that they were not familiar with. The only indication of the words' meanings came from the context in which they were used. Even the two-year-olds were able to quickly narrow down the meaning of the words from directions such as, 'Give me the *chartreuse* one, not the red one' or 'Put the *parallelogram* beside the square.' Shape names were acquired more readily than colours or textures.

An important consideration in interacting with toddlers is the ability of the caregiving adult to make a concerted effort to understand the meaning implied by these often truncated and idiosyncratic utterances. Mismatches between toddlers' implied meaning and caregivers' inferred ones may not only delay language acquisition—they can also make communication an unrewarding and perhaps alienating experience for the child. Indeed, successful conversations with toddlers may involve a fair degree of sleuthing. Clark (1983) gives the following puzzle to illustrate the point. See if you can determine the common characteristics of all the referents the words are used for.

Child's word[a]	Situations for which it is used
1. Car	Car, motorcycle, bicycle, aeroplane with a propeller, helicopter
2. Hi!	Hands under blanket, hands in gloves, wiggling finger puppets
3. Cotty-bars	Abacus, toast rack, photo of a Greek temple
4. Kutija	Matchbox, bedside table, cardboard box, chest of drawers
5. Kuck	Cat, fluttering moth, turtle on TV, throwing a ball

[a] 1 = Something with a wheel; 2 = Something that hides a hand; 3 = Something with bars, like a cot; 4 = A container that opens and closes; 5 = Something with moving arms, legs or wings.

Conversations with the toddler

No influence in a young child's life can be as powerful as having a caring adult communication partner to talk to, listen to, share with and grow with. The mother's presence alone can be a potent motive for language acquisition, as babies enjoy being talked to and understood long before they have the formal linguistic structures in place. As we see in Chapter 5, caregivers fulfil this role admirably, providing *motherese* or *baby talk* from the first days of birth and adjusting its complexity instinctively to the comprehension level of the growing child.

- In an Australian study of the effects of motherese on language acquisition, Cross (1981) found that mothers who made the most fundamental and frequent simplifications of language input to their toddlers had children with the most advanced language skills by 36 months of age.
- The child's age, his level of cognitive development and rate of language acquisition were also found to be important determinants of the style of input language employed by the mother (Cross, 1978).
- Mothers use mostly repetitions, followed by naming objects, with *no* expansions for their 11-month-old; almost equal measures of repetitions, naming of objects and expansions with their two-year-old; and minimal repetitions and expansions but more naming of objects when their child is five years of age (Nienhuys, Cross & Horsborough, 1984).
- Examining the use of motherese in *daycare centres*, it was found that daycare staff made somewhat less effective use of motherese compared with full-time mothers; however, in centres with adequate staffing ratios, both groups of children were found to develop language at the same rate (Cross, Nienhuys & Kirkman, 1983).
- Signing mothers of deaf children found it considerably more difficult to communicate with their child than did parents of hearing children. The child's hearing problem limited the mother's awareness of the amount of language understood by the child and the mother's ability to formulate a

message commensurate with the child's comprehension (Nienhuys, Horsborough & Cross, 1985).

> The truth may be that the child is responsible, not only for his/her own pace but also for the parent's pace in the language learning process (Cross, 1981, p.120).

DEVELOPMENT OF PLAY AND SOCIAL SKILLS

Toddlers' newly acquired skills in language open up a whole new array of social interactions and exchanges. These will be evident in the development of social play with peers, and the assertion of autonomy from parents and verbal negotiations with them.

Social play

Infants as young as ten months are likely to touch each other and engage in pulling toys away from each other if they are seated in proximity. By 18 months, children who have had regular contact with peers may begin displaying rudimentary cooperation, although such attempts are largely volatile and inept (Garvey, 1977). Language use in such exchanges has been described as 'collective monologue' by Piaget, where each child talks more about what he is doing with little true reciprocity.

The group care experience many toddlers participate in provides a rich context in which these skills can be refined and elaborated. The functional use of language during social play can be observed to include the following (Pellegrini, 1984):

- *instrumental communication,* where language is used to further the goals or to influence the other's behaviour; i.e. 'give me my book';
- *social facilitation,* where the use of language is directed to facilitate or harmonise social relations; i.e. 'come play with us';
- *imaginative mental stimulation,* where language is used to generate new and complex ideas or to explore the environment; i.e. 'why does that one sink?'.

In the same study, the quality of functional play language seemed to be negatively affected by adult intervention. When left alone by an adult, four-year-olds took initiative more than two- and three-year-olds, who were relatively dependent on adult guidance in generating play schemes.

It seems that the adult's best facilitative role is in orchestrating the environment that will be conducive to engaging young children in social play.

Language of assertiveness

Regardless of the level of high or low compliance of the infant before the age of 18 months, naturalistic observations of mother–child interactions indicate a sharp increase of *negativism* between 18 and 24 months. The toddler's emerging sense of self is made obvious, much to the parents' shock. By age three it shows a significant drop, with further reductions in the following two years (Wenar, 1982).

In a Brisbane study (Siegal & Storey, 1985), toddlers who attended daycare were found to be *more* negativistic than those who were reared at home when it came to complying with parental directives. However, these youngsters were also found to have a better understanding of social norms and rules of peer social interaction than did those who stayed at home. Daycare teachers were found to spend less time reprimanding the toddlers than their mothers did. It was concluded that rule-guided social behaviour was practised and refined in social contexts with peers, and discrepancies in expectations between the centre and home settings were the practice grounds for testing the boundaries of compliance for the toddler.

The extent of compliance also seems to be related to the language skills of the toddler. In a study examining the contribution of parent–child interaction towards compliance of the toddler in household tasks, the following findings were noted (Lawrence, 1984):

- Toddlers at the single-word stage were much more inclined to defy or ignore parental pleas for cooperation.
- Those children who were able to use telegraphic utterances with two to three words were significantly *less* defiant than their less-able peers.
- With single-word users, parents' strategies which acknowledged what the child was doing *positively*, before presenting him with the request, elicited more compliance.
- With multiple-word users, forceful, loud, explicit and direct commands elicited better compliance (i.e. 'Pick up those blocks and put them in the box now') than did indirect, and more complex requests (i.e. 'Would you mind helping me pack away?').

It seems that toddlers are initially more likely to respond by verbal negotiation than by outright non-compliance; however, when negotiations fail and frustration sets in, tantrums may be on the horizon. Things have to get worse before they get *much* better by four years.

Cultural factors towards verbal assertiveness and compliance contribute significantly to the mode of negotiation and conflict resolution in children. A study of Anglo-Australian and Lebanese-Australian parents' expectations about their children's verbal assertiveness indicated that, on the dimensions of resolving disagreements without fighting, stating their own preference when they were asked, and standing up for their own rights, Lebanese-born parents expected assertiveness in their children to develop at a later age than did Anglo-Australian parents (Goodnow, Cashmore, Cotton & Knight, 1984).

In contrast, in a study of parent-child interactions at home with urban Aboriginal and Anglo-Australian families, Aboriginal parents were observed to take a much more egalitarian approach. They did not see their children's non-compliance as a threat to their authority, gave independence to the toddler as soon as he seemed ready to assume it, and involved young children in the activities of the older members of the community from an early age (Bavin, 1993).

Learning is child's play

Play is the medium in which children construct their knowledge. The stages in which play changes seem to follow Piaget's stages quite closely (Rubin, Fein & Vandenberg, 1983; Smilansky, 1968):

- *Sensorimotor/functional play*, evident in the first year, centres on exploring and manipulating objects using all the sensorimotor schemes available to the infant.
- *Constructive play* contains these elements, particularly with novel objects; however, by two years the toddler begins to use objects to *construct* things, like towers with blocks, which makes up nearly half of his playtime between three and six years.
- *Pretend/make-believe play* begins at about the same time, in the second year. The toddler moves from using toys acting on the self in pretence, to the toy or the person becoming the *recipient* of the pretend play.
- *Substitute pretend play* arises between two and three years of age, when toddlers begin using objects to stand for something entirely different (i.e. riding the broom as the horse).
- *Sociodramatic play* emerges when children are able to assume others' roles. Several children join the play, creating mutual pretence. Some two-year-olds begin engaging in sociodramatic play; by four years virtually all children are involved in this type of play. The creation of *imaginary friends* seems a normal byproduct of this activity.
- *Rule-governed play and games*, occurring in early school years, is where children understand and conform to the rules in games and more structured play (hopscotch, board games) emerges.

By playing roles, acting out often elaborate fantasies and pretending to be others, children become increasingly aware of how the world of social relations works. In the process, their egocentric approach to the world diminishes, paving the way for friendships, empathy and social cognition. Let's take a closer look.

COGNITIVE DEVELOPMENT

You will recall that the *sensorimotor* stage dominated infancy, and Piaget believed that during this period the following attributes characterised the baby:

1. He responds to the world basically through sensory and motor schemas.
2. He functions in the here-and-now, responding to available stimuli only.
3. He is not able to plan ahead or have intentions, but anticipates recurring events.
4. He does not have an internal mental representation of objects, or symbols (words) which stand for objects that can be mentally manipulated.

Toddlerhood presents this major transition into *internal representation and symbolic functioning*. It also marks the onset of *preoperational thought*. Emerging language is the hallmark of representational activity. Children's growing mastery of symbolic activity is also seen in several aspects of their play (Corrigan, 1987):

- Children move from using real-life resembling objects in their pretend play, to less realistic and more symbolic objects. For example, the use of a toy telephone may soon be replaced by a wooden spoon as a communication device.
- Make-believe play moves away from the self, and play objects become the recipients of actions. Whereas the 14-month-old may be busy combing his own hair, a two-year-old may have the mummy doll combing the baby doll's hair. This progression indicates that the toddler is aware of the fact that the recipients of actions can act independently of him.
- Early pretend play may be limited to a single schema; for example, the child can fill the truck with sand, but cannot combine filling with carrying. Soon, play involves complex coordinations of schemes, and gradually *sociodramatic play* appears at around two-and-a-half years. Sociodramatic play, too, becomes increasingly complex, requiring a combination of social, language and cognitive skills, and is the cornerstone of development in the preschool years.

Constraints of preoperational thought

According to Piaget, the representational thinking of preoperational thought does not yet obey logical rules, or *operations* (hence the term *preoperational*). It is typically rigid, inflexible and perceptually bound; therefore it is *prelogical* and *intuitive*. Judged by the *rational* thought processes of the adults or older children, it may appear incorrect or distorted. Piaget saw many limitations in preoperational thought. As we look at his views on 'deficiencies' of this period's thought patterns, please bear in mind that quite a few of his assertions have been challenged. Not all will be applicable to toddlerhood; we put them all in perspective in Chapter 7.

■ *Preoperational egocentricism* describes the child's inability to consider others' viewpoints, hence self-centredness with respect to his own symbolic views.

■ *Animistic thinking* is the young child's belief that inanimate objects have life-like qualities. For example, my daughter at 30 months was convinced that her life-sized stuffed toy koala bear was miserable and cried each night, because we had to leave it behind while we were overseas (just *one* of the many stuffed toys she commiserated with).

■ *Transducive reasoning* means that young children rely on associations in time and space between events for causal explanations of phenomenon, rather than logical processes. Such magical thought is evident in comments like 'Let's go shopping mummy so we can buy some money'.[1]

■ *Lack of transitivity* describes the inability of the two- and three-year-old's to arrange items from the smallest to the largest, or the shortest to the tallest.

■ *Perception-bound thought* refers to paying more attention to the physical appearance of objects in reaching decisions about their capabilities.

■ *Centration* is focusing of the child's attention on one attribute at the expense of others in problem-solving.

These patterns of thought make *conservation* tasks a serious challenge for the preoperational thinker in the preschool years (see Chapter 7). In conservation tasks, the young child uses the perceptual attributes of a task to override its logical properties when asked to make judgments of equality: for example, of the two glasses with equal amounts of liquid in each, one is poured into a tall thin glass as the child watches. When asked which glass now has more liquid, the preschooler is likely to point to the tall one, *because* it is taller.

Perspective taking

Was Piaget being fair to preoperational children? Children as young as two and three years seem to have some rudimentary *perspective taking* ability—that is, an understanding that others can have different experiences from theirs. A three-year-old will alter his speech patterns when talking with a younger partner or a child with a handicap (Guralnick & Paul-Brown, 1984), indicating that there is a level of understanding of the other's reality. This ability is going to be crucial in developing a *theory of mind* later, and seems to evolve in stages (Flavell, Green & Flavell, 1990):

■ At level 1, the child understands *that* different people may see things, feel things or experience events differently. Toddlers operate on this level.

■ At level 2, the child is able to figure out *what* the other person sees,

1   Deniz, my daughter, thoroughly believed in the power of the automatic teller machine to indulge us with unlimited amounts of cash prior to our food and goods shopping.

believes or experiences by going through a complex series of rules. This level is not reached until four to five years of age.

Appearance or reality?

An extension of perspective taking is the ability to understand that appearances may be deceiving, and that the way things look may not be the only way to judge what they really are. Toddlers seem to judge things by the way they look. Here is an interesting experiment to study this phenomenon developmentally (Flavell, Green & Flavell, 1989):

- The experimenter shows the child a sponge painted to look like a rock. When the toddlers are asked to declare what this object is, they base their judgments on appearance alone: they *either* say that it looks like a rock and it is a rock, *or* that it looks like a sponge and it is a sponge. The child at this age is not able to understand that an object may *look* like something but *be* another.
- The four- and five-year-olds can make the distinction that the object may look like a rock but that in fact it is a sponge; the same object can be represented differently, depending on one's point of view.
- When, on the other hand, the children are allowed to feel the object, and are asked what a child who does know what it is will say it is (*false belief test*), the three-year-olds think that the naive child will think it is a sponge, because younger children act on their beliefs of the primary properties (squeezability) of the sponge.
- Older children believe that the naive child will think it is a rock. They realise that because the newcomer has not felt the sponge he will have the false belief that it is a rock; thus, by four to five years of age, children understand that *someone else* can believe something that is not true and act on it (Gopnik & Astington, 1988).

As we have noted, this complex ability to read the mind of the other is the basis of the child's *theory of mind*. It is this skill that seems to remain underdeveloped in children with autism (see Chapter 15).

EFFECTS OF DAYCARE

It is fairly typical for infants and toddlers to be cared for outside the home—particularly in industrialised countries, where mothers constitute a significant portion of the workforce. In Australia in 1993, 19% of children under 12 had experienced some form of formal child care outside the home, and an additional 29% had been placed in informal care with other family members, baby-sitters or neighbours. The incidence of infants under 12 months of age in formal daycare is 4% and rises to 10% for children under two years of age (Australian Bureau of Statistics, 1994). The systematic investigations of the effects of daycare on young children are fraught with confusion and complexities. Here are some of the reasons why (Bee, 1997).

- A huge number of different care arrangements are grouped together under the one umbrella of daycare.
- Children enter these arrangements at different points in their development, and stay in them for varying lengths of time.
- Some children have the same substitute caregiver for extended periods of time; others experience frequent changes.
- The quality associated with daycare varies enormously from setting to setting.
- The effects of daycare cannot be studied independently of the dynamics and experiences operative in the families whose children are in care.

The conclusions presented below need to be interpreted with these levels of complications in mind.

Daycare and attachment

The effects of daycare on the attachment of the infant to his mother or father has been an issue of contention. Recently, researchers sounded a well-publicised alarm on the negative effects of daycare on infants under one year of age, claiming that it increased the risk of insecure attachment (Belsky, 1992; Belsky & Rovine, 1988). Other studies show similar results: Lamb, Sternberg and Prodromidis (1992) summarised the findings of 13 studies with close to 1000 infants, and concluded that 35% of infants who had experienced at least five hours a week of non-maternal care were insecurely attached, compared with 29% of infants who were cared for by their mothers only. The risk of insecure attachment did *not* rise as the mothers' employment hours increased.

On the other side of the debate, Lori Roggman and her colleagues (1994) conducted a large replication study using the same kinds of daycare settings used by Belsky. Results revealed that *no* effects of daycare on attachment were robust enough to emerge consistently. Toddlers were *more* likely to emerge with a secure attachment if they attended daycare for more than 20 hours than if they attended part-time for four to 15 hours a week. The team cautioned strongly against basing either personal or governmental policy decisions on the belief that daycare has harmful effects.

Perhaps the issue at hand is not whether or not daycare has adverse effects but the *quality of care* that young children should experience, as good quality of care is generally associated with positive outcomes (see below). Some characteristics of *good quality in daycare* are noted in the following (Clarke-Stewart, 1992; Scarr & Eisenberg, 1993).

- *low teacher-to-child ratio:* a maximum of 1:4 with infants younger than two, and a maximum of 1:10 with two- to three-year-olds;
- *small group size:* six to eight babies in a group for those younger than 12 months, six to 12 for one- to two-year-olds, and 15 to 20 for older toddlers;
- *clean, colourful, ample space adapted for child play:* a variety of activities that the children find engaging; environment organised in a way that encourages play;
- *a daily plan with some structure:* balance between free play and structured teaching activities is called for;
- *caregiver(s) who are positive, involved in and responsive to the child:* safe and custodial care is not sufficient;
- *caregiver(s) with knowledge of child development.*

 Daycare and social and cognitive development

You may recall the beneficial effects of daycare in early intervention studies with children from underprivileged backgrounds (Chapter 4; Abecedarian Project). Other findings are as follows:

- Regardless of the economic status of the family, the higher the quality of care with cognitive enrichment and stimulation, the higher the child's later cognitive performance (Clarke-Stewart, Gruber & Fitzgerald, 1994).
- Children from poor families who began daycare *before* age one had higher reading and maths scores at the start of school, while those from middle-class families who entered daycare in infancy had poorer scores (Caughy, DiPietro & Strobino, 1994).

It seems that if the quality of care is good, and the enrichment the child obtains is more than he would normally get at home, the effects of daycare are facilitatory to cognitive development. In terms of social development:

- Children in daycare seem to be more popular and sociable, and to have better play skills with peers, than are those reared primarily at home (Scarr & Eisenberg, 1993).
- A small negative effect was found in terms of aggression and being less popular by school age for children who had spent the most time in daycare; the important variable did not appear to be *very* early experience from infancy, but the *total length of time* spent in care (Bates, Marvinney, Kelly, Dodge, Bennett & Pettit, 1994).

Despite evidence that appears contradictory, the crucial variable on positive outcomes holds for *good-quality care.* The small negative effects in aggressive behaviour are not observed in good-quality daycare (Clarke-Stewart et al., 1994).

GROWTH AND PHYSICAL DEVELOPMENT

Toodlerhood is a time for rapid physical growth and development, although the rate of growth is not so rapid as in the first year of life. Yet many behaviour patterns that typify toddlerhood are at least in part related to the increased growth and motor proficiency during this time. *Physical development* is a significant domain, which needs attention beyond descriptions of children's progress. Below are some of the reasons highlighting its importance (Bee, 1997):

Children's growth makes new behaviours possible.   Certain complex sequence of underlying motor and physical changes make possible movement skills, such as the ability to walk, be toilet-trained or ride a bicycle. In the absence of the motor development that underpins certain behaviours, those cannot be achieved regardless of training efforts: for example, nappy training before one year of age, before the achievement of sphincter control, is simply not possible.

Children's growth determines experience.   A range of physical capacities can have a major, indirect effect on cognitive and social development by influencing the variety of experiences children may have. The skills of independent walking and physical manipulation, for example, are likely to influence their exploration, and thus cognitive development.

Children's growth affects others' responses.   Newly acquired physical skills also affect others' response. An infant who is crawling is likely to elicit many more 'no's from the caring adults, as may a young child who has very high activity levels. Later on, children who are tall, well-coordinated and good-looking may be treated differently from those who are small and clumsy (Lerner, 1985).

Children's growth affects their self-concept.   Body image, which is an *internalised* part of self-concept, is often shaped by environmental and cultural influences, such as coordination and muscularity for boys and shapely and thin body for girls. Regardless of the objective reality of their physical characteristics, children's subjective or internalised knowledge of their bodies determines their feelings about themselves. (Anorexic young persons with a skeletal appearance often see themselves as being fat. Where, along the developmental process, is such distorted imagery consolidated, one wonders?)

Physical growth

We all know that kids get bigger as they get older. But the relative rate of growth holds surprises:

- While at birth the infant is about one-third of his adult height, at two years he is about *half* his adult height.

- In the first year, the infant adds 25–30 cm to his height, and triples his birthweight.
- In the two-year-old, the head is about one-quarter of the total body length, whereas in the adult this ratio is about 1:8.
- From two years, he will gain, on average, 5 cm in height and 2.5 kg in weight per year until adolescence.
- *Fontanelles*, the soft cartilaginous spots between the cranial bones, allow the skull bones to slide over each other during the birthing process to ease the passage from the birth canal. The largest one, the *anterior fontanelle*, fills in by two years of age.

Growth curves chart the growth of various measurements over age, usually from birth to 20 years of age (Petersen, 1996).

- The *general growth curve* charts height and weight measures. It shows rapid growth in infancy, slow and steady growth during preschool and middle childhood years, and rapid growth again from early adolescence on.
- The *head and brain growth curve* indicates a *very* rapid growth in infancy and toddlerhood, so much so that the brain attains 70% of its adult size by three years and 90% by age six. The brain and skull growth is fully attained by puberty.
- The *genital growth curve* indicates a slight early rise, but is essentially flat during childhood until it hits adolescence, during which time it shows a marked rise.
- The *lymphoid curve,* which shows the growth of the lymph system, whose function it is to filter out and fight harmful bacteria in the body, reaches 100% growth by seven years of age and continues to grow and peak until puberty, after which it starts to decline and returns to the levels attained at age seven.

Hormones

Various endocrine glands secrete hormones crucial to growth and development. Of these, the *pituitary* is the most important, as this master gland secretes the trigger hormones which then stimulate the secretion of hormones from other glands. For example, the thyroid gland, which secretes the crucial growth-stimulating hormone *thyroxine*, cannot do so until it gets the go-ahead from the pituitary. Here are some other facts:

- Prenatally, *thyroxine* is present from about the fourth month of gestation, and is mainly responsible for *brain growth*. Thyroxine hormone is secreted in greater quantities in the first two years of life, falling to lower, steady levels until adolescence.
- The *growth-stimulating hormone* sometimes used to stimulate physical growth in children who remain considerably smaller than their age mates is a derivative of the secretions of the pituitary.

- Pituitary secretes *gonadotrophic* hormones, which stimulate the release of *testosterone* in boys and *oestrogen* in girls, hormones responsible for reaching sexual maturity during adolescence.
- From 1880 to 1960, physical growth has accelerated over each generation. This *secular trend* is most obvious in the onset of the menstrual period in girls, which has advanced about three months per decade (Tanner, 1978) and seems to be related to better nutrition, as it is mostly evident in industrialised countries.

Nutrition

Essential human nutrients for growth and development include carbohydrates, fats, protein, water, minerals and vitamins.

- *Proteins* are essential for growth, maintenance and the repair of body tissue.
- *Carbohydrates* supply the primary fuel to meet the body's energy needs.
- *Fats* supply the energy reserves, and provide the body with insulation against heat loss.
- *Calcium* is essential for bone tissue, *iron* for red blood cells, *iodine* for thyroid functioning, *vitamin A* for vision and *vitamin D* for bone growth.

Balanced nutrition is *essential* to proper growth and development. Unfortunately, in images from countries ravaged by famine, poverty and war we are constantly reminded of the effects of poor nutrition on young children.

- *Marasmus* is a condition of slow and constant starvation. In its mildest form, *failure to thrive* involves food intake that is insufficient for normal weight gain. In severe cases, the mother's milk in the first years does not contain sufficient nutrients for the infant, as she may herself be starving. The result is emaciated babies, with wasted limbs and listless bodies.
- *Kwashiorkor* is caused by greater deficiency in *proteins* than calories. Children with inadequate protein intake have swollen bellies and swollen limbs. When such severe malnutrition occurs so early in life, growth is permanently stunted.
- *Obesity* occurs when children's activity levels are not sufficient to burn all the calories they obtain, usually due to excessive eating. It is a serious problem among developing children and appears to be a risk factor in cardiovascular health in adult years.

CONCLUSIONS

Toddlerhood is a time of qualitative change in cognition, which is reflected in all domains of development, from a sense of self, assertiveness, play and language to learning and knowing. The baby emerges as a little person, much better equipped to take on the challenges of the preschool years. Physical development and the social context are just as important in driving the young child towards maturity. We look at how all these forces act on the young child's personality formation and social emotional adjustment, as well as his cognitive and communication skills, in the following chapters.

7

Preschool years

Preschool years cover the period of three to five-to-six years of age, which encompasses the Piagetian *preoperational* stage of development in early childhood. The developing child is accomplishing marvellous feats in social and interpersonal relations. Although we present the Piagetian framework here as the prevalent one in cognitive development, you are invited to evaluate it critically and to develop an appreciation for the *social–contextual* forces acting on development as those presented by Vygotsky and the neo-Piagetians. You will also find the child's ability to appreciate the views of others in her environment to be a pivotal point, which is largely responsible for most of the integration and growth during this period.

COGNITIVE DEVELOPMENT: PREOPERATIONAL THOUGHT

According to Piaget, the *preoperational thought* of the preschool-aged child lacks *logical operations*. The child between the ages of two and seven uses a reasoning and logic that is qualitatively different from that of the *operational* child. By seven years of age, children are able to use *operations* which would allow for logical deductions, but even then the operations can be applied to concrete objects and current events only; thus the *concrete operational stage* follows the *preoperational stage*. Three basic features contrasting these stages can assist us in explaining the difficulties the preoperational child faces in understanding *conservation tasks*, *transitivity tasks* and *class inclusion tasks* (Piaget, 1929/1973):

1. Preoperational thought moves from *centration* (focusing on, thus being centred on a single attribute) towards *decentration* (unlocking attention

from a single attribute and taking into account various attributes) of concrete operational thought.

2. Preoperational thought moves from paying attention to *states* (the information available at the moment, without taking into account the previous or subsequent state) towards focusing in on *transformations* (changes from one state to another; initial *and* final state) of concrete operational thought.

3. Preoperational thought moves from making *absolute judgments on attributes* (e.g. being either short *or* long) towards the ability to make *relative judgments* about attributes (one being *longer* between two items, or *longest* among three items) in concrete operational thought.

Now let us review these tasks that are solved incorrectly by the preoperational child in view of the above constraints. In these tasks, which display the preschool child's logic in wonderful experiments devised by Piaget, there is an *initial state,* followed by a *transformation.* The child is asked to answer the question based on the *final state,* which results after the transformation.

Conservation tasks

The challenge in the conservation task is the recognition of invariance; that is, despite altered appearances, inner qualities of objects stay the same. Concrete operations permit an understanding of the *reversibility* of these transformations, whereas preoperational logic focuses in on their appearance. Some examples follow (the first procedure details are applicable to the others).

Number conservation.   The child is presented with two rows of coins, each containing the same number, laid out in exactly the same way (*initial state*). The *transformation* happens in front of the child's eyes, when the experimenter bunches up the coins in the bottom row, without taking away any coins but simply making it a shorter row. The *final state* question to the child is: 'Now are there the same number of coins in each row, or does one row have more?'[1] The preschooler's answer is likely to be 'More on the top row', because lack of logical operations confines her to *centration* on *one* attribute alone (length), without taking into account that although the *length* has changed the *number* of coins has remained unchanged. Also, the child pays attention only to the *final* state, and discounts the initial state.

Liquid quantity conservation.   The child is presented with two identical glasses with equal amounts of liquid in each. The liquid in one of the glasses is poured into a taller, thinner glass while the child watches (*transformation*), and then the child is asked which glass contains more liquid. The preopera-

1   Do you notice how sugestive the question is? The nature of these questions has been used as a basis for criticising the results obtained in Piagetian conservation tasks with young children, in which they are led by the adult to answer in favour of a difference between the initial and final states of the tasks.

tional child is likely to say that the taller glass contains more liquid, as it is taller.

Mass conservation.   The child is presented with two balls of playdough of identical size. The experimenter transforms one by stretching or rolling it so it becomes a snake shape, and then asks the child to indicate whether one has more playdough than the other. The preoperational child is likely to say that the longer-shaped one has more, as it is longer.

Length conservation.   The child is presented with two sticks of identical size, one resting exactly above the other. The experimenter moves one stick to the right, and asks the child whether one is now longer than the other. The child is likely to say that the one sticking out is longer.

Area conservation.   The child is presented with two lots of identical squares in two frames bunched together so that they form one surface area. One of the bunches containing the squares is spread out within one frame, and the child is asked to make a judgment as to whether there is more or less area covered within each frame. The child is likely to say that the spread-out squares are more than those lying together.

Class inclusion task

Here the child's challenge is to compare a class of objects with the larger class (*superordinate class*) to which it belongs. For example, the child is presented with six identical pictures of cats, and three identical pictures of dogs, and asked, 'Are there more cats than there are animals?' The category is cats, the larger superordinate category that cats form a part of is animals; the child is likely to say more cats, as she is not able to think of cats *both* as a class *and* as part of a larger class simultaneously.

Transitivity task

Here the child is asked to make comparisons between three rods of diminishing lengths—let's call them 1, 2, and 3. First, she is presented with 1 and 2, and asked which one is longer. She can correctly identify the longer rod (1), since she is basing her decision on a single attribute, (i.e. length). Then she is presented with 2 and 3; no problem there with identifying 2 as being longer either. But when she is asked to decide which one between 1 and 3 is longer, *without directly comparing the two but relying on logic alone* (if 1 is longer than 2, and 2 is longer than 3, then 1 must be longer than 3), she is unable to give the correct answer. This process is known as *transitive inference,* and is achieved by the concrete operational child.

When the *formal operations stage* is reached, at about 12 years of age, the mental operations will be freed from the here-and-now, and abstract, hypothetical and scientific thinking may emerge.

Other characteristics of the preschooler's mind

Piaget conducted probing conversations with young children in order to study the characteristics of their thought processes. Termed *'clinical interviews'*, these vignettes have often been criticised for lacking sufficiently standard techniques, which would allow comparisons between children. Nevertheless, they provide us with an insight into how the preschooler's view of the world is different from that of an older child, or an adult. Here is an example (Piaget, 1929/1973, pp. 200–201):

Adult: If you pricked this stone, would it feel it? *Child:* No.
Adult: Why not? *Child:* Because it is hard.
Adult: If you put it in the fire, would it feel it? *Child:* Yes.
Adult: Why? *Child:* Because it would get burnt.
Adult: Can it feel the cold or not? *Child:* Yes.
Adult: Can a boat feel it is in the water? *Child:* Yes.
Adult: Can the grass feel when you pick it? *Child:* Yes, because you pull it.

While the preschooler may not yet have a mature command of the linguistic structures that adults direct at her, Piaget thought that misunderstandings stemmed more from conceptual differences between adults and young children. Some conceptual characteristics of the preschooler's mind include the following:

■ *Animism*—thinking that non-living things can have attributes of live beings like people, or animals—is exemplified in the above conversation, when the child says that the stone will feel the fire. Toy manufacturers capitalise on the preoperational thinker's belief that stuffed toys and dolls are alive.

■ *Artificialism* reflects the young child's belief that natural phenomena are engineered by human beings—for example, night falls because people send smoke from their cars' exhaust pipes. Piaget also noted young children's dreams being like movies outside themselves: children were reported to dream with their eyes, and think with their ears (because they were hearing voices in their head!).

■ *Transducive* or *syncretic* reasoning associates specific instances as being causally related, and makes the young child's reasoning illogical. In contrast, adult reasoning is *inductive* (many examples with similar features lead to a conclusion; i.e. everybody is wearing purple—it must be the hot colour this season), or *deductive* (general principle accounts for individual cases; i.e. all fads pass—purple will be out next season).

■ *Belief in immanent justice* leads young children to conclude that illnesses or accidents are magically induced by disobedience and other forms of misbehaviour, or they may have other magical attributes for sickness and healing (i.e. my grandma got sick because I broke her vase, and she will get better if I wear a bandaid on my finger).

PIAGET: A REVIEW AND CRITICAL EVALUATION

As we near the millennium, Piaget remains by far the most influential developmental psychologist of this century. Many experiments have been conducted using methods similar to those Piaget devised, and on larger numbers of children (his initial observations were based solely on his own three children), in cross-cultural contexts (USA, Africa, UK, China), which showed the prevalence of similar thought patterns (Goodnow, 1969).

Formal operational reasoning, however, was reached only by a small portion of adolescents and adults, even in industrialised societies, particularly on scientific reasoning problems (King, 1985). It has also been suggested that the format for Piagetian tasks are culture-bound, and reflect cognitive styles demanded by Western-industrialised societies (Butterworth & Harris, 1994). Other arguments have questioned his conclusions.[2]

Donaldson (1987) makes a strong argument that young children might fail Piagetian tasks because neither the language used, nor the tasks themselves, made much sense to them. Many researchers have since demonstrated that, when the task and its context are made clear to the child, she may be able to exhibit logical thought well before the limits suggested by Piaget.

Piaget himself recognised, for example, that there may be unevenness in development in his stage theory: a child can achieve conservation of liquids but may fail at a class inclusion task. Indeed, conservation of number precedes others, particularly that of weight. Piaget termed this uneven development *horizontal decalage*. A case in point: when counting procedures are modified, three-year-olds demonstrate an understanding of number conservation concepts (Gelman, 1972). Also, children as young as two-and-a-half can understand some basic principles of counting, such as (Gelman, 1979):

- There is a one-to-one correspondence between objects and number names.
- Number names must be listed in a stable order.
- A list of numbers runs through the same order every time.
- Any set of objects may be gathered for a count.
- The last label used tells how many items there are in a collection.
- If all other principles have been applied, the order in which objects are counted does not matter.

While conservation can be taught to children four and five years of age, the procedure seems very laborious (Gelman, 1969).

Other developmentalists question the very notion of stages existing in development, suggesting that instead of going through stages children develop a repertoire of task-specific skills and strategies. Fodor (1983) has postulated a theory based on *modules* and *domains:*

---

2   Theorists who basically agree with Piaget but offer alterations to some of his notions and claims are known as neo-Piagetians.

- *Modules* are different neural networks that are genetically preprogrammed for processing different kinds of information (i.e. language, maths or musical information, which are modified through experience). Modules pass the processed information to a 'central executive', which builds up information in memory, generating new hypotheses and decisions about the world.
- A *domain* is a set of representations, a particular kind of knowledge or cognitive process. Development is domain-specific: maturation in one domain is independent of the development of another. Children can develop in drawing while being delayed in language; hence, development is also *modular*.

Chomsky's approach to language (see Chapter 10) and Gardner's approach to intelligence (see Chapter 11) exemplify such modularity in development.

And that brings us to another very interesting theorist, one born in Russia the same year Piaget was born in Switzerland (in 1896)—Lev Vygotsky. Vygotsky admired Piaget's work, although he thought Piaget had overlooked the social context in development. Although Vygotsky wrote in the 1930s, his works were translated rather late. His influence has been substantial over the past few decades, particularly in education.

VYGOTSKY: THOUGHT, LANGUAGE AND INTERACTION

There has been increased interest in cross-cultural studies of child development, particularly in investigations of the *culturally specific* practices affecting the developmental process. One major contributor to this orientation is the Soviet psychologist Lev Vygotsky (1896–1934), whose early writings have had a significant influence on the field since their relatively recent translation into English (1930/1978; 1934/1962).

Vygotsky was deeply affected by Marxist ideas and argued that interactions with adults and peers, as well as instruction, were essential to cognitive development. He believed that the *dialectic*, or the discussion and reasoning that occur in cooperative social dialogues between children and their socialising agents, were crucial in children's cognitive development and understanding of culturally significant activities. Piaget thought cognitive development to be a spontaneous process achieved through interactions with and exploration of the environment, which did not necessarily depend on direct instruction from adults; Vygotsky argued that concepts, language, attention, even memory, are functions that originate in culture and are acquired in interaction between the child and another person in the course of development. The following are some prominent points to compare and contrast the views of Piaget and Vygotsky.

Unlike Piaget, who saw language as a byproduct of conceptual growth, Vygotsky thought *language* was the most significant symbolic system for cognitive growth. Although, in reality, it may be a circular argument to decide which one comes first (i.e. language or thought), Vygotsky felt that language shaped cognition.

Even in very young children, the often observed self-talk is a tool for *problem-solving.* What Piaget called egocentric speech was seen as *private speech* by Vygotsky, who believed that language proceeded in cumulative stages. The next stage is language for social interaction, followed by *inner speech,* where language goes underground and becomes thought, which is essential to all higher mental functions, including memory, reasoning, planning and evaluating. Look at this self-talk of a three-and-a-half-year-old before an easel, who is busy creating some artwork but cannot find green paint:

> . . . and there's the yellow sun, and here's the blue lake, and here's the trees . . . and the leaves . . . no green leaves . . . I need to make green leaves . . . I'll put some blue, and maybe . . . white . . . no, yellow . . . here! Green leaves!

Piaget contended that children solved cognitive problems independently. Vygotsky argued that the impact of the social interaction between the child and mediation by a more capable person was crucial to promoting cognitive growth. Children have a *zone of proximal[3] development (ZPD),* in which they perform better and achieve greater cognitive growth when scaffolded by an adult or a more capable peer. *Zone of proximal development* may be seen as the difference between what the child achieves unassisted by the adult, and what she *can* achieve with the help of another person.

Vygotsky conceived of a qualitatively different role for social interaction compared to Piaget, claiming that social interaction *determines* the structure and pattern of internal cognition. Aids to instruction (such as computers) and social institutions (schooling) are transmitted to children with the rest of a culture.

> The very mechanism underlying higher mental functions is a copy from social interaction; all higher mental functions are internalised social relationships (Vygotsky, 1988, p.74).

Revisiting Vygotsky has strengthened our more contemporary views of the contextual and cultural forces acting on the developing child.

---

3   Proximal, meaning next, which indicates that Vygotsky assumed learning to occur in small successive steps, with adult guidance or instruction at points of experienced difficulty.

MEMORY DEVELOPMENT

Memory *span* or *capacity* refers to the innate reservoir of memory a child may have. Memory *strategies,* on the other hand, are groups of acquired skills used to facilitate the transference of material from *short-term* to *long-term memory.* If you were given a list of items to look at for 30 seconds and then asked to recall as many items as you could, how would you go about this task? Try it:

fish	laugh	chocolate	pen	tears	net	coffee	hook	paper
cry	shrimp	salmon	tea	sea	dog	book	clip	ink

Memory strategies (or *mnemonic devices*) include:

■ *Organisation* of material into meaningful, semantically related *chunks.* Two- to five-year-olds seem to use spatial organisation rather than semantic organisation (chunking) in recall (DeLoache & Todd, 1988). However, when children as young as four are trained to use semantic grouping strategies, they improve their skills in grouping like items together (fish, shrimp, net, hook/paper, book, pencil, pen, ink), as well as their ability to recall them (Sodian, Schneider & Perlmutter, 1986);

■ *Rehearsal,* or conscious repetition of the material for improved recall. Children younger than five are not likely to employ rehearsal successfully (Keeny, Cannizzo & Flavell, 1967). However, when preschoolers were given a group of familiar toys and instructed to remember as many as possible, they named, manipulated and evidenced some intentional memorisation strategies (Baker-Ward, Ornstein & Holden, 1984);

■ *Labelling,* or giving names to non-verbal items, such as locations or images attached to the items;

■ *Elaboration* or *visualisation,* where mental images are constructed and even linked together in a sequential and related order between items that are otherwise unrelated. (For example, in the list above you may have visualised fish and shrimp enjoying their coffee, tea and chocolates while laughing until they cried tears, while you were studying from your book, with papers, pencils and pens strewn on your desk . . . The possibilities are endless, and the more absurd they become the more likely you are to recall them!) Preschoolers can be taught to insert a verb or a preposition to construct images, but elaborate visual imagery improves by school age.

Memory also seems to be highly influenced by *cultural experience,* and to be particularly efficient in domains valued in that particular culture. Kearins (1981) investigated the memory skills of a group of Aboriginal children who still lived in traditional tribal communities of remote desert regions of Western Australia, and a group of matched suburban Anglo-Australian children. The task was to recall the items in the two trays, after 30 seconds of studying them. One tray had 20 compartments, with a manufactured object (e.g. thimble, button) in each compartment, and the other tray contained 20 natural objects (e.g. twigs, seashells and nuts). Aboriginal children did significantly better with both sets of items, but excelled in the recall of natural items (18 out of 20, vs six out of 20 for Anglo-Australian children), suggesting that their expert attention may be related to their lifestyle.

Long-term memory

Long-term memory is a memory bank from which we wish to access our account and retrieve the stored items. We can do this by *recognition, recall* and *reconstruction*.

Recognition
Recognition is the easiest retrieval mechanism, since one needs to compare old (already stored) information against new information. Preschoolers' recognition memory is amazingly good—in fact, it is as good as adults'. One week after they were presented with pictures of 80 items, four-year-olds were able to recognise 72 of the initial pictures in a new but identical set (Brown & Campione, 1972).

Recall
Recall is the ability to remember something that is not currently at hand, except perhaps some of its cues, and thus relies on *productive* memory. Preschool children's skills in recall are much poorer than in recognition and, as can be expected, show a steady improvement with age. Semantic organisation, clustering and chunking into categories are refined as the child gets older and practises her memory skills at school, which also contributes to the improved recall abilities (Perlmutter, 1984).

Reconstruction
Reconstruction is basically a recall process, except that the material recalled is quite different. In the reconstruction process, memory has been reorganised, embellished, interpreted, altered and doctored in accordance with the child's expectancies or experience. Piaget would very much agree with such a *constructivist* notion of memory, where knowledge is built from experience and adaptation. As a matter of fact, the following vignette illustrates the reconstruction of memory admirably (Peterson, 1996, p.241):

> One afternoon in Geneva, Switzerland, a nanny was pushing a baby in a carriage through the park. The baby was wide awake and looked around brightly at the trees, the buildings and the tram stop. Suddenly, a big, ill-shaven character charged up to the carriage, forced the nurse aside and made as if to abduct the baby. The nurse fought off the vagrant bravely, and, in the process, received two long

scratches across her cheeks from his unkempt fingernails. Just then, a policeman in a short cape hurried over and chased the intending kidnapper away.

The baby in the pram was Jean Piaget, and for many years Piaget believed this incident to be one of his earliest memories of a true event. This was because, even though the adults around him had often talked about the attempted kidnapping in his hearing when he was older, he remembered the details of the visual scene which [only] he and the nurse could have known . . .

Imagine Piaget's disillusionment, therefore, when his parents received a letter from his former nurse confessing that there had been no kidnapping, no kidnapper . . . and she had scratched her own face for authenticity. Now, as a convert to the Salvation Army, she wanted to confess her misdeed and to return the gold watch that had been awarded as a prize for her bravery.

Reconstruction applies to recently learned material as well, and improves with age, apparently providing young children with a multitude of retrieval cues to facilitate recall.

Episodic versus semantic memory

There seems to be two different ways of organising and storing events in the memory bank (Tulving, 1972):

- *Episodic memory* refers to chronologically organised events in our lives, which are personal.

- *Semantic memory* is what we know about the world, and the events, objects and relations in it.

Children as young as three years remember familiar daily events in terms of *scripts*, which are organised representations of event sequences (Nelson, 1986). Scripts describe routine events in children's lives and, because they have been committed to long-term memory by repetition, they provide predictability and stability. A four-year-old will have little trouble recalling how to buy a carton of milk (you go to the shops, pick up the milk with the green writing on it, go to the checkout counter, pay for it and leave). Scripts are often reflected in children's fantasy play, and are probably the developmental link between early episodic memory and a mature, semantically organised, long-term memory (Nelson & Gruendel, 1981).

Metamemory

Metamemory involves the ability to think about memory and the factors affecting it. Five-year-olds did not exhibit this skill, while school-aged children did, in an experiment in which the children were asked the following question (Kreutzer, Leonard & Flavell 1975): 'If you wanted to phone your friend, and someone told you the phone number, would it make any difference if you called straight away after you heard the number, or if you got a drink of water first?' Older children seemed to be aware of the fact that immediate memory decays rapidly, and that they needed to attend to the task straight away; younger children did not.

However, five-year-olds *are* aware of the following characteristics of memory, like their older counterparts (Wellman, 1977):

■ It is easier to learn items they once knew than totally new items.
■ A long list of items is harder to remember than a short list with a few items.
■ Noise interferes with memory, and adults remember better than babies do.
■ Cues facilitate recall, as does a longer time to study the items.

Children as witnesses and recalling of repressed memories

Children sometimes find themselves in situations of providing corroborating court evidence in allegations of various forms of abuse. In other instances, adults recall their early childhood memories of physical, sexual and emotional abuse, and want to pursue justice. For obvious reasons, the evidence given may be fraught with legalistic problems. The accuracy of distant memories, with possible distortions in their retrieval or reconstruction processes even when they are relatively new in childhood, is questionable. Reported memories, either spontaneously or through the aid of a therapeutic or hypnotic process, may be accurate, inaccurate, fabricated, or possibly a mixture of all these possibilities (McConkey, 1995).

LANGUAGE AND COMMUNICATION SKILLS

The length of the child's sentences expands in the preschool years, as well as her ability to link the ideas coded in utterances with her use of conjunctions (e.g. I had a chocolate ice-cream *but* I didn't have a drink). Also, some salient *grammatical* advances happen in the mid-preschool years which add to the complexity of the linguistic structures the child uses.

Negatives. The *semantic categories* of non-existence (e.g. 'allgone milk'), rejection (e.g. 'no want milk') and denial (e.g. 'that not milk') can now be coded using the adult-like form. Whereas in earlier utterances the *no* and *not* were either outside the utterance or used before the verb, the more mature sentences of the preschooler have structures like 'There isn't any more milk' (*non-existence*), 'I don't want more milk' (*rejection*), and 'That isn't milk' (*denial*).

Yes–no questions.   Earliest questions are asked by the aid of rising intonation at the end of the utterance. This convenient device allows for coding questions semantically even with single-word utterances: 'Out?' may well mean 'Are we going out to the playground, dad?'. The next phase in toddlerhood may sound like 'We going out?', before more mature patterns are employed, where the auxiliary verb is used for inversion, as in '*Are* we going out now?'.

Wh- questions. The earliest wh- question words acquired are those with a concrete referent, such as *what, where, which* and *who*. Those probing less tangible concepts, like time *(when)*, manner *(how)* and reason or causality *(why)*, are acquired later. Increased understanding and the use of syntactic complexity allows the preschooler to ask these questions with standard inclusion and inversion of the helping verbs: 'What you eating?' changes to 'What you are eating' (*inclusion* of the auxiliary), and finally to 'What *are* you eating?' (inclusion and *inversion*).

Passive voice. Preschoolers do not yet understand *passive voice* constructions clearly. When asked to actually show the action with the objects in such a sentence as 'The cat was bitten by the dog', they would have the cat biting the dog, which indicates that they are still going by the word-order rules. Full understanding of the passives are not accomplished until mid-primary school years (Pinker, Lebeaux & Frost, 1987).

Semantics. The preschooler's vocabulary continues to expand, and her semantic knowledge becomes better organised. The use of *overextensions* may continue but is often observed in contexts when the preschool child either is unaware of the new word meaning (i.e. cat for puma) or is not able to recall the right word.

Pragmatics. The preschooler is becoming a much better conversationalist. The conversational exchanges grow in number, while a topic is maintained with greater focus. Another development is in the skills of joining in the conversations of others (Dunn & Shatz, 1989). At the same time, the use of language in social context, such as using polite requests and greetings, is refined. Parents rarely correct incorrect grammar, and they would often expand the child utterances with limited semantic elements; however, they start teaching social forms practically before the onset of the first words ('Say bye-bye'). Failing to use socially acceptable speech would quickly lead to rejection and criticism. Parents seem aware of such unpleasant consequences, and start tutoring their children in the social niceties quite early (Greif & Berko Gleason, 1980).

Metalinguistic skills. Preschoolers also begin developing skills through which they can think about language and exhibit a conscious awareness of the rules governing it. For example, they can pick out words that rhyme, reject ungrammatical sentences that do not have the correct word order, and develop an appreciation that different languages can have different labels for objects (Smith & Tager-Flusberg 1982).

SOCIAL COGNITION

The skills acquired by the preschool-aged child in the domain of general cognitive processes have applications for her understanding of self and others, as well as for social relationships. As Flavell (1985) points out, the same head that tackles conservation problems will also attempt to understand people. Indeed, the principles applying to general cognitive development are those at play in social relations as well. However, people are substantially different from objects: unlike toys, they behave intentionally, they talk back, they get angry, they can hurt one's feelings and do all sorts of unpredictable things.

Children have to learn to establish *reciprocal* relations and to be able to achieve mutuality, they need to be able to infer other people's feelings and motives; they also have to learn social *scripts*, which will allow them to act by special rules governing different types of social interactions in particular settings.

As children mature, their development in object and person relations are reflected in some principles, as you can see in different facets of development.

Superficial to inner characteristics. As they get older, children's attention shifts from superficial and perceptually bound characteristics (i.e. what things look like), to looking for their causes and underlying principles (i.e. why things happen).

Observation to logical inference. Young children's conclusions are initially based on what they can see and feel; later they make inferences about what might or should be.

Rigid to flexible. Early 'rules' are definite and resistant to change; later years allow for reflective evaluation and flexibility.

Self-centred to other-considered. Diminishing egocentricism of the young child allows for considering not only the 'view from the self' but also for constructing a model of 'views of the others'.

Empathy

Comprehending the other's emotions and feeling similarly is *empathy; sympathy* is empathy, followed by a sense of concern or sorrow for the other's emotional state. Children's empathic responses show variability; those with a secure attachment history seem to be more empathic than others (Kestenbaum, Farber & Sroufe, 1989). Empathy follows a developmental progression (Hoffman, 1988):

Stage 1: Global empathy. In the first year of life, if the infant witnesses someone expressing a strong emotion (i.e. crying) she may match that emotion (i.e. crying herself).

Stage 2: Egocentric empathy. When the child begins to develop a separate sense of self at around 18 months, she tends not only to respond to another's distress but attempts to alleviate it in a way that *she* would find most soothing (i.e. she may show sadness when another child is crying, so she goes to her *own* mother for help).

Stage 3: Empathy for others' feelings.   From toddlerhood through to the early school years children note others' feelings, and partially match them; they also respond to the other's distress in non-egocentric ways. The range and subtlety of the recognised emotions diversify with age.

Stage 4: Empathy for another's life condition.   From late childhood on, children recognise that the sadness of the other person may not be momentary but an ongoing feeling associated with an event or circumstance.

The ability of the young child to make correct assumptions about another person's emotional states constitutes an important development towards social competence and the formation of reciprocal human bonds.

THEORY OF MIND

While Piaget examined the thought processes in the preschool child, he developed a task known as the *'three mountains task'*, in which he demonstrated the *cognitive egocentricism* of the preoperational thinker. This task is probably an early version of what is now known as the *theory of mind,* which is the child's ability to read the mind/assumptions/beliefs/desires of the person with whom she is interacting. The child was presented with a model of superimposed mountains, one behind the other. The first one had a snow-capped peak, the second had a cross at its peak, and the third mountain had a cottage situated at the summit. The child's task was to report how a person sitting across from her would view the mountains. The preschooler typically described the view from *her* vantage point, because, Piaget thought, the child was not able to *decentre* from her own perspective.

You may recall from our discussions of toddlers (Chapter 6) and their *perspective taking* and *false belief* applications that two- and three-year-old children cannot figure out *what* the other person experiences, or distinguish the appearance of an object from its physical reality.

By four years, children in a false belief task will understand that someone else can believe something that is not necessarily true. Observations such as these have led theorists to claim that children by this age have developed a new and quite elaborate *theory of mind* (Astington & Gopnik, 1991; Gopnik & Wellman, 1994). The child now has developed various theories about other people's ideas, beliefs, desires, thoughts and feelings. What the other person will do can no longer be predicted solely based on the situation; the ways in which the other person thinks and feels about it also need to be considered. This is

an appreciation that each person's actions are based on his/her *own representations of reality*, which may be different from what is observable, alone.

- The four- to five-year-old understands that other people think (i.e. I know
  that you know); what she does not yet understand is that others may
  think about *her* (You know that I know).
- Such a *reciprocal* nature of thought is crucial to genuine, mutual
  friendships, and seems to develop between five and seven years of age
  (Sullivan, Zaitchik & Tager-Flusberg, 1994).

It is this ability in reciprocity in social cognition which seems to be the most
important aspect of aberrant development in children with *autism*, even when
there is no significant associated intellectual impairment (see Chapter 15).

Another aspect of development underlying social cognition is that of
metacognition, or the ability to think about the thinking process.

- By age four, children understand that there is this process called thinking,
  which is different from knowing or talking, and that people can think
  about both real and imaginary objects (Flavell, Green & Flavell, 1995).
- By five years, however, they still do not understand that other people
  can think continuously (Wellman & Hickling, 1994).

Theory of mind research opens up many exciting avenues in exploring the
mind of a child, and has demonstrated that young children are considerably
less egocentric than Piaget led us to believe.

PLAY AND PEER RELATIONS

From interacting with sensitive, responsive adults, children learn to send and
interpret emotional messages in peer relationships; thus attachment behaviour may
affect children's friendships. Babies who experience a warm and sensitive parental
relationship engage in more extended peer relationships (Howes & Stewart, 1987).
In turn, these children are more inclined to display more competent social
behaviours towards their peers in preschool years (Howes, 1988).

While two-year-olds may simply observe their peers from a distance,
retreat from conflict or cry and approach the adult, the preschoolers come
closer together in play, engage in longer verbal exchanges and use attention-
getting devices such as smiling, eye contact, touching and calling a playmate
by name. This suggests a fundamental change in sociability with peers, and
a significant growth in reciprocal and coordinated interactions.

Play

Parten, in very early observations of young children's play in nursery school,
concluded that social development proceeds in three stages (Parten, 1932):

- *solitary play* and unoccupied, non-social, onlooker behaviour;
- *parallel play*, with a limited extent of social participation, where children play side by side, often with similar materials;
- *cooperative social play*, which emerges towards middle preschool years, where children share toys, converse, and engage in complementary role-playing.

Closer scrutiny, however, reveals that children do not simply evolve from one such stage to the next; rather, it is a matter of *distribution of time within each mode* of play, as well as the *type* of play that undergoes some developmental changes (Rubin, Watson & Jambor, 1978):

- Although onlooker play diminishes with age, it is still the most common form of behaviour among preschoolers, and constitutes about one-third of children's free playtime in kindergarten.
- Solitary and parallel play between the ages of three and six take as much time as highly cooperative social play.
- When the cognitive maturity of play is taken into account in categories of play (Smilansky, 1968; see Chapter 6), five-year-olds engage in more mature behaviours than four-year-olds.
- *Sociodramatic play* becomes increasingly prevalent with age.

A child who wanders aimlessly, or engages in functional play with repetitive, immature motor actions *as her preferred play mode*, may be exhibiting delays in cognitive social development. However, most preschoolers engage in *both* onlooker *and* parallel play. Contrary to common belief, children who spend much of their playtime in constructive play may be bright, socially competent youngsters, who do well at complex problem-solving tasks (Rubin, 1982).

Play that incorporates elements of *fantasy, imagination and make-believe* is rich in representational symbolism and, since it often involves more than one child, it is framed by social interaction. Most of its themes are character-oriented, and their re-enactment can have, as their stage, a range of venues from *Star Wars* to the local grocery store.

- Highly imaginative Australian children are found to watch less television than their matched controls (Peterson, Peterson & Carroll, 1983).
- Frequency and variety of dramatic play in preschool, and the length of time for which preschool children engage in it, correlate significantly with children's affective perspective-taking ability (where they were able to infer what the others were feeling) and their exceptional competence at social role-taking with peers at school (Connolly & Doyle, 1984).
- Children who score high on fantasy play are found to be more creative, more linguistically expressive and fluent, more skilful and imaginative in making up stories, and more patient when required to sit quietly for 15 minutes (Singer, 1973).

- Adolescents who had *imaginary friends* during early childhood score significantly higher in measures of creative achievement in academic, artistic and literary fields (Singer, 1973).

- Piaget also concluded that fantasy in children's play assisted solutions to real-life problems, facilitated generalisation of the discovered solutions, and promoted development of logical thought.

- Similarly, Vygotsky (1962) claimed that children learn about the solutions that apply to problems in real-life situations from the reproduction of meanings and rules in the context of fantasy play.

Family influence

Families seem also to influence children's fantasy play by creating a warm, safe and relaxed atmosphere. Mothers of children who were doing exceptionally well in early years of school were investigated for their teaching methods at home (White, 1975a). They were found to have more casual attitudes towards keeping a tidy home, provided the preschoolers with lots of often messy but interesting play materials, and plenty of room to move about. While they spent little direct teaching or play time with the youngsters, they were keen observers of the child's play, often being able to make a facilitative suggestion to suit the context of the ongoing activity. Also, their standards and applications on limit-setting and discipline were high on prohibiting dangerous, unsafe or antisocial acts.

Fathers of preschoolers with plenty of imagination and intellectual competence spend more time with their children than other fathers. Also, the security of attachment of the infant to the mother and/or father at 18 months of age predicts the child's quality of fantasy play at two years, suggesting that sensitive caregiving from infancy contributes to these positive effects (Fein, 1981).

Children are found to play less imaginatively in households in which there are high levels of tension and marital discord, as well as in those where the use of physical punishment is frequent and severe (Singer & Singer, 1981).

Young children's friendships

You may recall that by three and four years of age children prefer to play with peers rather than play by themselves. Also at this time, the nature of play appears to be much better coordinated and cooperative. Various forms of pretend play are evident, and the preferred playmates are the same-gender ones. Stable friendships often emerge among preschoolers who have shared the same early childhood setting over a few years. Friendships among preschoolers clearly move towards better-defined and more stable associations:

- Using the definition of friends as any pair of children who spent at least a third of their play time next to one another (Hinde, Titmus, Easton &

Tamplin, 1985), only about 20% of three-and-a-half-year-olds exhibit stable friendships.

■ By four years of age, 50% of the same group of children met this criterion of friends, providing early evidence for the consistent preference of playmates.

According to Gottman (1986), coordinated play activity is the central organising process, not only for preschool friendships but for other processes, such as conflict resolution, self-exploration and problem-solving. Among other attributes of early childhood friendships are:

■ *amity,* which is an expression of mutual affection and approval between friends;

■ *common ground,* which is the agreement to participate jointly in an activity;

■ *information exchange,* which may include both task-centred and self-disclosure information.

As children mature, so do their friendships. Indeed peer relations may play a role in children's development that is unique, and unrivalled by parents. During preschool years, young children are becoming cognitively equipped to start to cultivate stable and reciprocal friendships.

Attachment revisited

In Chapter 5 we talk about the infant behaviours leading to, and the strange situation test as a measure of, *attachment.* In Chapter 6 we discuss the effects of daycare on attachment. During toddlerhood, most attachment behaviours become less obvious. The fact that the child can appreciate the promised return of the parent when she/he departs reduces the separation anxiety. The toddler can even look at the photograph of the mother as a safe base and feel more confident in exploring the environment in a strange situation (Passman & Longeway, 1982). Wanting to be close to the parent on her return is still present, but the toddler has become more adventurous in non-stress-provoking, supportive environments.

By four years of age another shift occurs: the child is able to appreciate that not only does the mother continue to exist in her absence, but that their *relationship too* continues when mother and child are apart. This shift towards *goal-directed partnership* (Bowlby, 1969) allows her even more freedom to be without the mother for prolonged periods of time, and attachment behaviours may not be evidenced unless the situation is highly stressful for the child.

A MODEL PRACTICE IN EARLY CHILDHOOD: REGGIO EMILIA

Reggio Emilia, a city of 130 000 in northern Italy, has recently become synonymous with excellence in early childhood education. Funded publicly through national and regional legislation, it refers to a system as well as a philosophy of education for young children which has flourished because of a special case of educator–parent partnership. It is as successful as it is perhaps because it originated in schools built by the parents, and has maintained many years of exceptional commitment and collaboration between the two groups, culminating in the development of exemplary programs. Its framework for child development is inspired by Piaget, Vygotsky and other contemporary theorists; its practice, however, is predicated on careful reflection and re-adjustment; Reggio Emilia is unique because of the *attitudes of the community to early childhood education.* It is a wonderful example of the cultural–contextualist approach in action.

Here are some principles of this approach, all of which are interconnected and interdependent, forming a coherent, unified philosophy and practice unique to that community (Gandini, 1993):

- *The image of the child* the educators have is one where children are seen as curious, able and interested learners, keen in engaging in social interactions and in negotiating their environment towards the construction of learning experiences. Teachers make it their job to construct environments that will maximise the potential of each child.
- *Each child is embedded in a matrix of social systems;* the teachers activate and support the child within and in relation to other family members, who are part of the school community, which is in turn viewed as a part of the community and society at large.
- *The rights of children to high-quality care and education* is recognised as their entitlement to the best that the society has to offer, which in turn ensures not only the children's but the parents' and teachers' rights and wellbeing.
- *The essential nature of parent participation in programs* may be in day-to-day interactions, discussions of educational or psychological issues, or special events such as excursions.
- *The stimulating nature of the physical space* encourages communication, interaction and social encounters, as well as facilitating discovery and problem-solving. Children change their environments each year in accordance with their changing developmental needs and interests, but their peers and teachers remain the same.
- *Children's own sense of time* rather than teacher-set times rules the day. The program is full-day, which seems to allow sufficient time for the completion of projects. Also, teachers who stay with the children for three-year cycles obtain an in-depth knowledge about each child within a more natural time frame.
- *Teachers act as partners in learning with the children,* who are observed and listened to closely. Based on the understanding gained, teachers

facilitate learning by asking questions, probing children's ideas and hypotheses, and providing opportunities for exploration and discovery.

■ *Team teaching on equal level* is where teachers continually examine their own work and attitudes, and discuss and interpret children's work. Both children and teachers are seen as researchers. Teachers' relationships among themselves and the community are supported by a team of pedagogical coordinators.

■ *Precision and care in attending to detail* permeate all facets of the program, from the teachers' schedules to children's diets.

■ *Emergent curriculum* allows for the expressions of general goals, from which a curriculum emerges during the course of the activities or projects undertaken. *Projects* allow for lengthy explorations of ideas, some lasting several months.

■ *Children express themselves through many visual arts media,* each of which is seen as one of the 100 languages they employ as an extension of their cognitive and symbolic development.

■ *Children's work, transcripts of their remarks, and discussions and representations of their thinking, are carefully and extensively documented and displayed.* This process facilitates professional growth for the teachers, strengthens the bond with the families, indicates how each child's work is valued, and provides a rich archive for the school.

Such practice has been in effect in Reggio Emilia since the late 1960s. It may not offer novel theoretical visions, but the refined quality and the finesse with which early childhood education is embraced has become a benchmark for many educators across Europe, the USA and Australia. It is also important to note that children with disabilities are given priority for enrolment in Reggio Emilia schools!

CONCLUSIONS

As you can see, there are many orientations and theories in the field of early childhood development; our continued questioning attitude towards theory and practice makes it a vibrant and challenging science.

This chapter reveals that the preschooler has come a long way and has quite a way to go yet towards maturity. Social, cognitive and linguistic skills will be greatly enhanced by the formal schooling experience that she will soon find herself in. The availability of concrete operational structures also will broaden her perspectives and make academic learning achievable. However, there will always be those children for whom school readiness questions are multifaceted and often very difficult. (We take a close look at those marginal children in Chapter 12.)

8

Early school years

Most cultures have their young starting school at around seven years of age. Piaget's concrete operational stage begins at around the same time. Moral reasoning and perspective taking indicate a huge leap into other-considerateness by seven years. The structural underpinning of such significant development is probably supported by brain growth:

- a sudden spurt in the growth rate of the brain occurs between five and seven years;
- myelination of nerve fibers is almost complete by six to eight years of age; and
- adult levels of synaptic connections are reached by seven years of age. (Halford, 1993)

That very important first day of school, which parents recall with delight and children remember with pride and apprehension, arrives: the formal education process starts, usually with kindergarten, and proceeds towards primary school. This is the time in a young child's life in which the growth and development achieved thus far will be consolidated. It is also a time of adaptation to a more structured learning environment, and gradual awakening to the value of industry in school work. Early school years tend to define a child's self-worth, which is often derived through his accomplishments or acquisitions relative to peers, and from the feedback given to him by adults. For the child with special needs who is attending in a mainstream setting, there are challenges as well as significant benefits. At any rate, the psychological development acquired during the early school years would constitute the stepping stones for many future endeavours, not only academically but also, and perhaps more importantly, for the adaptive, creative, productive, emotionally resourceful and societally responsible person the child will hopefully become.

COGNITIVE DEVELOPMENT AND SCHOOL ACHIEVEMENT

Within the Piagetian framework, children between the ages of seven and 11 years are said to be in the *concrete operational stage*. This is an important attainment; children's thought processes now resemble adult thinking, in that concrete operational reasoning is flexible, logical and organised. Tasks involving conservation, transitivity and hierarchical classification (reviewed in Chapter 7) can now be tackled with success, forming the bases for *logico-mathematical operations*. Furthermore, children become increasingly proficient in their reasoning about spatial relationships among objects, making distance and projection judgments, as reflected in their ability to produce representations of large-scale environments.

School experience necessitates and facilitates the integration and coordination of cognitive functions and operations such as attention, memory, classification, inference, logical grouping and planning. Many of these functions can also be conceptualised within an *information processing framework*. The information processing approach is in part a reaction to Piaget's unified theory of cognitive development: it strives to uncover various aspects of cognition, from basic processes such as perception, attention and memory to complex problem-solving strategies. It makes the analogy of the human mental apparatus to that of a computer, conceiving of both as complex, intricate, symbol-manipulating structures. Research in information processing has been applied to children's learning of reading, maths and problem-solving skills. We examine this approach with reference to learning disabilities and attentional disorders in Chapter 12.

Motivation: key to learning

Children of similar cognitive ability may perform quite differently in school, and while a 'slow learner' can excel, his 'bright' counterpart may flounder. A key element in children's learning and ability to perform in school is the *emotional* energy that drives their desire to learn. Let us begin by looking at forces which propel a child to achieve in school.

Achievement motivation
A crucial factor affecting the educational career of a young child is *motivation*; this determines his attitudes towards school and learning. Children with drive and zest for school are not only better learners but are better adjusted and happier. There may be a host of problems contributing to poor motivation, such as low self-concept, school anxiety or phobia, familial stresses, personality

and learning styles, and academic underachievement. Another significant determinant of *achievement motivation* is the way children *interpret* the feedback given to them by their teachers.

A group of children with identical ability who received identical feedback from their teachers nevertheless exhibited contrasting patterns of interpreting such input (Licht & Dweck, 1984):

- *Mastery-oriented* children maintained a self-confident attitude, did not dwell on their failures, and focused their attention on strategies for solving the problem. They interpreted failure as either bad luck, or as not having tried hard enough, and attributed their success to their ability.
- *Learned helplessness*-exhibiting children adopted a defeatist and passive attitude, where they saw themselves as unable to achieve success and thus did not attempt the tasks with vigilance. They opted out of tasks they thought too difficult, and they gave up too easily. These children underestimated their performance in tests and did not view teacher feedback as realistic; they attributed their success to luck rather than ability.

One in every five gifted and talented ten-year-olds was found to exhibit such helplessness attitudes, where they ignored or distorted positive teacher feedback (Phillips, 1984).

Teacher expectancies and cultural influences on motivation

While these studies suggest *child-centred* evidence for poor achievement motivation, as you would expect, *teachers' views and expectations* of the children exert a substantial influence on their achievement outcomes as well (Rosenthal, 1994). Some teachers with multicultural students in their classroms demonstrate these interactions (St George, 1983):

> Teachers of 67 white and 20 Maori nine-year-old students in New Zealand were found to be rated as high achievers (87% white) and low achievers (54% Maori) at the beginning of the study. Teacher interactions and questions directed to those who were expected to be low-achievers tended to be simple, short and unchallenging, with a one-word answer requirements. The high-achievement expected students on the other hand, were presented with more complex questions, their lengthy explanations were encouraged, and less criticism was directed to them.

The ability of the students to match the student behaviours that teachers deem desirable may vary significantly due to ethnic and gender differences (Randhawa, DeLacey & Saklofske, 1986):

> Aboriginal students display an overly reserved manner in mixed ethnic classes, being guided by a different set of politeness norms than their Anglo-Australian peers, and thus rate lower on voicing their ideas, volunteering for public speaking,

offering to ask or answer questions, and maintaining eye contact in conversing with the teacher. Girls from both ethnic groups were rated as being closer to the ideal student behaviours.

We know how children begin to internalise their sense of self from adults' expectations of them. Teachers may need to display a greater sensitivity of cultural influences, and the powerful influence of the adult on a child needs to be more fully realised. In many Western cultures today, the reality of multiculturalism cannot simply disappear; teacher sentiments such as 'the child (coming from a non-Anglo-Australian background) was expected to adjust to school, rather than the school adjusting to the child' (Harris, 1980, p.34), would probably continue to erode achievement motivation in children from diverse cultural and ethnic backgrounds and experiences.

LANGUAGE, LEARNING AND LITERACY

The language skills of the school-aged child continue to develop in vocabulary, syntactic complexity and conversational pragmatics. Language has now become the currency of learning and the key to literacy acquisition. In addition to a growing proficiency with language, children develop an increasing awareness of language itself (*metalinguistic skills*). They also become verbally playful, enjoying and producing jokes, stories and other texts. As we discuss learning disabilities and reading problems in Chapter 12, the pivotal importance of language-related skills becomes even more salient. Indeed, all facets of language, including listening, speaking, reading and writing, are all inseparably interrelated.

Emerging literacy

Acquisition of reading readiness requires the child to construct meaning by bringing together what he knows about the world and language to help him predict his way through the visual cues on a page. The child's previous experience with *awareness of print*, as well as his skills in *phonological awareness* (the ability to recognise rhymes, to segment words into sounds and to put them together again) have significant effect on the ease with which literacy emerges.

■ Children begin to read familiar *signs and logos* within the environment, and come to recognise words as visual wholes. 60% of three-year-olds, and 80% of four- and five-year-olds, can read environmental print (Goodman, 1987).

■ Children's *picture-book reading* with parents is regarded as an important introduction to reading and writing, laying the foundations not only of effective language-learning experiences but of an awareness of story schema, structure of plots, anticipation of events, and use of language to create surprise, climax and humour (Clay, 1991).

- *Decontextualised language*, where the use of language to represent events, relations and ideas may be removed from the here-and-now, can be found in book-reading activities, home mealtime conversations, and during pretend play. Particularly when such activities bring the child into conversation with a mature speaker of a language, it has been found to relate positively to language comprehension and literacy acquisition (Snow, 1991).
- In addition to oral language skills, *phonological awareness*, where children gradually come to appreciate the speech sound structure of language, has consistently been shown as a precursor of the decoding of linguistic symbols and their combinations into reading, and combining them, or encoding, for writing purposes.
- Phonological awareness can be increased by appropriate preschool and kindergarten activities. Such training results in significant increase in word-recognition and spelling skills in early school years, particularly if they have been combined with practice in recognising letter–sound correspondences (Stanovich & Stanovich, 1995).

Metacognitive skills, which *good readers* bring into play as they read, are the following (Paris, 1986):

- *periodic monitoring* of comprehension of the read material;
- *paraphrasing*, which entails the transformation of complex sentences to their own words and structures;
- *searching the context,* where the skilled reader checks his understanding against other evidence that supports the meaning, such as redundancies in the passage or pictures;
- *formulating hypotheses* about the most important parts of the passage and making it accessible for reference by skimming it again or otherwise locating the information.

Language and context

Studying the use of language in social contexts such as conversations, story-telling and writing for different purposes is broadly labelled *discourse analysis*. It is a useful way of looking at the language skills of school-aged children, since reading and writing become increasingly important in their learning environment.

Linguists use the term *genre* to refer to the structure of language used for a specific purpose, in a particular social context. Different genres may include the following (Martin, 1985):

- the *expressive and imaginative* genre, which includes *recounting* an event or experience, the use of *narrative* to tell stories or a series of events in a time sequence, or a *poetic/literary* style to foster creative expression;

■ the *factual* genre, which includes *descriptions, reports* and *explanations.* Children gain experience in using different genres to suit their purposes as their schooling advances.

In using different genres or texts, children acquire the means with which to make the world of meanings comprehensible not only to themselves but to their listeners (see *Social perspective taking* below). They also employ *cohesive ties*, which are linguistic structures whose use makes the text hang together as a cohesive, understandable piece of speech or writing. Their appropriate use yields some developmental information. Here are some *cohesive ties.*

■ *Reference* establishes a relationship between an item (usually a noun) and its referent (usually a pronoun). For example, in '*The dog* had black and white patches. *It* was lost in the park', *it* is a referent for the *dog.*
■ *Substitution* refers to replacement of one item by another. For example, in 'I love chocolate. So does she', the second sentence is a substitute for 'She loves chocolate too'.
■ *Ellipsis* is the omission of an item altogether, where the meaning is derived from previous information. For example, in 'A snake is well equipped to survive in the desert, and the penguin in the Arctic', we can convey the meaning without saying 'survive' in the second part of the sentence.
■ *Conjunction* serves as a cohesive device by linking what has gone before with what is to come. Conjunctions include words such as: and, or, in addition, but, however, nevertheless, because, therefore, when, while, after and during.
■ *Lexical cohesion* involves the use of vocabulary which is related to previously appearing items by repetition of a word, or using a word which is in the same meaning field. For example, 'The *penguin* is a bird, although the *coat tails* can't fly'.

Children develop their proficiency of using cohesive ties well into adolescent years. Some findings are as follows (Chapman, 1979):

■ In children aged eight, 11 and 14 years, the perception of *reference* and *conjunctions* improves until 14 years.
■ The ability to process *reference ties* discriminates fluent readers from non-fluent ones at eight years of age.

Language is involved in all aspects of the learning process. The debate as to whether cognition or language comes first is not so relevant for the school-aged child as is the *interdependence* of these two domains. Language facilitates learning by (Emmitt & Pollack, 1992):

■ acquiring and generating knowledge by listening, reading and writing;
■ processing information and making connections by sharing ideas, identifying cause–effect relationships, and grouping similar ideas together;

- drawing conclusions and hypothesising by writing and giving oral reports, answering questions, and debating;
- consolidating and applying knowledge, as well as evaluating one's own knowledge by asking new questions and creating new productions.

SOCIAL COGNITION AND MORAL DEVELOPMENT

As children get older their self-knowledge and their understanding of other people become more sophisticated. You may recall from Chapter 7 that preschoolers often perform poorly in perspective-taking tasks. Theory of mind and social cognition are both based on an appreciation of other peoples' perspectives. While younger children's self-descriptions are tied to the more visible characteristics, school-aged children tend to describe themselves in more comparative and generalised ways.

Self-concept

Early school years mark the child's transition to an *abstract categorical self,* which is much less focused on external characteristics and more on stable internal qualities. Because the child can assess his own as well as others' characteristics as being stable, a *global* sense of self begins to emerge where, for example, seven-year-olds can talk about how well they like themselves or how happy they are (Ruble, 1987). Teachers' as well as parents' expectations of children also have a significant impact on self-judgments in school.

At the beginning of a school year, the teachers were informed that a group of (randomly chosen) children in their class were underachievers who were ready to 'bloom', implying that those children had more potential. The 'pygmalion' children, in fact, *did* have better academic outcomes at the end of school year than children who were not similarly nominated (Rosenthal, 1994) (see discussion of teacher expectancies, above).

Girls seem to have a lower perception of their academic ability. When they receive academic recognition for success, they are more likely to attribute it to hard work, as do their parents, while poor work is seen as their own fault. Boys attribute their high achievement to their ability or talent, as do their parents (Stipek & Gralinski, 1991).

Self-esteem

The global evaluation of the self reflects, to some extent, the child's self-esteem. Self-esteem is determined by the *discrepancy* between what the child *would like to be* and what he thinks *he is* (Harter, 1990). The key in self-esteem is the *child's own assessment* of the value of a particular skill or achievement in his world. Children who feel that their parents, other significant adults and peers generally like them for being the way they are tend to have higher self-esteem scores than do children with lower degrees of support.

Social perspective taking

Selman (1980) has proposed a cognitive developmental model for social perspective taking, which dovetails Piaget's concepts but is situated within an interactive context, from which mutuality in social relatedness emerges:

1. *Egocentric or undifferentiated perspective.* From about three to seven years, children do not always recognise that others may have a subjective experience different from their own. They tend to confuse social and physical realities.
2. *Subjective or differentiated perspective.* Between four and nine years, children begin to appreciate that each person may construct a different subjective reality, with unique feelings and thoughts.
3. *Self-reflective or reciprocal perspective.* From about six to 12 years of age, children are able to put themselves into the other person's shoes. Children can now understand how others see them; based on this understanding, they can form reciprocal appreciation of thoughts and feelings.
4. *Third-person or mutual perspective.* Between the ages of nine and 15, children are able to coordinate the perspectives of a number of persons, not only those of their interactive partners.
5. *Societal or in-depth perspective.* From adolescence onwards, perspectives are generalised to the society level, incorporating legal and moral views.

Children seem to go through these stages successively. Social perspective-taking ability is at the crossroads of social cognition and social behaviour, and accounts for variability in children's reasoning and actions.

Moral reasoning

Moral reasoning is the *cognitive process* that justifies decisions regarding right or wrong. Truthfulness is one aspect of morality. Piaget, in his clinical interviews (1932/1965; see Chapter 7), discovered that children aged six to nine had very different notions of what constituted a lie than did adults. Here are some of his findings:

- Lies are those things a child can get into trouble for saying, like 'swear words'.
- Lies that are not caught by the significant adult or receive a punishment are not considered to be serious lies. Piaget asked which of the below was a greater offence:

  1. A boy is frightened and tells his mother that it is because he has seen a dog as big as a cow;

2. A boy tells his mother that he has received perfect marks at school, when in reality he has done poorly.

- Most children younger than nine years felt that the first lie was a greater offence, as the mother would know that it was a lie immediately. However, preplanned deceptions (on marks) may not be seen as lies, particularly if they are not discovered by the mother.
- On the other hand, innocent miscommunications, such as giving confused, though well-intentioned, directions to a stranger, may be viewed as a serious lie, suggesting that mistakes may not be distinguished from lies at that age.

Stages of moral development

Moral rules define the right and wrong behaviour in ways that are applicable to all people and all cultures; as such, they carry a universality dimension. Piaget believed that morality was determined by the child's ability to take the other's perspective, and that it operated at two levels:

- *Heteronomous morality* is seen until about eight years of age. The basis of morality is the acceptance of authority. Because children at this age are egocentric, they cannot understand why adults make the rules, but out of respect for them the adults' morality becomes the childrens' morality as well.
- *Autonomous/cooperative morality* evolves after eight years, when the child has developed a sense of peer relations and moved away from egocentric thought. Moral decisions are based on mutuality and egalitarian relationships among peers.

Lawrence Kohlberg postulated *stages of moral development,* based on Piagetian notions. He, too, is a cognitive–developmental theorist, in that he believes in the sequential and orderly acquisition of morality, as well as certain principles guiding each stage of development. Instead of a clinical interview, he presented his participants with little stories, each containing a moral dilemma, the most famous of which is Heinz and his sick wife:

> In Europe, a woman was dying of a rare cancer. There was one drug which could cure her, discovered and developed by the chemist in the local pharmacy. The drug was expensive to make, and the chemist was charging $2000 for a small dose, although it cost him $200 to manufacture that much. Heinz, the sick woman's husband, wanted desperately to buy the drug, but could only raise $1000 towards its purchase. He went to the chemist and explained that his wife would die soon if he did not sell him the drug, but that he could only pay half of the price now. Heinz asked him to sell the drug more cheaply, or let him pay for it later. But the chemist said, 'No, I discovered the drug and I am going to make money from it'. Heinz got so desperate that he broke into the pharmacy to steal the stuff for his wife.

This episode would be followed by a series of questions, such as:

■ Should Heinz have stolen the drug?
■ What if he really did not love his wife; would that matter?
■ What if the dying person was a stranger?

Based on their answers, he formulated three levels (Table 8.1), with two stages in each level, in the development of morality (Kohlberg, 1976; 1981).

TABLE 8.1	Level I	**Preconventional morality: authority external to self**	
Kohlberg's developmental levels of morality	Stage 1	*Punishment and obedience orientation*	Child obeys for fear of punishment; obedience is valued for its own sake.
	Stage 2	*Instrumental relativism*	Rules are followed when they bear pleasant and self-serving consequences: 'I'll do it for you if you do it for me'.
	Level II	**Conventional morality: authority not analysed or questioned**	
	Stage 3	*Interpersonal concordance*	Actions are moral if they live up to the expectations of the significant group; being good is valued for its own sake.
	Stage 4	*Law and order orientation*	Social system and its rules, regulations and laws determine what is moral and what is not; laws should be obeyed.
	Level III	**Postconventional morality: authority based on self-chosen principles**	
	Stage 5	*Social contract and individual rights*	Acts for the greatest good for the greatest number are moral. Fairness; each person's life and liberty may supersede the law.
	Stage 6	*Universal ethical principles*	Reflective, carefully thought-out principles which apply universally, with justice, human rights and respect for life at their core.

Kohlberg's theory of moral development has spawned considerable research and his findings have been amply replicated, although some critical opinions remain (i.e. stages pertain to fairness and justice, and not to morality in its full scope). Preconventional reasoning (stages 1 and 2) is dominant in primary school; conventional reasoning (stages 3 and 4) emerges in middle adolescence and remains the most common form of reasoning in adulthood. Postconventional morality is achieved by a small percentage of the adult population only (Walker, deVries & Trevathen, 1987).

Prosocial reasoning

As you can see, Kohlberg's dilemma involves a wrongdoing, placing the person in a conflict situation in which one of the choices is stealing. Eisenberg (1986) postulated a developmental trend in morality in young children, basing it on *prosocial* and *altruistic* behaviours. Children are posed a question which faces them with balancing their self-interest with the welfare of another person, such as: 'You are on your way to your friend's birthday party, and see another child fallen and hurt. If you stop to help, you will miss the cake. What should you do?'.

Eisenberg's findings indicate that children move from *hedonistic* (self-serving) modes in preschool to *needs-oriented reasoning* (other-centred) by late childhood. Children who express more hedonistic modes of thinking on prosocial dilemmas tend to be less helpful and generous towards others, suggesting that prosocial reasoning influences prosocial behaviour.

PARENTING INFLUENCES ON SOCIALISATION

Traditionally, developmental psychology has focused on the parents as the agents in their children's socialisation process. We realise today that children influence parents, just as parents influence children. Such reciprocal effects need to be borne in mind in our attempts at understanding the interactive styles in families.

Patterns of parent–child interactions, and emerging parenting styles, were studied extensively in a classical work by Baumrind in 1971. Before we take a look at her system, and its elaboration by Maccoby & Martin (1983), let us review the basic dimensions that are operative in the ways in which parents approach children.

- *Warmth.* Low warmth is associated with rejection, insensitivity to child signals, insecure attachment, and generally a negative emotional atmosphere in which children are reared. High warmth, a crucially desirable attribute for favourable child outcomes, is characterised by sensitivity to child signals, secure attachment, nurturing, caring and expressions of positive emotions.
- *Control.* Setting age-appropriate behavioural limits and expectations, enforcing them consistently, and communicating the reasons behind their implementation define the positive aspects of parental control. On the negative side, control may entail power assertion through employment of physical punishment, deprivation and other punitive means.
- *Involvement.* Although parents who are warm and use positive control tend to be highly involved with their children as well, this dimension may exist independently of warmth and control. The character of the father in the movie *Shine* comes to mind as a very involved yet strongly negatively controlling parent.

The styles of parenting described by Diana Baumrind (1971) are summarised below:

- *Authoritative parents.* These parents are characterised by firm control and high expectations of independence and obedience, and rate high on warmth. They often employ open communication to reason with their children about the limits they set.

- *Authoritarian parents.* These parents expect obedience from their children without feeling the need to communicate to them the reasons for such compliance or its consequences. They rate high on control and consistency dimensions, and do not value independence or autonomy in their children.
- *Permissive parents.* These parents rate very low in control and involvement, and often rate low on warmth as well. They have a laissez-faire (non-directive) attitude towards their children.
- *Non-conforming parents.* These parents value independence and self-expression in their children, as well as engaging in open communication with them, particularly in negotiations of limit-setting and punishment of transgressions. They are moderately controlling.

A modification of this typology, by permutations of the control and warmth dimensions in parenting, is presented by Maccoby and Martin (1983):

DIMENSIONS	Warmth ⇒ High: responsive	Low: unresponsive
Control ⇓ High: directive	Authoritative	Authoritarian
Low: non-directive	Permissive	Non-conforming (uninvolved)

The authoritative parenting style, with its firm but warm interactive style, has consistently been found to be related to positive child outcomes (see *Social status* below). Parental discipline is another variable affecting the development of social cognition and conscience.

Parental discipline

Parents may use a variety of means to discipline their children and to instil in them an appreciation of the difference between right and wrong, which incorporates combinations of the dimensions we mentioned above (Hoffman, 1994):

- *Induction* (or inductive discipline) is when parents present the reasons for the limitation put on the child's behaviour. When used in conjunction with highlighting the affects the child's behaviour may have on others, it seems particularly useful (e.g. 'When you talk too loud, it hurts my ears').
- *Withdrawing of love* is when the parent punishes the child by withholding her attention and love from him, without necessarily explaining what the child has done to bring about this reticence.
- *Physical punishment* or power assertion is when the child is forcefully disciplined, as in smacking or hitting, or physically removing him from a circumstance.

For discipline to be effective, the child needs to *internalise* the transgression episode with its consequences, and develop cognitive appreciation of

- why the transgression was unacceptable,
- the effect of his behaviour on others, and
- the match between 'crime and punishment': parity or justice in the discipline received, in relation to the gravity of the misdeed.

Discipline based on natural consequences, and withdrawal of privileges based on a good understanding of why this occurred, assists young children in self-regulation and internalisation of discipline.

Unless internalisation occurs, parental discipline may lead to the reduction of that behaviour when the parent is around (fear of punishment) but not when the child is at liberty to behave so without adult knowledge (conscience). In other words, the child must have an *active* role in *accepting* discipline for it to become assimilated into his developing sense of morality. School-aged children can begin to understand induction as it affects others; preschoolers are too wrapped up in their own perspectives to have a full sense of such realisation. Grusec and Goodnow (1994) elaborate on other variables which affect the internalisation of discipline:

- Secure child–parent attachment makes the child more sensitive to parental disapproval.
- Accurate perception of the message is essential: it should be understandable, relevant, redundant and consistent, as well as carrying a positive parental intention.
- The discipline should fit the misdeed, and be perceived as appropriate by the child.
- Discipline should be appropriate to the temperament, mood, developmental status and other motivating factors of the child.
- Low-level power assertion, and minimal threat to the child's autonomy, also facilitate internalisation of parental discipline.

FRIENDSHIPS AND PEER RELATIONS

Friendships are characterised by the following criteria for five- to 11-year-olds (Burns & Goodnow, 1985):

- mutual avoidance of acts of aggression and hostility; prevalence of amity;
- having common interests in games, sport, activities, pets and other recreation;
- being available, and experiencing an attitude of caring from the peer as well as family.

While younger children place greater importance on having fun with their friends, as children get older and mature cognitively as well as emotionally, the criteria for friendships shift to psychological constructs, such as mutual trust, understanding and loyalty.

Peer relations and friendships rise to prominence in early school years. Among children aged seven, eight, nine and ten, playing with friends takes up almost all their time, when they are not in school, eating, sleeping or watching television (Timmer, Eccels & O'Brien, 1985).

- *Common activities* are the major basis for definition of play groups at this age; common attitudes and values as crucial determinants of friendships emerge in later years.
- Across most cultures, boys and girls aged six to 12 play with *same-sex* peers, with each in their own areas and their own kinds of games.
- Friendships in early school years are likely to last a year or longer; they are also collaborative, and oriented towards conflict resolution in disagreements (Newcomb & Bagwell, 1995).
- There are some *qualitative* differences between girls' and boys' friendships: boys' friendship groups are larger, more oriented towards outdoor roaming and less concerned with inclusion *(extensive)*, while girls' groups are smaller, often in pairs, more exclusive, and more oriented towards indoors and home play *(intensive)* (Waldrop & Halverson, 1975).
- Boys' friendships tend to be more organised around competition and dominance, with frequent use of 'controlling' speech (rejection, manipulation, challenging, ordering, resistance and defiance comments); girls' friendships cluster around more agreement, compliance and self-disclosure (Leaper, 1991).
- Boys and girls both seem to learn to control *aggressive behaviour* as they internalise the societal rules transmitted to them, so that anger is increasingly disguised and aggression (expression of anger) is increasingly kept under check with increasing age (Underwood, Coie & Herbsman, 1992).
- Careful analysis in boys and girls reveals that they display their aggression in *different* ways: girls tend to use *relational aggression*, where the hurt is directed to the other's sense of worth and status (e.g. I won't be your friend and I'll tell all your secrets); boys tend to use *physical aggression*, which hurts the other with actual or threatened physical damage (Crick & Grotpeter, 1995).

Social status

The *sociogram* is an evaluation tool which measures a child's status within a group of peers. There are a number of methods for obtaining sociometric nominations or sociometric ratings. Typically, children are asked to indicate the friends they like to play with the most, or to name two or three that they would invite to their birthday party. Based on the obtained results, children can be classified into one of four groups. Such classification seems to be stable over time, particularly in such continuous settings as a school or class (Hartup, 1992):

1. The socially accepted, or *popular*, children are those who are named most often by their peers. Popular children seem to be more capable than their peers in initiating and maintaining *positive* relations in social groups, expressing friendly interest in others, joining in social groups by engaging in non-obtrusive tactics, and volunteering information (Putallaz, 1983).

2. The *average* children constitute the greatest part of the group. They get nominated by other peers, but not as frequently as the popular children.

3. The *neglected* children are those who are not mentioned in the shortlist of preferred friends. They may be socially isolated because they are shy, withdrawn or socially anxious, but are not necessarily actively disliked by their peers.

4. The *rejected* children are named in response to the question 'Who do you least like/dislike?'. While the ethical considerations in asking such a direct question have been debated in the field, these children seem to be actively avoided by their peers, and are often associated with *aggressive and hostile* attempts to integrate themselves into a group. They also have an internal working model, 'hostile attributional bias', through which they interpret random or accidental events as aggressive acts directed at them (Dodge & Feldman, 1990).

Some children can be intensely disliked by some, and liked by a closer circuit of friends; such polarised opinions mark those children as being *controversial*. Having a single stable friend can reduce the vulnerability of the child; it is the totally rejected youngsters that we need to be concerned about, as these are the ones most at risk for maladjustments in life.

Research shows that rejection by peers in early school years is one of the few dimensions in early childhood that reliably predicts later conduct and behaviour problems, as well as emotional disturbance such as depression in late childhood and adolescence (Dishion, 1990; DeRosier, Kupersmidt & Patterson, 1994; Kupersmidt & Coie, 1990).

Parenting patterns seem to influence children's social status:

■ *Parental warmth*. Children of warm and sensitive parents tend to be popular; cold and rejecting parents are more often associated with rejected children (Putallaz, 1987).

■ *Parental involvement*. Parents of more popular children tend to spend more time playing and talking with them.

■ *Parental discipline*. Neglected and rejected six-year-olds were reported to have highly controlling parents, particularly in play situations (Putallaz, 1987). Nine-year-olds who tended to be rejected tended to have parents who failed consistently or effectively to discipline them (Dishion, 1990). Moderate control coupled with warmth in parents is associated more often with popular children.

GENDER AND SEX-ROLE CONCEPTS

School years consolidate the appreciation of gender and sex roles. You may recall from Chapter 6 that gender concepts form from quite an early age, and encompass the following components:

1. *Gender identity,* by which the child makes correct identification of male and female;
2. *Gender stability,* where the understanding that gender is stable over time occurs;
3. *Gender constancy,* where the child appreciates that changes in appearance or superficial characteristics of a boy or a girl will *not* alter his gender.

   - The words 'boy' and 'girl' become descriptives in a two-year-old's vocabulary, although he may not be able correctly to identify his gender until later.
   - By 30 months of age children can label their own gender correctly, both when asked orally and when shown a photograph of themselves (Thomson, 1975).
   - After three years, children can make correct judgments about gender and age (boy, girl, man, woman) from photographs of adults and children (Bem, 1989).
   - Gender constancy, however, is not yet understood by the preoperational child, and is achieved after the conservation tasks are understood (see Chapter 7).

The child's learning of *sex-role stereotypes* can be influenced by sex-role contexts he is presented with in his *television*-watching experience. Content analyses of British and US television programming indicated that women were typically shown as weak, passive, and in home-related roles, while men were typically portrayed in more exciting, cool-headed and aggressive roles (Durkin, 1985). In an examination of sex-role stereotyping in 281 Australian television commercials shown in the evening hours, the pattern found promulgated highly stereotypical roles for men and women (Mazella, Durkin, Cerini & Buralli, 1992):

- Men outnumber women nearly 2 to 1.
- Men are portrayed as being authority figures, experts, acting logically and competently.

- Women are portrayed as young, thin, and preoccupied with buying products concerning the home or the body, more efficiently or less expensively.
- The 'voice-over' in the commercials is most often a male voice.

The authors comment on the conformity of Australian television to the widely criticised patterns of sexist representations of women and men on Western television, which has not changed despite public debate.

Television reflects the values of its viewers; thus we may make the assumption that men are more valued members of the society than women. By the time he is 18, the average child has spent more time in front of a TV set than in a classroom (Calvert & Huston, 1987). How does such a skewed representation affect young children's views on gender?

- In a study asking girls aged five to 15 whether they would rather be boys, groups of Swedish, Australian, American and Canadian girls all indicated that they would rather be boys in varying percentages (7%–27%), with the exception of the 11-year-old Swedish girls, who did not want a change (Goldman & Goldman, 1982).
- Australian boys of all social classes are found to show unequivocal preference for masculine toys, games and models from three years of age on (Bussey, 1983).
- Elementary and high-school students who watch a lot of television are reported to have more traditional sex-role stereotyping (Morgan, 1987).

Androgyny

Androgyny reflects an understanding of femininity and masculinity not as the opposite ends of a continuum, but rather as two separate dimensions. It demonstrates a flexible blend of socially desirable masculine and feminine sex-role attributes associated with effective psychological functioning in men and women, so that a person can be high or low on either or both (Bem, 1975). According to this model, a person can be both compassionate (ranked high on femininity) *and* independent (ranked high on masculinity).

It is an interesting model, and challenges traditional views on gender roles. Take a look at this representation of sex-role types in quadrants:

	Femininity ⇓	Masculinity items ⇒
SCORE	**High**	**Low**
High	Androgynous	Feminine
Low	Masculine	Undifferentiated

- *Androgynous* persons are high on both masculinity and femininity items.
- *Feminine* persons are high on femininity and low on masculinity items.

- *Masculine* persons are high on masculinity items and low on femininity items.
- *Undifferentiated* or diffuse identity persons are low on both sets.

Children younger than nine or ten seem to show little sign of androgyny, perhaps because children have rigid ideas about sex roles, or because role models in the environment do not exhibit it. However, parental efforts to encourage androgyny may actually be effective.

In a study with 400 children and their families, where parents were prompted to encourage their children to do cross-sex household chores (i.e. girls to mow the lawn, boys to do the dishes) and have cross-sex career considerations (i.e. girls to become firefighters, boys to become nurses), and actively cultivated interest in cross-sex film, literature and other entertainment, children were found to have less rigid attitudes in conformity to biologically based roles (Katz & Ksansnak, 1994).

Breaking free of sexual stereotypes to cultivate androgyny can be partially achieved through parents' active cultivation of such practices as giving cross-sex toys as presents, spending more time with the opposite-sex parent and grandparents, playing games with mixed-sex peers and considering non-conventional career choices (Peterson, 1995).

Explanations for sex-role development

Major traditions and orientations in child development also have approaches to explain sex-role development:

- *Psychoanalytical approach* claims that identification with the same-sex parent would culminate in the child's sex-role development. This process occurs by four to five years of age. As children are able to discern sex roles considerably earlier, this orientation is not sufficient as a causal explanation.
- *Social learning theory* gains a degree of support in explaining sex-role development, since parents seem to reinforce sex-typed activities in children as young as 18 months of age (Fagot & Hagan, 1991). Fathers, more than mothers, tend to treat their sons more differentially, and are more concerned with gender-appropriate behaviour in them than in their daughters (Siegal, 1987).
- *Cognitive developmental theory* explains the process as the child's understanding of the gender concept. Indeed, children seem much more sensitive to same-sex models after they have understood gender constancy (Frey & Ruble, 1992), although differential sex-role behaviour is evidenced considerably earlier.
- *Gender schema theory* (Martin, 1991) states that child's understanding of gender can be seen as a function of the developing gender schema, which commences as soon as the infant is able to notice the differences between

genders; gender constancy need not be established before such social rule-based behaviour emerges.

CONCLUSIONS

Having reviewed the basics of typical development in early childhood, we can hardly say that we have covered all there is to know, because child development is one of the most extensive, exciting and dynamic fields of science. The information presented here alerts you to some prominent issues, and perhaps allows you to develop a further interest and critical analysis of these topics by further reading. If you find yourself asking more questions than finding answers, you are probably on the right track!

In the following chapters, we keep in mind the backdrop of normal development we have reviewed from birth to middle childhood, as we examine different perspectives on domains of atypical development and difference, delay and disorders. Our challenge is to maintain the unity of the child, and the interrelatedness and interdependence of the domains of development within the social context of the child, the family and the society.

PART III

Atypical development

Principles to remember as we take a closer look at special conditions in early childhood:

1. Normal child development in all facets and domains serves as the springboard to understanding the nature and course of atypical development and to planning facilitative experiences, as development is on a continuum of a hierarchical and progressively complex organisation.

2. Diagnostic categories may have their greatest utility for functions that are least important in the child's life: namely, professional (medical, educational) bureaucracy.

3. Categorical approach is not necessary to the provision of optimal services and facilitative intervention to young children and their families. All children, regardless of their developmental status, have the same needs of inclusion, acceptance, interaction, playfulness, stimulation and attention. These are the tools of fostering each child's development, whether such fostering process be called education, treatment, management, intervention, facilitation or therapy.

4. A diagnosis, or a label, or a category does not define a child, but pertains to a subset of her capabilities. A child is a child first and foremost; a disability may affect the adaptation of the child to the environment, but should have nothing to do with the sense of acceptance, regard and respect every child is owed.

5. The line between typical and atypical development may be an arbitrary one, either because the young organism's immense powers of resilience and compensation for a dysfunction are at play, or because assessment processes are inaccurate.

6. The most predictable aspect of development is change. The nature of change in atypical development towards more adaptive patterns may depend more heavily on the nature and compatibility of the environment to the needs of the child and family.

7. The child lives in a family which exists in a community. The unit of social context is the product of the reciprocal forces acting on the whole of the child, family and community; each child represents this unit.

Let us call them the *seven principles of sound judgment* of development and use them as the basic framework in interpreting children with atypical developmental trajectories.

As you develop your own principles, slot them into the above seven; seven is an easy number to remember!

9

Families, children and developmental psychopathology

Bronfenbrenner was a pioneer who focused the attention of many professionals working with children and families on the fact that the laboratory approach to psychology was inappropriate. He asserted that formal psychological assessment reflected 'a science concerned with the strange behaviour of children in strange situations with strange adults for the briefest periods of time' (Bronfenbrenner, 1977, p.513), and thus had limited usefulness. The argument was that child evaluations needed to be referenced against the social, behavioural and educational expectations in the child's natural environments: all living things can best be understood within their ecology.

Indeed, understanding maladaptive behaviour in isolation without the context in which it is embedded is not understanding it at all. A good example of the *ecological perspective* of children labelled as emotionally disturbed was presented decades ago: Rhodes (1967) asserted that viewing disturbance as something residing in the child led to a preoccupation with attempting to fix the child, whereas the disturbance was more readily attributable to a tension between the child and the demands of the environment. Focusing on the child, with little regard for the precipitating and sustaining environmental and familial factors in emotional disturbance, is akin to missing the woods for the trees. As you will see, the current thinking in developmental psychopathology is solidly embedded in developmental, contextual and interactional-transactional matrices (Katz & Kahn, 1969, p.91):

> Living systems, whether biological organisms or social organisations, are acutely dependent upon their external environment and so must be conceived of as *open systems* . . . (which) maintain themselves through constant commerce with the environment, i.e. a continuous inflow and outflow of energy through permeable boundaries.

FAMILY SYSTEMS

As a social system, family members continually affect and are affected by each other. Structural family theory and therapy describe the family in terms of dynamic relationship patterns that evolve as a consequence of parent–child and contextual interactions, which include those individual characteristics (such as temperament) as well as the numerous social interactional contexts that the individual is exposed to (Minuchin, 1980).

The family is made up of dynamics, structures, functions, change mechanisms and dysfunctions, all of which contribute to the development of the individual in the first degree. Within families, subsystems exist that are formed by interest, generation and gender, involving one or more members in roles that may be temporary or changeable, such as a *spouse dyad* (husband and wife bonds), *parent dyads* (those in parent–child roles), and the *sibling subsystems* (Minuchin, Rosman, Baker, & Liebman, 1978).

Functional families are defined as those in which communication, boundaries, hierarchies and subsystems meet the needs of the family members' developmental stages.

Dysfunctional families are those in which one or more of these dimensions contribute to the family's failure to meet an individual's developmental needs. Here are some dysfunctional patterns (Liebman & Ziffer, 1985, pp.185–186):

- *overprotectiveness:* the tendency of parents to hover over the child, and not to allow any competencies of autonomy or problem-solving to be exercised;
- *enmeshment:* an overinvolvement between two or more family members resulting in a lack of age-appropriate autonomy, independence, privacy and peer relationships for both parties;
- *rigidity:* the family's tendency to rely on accustomed patterns of transactions when circumstances call for flexibility and change;
- *detouring:* a means of avoiding conflict between two family members by focusing on a third person or event as the topic of the disagreement;
- *disengagement:* the lack of affective bonds, limits or nurturance between two or more family members.

All families may find themselves engaging in some or all of these patterns *some time* in their lives, which may merely be situation-specific, as in nurturing a child overprotectively during sickness. It is the nature and the extent of these patterns, and the habituality with which they are operative that mark dysfunctionality in families. When families are not able to solve the conflict interactions become stressful, which can create some problematic family types, such as those listed by Liebman and Ziffer (1985), below.

Triangulated family system.   Characterised by shifting of alliance between the partners, and splitting of the spouse dyad. Children experience stress because agreement with one parent has to be at the expense of the other.

Detouring protective family system.   Parents exhibit a superficially appropriate nurturant and supportive response to the child, whereas their typical response may be enmeshment and overprotectiveness.

Detouring attacking family system.   Parents present a united face of strength in the spouse dyad and put all the blame for the family problems on the child.

Stable coalition family system.   An identified child and a parent form a close and personal relationship, excluding and/or attacking the other parent.

Disengaged child family system.   One family member openly declares her/his lack of interest in being involved in the problems of the family.

When the family system works well it accommodates the needs of the individuals in it and its subsystems, and moulds to their developmental needs and changes over time. When it fails to function adequately, family dynamics lead to patterns of behaviour that hinder the growth and wellbeing of one or more family members.

Family and parenting life cycles

Another dimension that needs to be considered in understanding families is the *time* element in its life course—that is, the development of a family over time and how the family is affected by various events. The family life cycle is based on a model of orderly changes in the family, based on stages and predictable evolutions in an array of complex family dynamics. To illustrate, *enmeshment* may be appropriate in certain stages of the family life cycle (e.g. during the early child-bearing years), when closeness and cohesion are adaptive, in contrast to the family's middle years and the children's adolescence, when family relationships tend to be more outgoing, and *disengagement* is more adaptive (Combrink-Graham, 1983). Dysfunctionality may result when the stage in the family life cycle and the events in the family do not match. Table 9.1 is a model of *parenting life stages*, with examples of functional and dysfunctional patterns of parents and children (Tseng & Hsu, 1991).

As you can see from Table 9.1, the tasks of parents and children are different in different stages of the family life cycle. Dysfunctionality can occur within each stage if task demands are not adequately met by parents or children, or if the patterns employed are not appropriate for that stage.

Stress, vulnerability and resilience

The family and its members are liable to experience stressful events and transitions in life. An unusual number of stressors may be overwhelming and impair the family's ability to cope, particularly if these go above and beyond the family's financial, relational and emotional resources. When the coping capacity of the family is taxed heavily, the cohesive elements of the family are under

	Parenting life stages	Functional patterns	Dysfunctional patterns
TABLE 9.1 **Parenting life stages (Tseng & Hsu, 1991; printed with permission)**	*1. Infant and parents' stage*		
	Parents	Nurturing, protecting, and caring for infant	Child rejection, negligence and abuse
	Infants	Total dependency on parents	Regression and withdrawal from forming relationship with parents
	2. Younger child and parents' stage		
	Parents	Adjustment of triadic relation to child; provision of behaviour models for child, as well as appropriate restriction and limitations	Inability to allow child to separate
	Children	Achieving psychological separation from parents; autonomy; imitation of parents' behaviour	Prolonged fused relationship with parents
	3. Older child and parents' stage		
	Parents	Sensitivity to child's growth needs; provision of opportunities for independence; enjoying life through child's experience	Insensitive to child's growth needs; inhibition of child's individuality
	Children	Search for individuality	Failure to seek individuality
	4. Adolescent and parents' stage		
	Parents	Assistance in establishment of role and identity; toleration of cultural/generational gap	Unwillingness to negotiate the gap; parents feel their child undervaluing them
	Adolescents	Development of self-image and identity	Believes the parents depreciate her; rebels against parents

increasing pressure to unravel. Stressors may include poverty, familial strife, lack of support structures, and caring for a child with special needs. Accumulated stresses may have detrimental effects and increase the *vulnerability* of children to maladaptive behaviour or enhance the *risk factors* for abuse (Sameroff, 1995).

Certain characteristics or circumstances may serve as *protective factors*, and increase the *resilience* of children to adverse effects from stresses in family and social life. Among such protective factors are good cognitive potential, easy temperament, competent adult parenting, secure attachment and effective educational experiences. We look at these factors below in children subject to abuse.

ATTACHMENT AND PSYCHOPATHOLOGY

Children who are securely attached to their parents are able to explore their world, safe in the knowledge that the parents are available when needed in case they are anxious or distressed (see Chapter 5). Insecure children are less autonomous, and are more likely to have emotional problems by school age, such as difficulties in concentrating or relating to peers. Parents who have a clear and coherent understanding of their children's needs and vulnerabilities are more likely to have secure children, whereas parents who do not empathise with their children and find it difficult to respond appropriately when they are in need are more likely to have insecure children. The knowledge about parent–child attachments has been extended to understanding how the family as a whole can provide a secure base from which children can explore and develop (Byng-Hall, 1991).

John Bowlby (1969), who has made the most important contribution to the formulation of attachment theory, has also claimed a relationship between quality of attachment relationship and psychopathology. Here is some recent research evidence which continues to demonstrate that when *attachment—* predicated on a positive interactive emotional climate between the infant and her caregivers—is compromised, the child is vulnerable to a host of maladaptive conditions:

- During the first two years of life, the infant's affective experiences with the caregiver influence the maturation of the prefrontal cortex, which mediates regulatory and attachment functions. Deprivation of interactive affective experiences, or prolonged episodes of intense interactive stress for the infant, appear to inhibit the development of this system permanently, predisposing the child to future psychopathology through damage to the self-regulatory mechanisms (Schore, 1996).
- A comprehensive Australian review of connections between attachment and eating disorders such as *anorexia nervosa* and *bulimia* indicates the presence of attachment disturbances in children and young adults with eating-disorder psychopathology (O'Kearney, 1996).
- In a group of 60 psychiatrically hospitalised adolescents, nearly half the adolescents *and* their mothers were shown to have insecure attachment classifications. Those adolescents showing avoidant attachment are more likely to have a conduct disorder and substance abuse, while those with anxious attachment are likely to exhibit affective disorders, such as unstable and fluctuating moods of depression and mania (Rosenstein & Horowitz, 1996).
- Attachment dysfunction is linked to psychopathological conditions in maltreated children, to children with depressed and substance-abusing caregivers, and to children with oppositional conduct disorders. Adult

attachment organisations in caregivers have a significant impact on how they relate to their children (Cicchetti, Toth & Lynch, 1995).

Relationships within a family context have four primary characteristics (Sroufe & Fleeson, 1986):

- Relationships are wholes.
- Relationships have continuity and coherence.
- Individuals internalise whole relationships, not simply roles.
- Early relationship patterns are incorporated into later close relationships.

The incidence of child abuse can be explained in this framework, which has attachment as its cornerstone: the abusing parent has internalised an abusing role from her parents and carried it forward to a present parent–child relationship (Egeland, Jacobovitz & Sroufe, 1988); the insecurely attached infant internalises a relationship model which sets the stage for maltreatment of her own child in due course. And so the circular causality of dysfunctional interaction continues, awaiting to be interrupted by intervention or insight.

VIOLENCE AGAINST CHILDREN: CHILD ABUSE

Physical abuse and neglect of young children

Physical abuse is defined as physical acts of commission that involve either demonstrable harm or endangerment to the child (National Center on Child Abuse and Neglect, 1988). Physical abuse includes injuries such as bruises or broken bones resulting from spanking, slapping, shoving or hitting with a fist or object, and neurological injury resulting from shaking the young child or baby. Pre- and postnatal exposure to toxic substances such as alcohol and drugs is also being included in widened definitions of abuse. *Child neglect* includes both physical and emotional deprivation of the child of the sustenance necessary for her to grow and develop normally. Estimates of incidence of abuse and neglect vary, but it is thought to be around 20% (Harrison & Edwards, 1983).

- Children under the age of five represent 64% of those receiving major injuries from physical abuse, and the mean age of those who have died as a result of abuse is 2.6 years (Walker, Bonner & Kaufman, 1988).
- Boys are more likely than girls to be the victims of severe physical abuse, and 97% of children who are physically maltreated are abused by a parent (Bonner, Kaufman, Harbeck & Brassard, 1992).
- Very young children may be more susceptible to abuse. According to Belsky (1993), this is because:
  - physical force is more often used against them in disciplining;
  - they spend more time with caregivers;

- they are more susceptible to injury because of their physical vulnerability;
- their less well-developed emotional control makes them more likely
  to evoke hostile care from their parents.

Physical abuse is the result of a complex interaction between environmental
stresses, parental characteristics and child characteristics. According to Holden,
Willis and Corcoran (1992), the *environmental and familial risk* factors include:

- low socioeconomic status and social isolation;
- work-related stress or unemployment;
- single-parent status of the mother;
- marital discord;
- disturbances in the parent–child attachment;
- large family size, with inadequate spacing between children;
- negative maternal attitude toward pregnancy;
- anger-control problems in the parent;
- prevailing negative emotional states, such as depression and anxiety;
- low educational achievement;
- low intellectual level;
- unrealistic developmental expectations;
- deficiency in child management skills;
- parental history of childhood maltreatment.

These risk factors are balanced against some *protective* factors in parents,
which may counteract the tendencies for child-abusive behaviour (Belsky,
1993):

- positive attitudes towards parenting;
- average or higher intellectual functioning;
- high educational attainment;
- good understanding of early child development;
- a repertoire of positive parenting skills;
- strong personal coping skills;
- access to family planning resources;
- access to a loving, supportive and guiding adult.

Some *child characteristics* have been associated with an increased *risk* of
abuse (American Humane Association, 1985):

- young children born prematurely and those with developmental problems;
- young children exhibiting challenges associated with developmental transitions, such as oppositionality, poor appetite, waking in the night or
  resistance to toilet-training;
- unwanted children, younger male children, and those with physical
  handicaps.

According to Mrazek and Mrazek (1987), child factors which serve a *protective* function include:

- flexibility and the ability to play independently;
- average or higher intellectual functioning;
- high level of compliance with parental commands;
- smooth acquisition of developmental milestones;
- access to a nurturing individual who provides love and affection.

Most physically abused children grow up in families with multiple stressors and dysfunctions; it may thus be difficult to determine which of these factors contribute to the various psychosocial deficits noted in these children.

Physically abused young children may be oppositional, aggressive, hyperactive and distractible. They score lower on measures of self-esteem and intelligence, show problems adjusting to the classroom environment and interacting with peers. They are less accurate in identification of emotional expressions, and do not show an age-appropriate understanding of emotional concepts. Such inaccurate perceptions of others' emotions may compound their relational difficulties (During & McMahon, 1991).

Other reported characteristics shared by children who have been abused and neglected include the following (Harrison & Edwards, 1983):

- They seem afraid of parents and are described as being different or bad by them.
- They are habitually unclean, are left alone without supervision, and are given inappropriate food, drink and medications.
- They exhibit extremes of behaviour; i.e. they may be extremely fearful of adults, or seem fearless when confronted with authority.
- They appear wary of physical contact, not risking proximity to others, and have poor relational skills.
- They may exhibit sudden changes of behaviour, and may show regressive behaviours such as thumb-sucking, bed-wetting, whining or shyness.
- They may have attentional difficulties in concentration and tend to become self-absorbed.
- School attendance is erratic, with frequent prolonged absences (during which the injured child may be kept at home), or they may linger in school with a reluctance to go home.
- They may be dressed inappropriately for the weather to conceal bruises or other marks of abuse.
- They may be tired and listless with a blank expression; they may often sleep in class.

Prevention of child abuse may be achieved via approaches including public service announcements, community crisis hotlines, and family support services for high-risk groups such as low-income teenage parents. Parent-training programs, which equip parents with the skills to manage a variety of childhood behaviour problems, may serve as a primary prevention, but parents with a known history of abusing their children need to be offered individualised, intensive, multi-modal treatment and parent-training services. These may include stress reduction, individual therapy (short- or long-term), relationship/marital counselling and job-placement services (Lyman & Hembree-Kigin, 1994).

Sexual abuse of young children

Child sexual abuse is defined as contacts or interactions between a child and adult when the child is being used for the adult's sexual stimulation (National Center on Child Abuse and Neglect, 1978). The median rate of sexual abuse across studies is 20% for girls and 7% for boys (Peters, Wyatt & Finkelhor, 1986), and one-third to one-half of sexual abuse victims are children under the age of seven (Berliner & Stevens, 1982).

Wurtele and Miller-Perrin (1992) list the following *child characteristics* indicating vulnerability to sexual abuse:

- social isolation;
- submissiveness to authority figures;
- limited knowledge about sexuality and sexual abuse;
- strong needs for attention, approval and affection.

Persons who abuse children sexually do not seem to fit a particular psychological profile. Some are reported as shy, unassertive, deficient in heterosexual skills, immature, dependent, lonely, and to have inadequate impulse control. The overwhelming majority of perpetrators are male; most are relatives or acquaintances of the family, and not strangers. Most offenders are adolescents and adults in their 30s. According to Wurtele and Miller-Perrin (1992), family characteristics that may contribute to the risk of child sexual abuse include:

- marital conflict;
- power imbalance between parents;
- family isolation;
- financial and other major stressors;
- inadequate supervision of children;
- overly stimulating or repressive sexual attitudes in the family;
- maternal absence from home due to employment, and the presence of a male caregiver who is not the biological father.

Times of caregiving with an increased risk for sexual abuse include bathing, cleaning, changing clothes and bedtime. Most intimate forms of caregiving, either maternal or paternal, *do not* elicit sexually abusive behaviour from the caregiver. However, offenders tend gradually to desensitise young children to sexual touch by blurring the boundaries of appropriate and inappropriate touching and stimulation. Some *cultural factors* have also been associated with child sexual abuse, which include:

- children being seen as possessions;
- availability of child pornography;
- cultural encouragement of sexual coercion by men;
- low rate of conviction of child molesters.

> *Dissociative symptoms* develop from the child's need to get away from the horror, the confusion, and the betrayal of the sexual attack. Understandably, the child is unable to accept the reality of his or her situation. In a way, the child's body is there to absorb the violation, and her mind is elsewhere to survive it . . . Children who are described as daydreamers or lazy or having trouble focusing may well be blanking out or dissociating (DeMaio, 1995, p.136).

Effects of child sexual abuse

Sexual abuse has the potential to profoundly and adversely affect the adjustment of young children throughout their lives. Findings in some of these ill-effects include the following (Kendall-Tackett, Williams & Finkelhor, 1993):

- Almost one-half of the abused children show post-traumatic stress disorder symptoms, including sleep disturbance, hypervigilance and traumatic play.
- More than one-third of the abused preschoolers exhibit inappropriate sexual behaviours, such as overt masturbation, sexual advances towards adults and children, and preoccupation with sexual themes.
- These behaviours may go underground during later school years; when they re-emerge in adolescence, they assume the form of promiscuity, prostitution or sexual aggression.
- As adults, these symptoms may extend to sexual dysfunction and sexual offences. Other disorders in the adult victims of child sexual abuse include higher incidence of depression, suicidal ideation, anxiety disorders, alcohol and drug abuse, poor self-esteem, high levels of stress and sleep disturbances.
- About one-third of the abused children appear to be resilient enough not to overtly show indications of ill-effects. However, an estimated 10%–24% of sexually abused children appear to get worse over time, particularly in aggressive and sexualised behaviours.

Most *prevention* programs for the sexual abuse of young children have been organised around enhancing the self-disclosure and assertiveness skills of young children, as well as teaching them many sexual abuse concepts and personal safety skills. Behaviourally based programs emphasising the protection of genitals seem to yield favourable outcomes (Wurtele, Kast, Miller-Perrin, & Kondrick, 1989). Greater focus should be placed on the prevention role of parents, professionals, policy-makers and the general public (Wurtele & Miller-Perrin, 1992). Healing for victims of sexual abuse may be a lifelong struggle.

DEVELOPMENTAL PSYCHOPATHOLOGIES

Our understanding of the dynamics of deviant behaviour in young children has recently been elaborated in a developmental framework. This greatly enhances our understanding of and intervention with families and their children. Here are some guiding principles (Cicchetti & Cohen, 1995):

- *Normal* and *abnormal* development both emerge from the *same* basic processes, which interact in their manifestations. For example, the study of attachment as a normal process paves the way for understanding developmental deviations leading to maladaptive patterns.
- In a developmental approach, the *pathways* and *sequences* of experiences are considered important in understanding how, for example, an early deviation may return to normal development, or take a deviant turn.
- Individual differences exhibited in *resilience* and *vulnerability*, where children in highly stressed and abusive environments grow up to be competent, intact and resourceful young adults, or those in supportive environments develop manifestations of maladaptive behaviour, may provide us with crucial information in developmental psychopathologies.

Developmental psychopathologies are categorised in two major groups (Rutter & Garmezy, 1983):

- *Externalising* problems are also described as disturbances of conduct, where the deviant behaviour is usually directed outward. This group of disorders includes attention deficit hyperactivity disorder[1] (see Chapter 12), *conduct disorder* and delinquency.
- *Internalising* problems are also described as emotional disturbances, where the deviant behaviour is directed towards the self, or inward. This group of disorders includes *depression, anxiety* and *eating disorders*.

Conduct disorders

Conduct problems in young children include *non-compliance, oppositional behaviour, destructive behaviour, overactivity, physical* and *verbal aggression,* and deliberate *cruelty* towards animals. Within a developmental framework, it is sometimes the case that such acting-out behaviours fall within normal limits compared to children of that age, as at certain developmental phases like the 'terrible twos'. However, preschoolers may progress from less serious to more

---

1   ADHD is believed to be of biological origin; nevertheless, the child outcomes and adaptive strategies utilised by children with the disorder are in part a function of the nature of the environment and the supports available therein.

serious behaviour problems more rapidly than their older counterparts, and their problem behaviours raise the familial stress levels significantly (Loeber, Green, Lahey, Christ & Frick, 1992). Difficult child behaviour and inadequate parenting strategies or coping resources may place these families at risk of developing abusive parenting practices (Abidin, 1990). Daycare and preschool staff are similarly stressed by the behaviour of conduct-disordered children, who often need one-on-one supervision to prevent injury to themselves or to others.

- Non-compliance is the most commonly seen psychological problem in clinics; the incidence of oppositional conduct disorders in childhood is reported to be 4%–9% (Earls, 1982).
- Oppositional and aggressive behaviours include disobeying parental requests, talking back, taunting and teasing, whining, tantruming, being destructive, hitting, kicking, biting and cursing.
- Parent–child interactions in these families are often characterised by a high level of parental directiveness, with a resultant low level of child compliance and escalating negativity.
- Non-compliance in early childhood seems to be strongly related to later conduct disorders.
- Combinations of child characteristics and parenting behaviours are the main determinants of enduring problems, which may be exacerbated by family dysfunction and social context variables (Campbell, 1990).

The development of conduct problems seems to follow a predictable sequence in young children, although not all children go through these problem behaviours (Loeber et al., 1992):

- Parents note hyperactive motor behaviour emerging in the first two years of life.
- By early preschool years, stubbornness seems to be prevalent.
- By four to five years of age, problems with inattention emerge.
- Cruelty towards animals may become evident at about five years.
- The child may start setting fires by six years of age.

Unfortunately, serious disruptive behavioural problems tend to persist, placing preschoolers at risk of behaviour disorders in their early school years, and even more serious problems with substance abuse and delinquency during adolescence (Hinshaw, 1992).

Early serious antisocial conduct problems include persistent and intentional lying, stealing outside of the home, and intentional fire-setting. There may be a history of parental antisocial behaviour (i.e. criminality, substance abuse, family violence, chronic unemployment), as well as inadequate parental supervision, which may precipitate and maintain such conduct problems.

Research report

A large epidemiological investigation was conducted on 320 preschool children between the ages of two-and-a-half and five years in New Zealand. Using the Behaviour Check List (an instrument filled in by parents) and clinical interviews, the study indicated that the prevalence of behaviour problems based on a clinical diagnosis was 22.5%. Poor family functioning, poor maternal health and parent separation were found to be significantly associated with child symptoms (Pavuluri, Luk, Clarkson, & McGee, 1995).

Intervention for young children with non-compliance and conduct problems involves working with the families in cognitive-developmental-behavioural models, which aim at creating and strengthening a positive and mutually rewarding parent–child relationship. Intervention aims at reducing problematic behaviours and enhancing prosocial behaviours by establishing appropriate boundary structures and limit-setting.

Depression

Adequate mothering in infancy is not a sentimental luxury but an absolute necessity for optimal physiological and psychological development; being deprived of mothering after the bond of love is forged results in dramatically deviant behaviour (Wenar, 1990). Classical studies of *maternal deprivation* by Spitz (1945) clearly showed the infantile depression which could even be fatal as a response to prolonged loss of contact with the caregiver.

Bowlby's (1980) observations of hospitalised infants and their reaction to maternal deprivation indicated the following stages in *anaclitic* or infant depression:

1. *Protest*, where the infant is severely distressed, cries loudly, searches the environment for the mother, shakes the bed, has tantrums and rejects all substitute caregivers. She still has hope that the mother will return.
2. *Despair*, where the infant becomes withdrawn and inactive, lying in bed with averted face, ignoring adults. Loss of appetite and sleep disturbance are present; attempts to initiate contact produce panic and screaming. She seems to have abandoned hope of the mother's return, and grieves for her loss.
3. *Detachment*, where the infant is again able to respond to caregivers, toys and food. However, she no longer seems to be attached to the mother, and treats her as a friendly stranger, with socially acceptable behaviours that lack depth of feeling. She now seems to be protecting herself from experiencing the pain of loss again by denying the existence of the bond of attachment.

Depression in early childhood has been traditionally underscored, except when major crises in a child's life such as divorce or the loss of a parent have been associated with it. However, the prevalence of childhood depression in the general child population is reported to range between 2% and 5%, with 1% of preschool-aged children meeting the diagnostic criteria for major depressive disorder (Kashani, Holcomb & Orvaschel, 1986). The criteria used for *diagnosis* of childhood depression are as follows (based on Kazdin, 1990; DSM IV, 1994). At least five of these symptoms must be present during a two-week period, with at least one of the symptoms being depressed mood, or loss of interest and pleasure. Other disorders such as bereavement must be excluded:

- depressed mood (irritable mood in children) most of the day, nearly every day;
- loss of interest or pleasure in all or most activities nearly every day; apathy;
- significant weight loss or weight gain when not dieting or binge-eating (i.e. more than 5% of bodyweight in a month), or loss or increase in appetite every day (in children, failure to meet expected weight gains needs consideration);
- insomnia or hypersomnia nearly every day (in children, sleep disturbances);
- psychomotor agitation or retardation nearly every day (in children under six, hypoactivity);
- fatigue or loss of energy every day;
- feelings of worthlessness or excessive or inappropriate guilt, real or delusional, nearly every day (not merely self-reproach about being ill);
- diminished ability to concentrate, or indecisiveness nearly every day;
- thoughts of being better off dead or suicidal ideation nearly every day; or suicide attempt.

Causes of depression are multivariate, with strong suggestions of genetic predisposition, as well as environmental factors:

- 27% of the children with one depressed parent, and 74% of those with both parents suffering clinical depression, were diagnosed as being depressed themselves. Although these findings are suggestive of a genetic basis to the disorder, behavioural modelling in the home also needs to be considered (Gerson, Hamovit & Guroff, 1983).
- A concordance rate of 76% for depression in monozygotic twins and 19% for dizygotic twins, and 67% for monozygotic twins reared apart, is reported (Cantwell, 1982).
- There seems to be a strong link between *maternal depression* and psychiatric illness in children: 41% of children who had a depressed mother were found to have a mental health disorder. Three children in the study who attempted suicide had parents with depression (Orvaschel, Walsh-Allis & Ye, 1988).

As an *assessment tool,* one of the often used and best-standardised instruments in diagnosis of depression is the *Child Behaviour Check List* (Achenbach & Edelbrock, 1983). Although it is used with a wide variety of children clinically, as a research tool it indicates developmental differences in the depressive symptomatology of preschool children:

■ Suicidal talk is associated with other depressive symptoms in boys aged six to 11, but not in boys aged four to five.

■ For girls aged six to 11 anxiety and feelings of persecution are a part of the constellation of depressive symptoms, while these are absent for girls aged four to five.

Treatment for depression has traditionally been supportive psychotherapy focused on parents of young children with depressive disorder, with the goal of improving the affective interaction between parent and child, and play therapy with children to assist them to develop the ability to more effectively express feelings and relate to others (Minde & Minde, 1981). Cognitive–behavioural interventions and social-skills training have also been shown to be effective. In recent years, medication in conjunction with psychological treatments has increasingly been used to treat depression in young children, to good effect.

Fears and childhood anxiety disorders

Young children's fears and anxiety have traditionally been low profile in research and intervention, presumably because they are less salient than externalising symptoms, more subjective and internal, and largely believed to be transient phenomena. The normative fears in early childhood can be gleaned as follows (Ollendick & King, 1991):

■ Between 12 and 30 months, most toddlers experience anxiety in relation to separation from their mothers or primary caregivers.

■ With the onset of toileting at around two years of age, fears and anxiety associated with toileting may be common.

■ Fear of dogs and other animals may be seen in three-year-olds.

■ Intense fears of imaginary creatures and monsters are evidenced between two and four years, when children's imagination supersedes their under-standing of the reality–fantasy distinction.

■ Separation anxiety may also re-emerge at this age, which may be manifested as fears of abandonment, of being kidnapped, or of death of a parent.

■ If separation anxiety is *not* mastered by age five, anticipatory anxiety and somatic complaints may be common with the advent of going to 'big school', and possibly develop into *school fears* or phobias.

■ By age six and seven, fears of imaginary threats and separation are usually replaced by fears related to more tangible events, such as bodily injury, death, crime, natural disasters, school performance and peer relations.

> Transitional objects, like the teddy bears and blankets children use to calm themselves, have not been shown to be related to insecurity or future psychopathology.

Specific fears in early childhood may pertain to a reaction to a perceived threat, as evidenced by motor reactions (e.g. avoidance or escape), subjective reactions (e.g. verbal reports of distress or terror) or physiological reactions (e.g. palpitations, sweating) (Barrios & O'Dell, 1989). *Phobias* may be simple phobias focused on an object, or social phobias centred on public embarrassment.

Generalised anxiety is the diffuse and moderate fear reactions that occur in the absence of an immediately discernible threat. Some characteristic behaviours of overanxious children may be (Lyman & Hembree-Kigin, 1994, p.170):

- persistent and unrealistic worry about future events, (i.e. being expelled from school for not getting their toys cleaned up fast enough);
- unrealistic worry about their past behaviour (i.e. believing that a parent won't love them any more because they made a sloppy picture);
- unrealistic worry about their competence, (i.e. worrying they will never be smart enough to learn to read);
- somatic complaints (i.e. stomach aches, headaches);
- excessive needs for reassurance (i.e. repeatedly checking on the parent's wellbeing);
- self-consciousness (i.e. being afraid of saying the wrong thing in front of others);
- physical tension (i.e. excessive motor movements, hair-twirling, nail-biting).

Anxiety and depression often coexist in young children, and they may in fact reflect the same dimension. The Diagnostic and Statistical Manual of Mental Disorders (DSM IV, 1994) does not differentiate between adult and child anxiety disorders, and further research in the field may be necessary to determine the need for such a differentiation.

Most *causal* explanations of fears and anxiety are couched in familial patterns; although such patterns tend to run in families, it is not clear whether these are genetic or modelled attributes. A transactional model that acknowledges the mutuality of influences between the child and other members of the family is probably the most likely causal framework. Generalised anxiety is more common in children of parents with high achievement expectations.

Intervention strategies to manage generalised anxiety in young children include a combination of parent counselling, parent–child relationship enhancement, and parent training for teaching children coping skills; with specific fears and phobias, behavioural techniques to systematically desensitise children's fears together with supportive techniques prove effective.

Eating problems

Problems involving quantity and quality of food intake and eating patterns are a common cause of concern for parents of young children. Although psychodynamic theory emphasised the importance of early feeding experiences for later personality development, no reliable and specific relationship between feeding and adult personality has been shown. Nevertheless, eating patterns may serve as an indication of broader parent–child problems and developmental concerns, manifesting as an *internalised* disorder.

Medical conditions such as food allergies, thyroid dysfunction, and neuromuscular abnormalities affecting swallowing responses can cause feeding problems. *Pyloric stenosis* refers to congenital obstruction of the gastrointestinal tract, which results in projectile vomiting in the first month of life. It can be cured by surgical intervention. Other conditions with psychological correlates include the following.

- *Non-organic failure to thrive* is where children up to the age of four show weight loss or fail to gain age-expected weight despite receiving adequate nutrition. Disturbed parent–child relationships with improvished interactions, childhood depression, improper feeding techniques and parental stress appear to be factors causing or maintaining the condition (Kotelchuck, 1980).
- *Pica* is ingestion of inedible substances, and is associated with mouthing patterns of children with developmental delays, and poor parental supervision in other children.
- *Bruxism* is excessive teeth-grinding. Most cases, especially those involving bruxism during sleep, resolve over time, although it is usually associated with stress symptoms in children.
- *Obesity* in early childhood is most commonly attributed to genetic patterns, excessive caloric intake, insufficient physical exercise and poor parental supervision or knowledge about nutrition. It has also been associated with family psychopathology.
- *Anorexia nervosa* is not a disorder of early childhood as such, although clinical reports of the age range being pushed down to late childhood exist. It is a complex set of symptoms which aims at voluntary self-starvation in pursuit of thinness. *Restricters* rely on strict dieting, while *bulimics* alternate between binge-eating and self-induced vomiting. It is a serious and potentially fatal disorder, with a death rate of about 9% (Garfinkle & Garner, 1982). It has been related to depression, social isolation and insecure attachment (see above).

OTHER BEHAVIOURAL PROBLEMS

Toileting

Learning appropriate and socially acceptable toileting is one of the major tasks of the preschool years, and child psychologists report that between 5% and 10% of parental concerns centre around problems concerning toileting and toilet-training (Roberts, 1986).

The physiological and psychological readiness for toileting includes the myelinisation of the nerve tracts for bowel and bladder control, and the ability of the child to sit, walk, understand some verbal content, to relate to adults and imitate some of their behaviour, and to control impulses. Since these are attained between 18 and 30 months, toilet-training should not begin before two years of age (Christofersen, 1988).

Clinical problems with bladder (*enuresis*) and bowel (*encopresis*) are classified as primary when the child reaches the age of four or five and has never achieved adequate bowel and bladder control, while secondary conditions are said to be present when control is achieved and later lost (Lyman & Hembree-Kigin, 1994):

Enuresis

Enuresis can be *diurnal* (daytime) or *nocturnal* (night-time), most cases occurring together. Its incidence in children aged five or older is more than 3%, with boys being affected twice as often as girls.

Physical factors that may contribute to poor urinary control include urogenital tract obstructions and dysfunctions, urinary tract infections, nervous system disorders such as epilepsy, small functional bladder capacity, and sleep arousal disorders. There seems to be strong evidence for the child's parents or close relatives having experienced a similar condition as children.

Psychological factors include indications of emotional disturbance, although emotional disturbance does not seem to be a primary cause of enuresis. Reactions to stress and anxiety the child faces may result in secondary enuresis.

Intervention strategies include medication, which should be combined with behavioural techniques for a positive outcome. Behavioural management strategies such as dry-bed training, enuresis alarms and retention-control training also seem quite effective.

Encopresis

Encopresis is clinically defined as soiling with bowel incontinence in children above four years of mental or chronological age in the absence of physical disorders. Its incidence is lower than 2% in children older than five years, with boys being four times more likely to have the condition (Lyman & Hembree-Kigin, 1994).

Within the psychodynamic framework, encopresis is interpreted as an indication of emotional disturbance, with the primary component being a conflict with parental figures during toilet-training. The behavioural perspective, on the other hand, sees it as arising from failures in environmental learning experiences. Secondary encopresis, or a relapse after successful training, may be associated with inadequate reinforcement for appropriate toileting, conscious negativism or manipulativeness. If toileting is associated with an aversive experience (such as parental punishment or pain associated with constipation), voluntary faecal retention may result.

Voluntary or involuntary faecal retention related to chronic constipation is a primary causal factor in nearly all cases of encopresis. Chronic constipation, which may also be due to inadequate roughage in diet, inadequate water intake, genetic predisposition or stress, may result in a compacting of the waste material in the colon. The result is a distended colon with some fluid faecal material discharge, where the child may be unaware of the fact that she has soiled.

Behavioural *intervention* strategies have been shown to be highly effective in treatment of encopresis. Positive reinforcement for appropriate toileting combined with other interventions such as medication, enemas, dietary change or family therapy yield the most positive results.

Sleep disturbances

Sleep disturbances tend to occur in the context of other associated problems, such as behaviour management difficulties, maternal depression, and developmental disorders. Sleep problems in infants and young children may be related to colic, middle ear infections or other medical conditions, or poor bedtime transitions, routines and interactions. In families where chaos and violence are prevalent, establishing good sleep routines may be impossible.

- Difficulty in falling asleep, bedtime struggles and night-time awakenings usually occur together in young children. Children's sleep problems may result in sleep deprivation in their parents as well, and as a stressor it may interfere with their parenting skills, work productivity, interpersonal relationships and mood (Douglas, 1989).
- To have lengthy periods of uninterrupted sleep, young children need to learn to make the transition from wakefulness to sleep on their own. Over two-thirds of infants and toddlers who sleep through the night are self-soothers, who are not nursed, rocked or comforted to sleep by their parents (Johnson, 1991).
- Fear and anxiety over separation from parents at bedtime, fear of the dark or lurking monsters, fear of being abducted or fear of not waking up once asleep are developmental and transitory for most young children. Persistent and intense night-time fears, panic and nightmares in early childhood are usually associated with a family history of anxiety disorders,

and also with other stressors such as marital discord, separation or divorce, financial or professional difficulties, parental affective illness, medical disorder or death, family move, start of school, toilet-training, and birth of a sibling (Ferber, 1989).

Psychosomatic problems

The term *psychosomatic* has been expanded to include not only the physical problems caused by emotional disturbance but the physical effects of difficulties in learning, development and personality, as well as the psychological effects of physical illness and disability (Wright, 1977). This broadened context offers wide applications.

Among other conditions, *asthma* seems to respond favourably to behavioural management strategies. A comprehensive self-management program to teach decision-making and attack-management skills to asthmatic children and their parents, including medication compliance, resulted in improved respiratory function, more positive attitudes towards asthma, decreased school absenteeism, and greatly reduced health care costs (Creer, Harm & Marion, 1988).

Mental health interventions with *paediatric cancer* and *AIDS* patients address issues of treatment compliance and adjustment to treatment side-effects, as well as issues of mortality. These may involve multidisciplinary and multimodal forms, from play therapy to school consultation, and appear to have a place in comprehensive treatment and eliciting more positive attitudes from young victims (Olson, Huszti, Mason & Seibert, 1989).

Childhood schizophrenia

Historically, autism and childhood schizophrenia were thought to be on a continuum (Bender, 1947); they are in fact two quite different psychopathologies. Autism is marked by a predictable aloneness, sameness and non-communication (see Chapter 15). Childhood schizophrenia presents an unpredictable and profound lack of integration between, and discrepancy of skills within, developmental domains. The behaviours in autism are highly ritualised, and the child looks like an odd outsider, while the behaviours in childhood schizophrenia are florid, excessive and bizarre (Wenar, 1990):

- Its onset is most common in preschool years. Emotional instability is evidenced by irritability, excitement, anxiety, unprovoked aggression and temper tantrums, fears, disturbed sleep and preoccupation with bodily functions. Motor skills and language development may be slow or accelerated.

- In middle childhood, those children who *internalise* the problem may have symptoms such as anxiety, phobias, obsessions and compulsions, along with severe thought disturbances, such as hallucinations and delusions, or bizarre preoccupations. Those children who *externalise* the problem may have symptoms of acting-out, such as stealing, fire-setting, truanting, sexual acting-out, as well as distorted reality perception and erratic cognitive skills.

■ The incidence of schizophrenia in the general population is lower than 1%; the child of one schizophrenic parent has a 16% chance, and the child of two schizophrenic parents has a 39% chance of manifesting the disorder. While this incidence suggests a genetic basis, the experience of being raised in a home environment with impaired affect and communications also needs to be considered in the causes of the disorder.

■ The earlier onset of symptoms seems to be related to more severe disturbance in adulthood, although at least one-quarter of this population shows adjustment to community life, with support from the family, social agencies and mental health facilities.

CONCLUSIONS

In this chapter we have considered those conditions which seem to have a *psychogenic* cause, often embedded in family interactional patterns. All atypical developmental patterns reflect an interplay of nature–nurture, risk and resilience; and *all* have an interactional/relational component. Developmental psychopathologies, however, are unique in that the child is assumed to start the journey with an intact biological system and with an optimum chance of developing normally. Adverse psychosocial factors, and the life and family circumstances the child is confronted with, interfaced with her resilience, result in these maladaptive patterns.

10

Language and communication: development and disorders

There is a communication impairment component in the overall profile of many conditions. The language disabilities associated with some of these are reviewed in later chapters. First we concentrate on disorders of language as a primary impairment, although the knowledge acquired here will have applications to conditions covered elsewhere.

DEFINITIONS AND DOMAINS OF COMMUNICATION

Communication is a complex set of behaviours which entail the sending and receiving of intended messages. *Speech* is the oral-verbal mode of communication; other modes include writing, drawing or manual signing. *Language* is a conventional system of shared codes within a community of users of that language, which represents ideas, objects, events, relations etc. through the use of arbitrary symbols and has a set of rules to govern their combination. Language exists because its users have made decisions on the symbols and the rules (the *linguistic code*). These rules form the basis of the user's ability to understand language (*comprehension* or *receptive language*) as well as formulate it (*production* or *expressive language*). The user's implicit knowledge of the rules of language and their uses form his *linguistic competence*. Children acquire such knowledge in the absence of formal instruction in a remarkably short period of time; as a matter of fact, the process of spontaneous acquisition can be arrested only by some developmental disruption.

Language is made up of several *interrelated* components, including form, content and use (Bloom & Lahey, 1978).

Bloom and Zahey (1978)

Form

Form is what makes each language unique and distinct from another. The rules governing *form* are: (i) a system of sounds and their combinations to form words *(phonology)*; (ii) the internal organisation of words, such as prefixes and suffixes (*morphology*); and (iii) how words should be combined in different sentences to convey the intended meaning (grammar, or *syntax*).

- A *phoneme* is the smallest unit of *sound* that effects meaning. We know that *b*ook and *t*ook are different words because *b* and *t* are different phonemes.
- A *morpheme* is the smallest unit of *meaning*. Some morphemes are able to stand by themselves, such as book (*free* morphemes or words); others need a base to anchor themselves to, such as book*s*, read*ing*, use*ful* (*bound* morphemes).
- *Syntax* governs the structure of sentences (grammaticality) and different sentence types (i.e. declarative, question, negative, active–passive constructions), as well as describing different parts of speech (i.e. noun, verb). These rules allow the generation of an infinite number of meaningful sentences by combinations of words in a particular language.

Content

Content involves the *semantics* (meaning) to be communicated. The semantic rules govern the meaning of the words, as those found in a dictionary. The personal collection of meanings coded onto words (or *lexical items*) is the person's own mental dictionary (*lexicon*). Content is dependent on the person's experience and knowledge of the world. It is the *content* of language which is translated from one language to another, although a different *form* is used in each.

Use   *Pragmatics.*

Use governs the rules of language within a social context *(pragmatics)*. It includes *functions* or intentions of communication, as well as rules for addressing people, structuring a conversation, and discourse/narrative skills.

These domains of language overlap; their rules are *interrelated and interdependent*, such that linguistic competence necessitates knowledge and integration of the entire system. Children reflect their knowledge of these rules in their communications. For example, a three-year-old passing by the pony rides in the park who comments 'Look, baby horsies!' has integrated: (a) the *form*, by using understandable utterances, and the plural morpheme *s*; (b) the *content*, by choosing words which reflect his understanding of the small-sized animal being a baby within the horse family, and by using the correct basic word order; and (c) *use*, by obtaining his mother's attention and describing the event. In children with disabilities these components may be disrupted. For example, a youngster with autism may repeat the question his

Smallest unit of meaning

teacher just asked him, instead of answering it, with perfect *form* but little evidence of *content* or appropriate use.

FRAMEWORKS IN LANGUAGE DEVELOPMENT AND DISORDERS

The field of language development is an interesting one, because its growth has been cumulative; in other words, our current understanding has incorporated many of the premises put forth by successive orientations, as it has evolved into a comparatively comprehensive framework. The following is a brief overview.

Behavioural framework *Conditioning + reinforcement*

The behavioural framework was presented by B.F. Skinner (1957), who claimed that language acquisition was dependent on an environmental reinforcement of selective utterances of the infant. As vocalisations were shaped and chained by *external* influences, child language gradually approximated the mature adult system. Behaviourist explanations were not adequate, in that they offered an explanation for *how* language was learned (by selective reinforcement) but not *what* the child learned. Nor did they provide an explanation for children's frequent use of those utterances not typically used by adults, such as 'foots' or 'goed'. The role of maternal input has gained attention as a significant variable in language development over the past decades (see Harris, 1992 for review), and the effective use of many behaviourally based teaching and intervention strategies in special education have been documented. Nevertheless, this framework remains a simplistic approach to the explanation of complex linguistic processes, and virtually ignores cognition.

Psycholinguistic–syntactic framework

The psycholinguistic–syntactic framework was championed by Noam Chomsky (1965), who claimed that children had an *innate* predisposition to use linguistic rules, which unfold as they test their hypotheses against the linguistic evidence. According to Chomsky, the human infant comes equipped with the neural circuitry (programming) necessary for language acquisition through a mechanism called the *language acquisition device* (LAD), which is activated by exposure to linguistic input. Nevertheless, Chomsky does not provide a model for early syntactic development in language acquisition, and discounts the cognitive process as a necessary substrate in the process. This framework has had a major impact on our conceptualisation of the 'competent' child, with his active hypothesising and problem-solving processes. It has stimulated vast amounts of research and argument, as well as highlighting the significance of naturalistic observation as a research format.

Semantic–cognitive approach

Semantic–cognitive approach followed Bloom's (1970) discovery that children's early utterances may have the same 'syntax' but entirely different meanings. For example, the utterance 'daddy shoe' can be used by an 18-month-old to mean 'Daddy's shoe', or 'Daddy is putting on his shoes', or 'Daddy is putting my shoes on'. Thus early utterances are highly dependent on the *semantics* or the contextual meaning the child is coding, which would reflect his present experiences and knowledge of the world. The emphasis now is on the child's *mapping* the meanings or relations he knows onto the grammatical structures that are within his repertoire at that stage in development. Thus, the above utterance may still show the *semantic relation* of *possession* at the three-word stage, but it might now be coded as 'That daddy's shoe', as demonstrated in the maxim 'meaning before form'. This approach stimulated the revisiting of many Piagetian concepts, and explorations of the cognitive bases of language development. The social contexts in development were yet to be recognised.

Pragmatic–contextual approach

The pragmatic–contextual approach considers the caregiver–child interactions to be the crucible in which early language develops. Bruner (1974/75), for example, claims that socialisation and affecting the behaviours of the persons in the social circle drive children to language learning. McLean and Snyder-McLean (1978) define a transactional context of language acquisition, which synthesises most of the viewpoints in this school of thought:

- Language is acquired when a child has a reason to talk and influence his environment through communication.
- The mature language-user and the child engage in a dynamic social relationship which facilitates language learning.
- The child is an active participant in this transactional process, and will benefit from it only if he can contribute to it in meaningful ways.

There has been a flurry of interest in developing young children's pragmatic language and intentional categories, particularly in infancy (Halliday, 1975; Bates, 1976; Dore, 1975), without a clear consensus among different researchers. Nevertheless, with the contribution of this approach we seem to have covered all the bases.

Classification of language disorders

With reference to our current conceptions of language development, our safest strategy is to understand them all and to use each in the developmental phase in which it is most appropriate and valuable.

Different approaches are used in attempts to categorise child language disorders:

Aetiological/categorical approach

The aetiological/categorical approach is the more traditional one, classifying disorders based on their *causes*. The common ones would include mental retardation, hearing impairment, emotional disturbance and autism, neurologically based disorders and social-cultural disadvantage.

Descriptive/developmental approach

The descriptive/developmental approach focuses on identifying the strengths and needs of children with language impairments without necessarily labelling them; instead, they are described according to the impairments in the *form, content* and *use* domains of language discussed above.

Perhaps a more useful classification is based on speech and language pathologists' professional organisation's definition, based on deficits in *expression (formulation)* and *comprehension (understanding)* of language, or a *combination* of both:

> A language disorder is the abnormal acquisition, comprehension or expression of spoken or written language. The disorder may involve all, one, or some of the phonologic, morphologic, semantic, syntactic, or pragmatic components of the linguistic system. Individuals with language disorders frequently have problems in sentence processing or in abstracting information meaningfully for storage and retrieval from short and long term memory (ASHA, 1980, pp.317–318).

STAGES IN LANGUAGE DEVELOPMENT

Communication in the sensorimotor period

During infancy, communication begins from birth, with the perceptual abilities of the neonate ready to engage in social interaction, rudimentary though it may be.

The infant within the *first three stages* of the *sensorimotor period* (reflexive, primary circular and secondary circular reactions) is said to be *preintentional*, initially displaying reflexive, random or accidental behaviours. However, the caregivers monitor the infant carefully and often *attribute* a communicative intent to such attempts; they often respond to infant behaviours *as though* they were initiations of a conversation. Such early conversations by four months, with long periods of eye gaze and alternating patterns of vocalisations, can be seen as *protoconversations* (Bateson, 1975). This practice is thought to encourage the infant to become more intentional in his communicative behaviours.

Intentional behaviour is achieved in *stage four* (coordination of secondary circular reactions). Interactions between infants and caregivers become increasingly *child-initiated*; infants enjoy repetitive games and anticipate the next event in games like peek-a-boo. Around ten to 11 months of age children use objects to obtain adult attention by showing and giving (*protodeclarative* behaviour), which gives way to labelling. *Protoimperative* behaviour, on the other hand, is helpful in getting the caregivers to comply with infants' requests and demands. As the child is not using constant vocal referents (words) for objects, events or relations, his communications are *prelinguistic*.

By *stage five* (tertiary circular reactions), *first words* are evident. Children learn to use words through repeated experiences in routine 'scripts'—for example, by looking through a picture book with the caregiver (Nelson, 1983). In this *linguistic* stage of development, they move from being dependent on the immediate referents, such as actions and objects, or names for activities or events which accompany words, to being less dependent on the immediate context, a process known as *decontextualisation*.

By *two years of age*, children have developed the ability to represent objects and events internally. The following outlines the main accomplishments in the domains of language (McCormick & Schiefelbusch, 1990):

Content.   Representational thought allows for full development of object concept. Objects may be grouped according to similar dimensions, although errors do occur. The children appear to comprehend much of what is said to them, obtaining information from the context as well as the verbal input. They can locate and act on an object, but will often do what is usually done with the object, regardless of what has been asked. Their play is *conventional;* they use objects according to their functions.

Form.   They move from single words to *combinatorial* utterances, or two-word sentences, based on semantic relations. Examples of semantic functions in the *single-word* stage (Bloom, 1970) include the following:

Semantic function	Possible words (lexical items)
Object	Ball, shoe, cup, car
Action	Up, open, give, go
Agent	Mummy, daddy, doggie
Recurrence	More, again, another
Negation: rejection	No
cessation	No, stop
disappearance	Allgone

As the child begins to use *two-word sentences*, these categories are combined:

Semantic categories	Example utterance	Implied sentence
Agent + Action	Dad kick	Dad is kicking
Action + Object	Kick ball	Kicking the ball
Agent + Object	Dad ball	Dad (kicked the) ball
Entity + Location	Ball chair	Ball (is on the) chair
Action + Location	Go park	(We) are going (to the) park
Demonstrative + Entity	That ball	(Not this one)
Attribute + Entity	Big ball	Big ball
Possessor + Object	Daddy ball	Daddy's ball

Use. The main communication functions for the two-year-old include commenting about objects and ongoing events, vocal play, regulating the behaviour of others, obtaining objects, social interaction, discovery and calling attention. The communicative functions evident from the prelinguistic stage can now be coded in utterances (Halliday, 1975):

- *interactional* ('me and you' function);
- *personal* ('here I come' function);
- *instrumental* ('I want' function);
- *regulatory* ('do as I tell you' function);
- *heuristic* ('tell me why' function);
- *imaginative* ('let's pretend' function).

In the *third year of life*, the child has entered the *preoperational stage*. Not having to depend on the sensorimotor experience, and the ability to have internal representations (ideas and abstract thought), will culminate in the following skills.

Content. The child enjoys simple pictures and toys, can indicate a missing object from a small array of familiar toys, and can use newly acquired behaviours in varied settings and novel problems. He is able to point to and name a few colours, and can match shapes as well as colours. He can group objects by one attribute at a time. Comprehension is better with very short sentences, and directions are followed within a predictable routine (Chapman, 1978). Play continues to develop by: using objects in a non-conventional manner; expansion of the pretend-play repertoire; and combining actions relating to a toy with the planning of activities involving others.

Form. Utterance length increases, combining three semantic categories, which often contain the elements of a *subject* (agent), a *verb* (action) and an *object* (e.g. 'daddy kick ball'). Grammatical morphemes, which serve to give early utterances that grammatical flavour, emerge in the following sequence (Brown, 1973):

Grammatical morphemes	Examples	Average age of emergence (months)
Present progressive 'ing'	go*ing*	19–28
Preposition 'in' and 'on'	Put *in* cup	27–30
Regular plurals '-s'	Eat cookies	24–33
Irregular past verbs 'came'	He *went* home	25–46
Possessive noun '-'s'	Daddy*'s* car	26–40
To be as the main verb	I *am* boy; she *is* bad	27–39
Articles 'a' 'the'	Throw *the* ball	28–46
Third person singular '-s'	Timmy go*es*	26–46
Third person singular, irregular	She *does* work	28–50
To be with main verb, uncontracted	Baby *is crying*	29–48
To be as main verb; contracted	She*'s* nice	29–49
To be with main verb; contracted	They*'re* playing	30–50

Use.   Communication functions expand, with more sophistication in the child's ability to carry on conversations, including initiating interactions, maintaining a conversational topic, answering simple questions appropriately (with a margin for error), and asking growing numbers of questions.

In *the fourth year,* the child is still in the preoperational stage.

Content.   The abilities to think about and solve problems and to engage in social interaction continue to grow. A major development in play is role-playing, reflected in the dawning of *theory of mind*, where the child is now able to take the perspectives of the others. Significant cognitive skills include placing up to ten shapes in place, making a tower with nine or more blocks, remembering the daily routine sequences, knowledge of basic shapes, colours, sizes and positions, and a growing sense of time-of-day awareness. Comprehension of full sentences occurs routinely, but is dependent on subject + verb + object word order: 'The cat scratched the man' will be understood; but 'The man was scratched by the cat' is likely to be interpreted as the man scratching the cat (Chapman, 1978).

Form.   The child is now finetuning his sentence production. He can elaborate the sentences using *conjunctions* (e.g. because, but, and, or). Embedded sentence patterns appear (e.g. My friend that has yellow hair comes to my house), and grammatically correct question and negative forms are used. In terms of phonological development, most of his speech is clearly understood by others (*intelligibility*).

Use.   Functions and conversational skills also become increasingly adult-like. The child refers more often to the activities of others, talks about things in the past and the future, and modifies his speech to suit the needs of the listener (four-year-olds would use a higher pitch and simpler sentences when talking to a two-year-old compared with their talk to adults).

By *five years* of age, the child's language sounds quite like that of mature language-users. The *school-aged* child will continue honing his linguistic skills in terms of vocabulary expansion, comprehension and use of more elaborate syntactical structures, developing metalinguistic strategies (actively thinking about and monitoring language) and conversational pragmatics. He will add to his repertoire various means for conveying intentions, including indirect expression. Consider the different uses of language by different-aged children in the same context (Bernstein & Tiegerman, 1993):

CONTEXT: a plate of cookies
Two-year-old to adult: Gimme cookie. *Four*-year-old to adult: Can I have a cookie please? *Nine*-year-old to adult: My, those cookies look good!

Much of the language growth will be scaffolded by schooling and literacy experiences. As reading is primarily a language-based skill, academic attainments will largely depend on an intact language system (see Chapter 12). The school-aged child displays the following communicative functions and abilities (White, 1975b):

- to gain and hold adults' attention in a socially acceptable manner; to direct and follow peers; to role-play;
- to use others as resources for assistance and information; to express affection, hostility and anger, as well as pride in accomplishment;
- to structure narratives and relate story plots with growing cohesion and orderliness.

ASSESSMENT OF BASIC PARAMETERS

The purpose of assessment is to determine the parameters of the speech and language disorder in order to be able to plan an intervention program. It may follow a *screening* protocol, where all children in a given setting are expected to pass some measure which marks a threshold; a hearing screening is a good example. Those children who fail the screening are referred for a *comprehensive assessment*, which entails the use of a battery of procedures. Screening does not constitute sufficient grounds to identify a disability.

Comprehensive assessment

Comprehensive assessment should result in a detailed profile of the child's communication *strengths* and *needs,* priorities for intervention and specific recommendations. It must document the child's typical performance, and use that as the *baseline* against which the efficacy of the intervention efforts can be evaluated.

Assessment tools may be *systematic observation* devices, such as the following.

Standardised tests. Standardised tests contain information on their validity and reliability. If the performance of that child is compared with others in that age group (on whom the test has been standardised), the tool is *norm-referenced.* Standardised tools need precise administration procedures, and thus require professional training in their proper use and interpretation.

Developmental scales. Developmental scales list behaviours and skills according to what can be expected of children in particular age groups. They can be administered by observing the child in unstructured activities, or in situations designed to elicit particular behaviours. Examples are *Early*

Language Milestones (ELM) (Coplan, 1989), and the *MacArthur Communicative Development Inventories* (Fenson, Dale, Resnick, Thal, Bates, et al., 1993).

Criterion-referenced tests. Criterion-referenced tests compare the child's performance by certain standards or criteria, rather than against the performance of other children. This attribute makes them particularly suitable and developmentally appropriate for young children with disabilities, who would not otherwise be judged fairly against their non-handicapped peers. One good example is the *Evaluation and Programming System for Infants and Young Children* (Bailey & Bricker, 1986).

Observational checklists. Observational checklists can be used to determine the presence and frequency of some skills, which are not compared with developmental information. A useful tool in populations with special needs, one example is the *Communication Skills Assessment* (Roberts, Cairns & Treolar, 1990).

Language samples. Language samples are collected while the child is interacting with an adult and/or a peer, and need at least to be audio-recorded (video-recording is preferable, as it provides a wealth of contextual information that might otherwise be missed) and then transcribed within a format. They should typically contain 50–100 child utterances to yield a representative sample (Bloom & Lahey, 1978). Language samples can provide invaluable information, and often give a better-rounded picture of the child being assessed, since his communication skills are being directly observed and not merely inferred.

- *Semantic relations* (discussed above) provide a helpful analysis of *content* on a language sample, although care must be taken to incorporate the contextual variables, particularly in interpretations of single-word-stage utterances.
- Another measure of evaluating *content*, is *vocabulary diversity*, which is determined by *type-token ratio (TTR)*. This is computed by adding up the number of *different* words the child uses in a sample of 50 utterances, and dividing that number by the *total* number of words (e.g. 40 different words in a sample containing 100 words altogether would yield a TTR of .40). This measure remains fairly stable at about .45 to .50 between the ages of three and eight (Miller, 1981). A child who demonstrates a very low TTR would be using a small group of words repetitively in his expressive language.
- *Emergence of morphemes* (above) provides evidence for emerging grammatical application in early combinatorial utterances (Brown, 1973).
- *Mean length of utterance (MLU)* is a measure to evaluate the *syntactical* aspects of the child's utterances, by indicating its average sentence length (Brown, 1973). To calculate MLU, at least 50 spontaneous (not imitative)

utterances are necessary. The total number of *morphemes* are counted within the guidelines provided (Brown, 1973) and divided by the total number of *utterances* in the sample. For example the utterance 'Doggie runn-ing' has three morphemes. It is useful with utterances containing up to four or five *morphemes*, and provides an approximation of the age-level expectancies in five stages (normative data are available for MLU ranging from 2.0 to 4.5; see below). Longer utterances do not provide additional information on syntactical skills, as the utterances resemble mature-user productions:

Linguistic stage	MLU	Approximate age (months)	Characteristics
I	1.0–2.0	12–26	Use of semantic relations
II	2.0–2.5	27–30	Development of morphemes
III	2.5–3.0	31–34	Different sentence types; negative, imperative, question
IV	3.0–3.75	35–40	Emerging complex sentences
V	3.75–4.5	41–46	Multiple embedded clauses

■ *Phonological skills* can be determined by analysing the language sample and noting the error sounds that occur in production. Speech sounds are mastered progressively in early childhood; correct use of some sounds does not fully stabilise until school years. Phonetic alphabet is used in detailed analyses of phonology. The norms below are derived from an Australian study (Kilminster & Laird, 1978):

Phonemes	Age at which used correctly by 75% of children
p, m, h, n, w, b, k, g, d, t, y	3 years
f	3 years 6 months
l, ch, sh	4 years
s, z, j	4 years 6 months
r	5 years
v	6 years
th, vision	8 years

Unlike in the other domains, no normative data are available on *pragmatic* functions; however, we know from Halliday's (1975) work (see above) that prelinguistic infants as young as nine months of age acquire these communicative functions. Additionally, it would be worthwhile to note verbal as well as non-verbal communicative functions, such as attention-seeking, greeting, naming, commenting, requesting object and information, protesting, informing and answering (Dore, 1974), and turn-taking, narrating, and adjusting one's speech to the speakers (Craig, 1991).

SPEECH AND LANGUAGE DISORDERS

Developmental language disorders (DLD)

DLD are those disorders of communication which are evidenced in the absence of other conditions (e.g. mental retardation, autism, hearing impairment, brain damage) which interfere with normal language development. *Specific language impairment* is another title that encompasses these disorders. Children with DLD do not seem to have a common causal or behavioural profile to suggest the presence of a homogeneous group. As stated by Leonard (1982, p.295):

> These children often seem similar only in that their intellectual abilities, as reflected on non-verbal tasks, exceed their linguistic abilities. Children may vary from slightly below normal, to above normal in their intellectual abilities. For some children language comprehension may present as much difficulty as language production, whereas for others difficulties may center principally on production. Children may vary too in the severity of their comprehension and/or production difficulties.

There are, in fact, different subtypes of DLD, which may be clinically impaired enough in their full-blown form to warrant formal referral and evaluation. Most of them may be on a continuum, where milder versions of the disorder can be noticed by developmental specialists such as the early childhood teacher, and planned for in the learning environment (Talay-Ongan, 1994). The classification used below (based on Allen, 1989) seems particularly helpful in bringing together descriptors of language domains, together with a non-categorical, developmental approach.

Verbal dyspraxia[1]

The child experiences a severe expressive disorder, in which he is very non-fluent, and the utterances are limited and poorly articulated. Often related to a *motor planning disability*, children with dyspraxia have difficulty matching the acoustic properties of a sound or sound sequences with the oral motor activities needed to produce them. Children with dyspraxia speak little and effortfully, often producing single words or truncated approximations, with missing and distorted consonants. The utterances may be single words, with some two-word combinations and little opportunity to use grammatical structures, while their pragmatic skills are often age-appropriate. Some researchers consider dyspraxia a severe speech-production disorder rather than a language disorder; nevertheless, a receptive language deficit often accompanies the expressive disorder. There is evidence for a genetic transmission of

---

1   *Praxia* is a suffix that generally denotes planned and coordinated movement. The prefix *a-* indicates the lack of a function, whereas *dys-* usually implies impaired function. *Apraxia* is a term used for adults who lose expressive speech after a brain injury; *dyspraxia* its milder version, is used for children.

dyspraxia (Hurst, Baraitser, Auger, Graham & Norell, 1990). Vocabulary and syntactic development would require active remedial training in children with dyspraxia. In its less severe forms it may be exhibited as difficulty in learning or retaining new and multisyllabic words, as well as word-finding difficulties.

Phonological production (speech-programming) deficit

These children tend to speak in long, phonologically incorrect, poorly intelligible utterances, which sometimes sound like jargon. Although they are fluent, their phonological production contains multiple sequencing errors, substitutions and distortions of speech sounds. Poor intelligibility often makes it difficult to determine syntactic complexity. When they are verbal, children with phono-logical production deficit often have difficulty organising coherent discourse (e.g. telling a story or providing an explanation, skills that call for semantic abilities). Their comprehension may also be impaired, providing support for the interaction of expressive and receptive language abilities. They respond to intervention quite well, many children gaining sufficient intelligibility by school age; the prognosis is considerably better than that for dyspraxia (Rapin, 1996). In its milder forms it may be exhibited as moderate articulation difficulties.

Verbal auditory agnosia[2]

The primary deficit is the child's inability to decode (or comprehend) spoken language. This inability to derive meaning through a phonological mapping of sounds which make up words to constitute meaningful utterances, results in a severe expressive deficit (*dysphasia*). These children have normal hearing acuity, but are not able to process the incoming auditory messages to attach meaning to them, a condition sometimes described as *word deafness*. Inability to analyse incoming speech messages at the phonologic level makes it impossible to engage in any higher levels of language processing. Many such children thus remain non-verbal; those who improve typically have defective phonology, and their comprehension and speech-sound discrimination are unlikely to recover fully (Klein, Kurtsberg, Brattson, Kreuzer, et al., 1995). This severe deficit is often seen in children with autistic spectrum disorders (Allen & Rapin, 1992). These are the children who benefit most from acquisition of language by the visual modality, and who profit most from augmentive communication systems such as communication boards, sign language, or computer-based communicative devices.

Phonologic–syntactic deficit

This syndrome appears to be a milder version of the *verbal auditory agnosia*, where although comprehension is impaired it seems considerably better than

---

2   *A-gnoisa:* lack of knowing/cognition. While *auditory agnosia* means inability to derive meaning from what is heard, *visual agnosia* means inability to derive meaning from what is seen.

the child's expressive capabilities. These children tend to speak in short, *telegraphic* utterances, and often omit the grammatical morphemes, as well as articles, prepositions, conjunctions and pronouns. This improvised use of language structure results in a very small vocabulary, and word-finding difficulties are common, with *superordinate categorical* words (defining large categories and branching down—as in animal, mammals, dogs, terriers, etc.) being used more often than the target words.

The deficit in the auditory processing mechanism is demonstrated in an impaired ability to perceive brief acoustic stimuli, like the sounds *p, t, k* (Tallal & Piercy, 1978). Phonologic–syntactic deficits are the most common disorder in DLD. Perhaps they are exhibited as having delayed language development with a deviant edge in less severe forms.

Lexical–syntactic deficit

This group includes children who are typically late in language acquisition and who use more *content* words (i.e. words with an immediate referent like nominals; naming words) than *function* words (articles, prepositions, conjunctions; words that mark the relationship between lexical items). These children exhibit severe *word-finding difficulties* and use frequent filler words, as well as experiencing comprehension difficulty with connected speech. Early in development they may appear to have *disfluency*, or a stutter-like speech characterised by repetitions and prolongations, because of the word-finding difficulties. Their speech may sound like jargon, with simplified syntax and a limited repertoire of vocabulary items. Phonology is usually intact and the grammaticality of the verbal output improves, although they typically have difficulties with producing connected language (discourse or narrative skills). In its milder forms, lexical–syntactic deficit may be present in delayed language.

Semantic–pragmatic deficit

This disorder is characterised by verbosity, with comprehension deficits for connected speech. Affected children have excellent auditory memory skills, and can use rapid, lengthy and fluent sentences; however, their *pragmatic and conversational skills* are impaired. The basic elements of functional language use, such as turn-taking, question asking and answering, providing and requesting information, and maintaining a dialogue with topic focus and cohesion, appear out of context. These children may use a speaking voice that is too loud, speak to nobody in particular, or digress from the topic of conversation, often showing an insensitivity to the needs or feelings of the listener. This disorder is most prevalent in children with autism who are verbal, in whom it may be associated with conspicuous verbal and non-verbal pragmatic deficits, immediate and delayed echolalia, and verbal perseveration (Allen & Rapin, 1992) (see Chapter 15). In its milder forms, it may include inconsistent but chattery speech patterns in children with comprehension deficits, or failing to interpret social context and language use correctly.

Other conditions

Dysarthria

Dysarthria is a production deficit, and is not considered to be within the spectrum of DLD, as it is a sensorimotor disorder of speech production and not a language disorder. Dysarthria results from a motor deficit in the muscles of the face and the speech organs (the mouth, lips, tongue or the air supply generated by the lungs to sustain vocalisation), known as *oromotor deficit*. It is often seen in children with cerebral palsy (see Chapter 16), and is associated with drooling, imprecise articulatory movements, and difficulty in chewing and swallowing. Although children with dyspraxia often exhibit oromotor difficulties, these are not sufficient to account for the verbal expressive problems. In its milder forms, it may include those children with low muscle tone around the mouth area who tend to drool, and those with retained tongue-thrust type swallowing (a reflex particularly suited to sucking and which usually extinguishes by 18 months of age), in which the teeth are not clenched during swallowing, such that the tongue protrudes between the lips.

Cleft palate

Cleft disorder occurs in the first trimester of pregnancy and is attributed to the failure of the palatal plates to fuse. Clefts may be on one side only (*unilateral*), both sides (*bilateral*) with varying degrees of severity, and may involve the lip, the lip and the palate, or the palate alone (Behrman, 1992). Phonological production skills are most readily impaired in children with cleft palate; often there is *velopharyngeal incompetence* (inability of the soft palate to seal off the oral cavity from the nasal cavity in the production of nasal speech sounds), and nasal production of all speech sounds results, with *f, v, k, g, r, l, s* and *z* distortions contributing to poor intelligibility. There can also be distorted and weak phonation, associated hearing loss, and a slower rate of acquisition of communicative competence (Peterson-Falzone, 1995).

Surgery is a necessary aspect of the correction of a cleft palate. There is controversy over the effects of the timing of palate repair on speech quality. Generally, lip repair occurs between two and four months, and palatal repair from 12 months to five years of age, depending on the type of cleft. Additional surgery may be necessary to enhance facial appearance and speech abilities as the child grows up; only 10%–15% of children retain residual hypernasality after surgical intervention (Kalland, 1995).

Disfluency (stuttering)

Early disfluencies and hesitations often appear between the ages of two and four, a period called *developmental disfluency*, when children normally begin to become aware of and use conventional syntax. Children who may be at risk of later stuttering typically have late onset of combinatorial language and a family history of disfluency. Young stutterers differ from their non-stutterer peers in greater number of single-word responses, simpler syntactic structures, number of grammatical errors, later onset of speech, and greater numbers of phonological errors (Eisenson & Ogilvie, 1983).

Hereditary predisposition, coupled with emotional stresses, can precipitate disfluency in a vulnerable child, who may start involuntary repetition of words and syllables, or prolongations. The child soon learns to anticipate those words and situations that are difficult for him. This anxiety is often heightened by the parents' negative feedback to the disfluent speech. The classic phrase 'stuttering begins in the mother's ear, not in the child's mouth' (Johnson, 1961, p.139) explains the interaction between a child's tendencies, and the environmental influences which may consolidate the disfluency into a clinical syndrome of stuttering.

Reducing the emotional stresses and anxieties of both parents and child, and strengthening the child's perceptions of himself as an effective communicator, is often sufficient to ease him into normal rhythms of speech. With persistent disfluency, it is advisable to seek professional assistance prior to the establishment of the communicative fears typical in stuttering.

Articulation errors and phonological disorders

Phonology is the ability to discern the rules governing the sound system of a language and, as such, is a *cognitive* process. It is considered disordered when it interferes with intelligibility (as above in *phonologic–syntactic deficit*), or normal developmental processes do not progress and/or defective systems are established. Most phonological rules are mastered by three-and-a-half years of age. Some early processes are (Edwards & Shriberg, 1983):

- *cluster reduction,* where a group of initial consonants is simplified (e.g. kool for school);

- *deletion of weak syllable,* where an unstressed syllable is omitted (e.g. tato for potato);

- deletion of the *initial* consonant (e.g. up for cup) or *final* consonant (e.g. cu for cup);

- *reduplication,* where the word is simplified by repeating one syllable (e.g. wawa for water);

- *assimilation,* where sounds influence each other towards similar production (e.g. gog for dog);

- *substitution process errors,* where *distinctive features*[3] of phonemes are incorrectly substituted (e.g. fronting: tup for cup; dun for gun).

---

3 *Distinctive features* are a collection of characteristics of phonemes making them different from each other, like voicing, consonantal, continuant or nasal (Jacobson & Halle, 1956). For example, *b* and *m* are produced alike except *m* is nasal; *t* and *d* are different on *voicing*.

Young children also make *phonemic* errors without necessarily having a poor phonological system development. *Articulation* difficulties are usually characterised on the basis of the listener's perception of the error sounds, and are categorised as (i) *substitution* of one sound for another, as in *th*oup for soup; (ii) *omission* sounds, as in _at for cat; and (iii) *distortion*, which is a sound noticeably different to the listener, as in a lateral lisp. Most articulation errors resolve spontaneously by school age; intervention may be necessary with persistent errors, as these may have implications for phonological processing, a prerequisite skill in reading.

Language delay

Primary causes for disorders of language may be cognitive disability, neurological impairment, hearing loss or deafness, autism, or developmental language disorders (as discussed above). These conditions are assumed or known to have biological bases. Severe environmental deprivation may also adversely affect language development.

Language development is sometimes delayed in the *absence* of known causal factors. These late bloomers often have parents who describe themselves in the same vein. Their communicative skills develop within the predictable developmental sequence, but at a slower rate; most have subtle processing or integration deficits that contribute to the delay. These youngsters are likely to benefit handsomely from language facilitation programs, implemented at home and in the care/educational setting.

Bilingualism

Children who are exposed to two languages at the same time before the age of three are said to have developed *simultaneous bilingualism*. Usually the normal process of development is evident in both languages, and progresses in two stages (Kessler, 1988):

■ In *stage one,* the two languages appear to function as one *undifferentiated* system. Children will take input from both languages and develop a single (*mixed*) system. Juxtapositioning of words from each language in one utterance is common, where words acquired in one language are not likely to appear in translated form in the other. Morphology from one language may be applied to the other as well.
■ In *stage two,* two languages become differentiated into separate systems, usually by two-and-a-half years of age. Structures shared by both languages will appear first (at the same rate and sequence); structures specific to each language will follow. As the child achieves differentiation, his fluency and conversational competence becomes evident.

A child who learns a second language (L2) after the first (L1) has been fully acquired (typically at three years) is said to have *sequential bilingualism*. Children with sequential bilingualism may be at risk of language problems

(Schiff-Myers, 1992). The L1 may be *arrested* or *regressed*: the child's development in his first language appears to reach a plateau or decline to an earlier stage. A *silent period*, while the rules of the L2 are being processed, is also common. Or the child may have *semilingualism,* where he can communicate in both languages but fails to reach proficiency in either.

In sequential bilingualism, the stages of development indicate that children take L1 as the starting point, so that errors in L2 will reflect the application of rules from L1. The syntactic rules of L2 are acquired according to communicative need, not syntactic difficulty. It is common for children to juggle aspects of phonology, semantics, syntax and morphology. In the acquisition process of L2, the child may use strategies to interact conversationally with others, such as using commonly stereotyped phrases, listening intently to others and trying to repeat what they have said, code-switching (mixing elements from both languages), and role-playing (Kessler, 1988).

Simultaneous and sequential bilingualism assumes normal cognitive and linguistic development. However, children from bilingual backgrounds may also have an underlying disability that affects the process of acquisition of both languages.

INTERVENTION STRATEGIES

Delivery of services

The traditional model of intervention for children with communication impairment has been one in which the speech and language pathologist (SLP) performs a comprehensive evaluation, decides on the therapy objectives, has scheduled therapy hours in the office or clinic with the child, and provides instructions to the parents on 'things to work on' until the next visit. One major problem with this approach is that it is unlikely to result in the functional use of language in situations outside the office or the clinic.

An alternative approach is known as *collaborative consultation,* in which the SLP and the teacher combine their respective expertise in the assessment and development of an intervention program for one or more children. The SLP has the major responsibility for evaluation and target-setting, while the teacher assumes the primary responsibility for implementing the program in a meaningful context with the child. This model offers some advantages:

- Professionals share their skills and learn about each other's special training domains.
- Problem-solving and owning the program becomes a joint venture; communication lines open up where the family and other professionals get involved in the process.
- The teacher can use the acquired knowledge base in programming for other children with needs for facilitation in communication.

■ A transfer of skills acquired by the child is more readily possible, as he has the opportunity for practice and to receive feedback in a real setting, with his everyday peers and teachers, for hours every day.

Whether it is a clinic, a classroom, or the home, it is important to present an environment to the child that offers communicative temptations, to prompt communication efforts and allow for language use so that the child can accomplish his desires (Fey, 1986). Some strategies to promote language skills include:

■ *Expansion:* repetition of the child's utterance with increased difficulty; e.g. 'truck big' is echoed as 'The truck is big'.
■ *Reduction:* repetition of the omitted target; e.g. 'truck big' is followed by 'is', child responds as 'Truck is big'.
■ *Repetition of error:* this technique allows for the child to self-correct.
■ *Request for elaboration:* if child says 'boy go shop', adult responds 'What sort of shop?'.
■ *Parallel talk:* the adult talks about what the child is doing, allowing him to access the structures he may use to map his actions to utterances.

Particularly useful in children with severe impairment, some techniques that can be used to encourage the child's learning and spontaneous use of new communicative behaviours are summarised below (Mirenda & Iacono, 1988).

■ *Most-to-least prompts:* the child is provided with maximum assistance, using a range of prompts (a model, physical assistance), particularly in the acquisition of new skills, which are then systematically faded.
■ *Least-to-most prompts:* the child is provided with as much assistance as appears necessary, and a partial model is provided.
■ *Mand model:* the child is requested to produce the target behaviour (tell me what you want); a model is provided if there is no response.
■ *Time delay:* the child is allowed sufficient time to communicate his needs or to respond to an opportunity; the length of time may vary, but 15 seconds is recommended.
■ *Verbal prompt-free:* verbal prompts are withheld, and are replaced by physical or visual prompts to elicit the use of communication.

Principles to remember

Effective communication intervention can occur:

• within social, meaningful and reciprocal interactions;
• in naturalistic environments, with opportunities to facilitate communication;
• with child-initiated activities that are followed by the adult;
• with a questioning attitude towards teaching strategies when the child fails to perform.

CONCLUSIONS

Communication is not necessarily verbal–oral, as we see in our review of hearing impairment in Chapter 14. In this chapter we have focused on speech and language, reflections of our unique evolutionary heritage as human beings, where we can use symbols to represent events, ideas and objects. Language is just as much a tool of emotional expression and social relatedness as it is a currency of learning. Helping a young child to improve his communication skills is giving him an opportunity to fulfil his potential in all domains of development.

11

Cognitive power and intellectual disability

There are three basic orientations to the study of cognitive skills. The first one is the *cognitive developmental* approach, championed by Piaget, which claims that cognitive development is *qualitatively* different over age. Its emphasis is on mental *structures* rather than intellectual power, and its interest lies in discovering the *similarities* among all children. We have considered the Piagetian perspective throughout the course of the developmental spectrum.

The second perspective is known as the *psychometric* approach, which tries to determine the *individual differences* in intelligence and its measurement. This perspective, which we explore below, assumes that intellectual *power* can be measured, and that determinations and classifications can be made based on the intelligence *scores* obtained on a test.

A third and more recent perspective, known as the *information-processing* approach, represents a combination of the concerns of these two approaches. It is interested in both the *underlying processes* in mental abilities and *how to measure* them. (We examine this approach when we look at learning disabilities in Chapter 12.)

MEASUREMENTS OF INTELLIGENCE

Psychometric approach: Stanford–Binet test

Around the turn of the century in France, Alfred Binet and Theodore Simon developed an instrument to measure the intellectual abilities of school-aged children for the purposes of deciding who among them might have special education needs. The test included tasks assessing vocabulary, comprehension of facts and relationships, and mathematical and verbal reasoning. Lewis Terman and his associates at Stanford University in California modified, extended and translated this early version; thus the *Stanford-Binet* intelligence test was formed (although why they did not credit Theodore Simon remains a mystery . . .). Stanford-Binet consisted of six items for each age group, the items becoming progressively more difficult. *Mental age (MA)* was the sum total of the items passed, converted to age (e.g two months' credit for each item passed). A measure which described a child's demonstrated ability (MA) in relation to her *chronological age (CA)* was termed the *intelligence quotient (IQ)*. This ratio can be seen in the following formula:

Mental age/Chronological age × 100 = IQ.

Accordingly, if a child performs above her chronological age, the IQ score will be above 100, and if she performs below her chronological age, she will have a score less than 100. This ratio allows the child to be compared to others her age.

As you can imagine, this approach presented serious problems, particularly with young children. Mental growth is far more rapid in the early years, and a year's difference between CA and MA at three years of age is *not* a difference of just one year, as in the case of a ten-year-old exhibiting the performance of a nine-year-old. The approach has now been abandoned. The current revision of Stanford-Binet consists of 15 subtests which permit a detailed assessment of mental abilities, and the computation of scores is based on standardisation procedures (Thorndike, Hagen & Sattler, 1986). The subtests are distributed as follows:

- *verbal reasoning* (four subtests): vocabulary, comprehension, absurdities, verbal relations;
- *quantitative reasoning* (three subtests): quantitative, number series, equation building;
- *abstract/visual reasoning* (four subtests): pattern analysis, copying, matrices, paper folding and cutting;
- *short-term memory* (four subtests): bead memory, memory for sentences, memory for digits, memory for objects.

Stanford-Binet is suitable for children two to 18 years of age.

Wechsler tests

The *Wechsler Intelligence Scale for Children—Revised (WISC-R)* and *Wechsler Preschool and Primary Scale of Intelligence (WPPSI)* were both constructed to differentiate a *verbal* and a *performance* scale in their assessment of cognitive ability (Wechsler, 1974). As separate tests of intelligence, the verbal and the performance scales correlate[1] significantly with each other, as well as with

---

1   *Correlation* is used as a statistical measure of relatedness, where the strength of the relationship between two variables or sets of measures are calculated, although no causal relationship is assumed between them.

the composite score obtained by the combination of the two scales (*overall IQ score*). These measures on different domains may provide helpful clinical diagnostic information in the assessment of some children, including those with learning disabilities. The performance scale also allows for the testing of children with limited verbal expression, such as those with hearing impairment or little English knowledge. WISC-R is appropriate for children aged six to 16; WPPSI is suitable for younger children, from three to eight years. The subtests in each of the domains are as follows:

- *verbal scale*: information, similarities, arithmetic, vocabulary, comprehension, digit span;
- *performance scale*: picture completion, picture arrangement, block design, object assembly, coding, mazes.

Both Stanford-Binet and the Wechsler tests are *standardised* instruments, which means that they have been administered on large groups of children in each age group and the scores have been distributed within statistical parameters. This process enables the comparison of a child with others her age; they are thus *norm-referenced* tools.

The use of norm-referenced tests for the assessment of populations of children with handicapping conditions is not deemed appropriate or a fair comparison, as norms are developed (essentially) on normal children.

The other serious criticism often brought up is that of the representativeness of the sample on which these tests have been normed. They have traditionally been standardised on white, middle-class American children and, as such, may not be suitable tools for assessing children from different cultural and experiential backgrounds. The more recent revision of Stanford-Binet, however, has incorporated the needs of children from minority backgrounds and those with special needs.

Standardised tools may be administered only by professionals who have had supervised training in its administrative procedures, i.e. psychologists. If the strict guidelines of test administration are not adhered to, the results are not considered to be valid.

Both of these tests have a standard score of 100 as their *mean* (statistical average), with a standard deviation (SD) of 15. The scores are distributed on a *normal curve*, which means that about 70% of the scores obtained are within (plus or minus) one standard deviation; i.e. *normal intelligence* falls between 85 and 115. The normal curve would indicate that the proportions of individuals on either side of these scores will decrease as one gets further away from the *mean*. For example, the proportion of individuals who obtain an IQ score of 116–130 (between +1 and +2 SD) is about 13%; the same proportion applies for the left side of the curve, for scores between 84 and 70 (between −1 and −2 SD). These measures have been used in the classification of various degrees of mental retardation as well as intellectual giftedness. The proportion of individuals falling below 70 is less than 2.5%

and, as we shall see below, one of the criteria for the diagnosis of mental retardation is a score of below 70 on an intelligence test. Because of genetic anomalies, infections, trauma and brain damage, all of which increase the incidence of cognitive impairment, there are slightly more low-IQ children than very-high-IQ children.

Infant intelligence tests

As you may have noticed, the Wechsler and Stanford-Binet tests do not assess infants. Some other tools attempting to obtain a measure of cognitive ability in infancy in order to make predictions on later development are summarised below.

- *Battelle Developmental Inventory* (Newborg, Stock, Wnek, Guidubaldi & Svinicki, 1984) covers 341 items in five areas: personal-social, adaptive, motor, communication, and cognitive. It can be scored by direct observation or parent interview.
- *Bayley Scales of Infant Development* (Bayley, 1969/1993) consist of three scales: mental scale (163 items) measures perception, memory, learning, problem-solving, and language; motor scale (81 items) measures gross and fine motor skills; and infant behaviour record, used for the rating of infants' observed behaviour.
- *Cattell Infant Intelligence Scale* (Cattell, 1940/1960) is a downward extension of the Stanford-Binet, and contains multiple items for the direct testing of mental development.
- *Gesell Developmental Schedules* (Gesell & Amatrada, 1947; Knobloch & Pasamanick, 1974) contain multiple items in four areas: adaptive, motor, language, and personal-social. Direct testing is supplemented with parent information.
- *Griffiths Mental Developmental Scales* (Griffiths, 1978) contain items in social, fine motor, gross motor, hearing, eye–hand coordination, and speech. Scale I is for birth to two years, and contains 27 items.
- *Denver Developmental Screening Test* (Frankenburg & Dodds, 1969) is a screening device only, but provides a short overview of development in the areas of personal-social, fine motor-adaptive, language, and gross motor.

Achievement tests

Another measure of intellectual ability is the achievement test, which is designed to evaluate a *specific* domain of information usually learned in an academic setting, or *acquired* knowledge. IQ tests are designed to provide information on how well a child *can* think and learn (underlying *competence*), while achievement tests measure *what* the child has learned (*performance*).

Is it truly possible to determine underlying competence when competence is inferred from performance? Intelligence tests may be considered achievement tests insofar as they measure the performance of the child at the time the test is administered based on what the child is able to or chooses to do. Interpretation of the results of such tests, and making predictions for the child's future adaptive profile, requires reflection and caution.

Reliability and validity

There are two major concerns with tests in general: reliability, which indicates how stable the test scores are over time; and *validity,* which indicates whether the test measures what it claims to measure. These concerns apply to the tests of intelligence in particular, as long-term educational placement and other decisions in a young person's life can be made (sometimes quite incorrectly) based on IQ scores. The most common method of determining the stability of IQ scores from a younger to an older age is to follow that group of children longitudinally, and to correlate the scores obtained at different times in development.

- The correlation between a 12-month-old Bayley test score and a four-year-old Binet IQ is about .30, indicating a weak predictive relationship (Bee, Barnard, Eyres, Gray, Hammond, Spietz, Snyder & Clarke, 1982).
- Analysis of several longitudinal studies of repeated IQ testing over the early years reveals that about half the children showed little fluctuation, while the other half demonstrated fluctuations in both rising and declining scores, in some individual cases by as much as 40 points (McCall, 1993).
- The correlation between a child's IQ score and her performance on achievement tests in school is reportedly about .60, which means that, while most children with high IQ scores will do well in school, some lower-IQ-score children will do quite well also (Carver, 1990).
- While the correlation between IQs at two and five years of age is about .32, it rises to .70 for consistency of scores between age five and eight, and .85 between ages nine and 12 (Honzig, MacFarlane & Allen, 1948).
- *Therefore,* it seems clear that the *younger* the child is at the time of the first testing, the *less predictive* the score will be of future attainment.
- Generally speaking, it appears that what is being measured in infant tests of intelligence is not the same ability being tapped by childhood intelligence tests (Colombo, 1993).
- IQ test scores increase their predictive power over later years in childhood.
- Intelligence tests *do not measure* skills such as social skills, ability to relate to others, creativity, insight, ability to read and respond to social cues, or 'street smarts'.

ALTERNATIVE VIEWS

The notion that intelligence is a unitary concept has been challenged. One view that presents an underlying difference in mental abilities is that of Cattell (1971), who claims that there are two different sets of cognitive abilities:

- *crystallised intelligence*, which relies heavily on informational content (and is thus influenced by cultural and environmental influences), is reflected in tasks such as general information, vocabulary and arithmetic problems;
- *fluid intelligence,* by contrast, makes little demand on acquired knowledge, and involves the ability to see complex relationships, spatial visualisation and problem-solving. It relies on speed as well as accuracy of response.

Interestingly, contrary to some findings that intelligence declines over the life span, particularly with ageing, crystallised intelligence actually *improves,* while aspects of fluid intelligence, particularly when related to speed, seem to diminish slightly.

Multiple intelligences?

An interesting theory of intelligence has been developed by Howard Gardner (1983), who claims that there are seven different kinds of intelligences, only two of which are traditionally measured by standardised tools of intelligence assessment:

- *Logical/mathematical* intelligence, measured by standard IQ tests, deals with inductive and deductive thinking, reasoning, numbers, and recognition of abstract patterns.
- *Verbal/linguistic intelligence* is related to written and spoken language, is often measured by verbal parts of IQ tests, and dominates most Western educational systems.
- *Visual/spatial intelligence* deals primarily with the visual modality, and involves the ability to visualise an object, and the skills to create internally represented mental images.
- *Bodily/kinaesthetic intelligence* is related to physical movement and the knowledge of the body, and is exhibited in fluidity and control of motion, and awareness of body in space.
- *Musical/rhythmical intelligence* is based on the recognition of tonal and melodic patterns, including various environmental sounds, and on a sensitivity to rhythms and beats.
- *Interpersonal intelligence* operates primarily through person-to-person relationships and communications between people, manifesting as an ability to listen, understand and negotiate with others.
- *Intrapersonal intelligence* relates to inner states of being, ability to reflect on the self and to engage in metacognition (ability to think about thinking), and an awareness of spiritual realities.

Recently Gardner has added an eighth intelligence to his list: *the apprehension of the natural world*, as epitomised by the competencies of a skilled hunter or botanists' (Gardner, 1997, p.36).

> Take a moment to think about yourself, and some people you know . . . Can you relate their inclinations or choice of vocations to Gardner's intelligences?
>
> Now try to match these professions with the different intelligences: an architect, a scientist, a special Olympian, a yoga teacher, a bush tracker, a musician, an attorney and a psychotherapist. Individual differences seem to be manifest in more ways than one.
>
> Have you also noticed that this reflection is not a formal intelligence assessment, as we have not accounted for the reliability and validity of our impressions?

Triarchic theory of intelligence

Another view claims that there are three aspects or types of intelligence (Sternberg, 1986):

- *Componential intelligence* includes abilities traditionally measured by intelligence and achievement tests, and is reflected in planning, organising, remembering facts and applying them to new situations.
- *Experiential intelligence* is manifested by a person's abilities to see connections among things, to be creative, to realise how principles may apply in novel situations, and to synthesise available information into a new and interesting whole.
- *Contextual intelligence* is reflected in being streetwise (having 'street smarts'), in having the ability to manipulate the environment, to understand how the person fits into the context, and to know which people to cultivate and how to go about doing so for better adaptation to the situational demands.

Because research has focused almost exclusively on the investigations and outcomes of componential intelligence, our views on intellectual impairment may be similarly biased. Both experiential and contextual aspects of intelligence may be called for in real-life adaptation. It is this *adaptive aspect of intelligence* that we need to be more aware of in understanding and planning for children with developmental disabilities.

INTELLECTUAL DISABILITIES

The broad range of *developmental disorders* includes mental retardation, pervasive developmental disorders (autistic spectrum of disorders; Chapter 15), and specific developmental disorders (learning disabilities; Chapter 12, specific language impairment; Chapter 10, ADHD; Chapter 13 etc.). Here we examine *mental retardation,* starting with its definition (DSM IV, 1994):

> Mental retardation is characterised by significantly subaverage general intellectual functioning, with concurrent deficits in adaptive functioning, and its onset is before 18 years of age.

In terms of IQ scores in the subaverage intellectual functioning criterion, the classification of mental retardation is displayed in Table 11.1.

Mild mental retardation	50–55 to about 70
Moderate mental retardation	35–40 to 50–55
Severe mental retardation	20–25 to 35–40
Profound mental retardation	below 20 or 25

TABLE 11.1

Mental retardation and IQ scores

The second criterion is that of *adaptive* behaviour, which includes the person's effectiveness in meeting the standards of functioning expected for her age in areas such as social responsibility, communication, daily living skills, coping with schooling demands, personal independence and self-suffi-ciency. Thus, a low IQ score is a necessary but not *sufficient* condition to determine mental retardation.

The third criterion refers to the developmental occurrence of the disorder. Brain trauma suffered in an accident at 12 years may result in mental retardation; the same injury in an adult would be classified as organic brain damage.

Causes and incidence of mental retardation

A summary of causes contributing to mental retardation and their distribution is exhibited in Table 11.2.

Intrauterine influences	10%
Perinatal trauma	10%
Postnatal trauma	6%
Teratogens/toxins	3%
Infections	6%
Congenital abnormalities	20%
Genetic abnormalities	45%

TABLE 11.2

Causes of mental retardation (Moser, 1985)

Of the genetic abnormalities, 15% of mental retardation is attributed to Down syndrome, 10% to fragile X syndrome, and the remaining 20% accounts for factors such as hydrocephaly, microcephaly and other brain disorders.

We examine Down syndrome here in some detail, and briefly review fragile X syndrome and fetal alcohol syndrome, as collectively these disorders account for a significant proportion of the aetiology in mental retardation.

Down syndrome

The chromosomal aberration that accounts for Down syndrome (three copies of chromosome number 21, or *trisomy 21*—see Chapter 2) was not discovered until 1959, although clinical descriptions of the syndrome are to be found in the medical annals of the 19th century. In *mosaicism,* and *translocation,* which accounts for about 5% of the disorder, the associated retardation may be less severe. *Physical characteristics* of Down syndrome include the following:

- obliquely placed eyes, with underdeveloped iris;
- low muscle tone (*hypotonia*), with short and stout stature;
- low-set, small ears, and excessive skin around the neck;
- atypical hand prints, and fine skin and hair;
- heart, digestive system and skeletal malformations.

The incidence of Down syndrome (about one in 700 live births) rises significantly with maternal age, and is thus attributed to the characteristics of the egg, although the defect occurs in the sperm 15% of the time (Dagna-Bricarelli et al., 1990).

Medical complications
In addition to cognitive impairment, Down syndrome has a number of associated medical conditions, which necessitates medical intervention and follow-up of the child (Bathsaw & Perret, 1992).

- In the newborn period, *congenital heart defects* (40%) may necessitate open heart surgery. Children remain vulnerable to upper respiratory infections.
- *Gastrointestinal blockage* symptoms may include vomiting, poor feeding, and aspiration pneumonia (where the lungs are inflamed due to inclusion of a foreign substance). While surgical correction is successfully achieved on the congenital malformations causing the blockage, the child may be at risk of failure to thrive.
- *Visual problems* include refractive errors (70%), strabismus (uneven muscle pull on eye movements; 50%), nystagmus (darting movements of the eye; 35%) and cataracts (3%).
- *Hearing problems* result from narrow ear canals and a predisposition to middle ear infections. Mild to moderate conductive hearing loss is found in 60%–90% of children with Down syndrome.
- *Dental anomalies and malocclusion problems* are common because of delayed eruption of the teeth.
- In later childhood, *obesity,* short stature, hypothyroidism and *depression* are among the most common disorders.
- Loose joints and hypotonicity seen in infancy predispose the child to joint dislocations in later years, most commonly at the hips or in the upper spine (atlanto-occipital instability). Upper spinal partial dislocation (sub-

luxation) needs to be diagnosed early to avoid possible motor damage in the spinal cord.

Most of these ailments can be treated successfully, *and the majority of individuals with Down syndrome live long and successful lives.*

Motor delay may be most evident in early development, with decreased muscle tone giving the baby a 'floppy' appearance. Although gross motor skills may be delayed, even the youngsters with severe hypotonia improve significantly over time, so that physical disabilities are rare by school age. Early intervention may significantly facilitate the reaching of motor milestones, with many babies being comparable to their normal peers in such skills as sitting and crawling (Hanson, 1987).

Language development in children with Down syndrome

The child with Down syndrome looks better in her first two years of life than she may later on, probably because of her typically happy personality, responsiveness and attentiveness to parents (Cicchetti, & Beeghly, 1990). However, significant cognitive and linguistic delays become apparent by the first birthday.

Cognition. Communication and language development in children with Down syndrome generally reflect the extent of cognitive impairment. Most youngsters reach the *concrete operations* stage, and have the communication skills of a school-aged child. However, the abstract reasoning and hypothetical thinking required in *formal operations* is not evident in mental retardation associated with Down syndrome. Additionally, both recall and recognition memory seems to be impaired in comparison to same-age peers. Storage and retrieval of auditory as well as visual information are significantly impaired in preschoolers with Down syndrome (McDade & Adler, 1980). Memory problems may be exacerbated by the absence of rehearsal strategies and an inability to store information.

The acquisition of information requires attention to the relevant stimuli. From a Piagetian perspective, retaining or recalling various complex representations in the environment, so that they can be compared with the existing schemata before they are assimilated, may not be readily possible. Consequently, the motivation to sustain attention which propels an unimpaired child to acquire knowledge may be lacking in children with mental retardation.

Semantics. The development of meaning, or semantics, in Down syndrome appears to progress in a similar pattern to that in normally developing children, but is delayed and/or deficient, possibly due to a symbolic processing deficit (Rondal, 1995). The progression of semantic relational concepts, sequential use of sentence types, and use of morphology and vocabulary to expand sentences, basically follows the normal developmental sequence (Gunn, 1985).

Opinions differ, however, as to whether 'delays' correspond to comparative mental and/or language levels of normally developing children.

Following a delayed use of meanings and functions expressed through pre-speech acts and gestures, young children with Down syndrome generally acquire their first words between the ages of 20 and 30 months (Miller, 1992). Such delayed acquisition and use of vocabulary may be related to:

- slow development through levels of cognitive functioning;
- fewer and poorer opportunities to map meaning onto words, possibly because the child has more limited experiences of joint attention and attachment;
- motor control and phonological production difficulties as well as hearing problems, which adversely affect the ability to comprehend and monitor the use of words;
- short-term memory deficit (Meyers, 1990).

Syntax.   Children with Down syndrome may have a specific learning deficit when it comes to understanding and using grammatical structures. The ability of young children with Down syndrome to use combinatorial language has been fairly consistently correlated to their current levels of cognitive functioning. Those children who fail to achieve object permanence, or fail to combine symbolic play acts, also fail to develop beyond single-word utterances. A common characteristic of these children as they grow older, and start using longer utterances, is that of an 'asynchrony' between the complexity of the ideas expressed and the simplicity of the linguistic structures used to express them. School-aged children may use single-word utterances to convey complex meanings (Meyers, 1990).

Limitations in abstract thought and concept development may impede the child's ability to comprehend grammatical relationships, and thus to produce them appropriately (Miller, 1988). There is evidence that grammatical growth reaches a plateau at around eight to ten years of age (Dykens, Hodapp & Evans, 1994). Thus, compared to their normal peers, children with Down syndrome generally display verbal language that is characterised by:

- less complex use of syntax, with limitations in abstract thought and concepts;
- a more limited repertoire of grammatical structures;
- use of less complex morphology and function words to elaborate meaning.

Articulation and phonology

Although babbling and phonological acquisition parallel normal development, phonological difficulties which adversely affect intelligibility are apparent in most children with Down syndrome (Borghi, 1990). Phonological ability is often influenced by oral and facial anomalies, including a large and forward-placed tongue, frequent respiratory infections, speech motor control problems, compounded by the general hypotonia associated with the syndrome. The phonological errors made suggest a simplification of rule-governed processes, and are most evident in fricative phonemes such as *f, v, s, z, sh* and *th* (Owens, 1993).

Pragmatic skills

Although choice of appropriate subject seems as well developed as in their mental age-matched peers, children with moderate retardation seem less skilled in requesting clarification of information when the context is not informative. Children with Down syndrome are less likely to keep interpersonal distance, less able to judge non-verbal messages during communication, and less able to respond appropriately (Marcell & Jett, 1985). Common strategies to fill in the gaps and hold a conversational turn include the use of echolalia or frequent repetition of utterances.

Intervention

The following suggestions are made to facilitate the emergence and use of linguistic structures in infants with Down syndrome:

- early coupling of words with *signs*, which makes initial communications easier, as well as reducing frustrations associated with non-intelligibility problems (Miller, 1992);
- use of intact utterance structure and words, together with slower rates of speech in the input interactive language (Harris, Kasari & Sigman, 1996);
- capitalisation on the visual attention, which is usually superior to auditory skills, in augmentation of communication skills. Early use of highly interactive computer software linking speech output to computer graphics has been shown to be effective in promoting imitation skills (Meyers, 1990).

Outcome

The most common life experience of a child with Down syndrome is to remain at home and be educated in a special class for moderate intellectual disabilities or in an integrated educational setting. Compared with those who were institutionalised, individuals who grew up at home demonstrated much better outcomes in terms of adaptive abilities, and had a longer life span (Schroeder-Kurth, Schaffert, Koeckritz, et al., 1990).

Fragile X syndrome

Fragile X syndrome was accidentally discovered in a genetics laboratory in Australia, when researchers discovered that a group of male residents in a facility for group care all had the same pattern in their X chromosome: the bottom end seemed to be pinched off. This finding explained why mental retardation occurred more often in males than in females. Furthermore, the physical features of the male carriers of the fragile X chromosome looked remarkably similar: elongated faces, large portruding ears, narrow nose bridges, high palatal arches and prominent jaws. Most had severe mental retardation, often accompanied by aggressive behaviours. Soon it became apparent that the disorder was inherited by X-linked transmission (see Chapter 2).

Fragile X syndrome accounts for 6%–14% of all males with severe mental retardation, marking it as the second after Down syndrome in readily identifiable causes of intellectual disability (Chudley & Hagerman, 1987). Approximately 10% of fragile X cases are reported also to have autism (Brown, Jenkins, Cohen, et al., 1986).

Interestingly, some males with fragile X chromosomes do not exhibit any of the characteristics associated with the disorder (about 20%), but can still transmit the trait to their offspring. This pattern is consistent with the *gene* identified in that location causing the disorder (Sutherland & Mulley, 1990). Common cognitive and behavioural characteristics of fragile X syndrome in *young male children* who are affected (Simko, Hornstein, Soukup, et al., 1989) are:

TABLE 11.3				
Common	Mental retardation	80%	Communication impairment	95%
characteristics	Hyperactivity	65%	Poor eye contact	80%
in fragile X	Self-mutilation	60%	Autistic-like behaviour	60%
syndrome	Conduct problems	60%	Seizures	20%

Females may also have fragile X syndrome, although the physical appearance is less conspicuous and the cognitive deficit associated with the disorder seems to be less severe, ranging from mild mental retardation (10%) to various learning disabilities (20%) (Borghgraef, Fryns & van der Berghe, 1990). Other associated patterns include visual spatial processing deficits, cluttered and repetitive speech, attention problems and withdrawn personalities (Reiss & Freund, 1990). Excessive talking is seen more in fragile X syndrome than in Down syndrome (Sudhalter, Cohen, Silverman & Wolf-Schein, 1990).

As fragile X syndrome is a relatively recently discovered disorder, long-term outcomes are not yet known. Prenatal diagnosis for the disorder is possible.

Fetal alcohol syndrome

The adverse effects of alcohol on the developing fetus were recognised relatively recently (Jones, Smith, Ulleland, et al., 1973). Fetal alcohol syndrome (FAS) is now estimated to be a leading cause of mental retardation, accounting for 5% of congenital anomalies, and 10%–20% of mild mental retardation (Olegard, Sabel, Aronsson, et al., 1979).

FAS is caused by ingestion of alcohol by the mother during pregnancy. Amounts in excess of 200 millilitres of distilled spirits are considered excessive drinking, and are likely to produce FAS. The earlier the alcohol abuse occurs in the pregnancy, the more severe the effects. If the drinking occurs later in the pregnancy, the physical anomalies associated with the disorder (listed below) may not be evident, although growth and cognitive development deficits are present. These children are said to have *fetal alcohol effects (FAE)*.

The alcohol consumed by the pregnant woman passes through the placental membrane; thus, the fetus is drunk each time the mother is drunk. Because women have less of the enzyme that detoxifies alcohol (dehydrogenase), they get intoxicated faster, and smaller amounts of alcohol can damage both mother and fetus. The known effects of alcohol on the fetus are the following (Pietratoni & Knuppel, 1991):

- decrease in protein synthesis, impairing intrauterine growth;
- impairment of cellular growth and neuronal migration, such that the neurones destined for the cortex never reach it;
- decrease in the production of neurotransmitters, and inhibition of nerve myelination.

Simply put, alcohol is poison to the fetus. No safe limits of alcohol consumption are available for pregnant women, and the best advice seems to be abstinence.

Children with FAS are usually small for gestational age, although they are usually full-term babies. Their characteristic features include the following (Graham, Hanson, Darby et al., 1988):

- microcephaly (small head size), with widely spaced eyes and narrow eyelids;
- strabismus, or poor eye-muscle coordination;
- short, upturned nose and large, low-set ears;
- underdeveloped jaw, with frequent malocclusion of the teeth; shortened fingers;
- high incidence of congenital heart defects, and hip dislocation.

The *developmental profiles* of children with FAS and FAE include the following (Streissguth, Barr, Sampson, et al., 1986):

- average IQ of 60–70, placing them in the mild retardation category;
- preponderance of stereotypical behaviours often associated with autism;
- behaviour patterns resembling ADHD, with high levels of distractibility, hyperactivity, impulsivity and inattentiveness.

Statistics obtained in the USA indicate that approximately two-thirds of the mothers of children with FAS die from alcohol-related causes such as car accidents, overdose, suicide and liver illness. Many children with FAS are removed from the family home and placed in foster care because of neglect and abuse. For the children who remain at home, the incidence of neglect is 86% and child abuse is 52% (Streissguth et al., 1991). It is a major social ill of our society and, as with most such problems, prevention is easier wished than put in place.

General characteristics in mental retardation

The characteristics of children with mental retardation that pose barriers to learning, when compared with their non-impaired peers, seem to be (Gow & Ward, 1985):

- deficiency in such learning strategies as the rehearsal of new information and ability to analyse and synthesise the presented information;
- poor self-management skills, which can be interpreted as behaviour problems;
- slower rate of skills acquisition;
- slower rates of development in accuracy and speed;
- passivity in learning situations, with more dependence on the adult for guidance; diminished initiative (learned helplessness);
- less on-task engagement (attention-focusing) time;
- poor ability to determine their own ability and its limitations;
- difficulty in switching from one task or concept to another (perseverative tendencies);
- low self-concept and low self-esteem, with low levels of intrinsic motivation;
- impaired ability to *generalise* skills across tasks, settings, persons and time.

With adequate opportunity, most people with intellectual disabilities can acquire even complex skills, and continue learning throughout their lives (Baine, 1986). Traditional assessment has not adequately accounted for the learning capability of individuals with mental retardation. Their response to instruction and repeated learning opportunities reveal a much more optimistic outcome than was previously expected (Feuerstein, 1979).

Among the principles of *effective intervention* with children with mental retardation, the following suggestions seem to have beneficial outcomes (based on Owens, 1993):

- Highlight new or relevant material against a backdrop of known material.
- Explain the learning task; preorganise information before presenting it.
- Teach and train memory strategies, such as rehearsal, which assists in generalisation.
- Use overlearning and repetition to facilitate generalisation.
- Train and teach in naturalistic environments, where learned skills can be meaningfully applied.
- Begin intervention and facilitation as early as possible; facilitate mother–infant interaction.
- Follow developmental guidelines.

CONCLUSIONS

Mental retardation is an impairment of the abstract thinking; it is the concrete attitudes and misconceptions of the normal population towards the condition that may pose the most significant barrier to the integration of individuals with retardation as functional and valued members of our society. From the Special Olympics to inclusive classrooms, many a child and young person with mental retardation can be an inspiration and enrichment to us all.

12

Learning disabilities and attention disorders

You may recall that we reviewed the *constructivist* approaches to cognition championed by Piaget and the neo-Piagetians when we looked at the child at different periods of growing up. In reviewing mental retardation (Chapter 11), we considered the *psychometric* approach to measuring intelligence. Here we look at a third approach in studying cognition—the *information-processing* approach—which is not a theory of cognitive development so much as it is a model for explaining *how* learning occurs with specific reference to the *processes* involved in learning, problem-solving and remembering.

INFORMATION-PROCESSING APPROACH

This approach has made significant contributions to our understanding of *learning disabilities* and *attention-related deficits*. As we will see, a learning disability does not occur because of low intelligence; it comes about because the nervous system extracts or *processes* information from the perceptual input, in a way that is fundamentally different. The information-processing approach looks at the different *components* necessary to arrive at a solution (one of which is attention); a dysfunction in one or more of these parts may affect how a child learns or where he faces difficulties. In this era of information technology, the human mind is thought to be analogous to a computer: the information-processing *types* and *strategies* are the programs, run by the brain, which is the hardware.

The information-processing model places a heavy emphasis on perception, attention and memory, and the interrelations among these mechanisms, by which we accomplish thinking, knowing and learning. The information-processing flow may be as follows:

1. External information is registered by the *senses* (visual, auditory, tactile).
2. We pay *attention* to a subset of that information, which is passed on to the holding bay of *short-term memory*.
3. The *executive component* then decides whether to act on that information or to transfer it to *long-term memory* for storage.
4. The executive component also controls the *retrieval* of stored information from episodic (personal) or semantic (general) memory.
5. Attentional mechanisms are brought into play, and *different levels of attention* are allocated to different kinds of tasks.

A conceptual model of a *cognitive information-processing system* is thought to have the following components (Andre & Phye, 1986):

■ *Input* or *sensory registers* include audition and vision, which are responsible for receiving information.
■ *Short-term memory* briefly stores and transforms the information in accordance with the executive decision.
■ *Long-term memory* has an unlimited capacity for storage of information.
■ *Executive function* controls the flow of information and decides on, selects and performs operations on the information.
■ *Output buffer* compacts familiar or routine information such that little attentional resource is allocated to it, while new and important information can get more attention.

Information processing is accomplished by the flow and reciprocal feedback and feedforward processes within these components.

Close your eyes and pay attention to all the sensory information being received by your other senses. What can you hear in the background (auditory channel)? Had you noticed how your clothing felt on your body (tactile sense), or how your legs are positioned (proprioceptive sense)? Would you be able to concentrate on reading this passage if you had to pay intense amounts of attention to all this sensory information? Children with attention-related deficits may have to.

Attention and processing styles

It is generally thought that attention is a finite resource; that is, from the vast amount of sensory information that the organism is subjected to every moment, only a small amount can be processed accurately and meaningfully. Furthermore, there seem to be two distinct types of attentional processing of information (Fisk & Schneider, 1984). *Automatic* versus *controlled* processing compare and contrast in the following ways:

Automatic processing	Controlled processing
Fast mode of processing	Slow mode of processing
Parallel processing (multiple stimuli)	Serial processing (one at a time)
Effortless/subconscious processing	Effortful/conscious processing
Not limited by short-term memory	Limited by short-term memory
Reflects well-rehearsed skills and familiar information	Works with new and inconsistent information
Not under direct control	Regulated by direct control
Once learned, hard to ignore, change or suppress	Easily changed, suppressed or ignored

We start out the learning of a new skill in the controlled processing mode. As we gain experience and proficiency, less attention is required to perform the task; automatic processing takes over. School-related learning, and perhaps a learning disability requires a balance between these two modes, which is critical for optimal functioning. For example, if certain cognitive tasks like sound-symbol associations in learning to read were not relegated to automatic processing after years of experience with print, imagine what a drain on cognitive resources it would be and how it would slow the system down, preventing fluent and efficient reading.

Another differentiation with respect to styles of information processing is akin to inductive and deductive modes of thinking in reaching solutions (Gerber, 1993): bottom-up, and top-down.

Bottom-up processing requires small bits of *sensory* data before the larger generality or rule can be ascertained. For example, in learning to read, the phonological approach of learning individual sounds and their written symbols, then decoding their combinations, is data-driven (*from* the bottom) until meaning is attributed to the combination, of letters and sounds (*to* higher levels of processing), somewhat like deductive thinking.

Top-down processing, on the other hand, relies on *semantic* expectancies based on prior knowledge. Context, or the general principle, or a collection of events, provides the opportunity to discern the solution. Going from general to particular (or inductive thinking), *from* the top *to* the bottom would be at play in the whole-language approach to literacy acquisition, as the phonological rules are discovered from experience with texts and their meaning.

Both of these styles are called for in different contexts. Learning disabilities may indicate an imbalance in the deployment of these strategies to extract meaning.

Attention dimensions

Attributes of attention differ for tasks of differing demands. You may notice that the amount of attention paid is often dependent on the significance of the event for the person, or the intensity of presentation:

■ *Arousal and vigilance* refer to a physiological state of readiness to meet task demands. New and important activities require more arousal than monotonous activities. Levels of high arousal reduce *distractibility* (Eysenck, 1982).

■ *Selective attention* refers to the ability to show a preference for some events over others. It can be involuntary (as in being jarred by a loud noise) or voluntary (as we strain to listen to a conversation in a loud club).

■ *Focused attention* can be active, where it contributes to maintenance of focus, or passive, where attention can be disrupted by shifting to irrelevant stimuli. Many students 'drift away' during lectures; they may focus again as they have to listen actively to the topics to be covered for the exam!

■ *Divided attention* is distribution of attentional resources between two events. If one is automatic and the other is controlled processing, the automatic one can be done with such efficiency that we may not recall having done it. The more controlled and effortful an event, the more likely it is to be remembered (Fisk & Schneider, 1984). For example, we rarely think about how to drive (automatic processing), but have to pay close attention to street names if we are attempting to find an unfamiliar address (controlled processing).

Attentional strategies and development

The attentional strategies used by young children seem to be inefficient, and to be held by perceptual dimensions of form and colour. More and more critical and relevant features are focused on with increasing age. The way young children inspect things is *incomplete, redundant* and *unsystematic*. The ability to employ selective attention strategies, processing and memory capacity seems also to improve with age.

Clear developmental patterns were observed in a study in which pre-schoolers and children in grades two, five and eight were shown an array of small doors behind which were hidden pictures of different classes of objects. Children were told to look behind the doors in an effort to remember as many items as they could (Woody-Ramsey & Miller, 1988):

■ Preschool children showed no selective attention or organised strategy in the task.

■ Children in the second grade tended to use a strategy (opening all doors in a row), but the strategy was not necessarily relevant to the task (ignoring the common pictures on the doors which held items of the same category).

■ Fifth- and eighth-graders made efficient use of selective attention strategies.

Memory

Memory involves the transfer of information from short-term storage to long-term storage. If the short-term memory is not functioning adequately, the knowledge base to be transferred to long-term memory will be limited.

Children who experience difficulties in short-term auditory memory, for example, typically do not follow directions well or recall the contents of a storybook just read.

What is in the long-term store needs to be retrieved into *working memory* for problem-solving and recall when necessary. Transfer of information to and from long-term memory is facilitated by the use of *mnemonic* strategies such as semantic organisation, rehearsal and the integration of new input by old knowledge (see Chapter 8). Developmental factors influence both the use of strategies and the extent of the knowledge base facilitating memory performance. Given that language and memory are intricately interrelated, disorder in one may adversely affect the other basic process.

Developmental changes in information processing

It is reasonable to expect that, as the brain grows in the developmental continuum, its *capacity*, *speed* of processing and *efficiency* in processing information also increase. After all, the process of development is all about differentiation, and increased complexity of functioning.

- *Memory capacity*, as measured by digit span (immediate recall of a list of numbers), increases with age. From two units at age two, increase proceeds linearly, to three units at age three, four units at age five, five units at age seven, and six units by 11, until it reaches the adult capacity of seven units from teenage years (Dempster, 1981).
- Cognitive processing also gains in *speed* with age. A cross-cultural study shows that, across different tasks such as reaction time and mental mathematical operations, children clearly process faster and more efficiently as a function of increase in age (Kail & Hall, 1994).
- Speed of processing, as measured by reaction time, also appears to be related to IQ in children (Saccuzzo, Johnson & Guertin, 1994).
- Another function that gains proficiency with age is the *executive*[1] *function*, which allows the child the ability to plan what to do, be aware of the alternative strategies in solving the problem, and finally to choose and implement a strategy. By doing so, the child is actually thinking about thinking (*metacognition*), or reflecting on the process, so that if a strategy does not work, the steps can be retraced and modified as necessary. This function emerges gradually, and improves rapidly in the early school years.
- *Flexibility* in the use of a strategy (or the ability to transfer and *generalise* its use to other situations), as well as the use of *alternative* strategies when one does not work, have been shown to be related to intelligence in studies

---

1   *Executive functions* are mostly reflections of frontal lobe functioning, together with initiative, insight, attention and motivation. Lack of maturity of, or damage to, the frontal lobes is typically associated with poor planning strategies and impulsivity. Does this sound like children with *ADHD?*

comparing young children with and without mental retardation (Campione, Brown, Ferrera, Jones & Steinberg, 1985; DeLoache & Brown, 1987).

■ However, expertise, or specialised knowledge, which is usually determined by the child's interest in and practice with a skill, can compensate for a slower processing mode and lower IQ scores: the scores for recalling soccer-related items were better in a group of children who were experts in playing soccer than in those who were beginners at the game, although highly intelligent beginners did as well as less intelligent expert children (Schneider & Bjorklund, 1992).

Such research evidence seems to suggest that children with learning disabilities can be *taught strategies* for more efficient information processing to facilitate their learning.

DEFINITION AND SCOPE OF LEARNING DISABILITIES

What differentiates learning disabilities (LD) from other conditions that have associated learning deficits (mental retardation, cerebral palsy etc.) is the fact that LD is not dependent on intelligence. Early descriptors of LD made reference to a subtle brain-related disorder, calling it minimal brain dysfunction. The current definition is broad, and not entirely free of controversy (see below). Traditionally, the child with LD is thought of as performing *below* his potential (i.e. IQ) because of processing deficits/differences or learning barriers that adversely affect performance. In the USA, 'learning disabilities' is the preferred term; the same group of children in Australia is known as having 'learning difficulties'. The definition gets lengthier each time professional organisations review it, possibly because of the complexities involved in this category of children. Here is the current one (National Joint Committee on Learning Disabilities, 1994):

> Learning disability is a generic term that refers to a heterogeneous group of disorders manifested by significant difficulties in the acquisition and use of listening, speaking, reading, writing, reasoning, or mathematical abilities. These disorders are intrinsic to the individual and are presumed to be due to the dysfunction of the central nervous system, and may appear across the lifespan. Problems of self-regulatory behaviours, social perception, and social interaction may exist with learning disabilities but do not themselves constitute a learning disability. Although learning disabilities may occur concomitantly with other disabling conditions (e.g. sensory impairment, mental retardation, social and emotional disturbance) or with extrinsic influences (e.g. cultural differences, insufficient/inappropriate instruction), they are not the direct result of those conditions and influences.

There are some points that need to be highlighted in this definition. It tends to define what learning disabilities is *not,* rather than what it really is. In that sense, it is a definition of exclusion, which presents a problem, as LD can coexist with other conditions, particularly with attention deficit/hyperactivity disorder (ADHD).

Also, the definition applies to the school-aged child, and has no reference to a developmental continuum on LD. Yet language and language-based abilities play a crucial role in LD. Given that more than two-thirds of all preschoolers with disabilities are diagnosed as having a speech and language disorder as their primary disability, and given that over 90% of school-aged students with LD were found to have a speech, language or hearing problem (Gibbs & Cooper, 1989), it appears that most children diagnosed with LD may be language-impaired.

Part of the difficulty arises from the fact that although a *neurological origin* for the disability is assumed, there is no hard evidence or an assessment method that can make such a diagnosis accurately based on neurological evidence. There is a collection of neurological *soft signs* (see below) sometimes associated with LD, but they are not consistent enough to make a reliable determination.

It may be that a significant number of small anomalies, such as abnormal patterns of neuronal migration or organisation, groups of underdeveloped or immature neurones, or congenital spots of scars, develop in the brain in prenatal development. The growing brain attempts to compensate for these problem areas by 'rewiring' around them, which in turn may scramble normal information processing just enough to make the above-named tasks quite challenging (Farnham-Diggory, 1992).

Prevalence

Many difficulties arise in making accurate estimates of incidence, mainly due to the definitional issues. In the school-aged population, it has been estimated at 4%–5%; when ADHD coexists with LD the incidence goes up to 11% (Pennington, Groisser & Welsh, 1993).

Characteristics commonly associated with learning disabilities

The summary in Table 12.1 amply demonstrates the *heterogeneity* of children with LD. Not all children have all of these characteristics; the individual profiles of children with LD are more diverse than similar. Although some of these characteristics (e.g. reading, writing difficulties) become salient by school age, they are all developmental attributes usually discernible at an earlier age with careful observation. Table 12.1 is a list of common characteristics (based on McCormick, Loeb & Schiefelbusch 1997, p.79).

Early language-based learning disabilities

As is made clear in the definition, language is the central domain of development (see Chapter 10) implicated in LD, although it may occur also in non-verbal domains (i.e. mathematical abilities). *Language processing-based classifications*

Characteristic	Child behaviour descriptives	
Metacognition deficits	Use of inefficient and/or inappropriate learning strategies; at times having a lack of strategy.	**TABLE 12.1**
Disorders of attention	Distractibility, impulsivity, favours speed over accuracy, 'sticky' attention (perseveration).	**Characteristics of children with learning disabilities**
Poor spatial awareness	Difficulty in orienting to new surroundings and finding his way; gets lost easily.	
Confusion with directions	Difficulty in sorting out directionality concepts such as right–left, up–down, and compass directions.	
Difficulty with opposite concepts	Appears unsure and confused with polar concepts, i.e. light–dark, small–large, light–heavy.	
Poor motor coordination	Generally clumsy; trips over and loses balance often, runs into things, poorly coordinated with body in space.	
Poor fine motor skills	Difficulty in small-object manipulations; poor pencil or scissors grip; lack of refined, precise movement, overshooting.	
Insensitivity to social cues	Inability to interpret facial expression or body language; inappropriate actions to social context.	
Inadequate sense of time	Poor understanding of time concepts and relating self to tasks in time; difficulty in understanding temporal sequencing, as in events of the day.	
Visual perceptual problems	Often evidenced as letter reversals in writing, or difficulties in shape discrimination, figure ground discrimination, focusing and accommodation problems.	
Memory problems	Inability to remember simple sequences or find objects in known locations; memory problems in auditory sequencing.	
Social immaturity	Appears to act younger than age with little awareness of impact of behaviour on others; inability to predict consequences of behaviour.	
Auditory processing deficits	Difficulty with phonological awareness, speech discrimination, difficulty in suppressing background noise.	
Receptive language deficits	Inability to follow oral directions without repetition; inadequate vocabulary skills; difficulty in following group conversations and discussions.	
Reading difficulties	Sound sequencing, word recognition and comprehension errors; difficulty in following lines and monitoring comprehension.	
Written language problems	Difficulties in handwriting, spelling, text structure, sentence structure, organising sequence of ideas in composition.	

of children with LD have been particularly helpful, as they highlight the variability in the profiles of these children, many of whom can be then identified during the preschool years (Wiig, 1990; Gerber, 1993; Talay-Ongan, 1994).

Auditory perceptual problems.   Characterised by inattentive, confused or distractible behaviour, a child with auditory perceptual problems is likely to experience difficulties in phonological and phonemic awareness, and speech sound discrimination (see below). Associated problems may be inability to attend to foreground auditory stimuli and difficulties in discriminating environmental sounds. Also noted are difficulties in locating the source of the auditory stimuli or associating the sound with its source, synthesising or blending speech sounds to form a meaningful whole or, conversely, segmenting or dividing words into their constituent sounds.

Linguistic processing deficits. Closely related to auditory perceptual problems, these hierarchically manifest themselves at phonological, morphological (word formation), syntactic (sentence structure) and semantic (word and contextual meaning) levels. These levels of linguistic information processing are sequential (see below), yet often they need to be analysed concurrently for correct and stable meanings to be attached to them. A child with LD may exhibit deficits in learning the rules at each level, and often fails to relate the surface meaning to the deep structure (implied meaning) of spoken language.

Cognitive-processing deficits. In addition to the above, and perhaps interacting with it, the child with cognitive-processing deficits may misinterpret non-linguistic signals such as facial expressions, intonational patterns, body language, gestures and environmental cues. Other areas of deficit may be associated with poor cause–effect relations and symbolic play, making illogical deductions based on previous knowledge, and insufficient generalisation of information across contexts. Linguistic information tends to be interpreted in a concrete/literal sense, rather than on figurative/abstract implications, a skill acquired developmentally.

Memory deficits. A child with LD who exhibits memory deficits may experience difficulty recalling phonemes or word sequences, or may substitute words in a sentence-recall task. He may show particular difficulties with structurally complex and abstract sentences that rely on semantic and syntactic transformations.

Evaluation deficits. Characterised by an impairment in monitoring and self-correcting of errors in content or production of language, by school age the child experiencing evaluation deficits may give the impression of functioning with reduced logical operation abilities. Frequent errors in reaching conclusions and drawing inferences can also be observed.

Language difficulties associated with learning disabilities are summarised in Table 12.2 (based on McCormick, Loeb & Schiefelbush, 1997, p.84).

Closer look: specific reading disability

Specific reading disability, or *dyslexia*, is the most common form of LD. Efficient reading depends on rapid, accurate and fluent decoding of phonemes and attaching word-level and sentence-level meaning to them. A very impor-

Language domain	Difficulties	
Phonology	Delayed speech-sound acquisition Perception and production deficits in complex sound configurations Inefficient use of phonological code in short-term memory	**TABLE 12.2** **Language difficulties in LD**
Syntax	Production of less complex and shorter sentences for age Failure to encode all relevant information in utterances Difficulty with negative and passive constructions, relative clauses and contractions Difficulty with verb tense, plurals, possessive pronouns Delayed acquisition of morphological rules for use of auxiliary verbs (i.e. is, am), modals (ie., might, could), prepositions (i.e. under, over), conjunctions (i.e. because)	
Semantics	Problems in word-finding and definitions Too literal and restricted word meanings Excessive use of filler and non-specific terms (i.e. thing, stuff) Problems in understanding some conjunctions (i.e. but, if, or) Problems in understanding and use of relational terms	
Pragmatics	Difficulty with questions and requests for clarification Difficulty in initiating and maintaining conversation	

tant subskill in the reading process is that of *phonological awareness*, which manifests itself in the ability to analyse and manipulate speech sounds within words and syllables, to identify, count, reorder and delete them. If this process is impaired, reading will be slow, laboured and inaccurate, accompanied by poor comprehension (Lyon, 1995).

Phonological awareness may be deficient as a result of impaired *rapid sequential processing* in both visual and auditory modalities (Tallal, Miller, Bedi, et al., 1996). It can also be related to a defect in phonetic representation in *working memory* long enough to comprehend its meaning (Mann, 1994).

Neural bases for reading

Let us put together the *neural* bases for reading and information-processing approaches in order to understand the problems involved in specific reading disability (please refer to Chapter 4).

In reading, the visual pathways of both eyes carry the image of the printed word to the visual cortex in the occipital lobes of the brain. The next stopover is in Wernicke's area in the left temporal lobe, which has the translation of written language into its speech sound equivalents as a part of its major responsibility in processing language and extracting meaning. Visual information received by the right hemisphere needs to be transmitted by the corpus callosum, the wide band of fibres connecting the hemispheres.

In reading out loud, the information is forwarded to Broca's area in the left frontal lobe, which is responsible for the motor planning of speech output.

Both visual and auditory channels have the responsibility to monitor the comprehension of contents of the read material to see if it makes sense against what we know about the world. In skilled readers, such feedback prompts reviewing the read word or sentence until it is 'sensical'.

It becomes obvious that the system can have a dysfunction along one or more points of organisation in this process. Remembering that reading is embedded in language, and that reading disability is a language-based disorder, right- and left-hemisphere processing styles also may come into play.

- *Successive processing*, which allows the synthesis of information serially, is important in processing syntactic structure and contextual grammatical aspects of language, and is controlled by the *left* hemisphere (automatised organised speech).
- *Simultaneous processing*, which allows spatial–conceptual comparisons of all units of information in relation to each other, is important in logical grammatical aspects of language, and is controlled by the *right* hemisphere (comprehension of visual-spatial relationships) (Das & Varnhagen, 1986).

Indeed, *neurological* findings in dyslexia seem to support the organisation presented above. Abnormalities attributed to early brain development are found in neuroanatomical studies of young adults with dyslexia (whose brains have been analysed after dying from other causes). Underdeveloped temporal-parietal (auditory processing and syntax) and parieto-occipital (visual processing) regions in the left hemisphere, and a smaller corpus callosum, are reported (e.g. Filipek, 1995).

Studies in neuroimaging using positron emission tomography (PET) and magnetic resonance imaging (MRI) (see Chapter 4) also suggest that reading involves the simultaneous activation of many cortical networks involved in language and visual processing, as well as attention and planning. Findings include:

- decreased activation in the left Wernicke's area during phonological awareness (rhyme detection), and semantic processing (understanding word meanings) tasks;
- dysfunction of the central visual pathways leading to the occipital lobe; and
- abnormalities in thalamus and frontal lobes, associated with attention and planning.

Furthermore, possibly because so many brain regions are affected, up to 50% of children with LD are reported to have additional coexisting (*co-morbid*) impairments that hinder school adaptation, which include the following:

Impairment in executive functions.   Executive functions include having a set of strategies/procedures to attain a goal, as manifested in the inhibition of certain responses (impulse control, self-regulation), formulation of sequences in problem-solving (selective attention, creativity), and a reference in memory for problem-solving resources in the future (Denckla & Reader, 1993). Essential in school-related tasks in the long run, these metacognitive skills are exhibited in completion of homework and projects, sustaining attention in class and in self-control of disruptive behaviour.

Attention deficit hyperactivity disorder.   ADHD is estimated to coexist in 35% of children with LD (Light & DeFries, 1995). Characterised by inattention, impulsivity and hyperactivity, these children often lack the motor inhibition and reflective skills necessary for task completion.

Memory impairments.   These are reflected in diminished skills in listening, remembering and repeating auditory stimuli, particularly in dyslexia, and are related to phonological processing skills (Clark & Uhry, 1995).

Social interactive difficulties.   These are reflected in poor social comprehension, inability in social perspective-taking, poor pragmatic language skills and misinterpretation of body language (Shapiro & Gallico, 1993). Consequently, children with LD may be socially isolated, overlooked or rejected by peers.

Emotional and behavioural disturbances.   These may be the effect of repeated negative school experiences and other contextual and temperamental mismatches (Talay-Ongan, 1997). Common manifestations include conduct disorders, withdrawal and depression, poor self-esteem and self-image, chronic frustration and anxiety reactions. Acting-out in class is often a call for attention that the child is not able to secure academically or socially. LD accounts for a significant proportion of children dropping out of school and getting into trouble with the law.

Identification and assessment

Core symptoms of LD that are detectable from preschool years include delays in language, scattered attention and behaviour, impairment in social interactions, poor impulse control and scattered motor skills (Reynolds, Elksnin & Brown, 1996). Unfortunately, formal assessment and intervention for LD are usually initiated during school years, only *after* a cycle of failure has begun, although LD is a developmental phenomena:

- Children who later developed reading problems were found to exhibit decreased mean length of utterance, syntactic complexity and phonological accuracy at 30 months, lower receptive language and object-naming scores at three years, and impairments in phonological awareness and letter-sound knowledge by five years of age (Scarborough, 1990).
- Infants whose speech-sound discrimination skills were poor at 12 months were found to have lower receptive language scores at three and five

years of age, compared to their peers with adequate phonological processing (Talay-Ongan, 1996).

■ Kindergarten children with difficulties in word-finding skills, listening comprehension and phonological processing were found to be more likely to exhibit problems with reading, and reached target levels after a six-week training program in these skills (Dermody, 1990).

School readiness evaluation tools which incorporate measures of language function, sound-symbol association skills, phonological awareness skills, short-term memory function and rapid retrieval ability from long-term memory appear to be better predictors of children who are likely to struggle with specific learning disabilities in school (Badian, 1995). Some of these tools include:

■ Test of Phonological Awareness (Torgesen & Bryant, 1994);
■ Test of Awareness of Language Segments (Sawyer, 1987);
■ Lindamood Auditory Conceptualization Test (Lindamood & Lindamood, 1979);
■ Digit Span Subtest, WISC-III;
■ Rapid Automatized Naming Test (Denckla & Rudell, 1976).

For the school-aged child, a comprehensive psychoeducational assessment is necessary. There may be associated problems that make learning difficult, which need to be considered. These include some medical problems such as epilepsy, diabetes, chronic kidney and liver disease, as well as the after-effects of meningitis, encephalitis and traumatic brain injury. Sensory impairments of vision and hearing also need to be ruled out. Psychosocial effects such as poverty, malnourishment, problems associated with dysfunction in the family, abuse, neglect and other stresses and traumas pose serious threats to learning as well as the overall wellbeing of the child. Common assessment tools for LD include the following:

■ *Kaufman-Assessment Battery for Children* (K-ABC), which yields measures of sequential processing, simultaneous processing, mental processing composite and achievement (Kaufman & Kaufman, 1993).
■ *WISC-III* (Wechsler, 1991; see Chapter 11), useful in measuring general ability, memory and spatial abilities. Scattering of scores among subtests, particularly between verbal and visual performance, often yields diagnostic and planning information.
■ Tests of executive functioning measuring ability to initiate problem-solving activities, to organise and implement flexible problem-solving strategies, to maintain sustained attention, and to inhibit impulsive behaviour and distractability (Denckla & Reader, 1993). Examples are the *Test of Variables of Attention* (Greenberg, 1990), and the *Wisconsin Card Sorting Test* (Grant & Berg, 1993).
■ Language functioning, assessed by *Clinical Evaluation of Language Func-*

tion—Revised (Semel, Wiig & Secord, 1995). A common measure for visual perception is the *Bender-Gestalt Test* (Bender, 1946). Achievement tests include *Woodcock-Johnson Psycho-Educational Battery—Revised* (Woodcock & Johnson, 1989) and *Wechsler Individual Achievement Test (WIAT)* (Wechsler, 1992), which assess the seven areas mentioned in the definition of LD (oral expression, basic reading, comprehension, maths calculation and reasoning, listening comprehension, and written expression).

INTERVENTION

Intervention for LD needs to be multifaceted, and must take into account the *adaptive and self-concept variables* of the affected child just as vigorously as it addresses the cognitive skill areas. It may be necessary to incorporate the child's skill areas as well as disabilities in programming and teaching.

■ Social skills training may be crucial in the development of a healthy sense of self in relation to others and the promotion of self-esteem.
■ The child and his family may benefit from psychological guidance services, which promote better understanding of and assistance in mutually facilitative interactions, as well as community and educational support services.
■ The child may need assistance in the areas of study skills, time management, organisational skills and self-regulatory strategies.
■ Teachers working with the child in the mainstream also have support and training needs that should be considered.
■ Most children with LD are within regular classes, but the challenges do not get any easier with age unless they acquire strategies and support for dealing with them. Schools need to adjust to the children, as children must make adjustments to educational settings.
■ The heterogeneity in the profiles of children with LD necessitates a multidisciplinary assessment and individual educational planning (IEP). Many instructional strategies can be integrated into the educational and home environments, as long as there are viable lines of communication and cooperation between home and school.

As *phonological awareness* has been established as a clear precursor of reading skills in young children, the implementation of activities to promote this skill in preschool may serve as a safety net for children at risk. Some activities that may be integrated into early childhood curricula (Catts, 1991; Talay-Ongan, 1994) include:

■ beginning speech-sound awareness activities, such as nursery rhymes, poems, fingerplays, and songs with materials that contain rhyme, alliteration or nonsense sound sequences;
■ sound-play activities, such as creating rhyming or alliterative sound

sequences, activities involving the 'sound of the day', making speech-sound collages;

■   rhyme, alliteration and sound judgment tasks, such as finding rhyming and non-rhyming pairs, identifying whether pairs of words begin with the same sound or not; judging the length comparisons between words, and decisions on the odd word out in a series with common phonological structures;

■   segmentation and blending tasks, such as counting the syllables in words, separately pronouncing each syllable, and isolating syllables in phonemes in words, then blending syllables and or phonemes into meaningful units;

■   sound-manipulation tasks, such as syllable or phoneme deletion, segment addition, segment substitution, and initial phoneme reversals (e.g. *lood guck*).

ATTENTION DEFICIT/HYPERACTIVITY DISORDER

Many of the behavioural features of LD may be present in this group of children as well because of the high incidence of coexistence of the two conditions. Although attention deficit/hyperactivity disorder (ADHD) is characterised by short attention span, impulsivity, distractibility and hyperactivity, without necessarily the specific learning disabilities, 25% of children with ADHD are estimated also to have a learning disability; an additional 25% have other academic problems (Barkley, 1990).

The 'disruptive behaviour disorders', which include *oppositional defiant disorder* and *conduct disorder*, are reported to coexist in 30%–50% of individuals with ADHD. There also seems to be an increased risk of mood disorders, including depression and anxiety, in this population. ADHD is reported to be the most common neurodevelopmental disorder of childhood, with an incidence of 3%–5% in school-aged children and a ratio favouring boys by as much as 4:1 (American Psychiatric Association, 1994).

ADHD has a considerable history of being defined and redefined; our understanding of the disorder does not yet appear to be adequate. Like LD, it used to be called minimal brain damage. In the last decade it has been called attention deficit disorder with or without hyperactivity. Currently, it is thought to have two major dimensions, those of *inattention,* and *impulsivity/hyperactivity.* The disorder can be:

■   ADHD–inattentive type;
■   ADHD–impulsive/hyperactive type; or
■   ADHD–combined type.

According to the most recent Diagnostic and Statistical Manual of Mental Disorders (DSM IV, 1994), prior to a proper diagnosis the symptoms of ADHD must:

- be present for at least six months;
- be maladaptive to a degree not consistent with developmental expectations;
- be present prior to seven years of age;
- be observable in two out of three settings (e.g. home, clinic/office, school);
- not be due to a pervasive developmental disorder (see Chapter 15) or psychotic disorder, or primarily due to another mental disorder.

The behavioural diagnosis of ADHD needs to meet the following criteria:

A. Symptoms of inattention
- Often fails to give attention to detail or makes careless mistakes.
- Often has difficulty sustaining attention.
- Often does not seem to listen.
- Often does not follow through on instructions and fails to finish tasks.
- Often has difficulty organising tasks and activities.
- Often avoids or dislikes tasks that require sustained mental effort.
- Often loses things.
- Is often easily distracted
- Is often forgetful.

The *ADHD–inattentive type* must meet seven out of nine of these criteria.

B. Symptoms of hyperactivity/impulsivity
- Often fidgets or squirms.
- Often leaves seat when remaining seated is called for.
- Often runs about or climbs excessively in inappropriate situations.
- Often has difficulty engaging in activities quietly.
- Is often on the go, like 'being driven by a motor'.
- Often talks excessively.
- Often blurts out answers before questions have been completed.
- Often has difficulty waiting a turn.
- Often interrupts or intrudes on others.

The ADHD–impulsive/hyperactive type must meet seven out of nine of these criteria. The ADHD–combined type must meet both sets of criteria.

Unresolved issues in diagnosis

Some issues in the diagnosis of ADHD with the DSM-IV criteria that have been highlighted and need further attention (Barkley, 1995) include the following.

Age-related issues.   The criteria, having been developed on children four to 16 years of age, may *falsely* identify preschool children. The ADHD-impulsive/hyperactive type may be a developmentally earlier stage ADHD–combined type, or a different disorder altogether, as longitudinal data suggest that childhood symptoms of hyperactivity are related to adolescent negative outcomes, while those of inattention are not.

Gender-related issues. Criteria need to be adjusted for the gender of the child diagnosed. Males with ADHD demonstrate more aggressive (oppositional defiant) behaviour and conduct disorder than do females.

Duration of symptoms. The six-month duration requirement seems unsubstantiated, as particularly preschool-aged children may show remission of symptoms within 12 months.

The difficulty in accurate diagnosis of ADHD, and the debate surrounding whether or not it really exists in some children, become understandable in view of the above criteria, which are quite subjective and imprecise. Many of these symptoms are observed in children in a preschool classroom, where the contextual demands of the learning environment and teaching philosophy tend to be much more accommodating of child characteristics. Yet many parents and early childhood professionals express concern in reference to particular youngsters whose attention and activity levels appear to be atypical. Certainly by school age, when the learning environment demands become considerably more structured, children with symptoms of ADHD stand out and face adaptive, emotional and cognitive challenges, the age factor being accounted for in the DSM-IV criteria.

Naturally, the list of symptoms provided in the above diagnostic criteria is not exhaustive. Individual differences among children with ADHD is considerable. In addition to short attention span, distractibility, impulsivity and hyperactivity, children with ADHD may display low frustration tolerance and a general lack of motivation. They are easily bored and discouraged. They also seem to lack the reflective skills to learn from their errors, or to appreciate the long-term consequences of their behaviour. Children with ADHD–inattentive type may have a high threshold of arousal and slow reaction times. Disinhibition of responses may affect their social relationships. It must be noted, however, that in the areas in which they are interested and enthusiastic, these children can get seriously involved and achieve highly successful outcomes.

Preschool children with ADHD

Developmental stages of attention (see above) are helpful in ascertaining attentional difficulties in young children. Activity levels are not always stable measures on which to base a diagnosis and, in children with coexisting language problems, there are further problems in determining developmentally appropriate levels of impulsive or antagonistic behaviour. The findings of a longitudinal study shed some light on the issue of ADHD in preschoolers (Palfrey, Levine, Walker & Sullivan, 1985):

■ Of a cohort of 174 children followed from birth to the second year at school, 41% exhibited attentional and activity level responses that were of concern to the parents; most of these concerns were minor and transient, peaking at 42 months.

■ Of this percentage, behaviours in 13% were judged serious enough to warrant intervention; in 8% symptoms settled before kindergarten; and in 5% of the total children definite and persistent problems of attention-related deficits remained in school years.

■ Persistent attention problems in these children were associated with preschool social-emotional difficulties, developmental lags and single-parent families.

■ Of the children with persistent attentional problems, 45% had reading problems by the second year at school (compared with 13% of children without attentional problems); 37% were reported as having poor academic output and received remedial educational services.

It should also be noted that communication disorders are consistently associated with behaviour problems: 59% of three-year-olds with expressive language delay were found to have behaviour problems, compared with 14% of their controls, persisting to eight years of age (Stevenson, Richman & Graham, 1985).

Preschool-aged children tend to reject peers who are aggressive and hyperactive. When defiance was associated with aggression in preschoolers, poor outcome at adolescence (delinquency, conduct disorder, antisocial personality and substance abuse) was found to rise significantly (Satterfield, Swanson, Schell & Lee, 1994). A recent review has also documented the chronicity of preschool hyperactivity and subsequent difficult behaviour into adolescence (Campbell, 1995).

Early identification of and intervention for preschool ADHD appears crucial in view of developmental evidence highlighting the social cost to society of ignoring the problem.

Causes of ADHD

The aetiology of ADHD is presumed to be neurogenic, and to be related to *executive function* impairment associated with the frontal cortex. Subtle structural and functional deficits are reported to exist in the brains of individuals with ADHD.

■ In particular, it is thought that the frontal lobes and the rest of the brain regions do not communicate adequately because of a deficiency in dopamine and norepinephrine, the very neurotransmitters enhanced with medication in the treatment of the disorder (Cook, Stein, Krasowski, et al., 1995).

■ The frontal lobes, basal ganglia and corpus callosum are found to have lower metabolic rates in ADHD, where various neuroimaging techniques, including PET, are employed (Mercugliano, 1995).

■ The most common aetiology of ADHD is *genetic* transmission, although the particular gene or genes that contribute to the disorder are still under investigation (Faraone & Biederman, 1994).

■ Also, there seem to be a number of *prenatal* and *postnatal* influences contributing to the disorder, which include brain infections, fragile X syndrome, inborn errors of the metabolism, low birthweight, prenatal exposure to lead, alcohol and narcotics, birthing complications, sex chromosome disorders such as Kleinefelter or Turner syndrome (see Chapter 2) and *neurofibromatosis* (Bathshaw & Perret, 1992).

■ Of children with Tourette syndrome, a neuropsychiatric disorder of childhood onset characterised by multiple motor and vocal tics which wax and wane, 80% are reported to have coexisting ADHD and LD (Robertson, 1994).

Assessment

A comprehensive assessment of a child with suspected ADHD needs to include *medical, developmental* and *educational* components. Many issues and assessment tools discussed in reference to evaluation of LD may also apply to young children with ADHD, particularly if coexistence of the two conditions is suspected.

Developmental assessment should focus on gross and fine motor abilities, visual motor integration, visual and auditory short-term memory, receptive and expressive language functions, sequencing abilities, and attention and related behaviours. *Educational assessment* is appropriate for school-aged children, and requires classroom observation as well as formal test administrations. Generally, individual testing, including WISC, have not been found reliably to discriminate children with ADHD from their normal peers (Barkley, 1991).

Some rating scales have been developed for teachers and parents to use in children with suspected ADHD, which may be helpful in assessment and planning:

■ *Conners' Rating Scale* (Conners, 1976). One of the most widely used rating scales, it contains a 39-item Teacher Rating Scale and 98-item Parent Rating Scale, as well as a modified 10-item Parent/Teacher Questionnaire, made up of overlapping items, which is useful for reliability indications in medication trials.

■ *Child Behaviour Check List* (Achenbach, 1978; 1991). Carefully developed and standardised instruments for the diagnosis of a wide array of psychopathologies of childhood, it is normed for age groups of four to five, six to 11 and 12 to 16 years. It is more suitable for use by professionals than by parents.

In recent years, a computerised testing known as *vigilance testing* has been developed to provide an objective measure of sustained attention, with norms for different ages:

■ *Connors' Continuous Performance Test (CPT)* (Connors, 1992). The child is instructed to press the appropriate key for any letter except X. Norms are available from four to 18 years.
■ *Test of Variables of Attention (TOVA)* (Greenberg, 1990). The child is presented with geometric shapes on a computer screen and instructed to respond accordingly. The test measures errors of omission, commission and reaction times. Norms are available from six to 15 years.

Intervention

Children with ADHD are likely to encounter a number of difficulties in academic, social and emotional domains. Comprehensive intervention should target as many of these as possible, and involve the child (where appropriate) alongside the family and teacher in management. Multi-disciplinary assessment and intervention may be necessary, particularly if LD coexists with ADHD. A speech language pathologist, psychologist, occupational therapist and teacher, together with the medical specialist and the family, are core members of the team. Frequent consultations and fluid communications, centred on empowering the child and the family, hold promise of positive outcomes. Home as well as classroom/school strategies are necessary to address common concerns in the child's educational planning.

■ Teaching needs to be directed to the child's strengths and abilities, and to organisation of the learning environment to make objectives achievable for the child.
■ Opportunities and strategies for maximising attention and concentration while countering impulsivity need to be actively planned.
■ Improving socialisation skills and offering opportunities to build self-esteem are crucial, and remain at the heart of positive outcomes.
■ Plans need to include assistance in overcoming learning difficulties, taking into account the child's motivation level, and an attribution of failures and gains to controllable versus uncontrollable causes.
■ Behaviour modification needs to be incentive-based, and cognitive behaviour therapy techniques should provide the child with default strategies and metacognitive skills to monitor performance and outcome in problem-solving skills in academic and personal–social arenas.
■ The family needs to be supported, guided and communicated with in an ongoing schedule.
■ The child's educational plan should be reviewed twice a year for progress, recalibrating the objectives as necessary.

Research report

The temperamental and behavioural characteristics of children (see Chapter 5) and their interaction with those adults responsible for their care and education may influence the manner in which some children with ADHD are viewed along the developmental spectrum. According to a recent study (Talay-Ongan, 1997):

- Of the four-, six- and eight-year-old children, all were rated as having a difficult temperament by both the teachers and the parents.
- Six-year-old children showed the best 'goodness of fit' in that they were not perceived to be so difficult, and elicited a more democratic teaching and parenting style; the trend was evident but less strong for eight-year-olds.
- The academic outcomes of the children and their socioemotional adaptation seemed to improve as the 'goodness of fit' improved.
- Two sets of identical twins with ADHD (each of whom was presumed to have the same behavioural profile), placed in different educational settings, were described as being 'hyperactive' and 'troublesome' by the teachers of one twin and as being 'full of energy and curiosity' by the teachers of the other twin.
- The teachers describing the children in a more positive light were found to employ predominantly authoritarian/democratic teaching styles compared with the teachers who viewed the children as having negative attributes.

Medication

Medications for many disorders act on immature or inefficient neurotransmitters which are localised or distributed throughout the brain, having a widespread effect on performance and behaviour. Stimulant medication such as dexamphetamine and methylphenidate (Ritalin) act on dopaminergic and noradrenergic neurotransmitter pathways and appear mainly to influence prefrontal, frontal and limbic systems, with benefits to behavioural inhibition, impulse control, selective attention, active working memory and executive functioning (Greenhill, 1992).

Their prescription and administration in children with ADHD must be medically initiated. Review of the medical literature indicates stimulants to be safe and effective in the management of child and adolescent psychiatric disorders (Gadow, 1992), although the long-term trials in ADHD have yielded mixed results, particularly where educational, behavioural and family support measures have not been put into place.

Alternative therapies

Alternative therapies such as diet modification and elimination diets, optometric training, Erlin tinted lenses, mega-vitamin dosages, kinesiology, patterning and sound therapy with modified acoustic characteristics do not have scientifically rigorous credibility, and have not been shown reliably to improve outcomes in ADHD. However, parents seek these solutions because *some* children appear to benefit from some applications. These interventions appear innocuous, and parents' choices need to be respected.

CONCLUSIONS

We have reviewed some basic characteristics of children with learning disabilities and attention deficit hyperactivity disorder. Both of these conditions are neurodevelopmental in nature, and exist in the years preceding formal school years. The children are of normal intelligence, and their difficulties are not necessarily precipitated by psychosocial stresses. Yet they often remain *marginal* children. Let's remember the nature–nurture debate: the biological predisposition to the condition may not change in the life span, but outcomes are dependent on the environmental variables.

Instead of expecting the *child to adapt to the environment* unilaterally, we should perhaps make an attempt *to adapt the environment to the child. The best predictor of future outcomes in children is the expectations put on them.*

13

Gifted and talented children

This chapter may challenge your traditional views, as *atypical development* is generally thought to include children with disabling conditions, where the *lack* of some attributes in certain developmental domains accounts for the adaptive problems. Here we are considering those children who have an *excess* of an ability or attributes within certain domains. Why should these children be seen as having atypical development? Is more of an ability always a ticket to better adaptive status? If not, what are the contributing factors to the outcome? How do the attitudes of society shape developmental course and outcome in gifted and talented children?

The previous two chapters, on cognitive power and mental retardation, and information-processing and learning disabilities, have set the stage for individual differences in cognition and adaptive development. Let us now consider the other end of the spectrum.

If you were the policy-maker . . .

In the 1980s many states in Australia embraced the wider definition of giftedness, and the special schools for the gifted were closed down while students with disabilities were progressively integrated into mainstream classes. Seeing this as the hallmark of egalitarianism in a society that scorns elitism, one state department of education proclaimed that all children had gifts and talents that needed to be fostered within an educational environment, and that special provisions were not necessary for children with superior ability.

It has also been argued that educating highly gifted and talented children within the regular classroom, which accommodates a spectrum of developmental needs, is against the contemporary view of inclusive education in the *least restrictive* environment, as confining these children to a heterogeneous classroom is the *most restrictive* option.

. . . what would your position be?

HISTORICAL PERSPECTIVES AND DEFINITIONS OF GIFTEDNESS

The dilemma presented above between seeing all children as having gifts and catering to the needs of children with superior ability suggests some controversy over issues surrounding the definition and provision of special services for gifted children.

With the psychometric approach to intelligence, IQ testing (see Chapter 11) has traditionally been the criterion for identifying gifted children, although current views reflect an evolution of ideas and concepts regarding this classification:

■ In the 1940s, it was held that having a high IQ score as measured by an intelligence test (135+) was associated with advanced emotional maturity, better reading scores, good health, advanced physical abilities, and possession of a wide range of interests, in addition to superior performance in thinking, reasoning and making judgments (Janos, 1987).

■ Such a unitary view of intelligence and giftedness was challenged by Guilford's multidimensional concept of intelligence, which included divergent and convergent thinking abilities, creativity, creative productivity, flexibility, fluency, originality, spontaneity, sensitivity to problems and improvisation (Guilford, 1967).

■ In the 1970s, an influential report advocated that gifted and talented children were those who were identified by professionally qualified persons, and who were capable of high performance by the virtue of their outstanding abilities in one or more of the following areas (Marland, 1972, p.10):
  ■ general intellectual ability
  ■ specific academic aptitude
  ■ creative and productive thinking
  ■ leadership ability
  ■ visual and performing arts
  ■ psychomotor ability.

Although objective and standardised assessment of creativity, visual and performing arts, leadership and psychomotor ability remains a problem area, such a multivariate definition pervades our thinking in giftedness today (Khatena, 1992).

The definition of giftedness may also reflect the purpose of identification. The *national resource* approach is based on an attempt to predict 'leaders of tomorrow', whereas the *special education* approach is primarily concerned with identifying gifted children to meet their current social-emotional and educational needs. Developmental needs of the children themselves seem to have a stronger support in research (e.g. Borland, 1986; Roedell, 1989). A working definition of giftedness is proposed as follows (Harrison, 1995, p.19):

A gifted child is one who performs or who has the ability to perform at a level significantly beyond his or her chronologically aged peers and whose unique abilities and characteristics require special provisions and social and emotional support from the family, community and educational context.

This definition seems to allow for individual intellectual and personality differences, cultural diversity and possible underachievement, as well as acknowledging that the regular curriculum may be insufficient for the gifted child. It also recognises a socioemotional vulnerability and the need for understanding and support of the gifted child and her family. If such children are constantly expected to accommodate to the norm, their exceptional potential in early childhood may never be realised (Harrison, 1995).

Children with *special needs* and *disabilities* are sometimes masked by a primary categorisation or label, which may prevent the realisation and cultivation of their special abilities. Children with learning disabilities, for example, are less likely to be referred for placement in a gifted program, compared with their non-disabled peers, although they are described in an identical manner (Minner, 1990). Children with visual, hearing or communication disabilities may often not be provided with the type of assessment that would unearth their special abilities.

Potential giftedness also needs to be looked at. There are children who have not had the platform to exhibit their special abilities and talents because of motivational or lack of opportunity factors. Children of migrant families, those from disenfranchised minority communities those living in remote communities, and those living in poverty are particularly underrepresented in programs for the gifted and talented.

Motivation, giftedness, practices: an intersection

Analyses of expressions of giftedness indicate some combination of above-average ability, creativity and task commitment, and motivation (Renzulli, 1978), or superior general abilities, special aptitudes, and the acceptance of the achievability of its expression provided that the person is motivated to achieve (Feldhusen, 1986).

Motivation seems to be the crucial element here, in that it bridges *potential* and the *performance* based on that potential (Gange, 1985). An individual may have superior potential in areas that relate to giftedness, such as intellectual, creative, socioemotional, sensorimotor and other domains, but for one or more of these domains to be realised as being a special talent the individual needs to be *motivated* to perform it.

Giftedness refers to the *ability*, while *talent* refers to *performance* of the giftedness in a specific domain, sparked by the *motivation* to express the giftedness. This concept allows for the *cultivation/development* of giftedness as the educational goal, rather than provision of specialised services for precocious children only. It also encourages the inclusion of *underachieving* children in gifted and talented programs. Motivation, then, is the window though which giftedness becomes visible as a special talent.

Different stages of development may allow for different expressions of gifted behaviour, interacting with motivation and the opportunity for such expression. Not all giftedness is obvious in early childhood, or discernible with standard measurement tools.

Facets of giftedness

Particularly when planning for the educational needs of the child, it is helpful to realise that giftedness is on a continuum. The following distribution is suggested with respect to IQ score intervals (Gross, 1993):

- *Moderately gifted* IQ scores fall between 130 and 145, with an incidence of 1:20.
- *Highly gifted* IQ scores fall between 146 and 160, with an incidence of 1:1000.
- *Exceptionally gifted* scores fall between 161 and 180, with an incidence of 1:10 000.
- *Profoundly gifted* scores are above 181, with an incidence of 1:100 000.

We have already commented on the limitations of the psychometric approach in the assessment of gifted and talented children. You may also recall that there are more contemporary approaches to conceptualisation and assessment of intelligence. Gardner's (1987) model of multiple intelligences suggests possible giftedness in one or more of the eight intelligences. Sternberg's triarchic, information-processing-based model of intelligence put forth that giftedness is associated with excellence in the following attributes (Sternberg & Davidson, 1986):

- deciding on the relevant problems that need to be solved;
- selecting appropriate means of solving those problems;
- deciding which intelligence components are called for in particular problems; and
- monitoring the obtained solutions against desirable outcomes.

Furthermore, gifted individuals are able to draw from two other means of knowing—insight and metacognition.

Insight allows for an efficient abstraction capability, by:

- distinguishing relevant from irrelevant information;
- synthesising the relevant bits of information into a meaningful matrix;
- incorporating new information with the old, based on the above.

Metacognition allows for reflecting on one's own thinking, by:

- *inference*, or discovery of relations between objects or events;
- *mapping*, or relating the aspects of different events to one another;

- *application,* or ability to make predictions based on mapping;
- *comparison,* or considering outcomes from alternative predictions; and
- *response,* or verification and communication of the solution.

Not all of these means of constructing knowledge, problem-solving strategies or metacognitive skills are normally evidenced in early childhood years, although gifted children may exhibit them. Let us briefly review the developmental course of giftedness in early childhood.

DEVELOPMENT AND GIFTEDNESS

From infancy, young children who are gifted appear to reach developmental milestones and norms considerably earlier than their same-age peers. The extent of earlier attainments may be related to the nature and extent of giftedness, and may cut across many domains of development, although the rate and distribution of skill acquisition show some variability. Such rapid rate of development and qualitatively advanced developmental profiles are not surprising, if giftedness is a biologically rooted phenomenon which culminates in advanced and accelerated integration of neural functions, including physical, sensory, emotional, intuitive and cognitive operations (Clark, 1988).

- In *motor development,* infants who are highly gifted are reported to sit unsupported at a mean age of 6.2 months, crawl at 7.6 months and walk at 8.7 months, and to exhibit precocious balance skills which contribute both to their advanced mobility and self-confidence (Gross, 1993).
- In contrast, *fine motor development* seems to lag behind the other areas, and may be exhibited in a child's understanding *how* to tie shoelaces, but an inability actually to perform the act with the necessary finger dexterity (Tannenbaum, 1992).
- In *cognitive development,* alert behaviour is exhibited as demonstrated by longer than expected periods of visual focusing on objects, intent listening and concentration, tactile exploration, intense curiosity, and a prolonged attention span.
- In *play,* children tend to display intensity of purpose and task commitment, particularly in exploratory and solitary play. A two-year-old may choose a book or a puzzle and be engrossed in it for more than half an hour; a four-year-old may be intensely involved with mastering an imaginative scheme she is absorbed in (Harrison, 1995). In interactive play, advanced development is evidenced in an interest in complex and rule-governed play, which may present a problem with preschool peers who drift to less challenging and age-level activities.
- Exceptional recall *memory* may also be evident, where toddlers can repeat songs or recite storybooks from cover to cover after a few readings.
- In *literacy* skills, early interest in letters and words followed by early

reading and writing are common, such that, by the time a child who is exceptionally gifted enters school, her reading accuracy and comprehension may be at the level of children who are three years older (Gross, 1993). The ability to understand complex mathematical concepts and logical operations at an early age is also often exhibited.

- Classification and labelling of, and an investigative attitude towards, objects of interest such as cars or animal and plant species are commonly reported. Children who are gifted appear to acquire knowledge effortlessly, to generalise it to novel situations, and to ask probing, often abstract and reflective questions.

Look at the narrative from a highly gifted young child presented below (David, age 3:1, cited in Harrison, 1995, p.34). What attributes seem to mark him as having superior cognitive ability?

> We got off the train and went to the Queen Victoria Building. A lady took a photo of the queen and a man took a photo of the king. It was just pretend, they were just pretend kings and queens. We saw teddies and some soldiers and some curling, winding stairs. We saw a big clock. The soldiers popped out the top and tooted their trumpets. And they had beautiful windows, beautiful cream sharks and a wooden pirate ship and a beautiful blue dinosaur popping out of the castle . . .

Children like David seem to share some characteristics:

- *Language skills* show a number of attributes that characterise giftedness. Advanced levels of *imagination and creativity*, as well as eloquence in the production of poetry, narratives and stories, are evidenced. It is not unusual for such children to be incessant talkers, and seekers of explanations.
- From a very early age children demonstrate an intense interest in the speech sounds and rhythms of language, and never tire of being read to. The onset of first words may be as early as five or six months of age (Hall & Skinner, 1980).
- *Syntactic and semantic skills* are marked by the use of complex constructions with extended vocabulary, where multisyllabic words can be correctly used in context. Children aged 30 months are reported to use words like 'ostracised' and 'incidentally' (Rogers & Silverman, 1988).
- Some children have an unusual development where, instead of producing language very early, they communicate non-verbally after the babbling stage, and start using complex constructions at the onset of verbalisation. Such children, however, maintain good receptive language skills during the silent period, which seems to be utilised for the rehearsal of various linguistic forms.
- Young children who are gifted often seek out older communicative

partners, and demonstrate an understanding of complex concepts and topics. They also have a keen sense of humour and take delight in creating jokes and puns.

In *social interactions,* advanced cognitive and linguistic functioning allows the young child who is gifted more mature and advanced-for-age relational patterns. The social skills of the young gifted child include more independence, social responsibility, prosocial behaviour and cooperative interaction, often exhibited in her play styles (Barnett & Fiscella, 1985). However, there are two elements that contribute to the nature and extent of *social adjustment*:

- *Degree of giftedness.* There is strong research support to indicate that children who are *moderately* gifted tend also to be well adjusted, popular among peers and socially competent, with fewer indications of psychological problems than the average population (Silverman, 1993). However, with highly and exceptionally gifted children, the discrepancy with same-age peers becomes so great that they are at risk of *social isolation* and are often found to be in solitary play, not because of social ineptitude but because of boredom and lack of satisfaction.
- *Age of the gifted child.* Younger children tend to be less cognisant of the differences between them and their peers, whereas older children become increasingly conscious of the difference, which may create feelings of discomfort and anxiety. These perceptions may lead the child to pursue various self-protective mechanisms, including denial of her own interests and abilities in favour of the socially popular ones, and even underachievement.

Some other characteristics of gifted children in the socioemotional domain include the following:

- Gifted children can develop *perfectionistic* standards for their peers as well as for themselves, prompting them to be condescending and competitive with other children. Such attitudes tend to increase the degree of social isolation of the gifted child, and may serve as motivation for underachievement, where she presents herself as being less capable in hopes of social acceptance (Delisle, 1992).
- Very high and unrealistic expectations of themselves may prompt children who are gifted to have self-doubt and feelings of inadequacy when they fail to achieve tasks in the first trial.
- A characteristic of gifted children is their ability to experience feelings and emotions very *intensely,* and to react to them with vigour (Silverman, 1993). Temper tantrums may ensue when they are frustrated. These children also have heightened sensitivity to others and a high ability to empathise. Emotional expression tends to be age-appropriate; nevertheless,

adults may expect the expression of their affect to be more restrained, on a par with their social maturity and cognitive and linguistic skills, which is often not developmentally justified.

- *Uneven developmental profiles* in children who are gifted, and the stresses put on them because of their superior ability, which does not always find its match in environmental and social facilitation, may make it difficult for parents, caregivers and teachers to know what to expect of them (Freeman, 1995).
- An area of precocious development in gifted children is in *moral reasoning*. It was Kohlberg himself (Kohlberg, 1964) who noticed that intellectually gifted children were able to make complex moral judgments considerably earlier than their same-age peers, and that some highly gifted primary school children showed evidence of functioning at the postconventional level, attained by less than 10% of adults (see Chapter 8).
- Young gifted children tend to develop a strong sense of *justice* and exhibit behaviours such as turn-taking, sharing equipment and negotiating conflicts verbally at an earlier age than their peers. In return, they feel vulnerable and are deeply hurt when peers are not yet developmentally able to show them empathy, or otherwise treat them equitably. This attribute also makes them prone to rebellion against arbitrary or authoritarian discipline, which demands compliance by the adult unilaterally (Delisle, 1992).

ISSUES FOR GIFTED CHILDREN

The *identification* of a child with lower levels of cognitive functioning rarely draws the controversy that the identification of intellectual giftedness may incur in early childhood. Some concerns are well founded.

- *Parents' initial reluctance.* Parents may be exploitative or be intimidated by the identification of giftedness in their child. Similar to the parents of other children different from the norm, parents of gifted children often experience difficulties in their interactions with the world of extended family members, school personnel, friends and others (Chamrad & Robinson, 1986). They have the same needs for support and informed discussion as other families with children with special needs.
- *Early childhood practice.* Introduction of literacy and numeracy skills in preschool (sometimes referred to as 'hothousing') is often seen as undue pressure placed on children to master academic skills at an early age, which is not compatible with developmentally appropriate practice if it disregards children's developmental levels. It is just as imperative, however, that educators do not 'hold back' children who are eager to explore at more advanced levels (Wolfle, 1990): children who become tuned out and

frustrated may seek attention in negative ways in an environment not responsive to their needs.

The advanced and distinctive development of the child who is gifted places demands on social and emotional development, which often results in *social isolation* and emotional sensitivity (Silverman, 1993). Since a sense of belonging is crucial to human development, early identification of giftedness is essential not only to the provision of learning experiences and interactions to match the genetic potential, but to minimising the possible social and emotional difficulties.

- Children who are gifted experience emotional problems mainly because they feel different from their peers and other people. Same-aged peers do not share the skills and interests of the child who is gifted, while older children tend to see her as being too young for a playmate. Loneliness as well as solitary play may result; children also develop a sense of reliance on adults (Whitmore, 1980).
- Advanced cognitive and social awareness may prompt gifted youngsters to be concerned about the ills of society such as ecology, conflict or racism, while their powerlessness to do anything about them leads to feelings of helplessness and depression. Their precocious imagination may also lead to development of fears earlier than other children (Porter, 1997).
- Gifted children are at ease with abstract and complex material earlier and construct knowledge in greater depth and breadth than expected for their age, while other domains of development (such as emotional or physical) may be at age levels. Such uneven development levels need to be accommodated in planning: children may intellectually understand some concepts while being emotionally stressed by their content (Morelock & Morrison, 1996).

EDUCATIONAL RESPONSIVENESS TO GIFTEDNESS

Gifted and talented children do not consistently receive special attention to cater to their needs, some reasons for which may be that society values certain forms of giftedness more than other forms. In Western societies talent in sports, for example, is allowed an entirely different kind of recognition, support and mobility than talent in science (Gallagher, 1991). Also, it is assumed that gifted and talented children will excel regardless of the obstacles they face; hence, special provisions for them are not necessary and are seen as being displaced from services to 'more needy' children.

There may be a limit to what teachers can provide for children with diverse and extensive abilities. The range of options outside the classroom includes acceleration, enrichment, withdrawal groups, streaming, special classes and special schools. Provision for gifted and talented students may be a complex process, involving branching or combined options (Braggett, 1994).

The following suggestions are made to accommodate the needs of the intellectually gifted youngster in early childhood settings (Harrison, 1995).

The *curricula* need to offer open-ended activities, aimed at promoting:

- higher-level (executive) thinking skills, such as analysis, synthesis, evaluation and problem-solving;
- ownership of learning, so that the child can pursue her own interests to a depth that satisfies her;
- intellectual risk-taking, as manifested in activities requiring creativity and divergent thinking;
- a higher degree of complexity and variety in content, process and product;
- less repetition and a faster pace than is usual for the child's age.

The *teacher* needs to:

- facilitate the child's achievement of skills, which are just ahead of present levels of development;
- make the tasks relevant, worthwhile and interesting, so the child has positive feelings of achievement associated with them;
- allow the child to feel safe about making mistakes and using trial-and-error approaches to solving problems.

ASSESSMENT OF CHARACTERISTICS

The following *characteristics* are *common in young gifted children* (compiled by Porter, 1997). These attributes also form the bases for an assessment tool for the identification of young gifted children, *Investigation of Talented Students* (Sayler, 1994), where each attribute is marked on an 11-point agreement scale, from 'strongly agree' to 'strongly disagree'.

Cognitive skills
- Masters a new skill with unusual speed.
- Has quick and accurate recall, demonstrating competence in a skill presented in the past.
- Has a keen sense of humour and often sees incongruities as being funny.
- Understands abstract concepts such as death and time.
- Displays great interest or skill in ordering and grouping of items.
- Remembers and makes connections between past and present experiences.
- Is unusually attentive to features in the environment.
- Understands things well enough to teach them to others.
- Exhibits deeper knowledge than other children of the same age.

Learning style

- Is attentive and alert.
- Is intensely curious and tends to become totally absorbed in one kind of knowledge.
- Displays a high level of planning.
- Uses unusual or imaginative methods to accomplish tasks.
- Displays unusually intense interest and enjoyment when acquiring new knowledge.
- Shows metacognitive skills in managing her own learning.
- Enjoys intelligent risk-taking.

Motor abilities

- Motor development proceeds considerably early compared with age norms.
- Makes interesting shapes and patterns with objects.
- Is skilful in putting together new or difficult puzzles.
- Is capable of locating herself in the environment.
- Takes apart and assembles objects with unusual skill.
- Identifies directionality (right and left).

Language skills

- Uses advanced vocabulary.
- Uses abstract language concepts such as metaphors and analogies.
- Makes up songs or stories spontaneously.
- Appears to modify her language for less mature children.
- Uses language for real exchange of ideas and information.
- Is able to carry instructions to do several things in succession.
- Reads, writes, or uses numbers in ways that are advanced for her age.
- Asks many questions, is driven by curiosity.

Social skills

- Is sensitive to the needs or feelings of other people.
- Uses verbal skills to handle conflict or to influence another child's behaviour.
- Might not display advanced behaviour in everyday situations such as dressing herself, possibly due to fatigue, perfectionism or stress.
- Has advanced play interests and behaviours.
- Demonstrates leadership skills.
- Is comfortable among older children and adults.
- Is often sought out by peers.
- Is looked up to by others for ideas and decisions.
- Accepts responsibilities usually given to considerably older children.

CONCLUSIONS

The young child who is gifted may be intellectually superior to her peers, and giftedness may manifest itself in precocious language skills, intuition, strong senses of aesthetics, social justice and humour, but the child is a *child, first and foremost.* Adaptive behaviour and learning are *emotionally* driven, and emotional acceptance and social support is where the gifted child is most at risk. An alienated, isolated child is not a happy child, whether gifted or impoverished. Wholesome development acknowledges the interrelatedness of all the domains of development; intellectual giftedness is not all that it *can* be if it is *not* couched in a positive sense of self reflected on the child from the peers and adults in her environment, and the socioemotional reciprocity and support implicit therein.

14

Auditory and visual impairments

Deafness and blindness are at the extreme end of the spectrum of perceptual disabilities. Degrees of hearing and visual impairment can be conditions accompanying such primary diagnoses as cerebral palsy, Down syndrome or developmental disabilities, or they can exist as 'stand alone' conditions. Those with normal hearing may think of deafness as a handicapping condition, while deaf persons in a hearing-impaired community may not be aware of a handicap in their everyday lives. Obviously, the context of interpretation is crucial to appreciating an experience which may be different from those considered normal. On the other hand, a child with a mild to moderate hearing loss *will* be at risk of receptive language disabilities, unless he is identified early in development and provided with appropriate services.

The disorders we review here pertain to the reduced *quantity* of auditory and visual information the brain receives via these two major input channels. (The group of disorders based on the *central processing* of visual and auditory information, which occur despite intact peripheral mechanisms of vision and audition, exhibit *qualitative* problems; these types of central perceptual disorders affect learning and language, and are discussed in Chapter 12).

HEARING MECHANISM

It is necessary to review some structural elements of the human hearing mechanisms before we talk about hearing impairment.

■ *The external ear* is made up of the pinna (the external ear cup) and the ear canal (external auditory meatus). It ends with the *tympanic membrane* (eardrum). The sound waves are collected by the pinna and carried through the ear canal, where the vibrations of the eardrum transmit the acoustic energy into mechanical energy in the middle ear.

■ *The middle ear* has three tiny bones (the hammer, the anvil and the stirrup), collectively called the *ossicular chain* because they are in touch with each other. The vibrations pass through the ossicular chain and are conveyed to the inner ear. Another important structure in the middle ear is the *eustachian tube*, which opens up to the nose and throat. Its function is to equalise the air pressure on both sides of the eardrum.

■ *The inner ear* contains the *cochlea* (the snail-shaped structure), which is lined with hair cells organised so that they respond to different sound frequencies. The mechanical energy is transferred to neural impulses in the cochlea, which extends to form the auditory nerve.

■ Also in the inner ear are the *semicircular canals*, which are three horseshoe-shaped tubes placed in three planes in space. These canals are filled with fluid, and contain tiny otoliths (stones) which move in the fluid as the head moves in space, stimulating the nerve endings. They are part of the *vestibular* (balance) system through which we can determine the position of our bodies in space. As we wait for the feeling of dizziness to subside after we spin around, otoliths are settling in after having sloshed around in the semicircular canals. (See Figure 14.1.)

■ *The auditory nerve* thus contains both vestibular and acoustic fibres. It passes through the brainstem and the thalamus, before the auditory

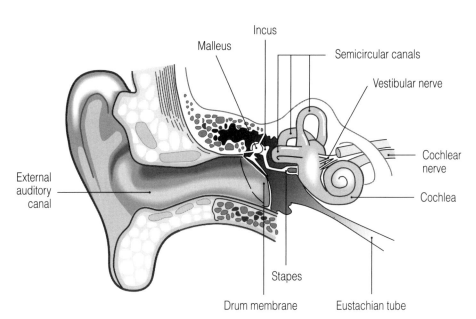

FIGURE 14.1

Structures of the ear

information is relayed to the temporal lobes of the brain, where it is analysed and connected with meaning (see Chapter 4).

HEARING ASSESSMENT

An *audiogram* is a graph that shows the two basic parameters of hearing: frequency and intensity of sound (Figure 14.2).

The horizontal axis charts the *frequency* (pitch) of the sound waves from a very low and base-sounding 125 Hertz (Hz; cycles per second) to the shrill and high-pitched 8000 Hz. Human speech production/reception is said to be within 500–4000 Hz.

The vertical axis indicates the *intensity,* or the loudness level of the sound. The flat line at the top portion of the audiogram which is marked zero decibel (dB) is the average human hearing *threshold,* where sounds are just barely heard across the measured frequencies. Thus, further away from zero means that more sound energy is needed to reach the barely audible level. Audiometric testing usually goes up to 100 dB, after which the intensity of sound can be perceived as vibrations through the tactile sense.

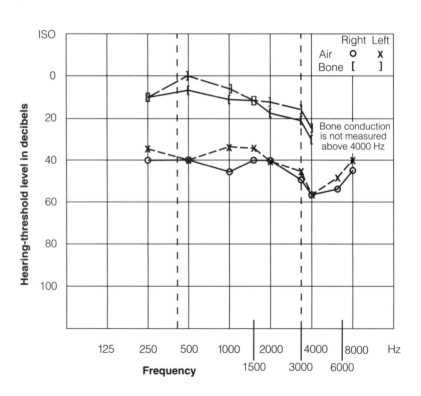

FIGURE 14.2

An audiogram and typical representations of hearing loss

Techniques in the measurement of hearing

Audiologists use various techniques and procedures in the assessment of hearing function. Some basic ones are the following.

Pure tone audiometry.   Presenting pure tones at each frequency, this technique marks the threshold of reception intensity in each ear. Delivered through earphones, hearing testing needs to be performed in a soundproof booth to eliminate the effects of ambient noise and environmental sounds.

Bone conduction testing.   This assessment involves the placement of a sound-generating device on the bone behind the ear (mastoid process), such that sound can travel to the cochlea by bypassing the external ear canal and the middle ear. The advantage of this procedure is that the inner ear function can be tested without being overshadowed by possible obstructions in the external and middle ear.

Speech discrimination testing.   This test involves the presentation of pairs of words that either are similar acoustically, but are different words (e.g. pat–cat), or are pairs of same words (e.g. pat–pat). The person is asked to indicate whether the two words, which are presented at comfortable listening levels, are the same or different. Such a test is useful in types of hearing loss with a significant sound-distortion element, and in assessing the efficacy of hearing aids.

Impedance audiometry or tympanogram.   The middle ear function is assessed by measuring the pliability of the eardrum. Normally the eardrum is not obstructed from free movement, and the movement response recorded is a bell-curve shape. A flat line is recorded if the tympanic membrane is prevented from movement by, for example, fluid accumulation in the middle ear cavity due to a middle ear infection.

Tympanography is particularly useful with young children because it does not require a behavioural response but can directly record the movement of the eardrum. It is a quick and non-invasive procedure, during which a plug placed in the ear delivers a stimulus. However, it is a *screening procedure only,* and is not to be seen as a proper hearing assessment.

Brainstem evoked potential measurement.   This assessment tests the integrity of the auditory pathways past the cochlea. It records the response to clicks of the brainstem nuclei with which auditory nerve fibres make synaptic connections. It may have clinical diagnostic significance in various brain tumours and pathologies of the neural auditory pathways.

Otoacoustic emission testing.   A fairly recent and non-invasive process, this test assesses the presence of an echo generated at the cochlea during normal hearing. Absence of the echo generally indicates impairment at the cochlear level. It can be used as a diagnostic tool to localise the damage causing the hearing loss, as well as a screening tool.

Assessment procedures for hearing need to be modified for infants and young children. When a behavioural response to sound is needed (e.g. raising a hand or lifting a finger), preschoolers are usually trained to manipulate objects, such as by placing pegs in a board or stacking ring towers in response to hearing in audiometric testing. Infants are tested by a procedure known as *visually reinforced infant audiometry,* where they are conditioned to respond to perception of a sound with the reward provided by the contingent clinician-operated toy animation. Formal testing begins after training.

HEARING IMPAIRMENT

Let us look at a possible format for average impairment to see how some of these clinical procedures can be used to describe levels of hearing loss:

```
0 dB⇓          Normal hearing
10 ─────────────────────────────
20             Mild hearing loss
30 ─────────────────────────────
40
50             Moderate hearing loss
60 ─────────────────────────────
70
80             Severe hearing loss
90 ─────────────────────────────
100
110            Profound hearing loss
```

Types of hearing loss can be described with respect to the structures involved, and can be classified as conductive, sensorineural, mixed or central.

Conductive hearing loss is usually associated with an intact cochlea and hearing nerve; the obstruction to hearing is in the external and/or middle ear and prohibits the sound from reaching the inner ear. In conductive hearing loss, there is uniform reduction in hearing acuity across all frequencies. The sound received is dampened, but there is little distortion to the speech signal. Conductive loss by itself would not exceed moderate levels of hearing loss, and tends to respond well to amplification. Furthermore, it may be reversible: hearing lost due to middle ear infection or a ruptured eardrum, for example, will return to normal levels with treatment.

Sensorineural hearing loss is caused by cochlear damage, or damage to the auditory nerve. The nature of the hearing loss is that higher frequencies suffer more damage than the lower frequencies. On the audiogram, this is known as a *sloping curve loss,* because of the decline of hearing as the frequency rises. Consequently, the incoming speech signal is distorted; i.e. those speech sounds containing high frequency such as s, sh, ch, z would not be heard fully, while the vowels, which are comprised of lower frequencies, can still be heard (see Figure 14.2). Sensorineural hearing loss is not reversible; the damage sustained is permanent, although amplification can be of benefit to improve the levels of hearing.

Mixed hearing loss is said to occur if a person has *both* a conductive *and* a sensorineural component in the impaired hearing profile. Of the two, the sensorineural hearing loss levels exceed those of conductive loss. Nerve loss is the more serious damage, and is the cause of severe to profound hearing deficits.

Central auditory deficits are said to occur if the structures responsible for carrying the auditory signals to the brain are intact, but the meaning to be derived from the stimuli is deficient, presumably due to a central nervous system *processing* deficit.

Sometimes hearing loss is described according to when in the life span the loss has been incurred (*age of onset*):

- *Congenital hearing loss* is present when the child is born, and is commonly associated with cerebral palsy, intrauterine rubella or Down syndrome.
- *Adventitious hearing loss* occurs any time after birth, and is usually attributable to such diseases as meningitis, or to accidents.
- *Prelingual hearing loss* is present before the child learns verbal language; most prelingually hearing-impaired children have congenital hearing impairments.
- *Postlingual hearing loss* is evidenced after the child has acquired spoken language; most postlingually hearing-impaired children have adventitious hearing loss.

The effect of a hearing loss on development of speech and language depends on three factors:

- Severity of the hearing impairment, and its stability. A mild conductive hearing loss due to chronic middle ear infection can clear with antibiotics or surgery, while some types of sensorineural hearing loss get progressively worse.
- Age of onset, identification and proper intervention. Prelingual deafness poses a significantly more serious risk for the development of oral/verbal communication.
- Whether the loss affects one ear (*unilateral*) or both ears (*bilateral*). Although a unilateral hearing loss is easier to manage, it accounts for only 20% of hearing impairment in children (Bess & Tharpe, 1984).

Causes of hearing impairment

Here are some common causes of hearing loss:

- Of all the *conductive hearing impairments* in children, over 90% are attributable to middle ear infections (Northern & Downs, 1991).
- *Sensorineural hearing loss* may be congenital and genetic. There are about 70 inherited syndromes associated with deafness, where deafness is usually transmitted as an *autosomal-recessive* trait (see Chapter 2).
  - *Treacher-Collins syndrome* is associated with a dominant gene disorder, and is characterised by atypical facial appearance with wide-set eyes, low-set ears with abnormalities to the ear canal and the middle ear.
  - *Waardenburg syndrome* is characterised by an unusual facial appearance, with different eye colours, a white forelock, and sensorineural hearing loss.
  - *Lawrence-Moon-Bidell syndrome* is associated with recessive genes, retinitis pigmentosa (progressive degeneration of vision; see below), and progressive hearing loss, general developmental cognitive delay and obesity.
  - *CHARGE association* is characterised by mixed hearing loss, as well as visual and other abnormalities.
  - *Down syndrome* is characterised by small ears and narrow ear canals, a high incidence of middle ear infections, and conductive hearing loss.
- Children with *cleft palate* (see Chapter 10) are susceptible to middle ear infections, as well as conductive (30%) and sensorineural (25%) hearing loss (Northern & Downs, 1991).
- *Prematurity* complications such as asphyxia, circulation problems and jaundice, particularly in neonates born under 1500 g, predispose the infant to sensorineural hearing loss (see Chapter 3). As noise can also induce hearing loss, the level of surrounding noise for a premature infant in an incubator, which can range from 60 to 80 dB, needs to be monitored carefully (Northern & Downs, 1991).
- *Maternal rubella* in the first trimester exposes the infant to a 30% risk of sensorineural hearing loss. Other *infections* which can cause hearing loss include toxoplasmosis, cytomegalovirus, herpes and syphilis (see Chapter 2).
- *Bacterial meningitis* carries a 10% risk of residual hearing loss, as do some antibiotic medications which can be toxic to the cochlea (e.g., neomycin).
- *Accidents* and *trauma* to the head or the ear can cause hearing loss, as can exposure to high-intensity (100 dB+) noise, associated with industrial noise and rock concerts. Protective earphones for the former are a necessary workplace safety measure; protection from the latter is unthinkable!

Middle ear infections

An overwhelming proportion of children (76%–95%) experience middle ear infection, or *otitis media*, at least once before they are two years of age (Bluestone, 1989). Chronic middle ear infection lasting more than two months causes mild to moderate conductive hearing loss. Antibiotic treatment (amoxicillin or ampicillin) usually clears the infection in less than a week; drainage of the fluid that has accumulated in the middle ear can take much longer. A series of infections may mean that the child spends most of his young life in reduced levels of linguistic input during critical periods for language, which may adversely affect language development and later academic performance. If left untreated, the infection can penetrate the bony structures or the cochlea, leading to serious complications.

One reason why fluid gathers in the middle ear is because in the young child the *eustacian tubes*, which connect the middle ear to the throat, are not yet sloping downwards to accomplish drainage effectively, but are level with gravity. Furthermore, they are usually clogged because of the infection.

Myringotomy is a surgical procedure where *grommets* (tiny aeration tubes) are inserted into the eardrum so that the *effusion*, or fluid buildup, is allowed to clear over a period of months. This procedure has significantly reduced the incidence of permanent hearing loss in young children with chronic middle ear infections (Bluestone, 1989).

Native populations such as Australian Aborigines, American Indians and Eskimos are at a greater risk of middle ear infections, and, because the availability of medical attention to these communities is limited, the incidence of persistent hearing loss is greater.

LANGUAGE DEVELOPMENT IN HEARING IMPAIRMENT

It is rare to diagnose hearing impairment in the first six months of life by the behavioural signs of the infant, because there is little discernible difference between the normal hearing and hearing-impaired child. It is therefore important for children in high-risk groups to be screened often for signs of hearing loss.

You may recall how the human infant is born primed to process and attend to auditory information, which constitutes a major input channel for the development of communication and socialisation skills. (For a review of developmental auditory skills in infancy, see Chapter 5.) The cooing and babbling will cease to be meaningful for the infant who is unable to hear others, to imitate or vocalise with caregivers, or to hear his own voice and sounds. Such vocal activity reduces in frequency and complexity after six months and disappears by one year of age in infants with hearing impairments.

An infant who fails to wake up from sleep to loud noises, or who fails to localise a parent's voice by turning to it by four months needs to be assessed for hearing function. If the child has experienced any of the factors associated with possible hearing loss, such as a family history of deafness, a maternal intrauterine infection, a postnatal infection such as meningitis, prematurity and NICU (neonatal intensive care unit) stay or anoxia, early assessment is imperative (American Speech-Language-Hearing Association, 1990).

The effects of hearing loss are most serious in congenital deafness. The interactive nature of cognitive, language, social and motor development means that lack of or problems with speech and language will invariably affect performance in other domains. Children who cannot hear speech do not learn to produce it in the absence of special training. Relatively few children with significant hearing loss develop *normal* oral-verbal language production and comprehension abilities.

Both physical indicators and behavioural indicators alert parents and teachers working with young children to seek referral for an audiometric assessment (DuBose, 1983).

Examples of *physical indicators* are:

- frequent complaints of ear aches and colds;
- discharge of fluid from the ears; sore red ears;
- complaints of ringing or buzzing sensation in the ears;
- persistent mouth-breathing and nasal obstruction.

Examples of *behavioural indicators* include:

- apparent lack of comprehension in following simple directions;
- failure to respond to questions or conversations appropriately;
- repeated requests for many words and sentences;
- inattentive behaviour; daydreaming;
- articulation (many omissions) and voice (monotone) problems;
- indicating a preference for high- or low-pitched sounds;
- disorientation and confusion when noise levels are high.

The degree of hearing impairment, and its relationship to the understanding and production of speech and language, is summarised in Table 14.1 (based on Anderson & Matkin, 1991; McCormick, Loeb & Schiefelbusch, 1997, p.90).

Some interesting findings in relation to severely hearing-impaired children include the following.

- About 90% of deaf children are born to *hearing* parents, and thus grow up in a world of spoken language.
- Among the deaf, those who have deaf parents usually do as well as or better on measures of written and spoken language than do those with hearing parents (Marschark, 1993). A possible explanation is that this

Decibel loss	Effects
25–35 dB (mild)	Some difficulty in hearing distant speech, unvoiced consonants, and difficulty in discriminating sound combinations; about 30% of speech signal is missed; listener fatigue and difficulty in keeping up with fast-paced peer interactions. *Interventions* include seating in front, hearing aids or FM system, speech therapy.
35–55 dB (moderate)	50% of the speech signal is missed; conversations within 2 m can be understood; problems with suppressing background noise are evident; articulation deficits, limited vocabulary, deficits in language use and reception are common. *Interventions* include hearing aids or FM system, lip-reading, speech therapy and remedial help in the classroom.
55–70 dB	Most speech signals are effectively missed; can understand loud conversations; but telephone conversations and class discussions are difficult; language is delayed and has reduced intelligibility; voice is monotone; syntactic deficits are common. *Interventions* include full-time amplification, special education placement, and speech and language therapy.
70–90 dB (severe)	All speech sounds are missed; loud voices close to the ear may be heard; vowels, but not most consonants, are discriminated; speech and language is defective, and likely to deteriorate without therapy. Full-time program for the deaf and total communication and amplification are needed.
90+ dB (profound)	All speech and environmental sounds are missed; vibrations are felt; vision is relied on as the major venue of communication; speech and language are of a very poor quality. School for the deaf and possible cochlear implant are needed.

TABLE 14.1

Relationship of hearing impairment to speech and language

group is immersed in sign language much earlier than the deaf children of hearing parents.

■ Profoundly deaf children have significant deficits in both spoken and written language. Although on non-verbal measures of intelligence hearing and deaf children exhibit *no* significant difference, deaf children are usually not very fluent readers, and experience difficulties with lip-reading and oral language (Braden, 1994).

APPROACHES TO LANGUAGE LEARNING

There is considerable controversy over how and where children with significant hearing impairment should be educated and taught to communicate. One group feels that they should be educated to become as much like their 'normal' hearing peers as possible; the other feels that the deaf community has little need to compromise, and can integrate the child within it. Naturally, the first group supports the *oral* mode of communication, while the second supports the *manual* or *signed* mode. Below are some of the approaches to communication for the deaf.

Oral method

Supporters of the oral method believe that the most normal mode of communication is the oral-verbal mode; thus, language should be acquired by encouraging lip-reading and utilisation of the residual hearing. The goal of this method is to integrate the person with hearing impairment into the hearing community.

Lip-reading

Visual information derived from the lip movements of the speaker, coupled with residual hearing, forms the basis of oral communication. The drawback of the lip-reading method is that many sounds that are acoustically different are produced with similar oral movements (e.g. pat, mat, bat), and some sounds are not produced visibly at all (e.g. k and g). Reliance on lip-reading alone (known as the *oralist* approach) does not seem sufficient for communication, with only about one-quarter of the children exhibiting intelligible speech (Trybus, 1980).

Cued speech

Used in conjunction with lip-reading, eight hand shapes are used to clarify the ambiguities encountered in lip-reading. Coupling lip-reading with manual cues seems significantly to improve the communication skills of deaf children in receptive language, but does not facilitate the acquisition of language.

Signed languages

Signed languages of deaf communities are not merely a collection of gestures but are valid, independent, rule-governed languages in themselves. Australian Sign Language is known as AUSLAN; in the USA, it is known as American Sign Language (ASL). These are not exact and parallel gestural translations of an oral language with signs for morphemes like the plural -s or past tense -ed, and finger-spelling of the words, which is known as Signed English. The grammatical forms of the two are different; in Signed English, the signs used are from AUSLAN but the grammatical form is spoken English.

Total communication

This approach combines *all* venues of communication, including lip-reading, AUSLAN, Signed English and residual hearing. Total communication develops both receptive and expressive communication skills, and seems to be a compromise between purely oralist and signing methods.

Amplification

Amplification can be achieved by a *hearing aid*, which has three components:

- a microphone, which converts sound energy to electrical signals;
- an amplifier and power supply, which increases the intensity of received sound;
- a receiver and speaker, which transmit the amplified sound through an ear mould placed in the external ear canal.

Hearing aids raise the level of sound intensity by around 20–60 dB (Sandlin, 1988). With proper training for their effective use and adjunct speech therapy, hearing aids benefit most children with hearing impairment. Most hearing aids fitted to children also have the capability to incorporate direct audio input, so that a teacher, for example, can transmit messages direct to the child from a wireless FM microphone that he wears (*FM system*).

> In Australia, the incidence of hearing impairment for children actually fitted with a hearing aid is 2.75 per 1000, and it is estimated that about 1% of the school population may be affected by various degrees of hearing loss (Upfold, 1988).

Bionic ear

In most cases of severe to profound hearing loss, the hair cells in the cochlea, which transform the auditory/physical information to electrical/neural messages to be carried to the auditory cortex by the auditory nerves, are destroyed. The bionic ear or *multichannel cochlear implant* is a surgically implanted device, which artificially stimulates the auditory nerve to produce hearing sensations by bypassing the hair cells and stimulating the auditory nerve directly. It contains a set of electrodes, a receiver stimulator, an ear-level microphone, a wearable speech processor, and a transmitting coil. Auditory signals entering the microphone are converted to an electric signal at the speech processor, which is then relayed back to the transmitter fitted behind the ear over the receiver. Australia is the world leader in the development, trial and manufacture of this remarkable technology, which has enabled profoundly deaf children to enter the world of sound.

In an intact cochlear system there are approximately 20 000 hair cells, each responsive to and responsible for resolving and transmitting a unique frequency in the spectrum of sound that the human hearing system is primed to process. The bionic ear, in contrast, has 22 electrodes planted in the inner ear which receive and transmit sound. As such, the device does not allow normal hearing but is an aid to hearing. However, the reports from adults with acquired hearing loss who have been fitted with a bionic ear indicate that the quality of received sound is quite adequate for the comprehension of speech (Mecklenburg & Brimacombe, 1985).

When hearing is augmented by lip-reading, speech comprehension is reported to improve significantly in most adults with cochlear implants (Dowell, Mecklenburg & Clark, 1986). Users of the device not only enjoy improved verbal communication skills, but are reported to hear environmental sounds, to monitor their own voices more effectively, and to be able to conduct telephone conversations (Brown, Clark, Dowell, Martin & Seligman, 1985).

The first children to be the recipients of a bionic ear were those who had had normal hearing and speech language, but had suffered meningitis with a subsequent hearing loss. All of these children adapted very quickly to the implant signal, and were able to comprehend language auditorily within five to six weeks (Nicholls, 1988). The next step was to see whether congenitally deaf children could utilise the degraded signals of the device and learn to listen to be able to acquire speech and language (Mecklenburg, 1988). Since then, the numbers of *prelingually deaf* children who have benefited from the device and acquired verbal communication have grown to hundreds.

VISUAL IMPAIRMENT AND THE VISUAL APPARATUS

Visual impairment varies considerably with respect to type, degree of visual limitation and extent to which the handicap interferes with daily adaptation and functioning. All visual handicap is likely to hinder learning; however, the extent of that barrier depends on such variables as the age of onset, degree of vision loss, aetiology of the visual impairment, and the extent and nature of associated disabilities.

Let us begin by reviewing some of the basic structures of the human visual system (Figure 14.3), as an image is refracted onto the transparent cornea and lens of the eye, until the image is deciphered at the occipital cortex:

- The covering of the eyeball is a leathery, thick, white substance called the *sclera,* which becomes the transparent *cornea* in the front of the eye. The sclera is covered by the *conjunctiva,* which nourishes it with the blood supply through tiny vessels (as manifested in the red eyes from a sleepless night or inflammation—*conjunctivitis*).
- The *iris* is the coloured part of the eye, and its function is to dilate or constrict according to the amount of light available. The *pupil* is the actual opening in the centre of the iris.
- The *lens* is behind the iris and is anchored to the inner surface of the eye by the ciliary muscle. It adjusts to focus visual stimuli by being pulled to become thinner or relaxed to become fatter, in a process known as *accommodation.*

FIGURE 14.3

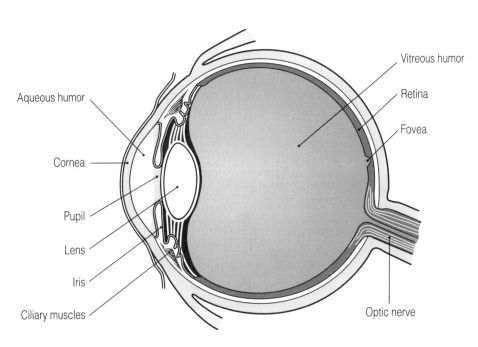

Basic structure of the human eye

- The eye is filled with a translucent jelly called *vitreous humour*, which prevents the eye from collapsing and nourishes it. The *retina* forms the inner lining of the eyeball. The retina is attached to the *choroid* (middle layer), which is then attached to the sclera (outer layer).
- Retina is actually composed of the *nerve endings* of the optic nerve, and is thus a window to the brain; examination of the eye with a light reveals the state of the brain in cases of trauma. The light-sensitive surface of the retina has *rods* (which process black and white information and are important in night vision) and *cones* (which process colour information). The image that falls on the retina is upside down, and back to front.
- The centre of the retina is called the *macula* (or *fovea*), and is made up of all cones. This is where the image is sharpest (20/20 vision). The projections of the rods and cones converge at the *optic disc*, which actually is the blind spot in our vision, forming the *optic nerve* and travelling towards the brain.
- Images fall on two halves of the retina (the nasal, toward the nose; and temporal, towards the temple halves). The optic nerve carries visual information from these halves, such that at the *optic chiasm*, the nasal halves *cross* and reach the opposite side (*contralateral*) *occipital lobes* in the cortex. Fibres from the temporal halves do *not* cross, and reach the same-side cortex (*ipsilateral side*) as each eye. Such neural organisation produces different *visual field damages* according to where the disruption or *lesion* is located (see Figure 14.4).

FIGURE 14.4

**Pathways of
the optic system**

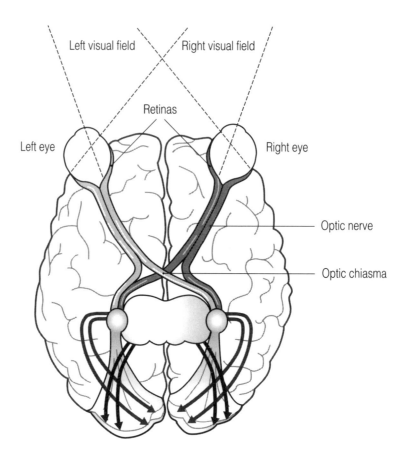

- The neural information received in the occipital cortex is righted from the upside-down position, analysed and connected with meaning.
- We can move our eyes without having to move our head, because each eye has six eye muscles that coordinate and move the eyes in synchrony. When the pull on these muscles is uneven, squint or strabismus results.

ASSESSMENT OF VISUAL IMPAIRMENT

Identifying infants with partial visual loss is considerably more difficult than identifying those who have total blindness. Assessing visual function in infancy is important, particularly if the infant's vision is obstructed because of a cataract or some other treatable condition. The visual cortex, in the absence of visual information transmitted from the eyes, will atrophy and cease functioning. Known as *cortical blindness*, this condition is not reversible once the stimulation-sensitive critical period is over (see Chapter 4). In human infants this critical period is the first three months after birth. Tests to evaluate visual acuity and functioning in infants are summarised below.

Fixating and tracking. As infants are able to *fixate on and track* objects in their visual field soon after birth, one test of visual functioning is to assess this skill. This is usually accomplished by observing how well the infant looks at and follows a person. Although it is a crude measure, the lack of looking and following response in a baby may be a sign of serious difficulties.

Teller test. Similarly, infants have a preference for looking at and processing complex visual information. In an assessment procedure known as the *preferential gaze* or Teller test (Teller, McDonald & Preston, 1986), the infant is presented with two stimuli, one with a solid colour, and another with stripes. Normally, infants choose to gaze at the one with the stripes, as that is the more visually complex stimulus. The stripes are presented in gradually finer lines, and the infant's visual acuity is determined by noting the point at which he stops showing a preference for stripes over solid colours. (If the spacing between the stripes is not resolved, the pattern will appear to be blurry like a solid colour, and the infant will no longer prefer it over the solid colour.)

Opticokinetic response. This response is elicited by having to focus on successive objects in motion. A good example is trying to count the power poles as you are driving: typically the eyes jiggle in trying to follow the object before the next one appears. This response is present in the young infant, and to evaluate it a black-and-white striped cylinder is twirled in front of his eyes. If the eyes do not move, the assumption is that the child has a vision loss, as normal focusing would result in a rapid tremor.

Evoked visual response (EVR). Similar to the evoked auditory response we mentioned above, EVR measures the cortical reaction to visual stimuli such as lights or patterns. Electrical recordings are made by placing electrodes on the back of the head over the occipital lobes.

ERG (electroretinogram). ERG records the electrical activity recorded from the retina as a response to visual stimuli. As it indicates the functioning of the retina, normal reactions in a blind child means that the impairment is either in the optic nerve or the cortex.

Ophthalmoscope. A specialised instrument that allows the examination of the inside of the eye, the retina, the optic nerve and the blood vessels feeding the system, the ophthalmoscope is used in routine visual function assessments.

Retinoscope. This instrument allows for determination of refractive errors without a behavioural indication from the child, by using multiple lenses until the correct refraction is obtained.

Development of visual skills

The newborn has a large cornea and a lens which is nearly spherical. The macular vision is not yet fully developed, although the occipital cortex is well myelinated. In all, 80% of children are born long-sighted (*hyperopia*). Visual acuity improves rapidly and reaches about 20/100 by six months (see below). Despite some variability, children reach adult visual acuity by three years of age (Peckham, 1986).

Binocular vision, which is essential for depth perception, is well established by six months of age. By then the accommodation ability of the lens has also improved significantly. (For a review of developmental visual skills see Chapter 5.)

Visual acuity evaluation

For older children and adults, the traditional way of evaluating visual acuity is by reading the letters on the *Snellen chart*. Based on this measure, perfect visual acuity is defined as 20/20, which means that at a distance of 20 feet (about 6 metres) the smallest objects or letters on the bottom row of the chart are legible. Modifications are necessary for children who are not able to identify the letters of the alphabet.

- For children aged two to four years, pictures of animals, toys and other familiar objects are substituted for letters, but their relative sizes (to the Snellen chart) are maintained. These images are projected onto a screen, and the child is asked to name them.
- For children aged four to six years, a common chart uses the letter E in various positions. The child is asked to demonstrate with his fingers which direction the arms of the E point towards.
- 20/40 vision means that the objects that are readable to that person at 20 feet can be read by a person with normal vision from 40 feet, a mild acuity problem.
- A *partially sighted* child has an acuity between 20/70 and 20/200.
- *Legal blindness* is defined as a visual acuity of 20/200 or less in the better eye. While the normal visual field covers about 105°, legally blind individuals are defined as those who have only a 20° visual field. Both of these measures are taken after wearing corrective lenses, where applicable.

Causes of visual impairment

The prevalence of blindness is much higher in the developing countries than in industrialised nations. The major causes of blindness include trachoma, measles, smallpox, gonorrhoea, syphilis, tuberculosis, bacterial meningitis, malnutrition and vitamin A deficiency; 70%–90% of such visual impairment is preventable. Among industrialised societies, prenatal causes are predominant in congenital blindness, although in Australia there is a high incidence of trachoma among the Aboriginal population (Lowe, 1990).

The *causes of early blindness* and visual impairment include inherited blindness, intrauterine infections and genetic mutations as the largest group (44%), although about 15% of children born will not have known causes. Maternal rubella during pregnancy accounts for 10% of children born with a visual handicap. The incidence of visual impairment due to oxygen poisoning associated with prematurity care (retrolental fibroplasia or retinopathy of prematurity) has fallen with better awareness and monitoring.

More than two-thirds of congenitally blind children have associated handicapping conditions such as mental retardation (25%), hearing loss (10%), cerebral palsy (6%), epilepsy (8%) and congenital heart defects (6%) (Lowe, 1990). Acquired cases of visual impairment encountered later in life are associated with neoplasms (tumours) and other disease processes of the visual system, injuries and poisoning.

Among blind children, about one-quarter are totally blind, with no ability to distinguish light and dark; another one-quarter have some light and shade perception; the remainder have sufficient vision to see up close or read with enlarged print (Buncic, 1987).

DEVELOPMENT AND VISUAL IMPAIRMENT

Visual impairment may not be obvious to the parents if the infant's eyes look normal. When the child's development is somewhat delayed, particularly in the areas of social interaction and motor milestones, parents become concerned about their child's difference. Developmental delay may be mistaken for mental retardation until a correct diagnosis is made.

Attachment and blind babies

Selma Freiberg's classic work with blind infants (1974; 1977) indicates that blind babies start to smile at about four weeks, at the same time as sighted babies; however they smile less often. Whereas sighted infants' smiles in response to seeing their caregivers increase by two months, blind babies' smiles become less frequent, less intense, and more fleeting by this time. This gives the impression of an indifferent and serious-looking baby, who does not take delight in mutual gaze, the very basic behaviour that underpins attachment. Parents often reach the false conclusion that the baby is rejecting them, and/or that he is depressed.

- Most mothers of blind babies were found to withdraw from their blind infants: they provided physical care, but gradually gave up trying to elicit smiles, initiate play or engage in social interactions. Some mothers felt that they did not love their infant.

- Freiberg's careful analysis, however, indicated that the mothers were not reading the proximity-seeking and proximity-promoting behaviours of the infants because they were concentrating on the infants' face. Actually, it was the *hands* and the body of the blind infant that expressed what the eyes did in a sighted infant.
- Parents were shown how their blind infant stopped moving when the mother came into the room, or how the infant moved his hands in response to the father's voice instead of smiling.
- When parents of the blind infants learned to respond to this alternative set of attachment behaviours, their relationship with the babies improved. As parents now provided them with the much-needed social facilitation, the blind babies developed more normally.
- The 'blindisms', which are characterised by behaviours such as rocking, head-banging, sucking and other repetitive, self-stimulatory behaviours, were not evidenced in blind babies who were responded to in a reciprocal and positive manner by their parents.

Language and blind babies

Children who are congenitally blind need special help to learn many concepts that are relevant to language acquisition, because of limited incidental/discovery learning opportunities. Delayed cognitive development and difficulties with social interactions are the two major factors contributing to language delay in infants who are severely visually impaired. In the absence of an associated disability such as cerebral palsy, the delay in cognitive development in blind babies is most likely the result of limited mobility and environmental exploration opportunities.

- Like their sighted peers, blind children use 'sighted' words such as *look* and *see.*
- By three years of age, most blind babies have a comparable *MLU* (see Chapter 10) for their age (Landau & Gleitman, 1985).
- Blind children tend to use *limited naming or requesting*, relying instead on reference to routine phrases and people's names.
- They do not refer to objects and events beyond their reach or touch, and they rarely use *function words* such as *there, gone* or *more* (Orwin, 1984).
- Children with a severe visual handicap may provide detailed explanations of objects in their environment with little real understanding. Such limited shared understanding in communication places a strain on social interactions (Andersen, Dunlea & Kekelis, 1984).
- Because children are not able to determine the proximity of their partner when communicating, they often speak too loudly, smile too often, and use eyebrow movements that appear inappropriate in the communicative context (Park, Shallcross & Andersen, 1980).
- Higher incidence of *echolalia* is reported: three-year-old blind children

used 20% echolalic utterances with their mother and 35% such utterances with unfamiliar adults in their spontaneous speech (Kitzinger, 1984).

Cognitive development

At no time in development are cognition and motor development intertwined more than in infancy, and *both* these processes are *significantly* affected by vision. Maintenance of muscle tone, for example, is in part mediated by vision; in its absence, motor skill acquisition is delayed.

Blind babies acquire all their motor milestones later than their sighted peers, and usually skip crawling. Walking may be delayed until well after two years. Fine motor skills are also delayed and may be atypical.

Limitations in the sensory experiences prohibit the child who is visually impaired from reaching for objects. This has the impact of delaying *object concept* from one to three years. Environmental exploration is delayed due to later onset of walking. Understanding similarities between objects and the ability to make generalisations may also lag, leading to rote and artificial-sounding verbalisation (Langley, 1980).

- Cognitive deficits are *less* significant when the child is *guided* to explore in the early sensorimotor period, together with verbal labels for descriptions of the experience.
- Blind children show equivalence to their sighted peers by preschool years, when logical thought begins to replace visual perception as the major learning channel (Reynell, 1978).
- After five years of age, the verbal subtests of the Wechsler Intelligence Scale for Children (see Chapter 11) yield a score with improved reliability for the assessment of intellectual functioning.
- Severe visual impairment may prohibit the development of an accurate body image, stemming not only from limited exploration but from parental overprotection (Cratty, 1981).
- The adverse affects of visual impairment on the development of play skills may be reduced by early intervention (Wyver, 1997).

INTERVENTION AND FACILITATION IN VISUAL DISABILITY

Referral for assessment

Significant visual handicap is usually salient enough to get the proper medical and educational attention. Parents usually seek medical attention when their infant fails to engage in eye contact with them, or does not show interest in brightly coloured and moving objects, or fails to protect himself from approaching objects (e.g. a ball). Abnormal jerky eye movements (*nystagmus*) or uncoordinated eye movements (*strabismus*) are often associated with visual impairment.

With mild and moderate visual impairment, teachers are a major source of referrals for children. Certain physical and/or behavioural indicators may constitute grounds for *visual assessment* (Hollins, 1989).

Examples of *physical indicators* are:

■ crossed eyes; watery or inflamed eyes;
■ recurring sties, and red, swollen or encrusted eyelids;
■ dizziness, nausea, frequent headaches.

Examples of *behavioural indicators* are:

■ frequent rubbing of the eyes;
■ tilting the head when looking at books;
■ holding material too close to the face in inspection or reading;
■ squinting and/or frowning; evidence of visual strain;
■ covering one eye when looking at printed material;
■ complaints about inability to see clearly.

Early identification and implementation of an infant stimulation (and parent support) program for visual impairment can start at six months of age. Home-based programs, where the teacher facilitates exploration, language and motor skills, as well as parent support, seem to be successful (Sonksen, Petrie & Drew, 1991). Preschool experiences need to be planned to emphasise language skills, self-help and functional independence, as well as social interactive skills, in which the blind child has needs for additional feedback. Self-stimulatory behaviours also need attention.

Children with better than 20/200 vision can be successfully integrated into mainstream classrooms with modifications in the teaching materials made available to them. Large-print books or technology-assisted magnification are needed. Although the child can move around without assistance, care is called for in the playground and in other safety/risk situations. Wyver and Livesey (1997) argue that the motor skills of children with a visual impairment should be assessed routinely and intervention programs for these children should target kinaesthetic and motor skills.

Those children who are totally blind utilise the tactile perception channel in reading (*Braille*). Audiotaped or talking books, and the computer-assisted interactive technology which can respond to verbal commands, make school adaptation significantly easier, as do devices such as Optacon, which can convert typed text into Braille, and others which achieve Braille conversions from computers.

As might be expected, the long-term positive outcomes in persons with visual impairment usually depend on intelligence and the severity of the impairment. Another crucial element is the social environment, which should foster empowerment rather than helplessness.

GLOSSARY OF TERMS IN VISUAL IMPAIRMENT

These definitions are compiled separately for ease of reference, but should be interpreted in light of the above information (based on Fielder, Best & Bax, 1993; Hollins, 1989):

Amblyopia: impaired vision in the absence of any apparent reason such as any disease processes of the retina or the optic nerve or the usual refractive errors.

- *Strabismic ambylopia:* double vision in poorly coordinated eyes, where the child needs to suppress the messages from the deviating eye; is often corrected by patching the correct eye, followed by medical intervention.
- *Vision-deprivation amblyopia:* impaired vision due to insufficient visual stimulation during the critical periods in infancy; may be due to marked ptosis, congenital cataracts or corneal opacities.
- *Ametropic amblyopia:* impaired vision because neither eye has received a clear retinal image from the critical periods in early childhood, due to a huge refractive error.

Aniridia: lack of part or whole of the *iris,* the coloured, light-regulating part of the eye.

Anisocoria: inequality in size between the two pupils, suggesting uneven innervation.

Cataracts: opaqueness of the *lens,* which may be associated with trauma, congenital rubella, CMV, toxoplasmosis, trisomy 13 and 18, diabetes, galactosaemia (intolerance to milk products), Lowe syndrome (amino acids in the urine).

Coloboma: a scar that occurs on the iris or the retina; seen in CHARGE association.

Glaucoma: raised pressure inside the eyeball due to poor drainage of the intraocular fluid from the tiny canal in the cornea; leads to perfusion of blood through the capillaries. If untreated, can result in visual field loss and blindness.

Goniotomy: surgical intervention for the relief of glaucoma.

Infantile macular degeneration: loss of most acute cone/colour central vision with functional peripheral vision (Best's disease).

Keratoconus: loss of curvature or irregular curvature of the *cornea,* the transparent structure over the lens, which may result in astigmatism not correctable with glasses; sometimes observed in postlatency years in children with Down syndrome.

■ *Corneal opacities:* cloudy appearance and loss of transparency of the cornea, which may be due to congenital eye defects, trauma, congenital glaucoma, rubella or external infections; likely to impair vision if present from birth.

■ *Keratoplasty:* corneal transplant in treatment of corneal clouding.

Miosis: unusually small *pupil* or one that fails to dilate in the dark.

Mydriasis: unusually large pupil, resulting in photophobia or aversion to light because of pain.

Nystagmus: involuntary rhythmic oscillation of the eyes, which can be horizontal, vertical or rotary, where the eye movements appear jerky due to the faster movement in one direction; a normal reaction if you are counting trees in a speeding car or spinning; often seen in neural disorders such as multiple sclerosis, brainstem and cerebellar tumours/disease and hydrocephaly.

■ *Nystagmus secondary to visual impairment:* bilateral visual loss from any cause may include nystagmus, especially if loss of vision occurs before two years of age and rarely if loss is after six years.

Optic nerve atrophy or hypoplasia: degeneration of the optic nerve related to developmental defects, malformation of the skull, hydrocephalus, intracranial tumours or other disease processes.

■ *Optic neuritis/papillitis:* inflammation of the optic nerve.

Red–green colour blindness: sex-linked recessive trait; ~8% of white males but only 0.5% of females are affected; normal visual acuity.

■ *Achromatopsia:* total colour blindness with severely reduced acuity, photophobia and nystagmus.

Ptosis: drooping of the upper lid, where more than the normal area (1.5 mm) of the cornea is covered; is usually accompanied by other visual disorders such as strabismus or ambylopia, or signalling third cranial nerve (regulating motor control to the eyelid) paralysis.

Refractive errors: unclear image falling on the retina due to (i) length of the eyeball, (ii) irregularities of the cornea, or (iii) lack of proper accommodation of the lens. In normal sight, refraction falls precisely on the fovea.

■ *Myopia (nearsightedness):* the eyeball is too long, so that the image falls *in front of* the retina; corrected by concave [)(-shaped] lens.

■ *Hyperopia (farsightedness):* the eyeball is too short, so that the image falls *behind* the retina; corrected by convex [()-shaped] lens.

■ *Astigmatism:* the curvature of the *cornea* is irregular, while the eyeball is the right size; corrected by a cylindrical lens.

Retinitis pigmentosa (RP): slowly progressive and steadily increasing bilateral loss of vision, starting with the rods and peripheral vision; more severe in the recessive and sex-linked cases (20/200 by age 20), resulting in degeneration of the optic nerves.

Retinoblastoma: malignant tumour or cancer of the retina, filling the eye.

Retrolental fibroplasia (retinopathy of prematurity; ROP): separation of the retina so that it looks like a fibrous membrane behind the lens; related to oxygen intake in premature and low-birthweight infants.

Strabismus: lack of coordination between the *movement* of the two eyes (wandering eye; cross-eyes; squint), which will impair depth perception if not treated in early childhood. However, because of lack of binocular vision and accommodation before four months of age, eyes may appear uncoordinated in infancy.

■ *Esotropia:* one eye turned in, often corrected in farsighted young children by corrective lenses; also known as accommodative esotropia.
■ *Exotropia:* one eye turned out, often because of uneven muscular pull on the eyes.
■ *Hypertropia:* one eye riding higher than the other due to disturbances in the vertically acting eye muscles.

Uveitis (choriditis/chorioretinitis/iritis): inflammation of the choroid, (the lining to which the retina is attached); common in juvenile rheumatoid arthritis and toxoplasmosis; may lead to cataracts.

Visual field defect: occurs because of damage to the optic nerve at different points between its exit from the eye and arrival at the cortex, *or* selective parts of the retina or occipital cortex.

■ *Optic nerve lesion before the optic chiasm:* loss of vision in both fields of one eye; total blindness in that eye.
■ *Optic nerve lesion at the optic chiasm:* loss of vision in the nasal retinal fields of each eye, which receive information from the (crossed) temporal *visual* field (what is out in the environment) for each eye; results in *temporal hemianopia,* or *tunnel vision.*
■ *Optic nerve lesion after the optic chiasm:* Loss of vision in *half* the visual field of *each* eye.

CONCLUSIONS

We have reviewed some of the medical, psychological and educational considerations in perceptual disabilities. Their profound impact on development is made more obvious by considering the disabilities in hearing and vision. Helen Keller, we salute you!

15

Autism and Pervasive Developmental Disorders

Autism is a perplexing disorder, and has been the subject of many debates with respect to its causes. Our current views place autism in a spectrum of conditions known as the pervasive developmental disorders.

HISTORICAL PERSPECTIVES

The description and diagnosis of autism as a separate entity from childhood psychosis were made by Leo Kanner in 1943 in a now famous paper. He postulated the features of autistic aloneness, desire for sameness, islets of ability and an innate inability to form relatedness with people from the beginning of life in his classic description of 11 children, calling their condition *early infantile autism* (Kanner, 1943). He also noted that the mothers of these children appeared to be cold and emotionally reserved, and that they had probably been at the root of the problems in their children. We know today that mothers do not cause autism in their children, and if they appear distant it is probably the *effect,* and not the cause, of battling with this enigmatic disorder.

Autism is not a progressive disorder; it does not get worse, deteriorate or become degenerative over the life span. However, it is a *developmental* disorder of early origin and, as such, affects the whole of development and the process of building up experience from infancy onwards (Frith, 1989). It is currently classified as a pervasive developmental disorder. The incidence of autism is about two per 10 000; the ratio of affected boys to girls is as high as 5:1 at the higher end of the ability range and 3:1 at the lower end (Lord, Schopler & Revicki, 1982).

The group known as Pervasive Developmental Disorders (PPD), according to the Diagnostic and Statistical Manual of Mental Disorders (American Psychiatric Association, 1994), include the following:

- autistic disorder
- Asperger disorder
- pervasive developmental disorder—not otherwise specified (PDD-NOS)
- Rett syndrome
- childhood disintegrative disorder (CDD).

The features common to these include communication disorders, impairment in reciprocal interactive skills, and a prevalence of stereotypical patterns of behaviour in interests and play (Volkmar & Rutter, 1995). Current thought in childhood psychopathology has recognised the commonality of these three prototypical impairments across the five disorders, and grouped them under the umbrella of PPD, of which autism is the most severe expression.

AUTISM

Autism is the most prominent disorder in the PPD group. It is helpful to review the criteria set by DSM-IV (American Psychiatric Association, 1994) in the diagnosis of autism. The child diagnosed with autistic disorder needs to have the onset of the symptoms of delay or abnormal functioning in *social interaction, language for social communication* and *symbolic or imaginative play* areas prior to three years of age, and must meet at least six of the 12 criteria listed below:

A. Social interaction
- Impairment in the use of non-verbal behaviours such as eye contact, facial expression, body postures, and gestures regulating social interaction.
- Lack of peer relationships appropriate to developmental level.
- Absence of spontaneous seeking to share enjoyment, interests or achievements with other people (e.g. by a lack of showing, bringing or pointing out objects of interest).
- Lack of social or emotional reciprocity.

B. Language used in social communication
- Delay or absence in the development of spoken language (without an attempt to compensate through alternative modes of communication such as gesture or mime).
- In verbal children, an impairment in the ability to initiate or sustain a conversation with others.
- Stereotyped and repetitive use of language or idiosyncratic language.
- Lack of varied, spontaneous make-believe play or social imitative play appropriate to developmental level.

C. Patterns of behaviour, interest and activities

■ Preoccupation with one or more stereotyped and restricted patterns of interest that is abnormal either in intensity or in focus.
■ Insistence on inflexible, specific, non-functional routines or rituals.
■ Stereotyped and repetitive motor mannerisms (e.g. hand or finger flapping or twisting, complex whole-body movements).
■ Persistent preoccupation with parts of objects.

Restricted social interaction

One of the earliest symptoms reported by parents of children with autism is a lack of moulding of the infant to their body as she was being held. Impaired social interaction is also discerned from an early lack of reciprocity in shared smiles, and a paucity of indications from the infant of pleasure at being picked up. Such an infant also appears quite content to be by herself, does not seek comfort when she is hurt, and fails to engage in eye contact or imitate the caregiver's facial expressions (Baron-Cohen, 1995).

Parents become increasingly aware of these patterns, which seem present from two to three months of age, and recognise other impairments which are more obvious as the child gets older (Seigel, 1996). The impairments in social interaction are manifest in a lack of interest in the thoughts and feelings of others, lack of empathy, lack of desire to establish friendships, a communication that is restricted to expression of needs and wants rather than a desire to acknowledge and be acknowledged by the caregivers, and impaired social understanding and imagination (see below).

Communicative impairment

Although delayed and deviant speech and language patterns are evident in autism, even in cases of relatively well-developed verbal skills the *pragmatics* of language, or its use for *social intentions*, is uniformly impaired (see Chapter 10). Many children appear to develop language in the first year of life only to gradually lose it; many such children remain mute and unable to use even gestural communication.

About half of children with autism do not use oral-verbal language, and are taught to utilise alternative augmentative communication strategies, such as communication boards, technology-assisted communication, or manual sign language (Prizant, 1996). Children who develop verbal language tend to show delayed onset of first words. Typically, the language used by children with autism is *echolalic,* stimulus-bound and idiosyncratic, while most of their normally developing peers use language creatively, interactively and generatively.

Features of difficulties associated with autism across language domains are summarised in Table 15.1 (based on McCormick, Loeb & Schiefelbusch, 1997, p.97).

Language domain	Difficulties and deficits
Pragmatics	Initiation and maintenance of conversations; paucity of eye contact and gestures; limited range of communicative functions; appearance of aloofness and lack of interest in interactions; echolalia; expressive speech sounds mere rote or memorised; not used for meaningful exchange.
Semantics	Unrelated or inappropriate answers to questions; better-developed vocabulary in particular interest area(s); verbal perseveration; an appearance of irrelevance of vocabulary which does not have personal use; word-finding difficulties; receptive language deficit
Syntax	Pronominal reversals (use of *you* for *I* or *me*); incorrect use of pronominal case (*her* for *she*), and gender confusions in pronoun use; use of shorter, less grammatically complex utterances for age.
Phonology	Difficulties with prosody: intonation inappropriate to the content of speech; monotonous pitch; sing-song, and pedantic voice quality.

TABLE 15.1

Language difficulties associated with autism

Echolalia

Echolalia may be defined as utterances repeated from an external source, with little apparent communicative intent for the listener. Often observed in the speech of a young child with autism, echolalia can be:

- *immediate* (the exact repetition occurs within seconds; often the last part of a sentence or question directed to the child is repeated);
- *delayed* (an approximation is produced some time after the original utterance; sometimes evidenced in repetition of TV commercial jingles, songs or prominent phrases);
- *mitigated* (echoing the utterance with some structural alteration or supplement; e.g. 'Would you like some milk?'—'Would you like some milk? Yes').

For the most part, echolalia is repetition without processing the meaning of the utterance, like parrot speech. However, there is evidence to suggest that it may have some communicative intent.

While not all echolalia is communicative, some is found to be used to gain adult attention (it begins when the adult's attention is diverted, and continues until the adult turns his/her attention back on the child), or to fill a conversational turn (Prizant & Rydell, 1984). Echolalia seems to decrease significantly by school age, at which time a substantial growth in vocabulary is seen.

The most persistent deficit in communication remains in the non-verbal domain of communication (eye contact, body language and gestural expressiveness), in which even the most high-functioning children experience difficulties unless they are immersed in specific behavioural interventions (Frea, 1995).

Autism and theory of mind

Given the fact that children with autism rarely engage in reciprocity of interaction, or mutual understanding and sharing, the communication problems cited above are to be anticipated. Recent advances in our understanding of such *lack of intersubjectivity* (absence of a shared reality between two persons) as causal explanations for autism within the theory-of-mind orientation have been an exciting and fruitful development (see Chapter 7 for a review).

Four progressive mechanisms culminate in a theory of mind, which allows children to decipher the needs, beliefs and intentions of others (Baron-Cohen, 1995):

- *Intentionality detector* allows for the capacity to interpret acts of motion as consequences of volitional mental states. It is dependent on vision, audition and touch.
- *Eye-direction detector* presupposes the ability to engage in mutual gaze and follow the other's visual regard.
- *Shared-attention mechanism* allows for the capacity to perceive that someone else is sensorially engaged in the same way as oneself, and that there is a common object of interest.
- *Theory of mind* is constructed based on the mental states cultivated by the first two mechanisms, and processed by the shared-attention mechanism, which forms the basis for the ability to understand and share the other person's thoughts, desires and intentions.

Baron-Cohen (1995) contends that the third (shared-attention), and therefore the fourth (theory-of-mind) mechanism, are absent in autism. Indeed, concepts of *shared* or *joint attention deficit* as a prominent marker of autism seem clearly established:

- Young children with autism are better able to request objects or events than they are to initiate joint or socially shared attention relative to an object or an event. A specific neural subsystem regulates and promotes social-emotional approach behaviour. Lack of this mechanism has a lifelong negative effect on social cognitive development of children with autism (Mundy, 1995).
- In comparisons of children with autism and their normal peers at their first birthday party, autism versus normal development was identified with more than 90% accuracy, based on four behaviours of joint attention: pointing, showing objects, looking at others and orienting to name (Osterling & Dawson, 1994).
- If children with autism lack universal, biologically based capacities for the affective perception of and contact with others, such restrictions in interrelatedness may constitute sufficient reason for their characteristic linguistic and cognitive deficits (Hobson, 1989).
- Lack of shared attention also reflects itself in attachment behaviours (see Chapter 5). Only 40% of the children with autism investigated show secure

attachment (in contrast with 65% of normally developing children who show secure attachment), and those children who are securely attached to their mothers also exhibit more responsivity to and more initiation of joint attention bids (Capps, Sigman & Mundy, 1994).

Parents whose children have autistic symptoms may be inclined, as a default position, to think that their baby is rejecting them. It is possible that mothers who feel unwanted and unloved only naturally and perhaps unconsciously withdraw their bids for attention and interaction, unwittingly contributing to the insecure attachment so often seen in children with autism, and thus exacerbating their withdrawal.

Parents have great support needs that have not adequately been recognised. They need to be convinced that the child's behaviours are not a personal affront to their parenting or a challenge to their value as a parent. They need to be supported in stepping up their thwarted interactivity efforts, for the young organism can benefit from intense social stimulation in the first years of life, perhaps more than at any other time in development.

Behavioural difficulties

A number of behavioural expressions, which are atypical in their intensity and frequency, are noted in children with autism.

Stereotypical behaviours. These involve repetitive and rhythmic actions (e.g. twirling fingers, flapping arms, spinning, toe-walking), and are sometimes described as compulsive behaviours. The child is drawn to stacking the cubes or lining up the toy cars in a particular way, as she might be insistent on what she eats, where she sits, and what she does in particular contexts. She may show an intense attraction to idiosyncratic objects and events, such as touching hair or playing one particular song.

Self-stimulatory behaviours. Behaviours such as rocking and spinning are considered to be self-stimulating. These are also marked by a restricted range of preferences, and may be indicative of the child's attempts to communicate discomfort, boredom or anxiety (Helmstetter & Durand, 1991).

Atypical play. Play is characterised by atypical attachment to inanimate objects and playing with parts of toys while ignoring the intended functions of that toy. A salient feature of autism is the absence of representational, symbolic and pretend play and of social role-taking in play, which is an expression of the child's inability to conjecture others' mental states (mind-reading, or a theory-of-mind deficit in autism).

Self-injurious behaviours. Children may be involved with head-banging, finger-sucking, biting, hair-pulling and scratching. *Pica,* or a tendency to eat non-nutritive items which may include screws and glass, may also be present.

Challenging/aggressive behaviours. These are fairly typical if a child's routine is disrupted or her attachment to particular order of events, objects and preferences is not indulged. Intense temper tantrums may come about as a result of what, to the observer, appear to be minor events.

Stimulus overselectivity. Referring to the child's tendency to focus attention on *one* aspect of the stimulus at the expense of the whole, stimulus overselectivity is not unlike missing the forest for the trees. For example, the child may exhibit an overselectivity for a visual aspect (such as the shiny lipstick she wears, or a particular hair texture) of the woman speaking to her, and appear totally oblivious to the auditory aspects of the message. This process prohibits normal language development, as the necessary associations between different modalities in forming abstractions are not realised.

Children with autism can also display prolonged sleep disturbances in early childhood, as well as hyperactivity and inattention.

Sensory abnormalities in autism

The US Federal Register (1992), in defining autism as a disability category for the purposes of providing educational services, basically includes the above parameters and adds *unusual responses to sensory experiences.* Although such experiences are often reported by individuals with autism, this cluster of symptoms is neither in the DSM-IV descriptives nor is it well represented in research on the disorder.

- Autobiographical accounts by authors who have sufficient control over their autistic disorder to lead functional lives (Williams, 1994; Grandin, 1992; Stelhi, 1991) provide vivid and insightful descriptions of the sensory oversensitivities and distortions of sensory input that seem to have held these persons captive. For example, while the sounds of being called by name are not registered, the drone of electrical equipment or even blood being pumped in the arteries may be perceived as intolerably distressing.
- There are clinical and anecdotal reports of successful intervention strategies based on modification of auditory hypersensitivities (Stelhi, 1991; Rimland, 1991).
- In a controlled investigation on sound sensitivity in children with autism, a significant reduction in sound sensitivity was reported following a treatment program based on an audiometric modification (Bettison, 1996).
- Recently, sensory sensitivities in the form of hyper- and hyperoreactivities have been documented across all domains (auditory, visual, tactile, gustatory and olfactory) in 30 children with autism, in comparison with their normal peers (Wood & Talay-Ongan, forthcoming).

Sensory overload may be hindering the child with autism to process information and understand the world of relationships adequately.

Associated deficits

Children with autism more often than not display other abnormal developmental patterns.

- Although most children with autism have mental retardation, the disorder can occur at all levels of cognitive functioning. Only 20% of individuals are reported as being within normal intelligence levels, another 20% are in the 50–70 range, while the rest have IQs below 50 (Gillberg, 1991).
- Islets of ability refer to the corralled areas of special abilities not necessarily commensurate with the rest of the child's developmental profile. Such abilities may include exceptional visual or rote memory, *hypercalculia* (ability to do complex mathematical calculations with super speed and accuracy), or exceptional musical ability. The term *splinter skills* are often used to describe such precocious but isolated and uneven development (O'Connor & Hermelin, 1991).
- The incidence of seizures in cases where mental retardation coexists with autism is reported to be higher, at one out of three cases, than in those without mental retardation (Tuchman, Rapin & Shinnar, 1991). Such seizure disorders tend to appear during adolescence.

Autism in its 'pure' form is hard to come by: it is much more likely to be found in combination with other developmental disorders. Uta Frith (1989) makes a cogent argument about the challenge for identification of the 'core features' of autism—those which lie deeper than the associated developmental disabilities such as mental retardation and severe communication impairment. She offers the child's inability to mentalise others' mental states as being the common thread that runs across autism (1989, p.187):

> The central deficit underlying autism is . . . the inability to draw together information so as to derive coherent and meaningful ideas [as] there is a fault in the predisposition of the mind to make sense of the world.

ASPERGER DISORDER

While Kanner was documenting infantile autism in Baltimore in the USA, Hans Asperger was describing it in Vienna in 1942. Although we tend to think of a higher functioning variant of autism as Asperger disorder (previously known as Asperger's syndrome), his initial descriptions of the disorder termed *autistic psychopathy* were, in fact, wider in scope than those of Kanner. Some of Asperger's initial descriptions included the following (Frith, 1991):

- characteristic peculiarity of gaze; lack of eye contact;
- poverty of facial expressions and gestures; stereotyped movements devoid of expression;

- abnormal and unnatural use of language; original word creations;
- impulsive behaviour with little regard for social demands;
- at times, excellent ability in logical abstract thinking; isolated areas of interest;
- disinclination to learn from adults;
- disturbance of social contact and adaptation.

Thus, Asperger disorder encompasses children and adults with the social and behavioural components of autism, but without the significant impairments in cognition and language.

- The *splinter skills* referred to above may be even more pronounced in these children, such that the ability for decoding language (letter recognition and reading, although without extracting the meaning) may be evident in the preschool years (Szatmari, 1991).
- Language use can border on pedantic, with an elaborate expressive vocabulary, while non-verbal, bodily and gestural communication may be odd and clumsy. Signs, symbols and language tend to be interpreted literally, rather than contextually or figuratively.
- In social interaction with peers, they do not seem to be on the same wavelength, not because of shyness, rejection or avoidance of human contact and wanting to be alone physically, but because of being alone *mentally* (Frith, 1991).
- Pursuit of *very narrow interests* bordering on minutiae are seen in older children, where they manifest a preoccupation with sports statistics, transportation schedules, and the like (Klin, 1994).

Dustin Hoffman portrays a man with Asperger disorder poignantly in the film *Rain Man*. Autobiographical accounts of autism by Williams, Stelhi and Grandin also depict this disorder. Asperger disorder is more difficult to recognise due to the subtlety of its cognitive and linguistic deficit, but is becoming better known and understood in the early childhood field.

OTHER PDDs

The remaining three disorders under the PDD classification are neither as well researched nor as prominent as autism, but they too contain autistic-like symptomatology.

Pervasive developmental disorder—not otherwise specified (PDD-NOS). PDD-NOS is used for transient disorders of early childhood, when there seems to be no other viable classification for mild autistic symptoms. The fact that learning disabilities and attention-related deficits are sometimes diagnosed in this category suggests that there may be some common neurogenic bases for these disorders. Autistic disorder, Asperger disorder and PDD-NOS are often thought of as a single disorder group, with different gradations of severity in impairment.

Rett syndrome.   A progressive neurological disorder, Rett syndrome manifest only in girls, which is strongly suggestive of a genetic aetiology. As the genetic causes of this disorder became better understood it may not be included with PDDs as it currently stands. Symptoms of Rett syndrome, characterised by autistic-like behaviours, may become apparent during preschool years. Another characteristic feature of the disorder is rubbing of the hands, resembling washing movements. Hagberg (1995) gives the stages of the disorder:

- early onset (6–18 months)—characterised by slowing up of head growth (*microcephaly*), subtle neurodevelopmental delays in play and communication;
- rapid deterioration (1–4 years)—characterised by hyperventilation and irregular breathing, loss of purposeful hand use and stereotypical hand-washing movements, onset of *ataxia* (loss of balance and compensatory wide gait), loss of mental functions with autistic features, and seizures;
- pseudostationary stage (4–6 years)—characterised by dampening of the autistic features but continuation of cognitive and motor dysfunction;
- late motor deterioration (6–15 years)—characterised by decreasing mobility, with spasticity, bodily deformity and growth retardation, and staring behaviour.

Childhood disintegrative disorder (CDD).   Another progressive neurological disorder, CDD appears to be a genetic or congenital metabolic error. Typically after the first two years of normal development, overall developmental disintegration starts to occur in the areas of language, cognition, social skills and toileting, and behavioural features associated with autism emerge (Volkmar & Rutter, 1995).

EVALUATION AND INTERVENTION

Causal factors

There seems to be consensus that the causal factors related to autism, Asperger disorder and PDD-NOS are biological and neurogenic.

- In an early study, EEG recordings from autistic individuals were shown to have abnormal patterns (DeMyer, 1975). Unusually high levels of neurotransmitter substances (particularly serotonin, a neural opiate) are reported (Shreibman, 1988), as well as various cortical and cerebellar dysfunctions (Courchesne, 1991).
- Incidence of autism is higher in certain diseases known to cause brain damage, such as PKU (see Chapter 2), congenital hyperthyroidism and

neurofibromatosis (see Chapter 16), and infections such as cytomegalovirus (Gillberg & Coleman, 1996).

■ The high incidence of mental retardation in autism, together with prenatal infections and other risk factors, such as prematurity and birth trauma, also suggest a biological vulnerability: 10% of children with mental retardation are reported to have PDD (Nordin & Gillberg, 1996).

■ Studies using neuroimaging techniques such as PET and MRI (see Chapter 4) look quite promising in shedding light on the brain organisation and chemistry in individuals with PDD, and may eventually be able to offer neuropharmacological interventions that dampen some of the behavioural symptoms in autism.

■ A genetic predisposition to autism is indicated in certain families, where recurrence risk of autism in subsequent siblings ranges from 2% to 9% (DeLong, 1994).

Differentiating autism from other conditions

The nature and the extent of avoidance of social contact is the most prominent feature distinguishing autism from other developmental disabilities and conditions. Mental retardation can coexist with autism, but not all children with mental retardation, most of whom enjoy social relatedness, have autism. However, some features of autism, such as severe language impairment and stereotypical and self-injurious behaviour patterns, are also observed in severe mental retardation.

Childhood schizophrenia is characterised by bizarre behaviours but also fantasies, delusions and hallucinations, and is not associated with mental retardation (see Chapter 9). These differences distinguish it from autism.

Children with congenital blindness (see Chapter 15) may have some mannerisms (e.g. pressing the eyes, rocking, emotional detachment) that resemble those in autism. Hearing impairment also may give impressions of autism, with selective hearing and inconsistent responsivity. Neither of these impairments, however, are associated with mental retardation or severe pragmatic language deficit.

Diagnosis

Initial diagnosis of autism is most often given by the paediatrician to the young child whose behavioural and adaptive patterns are sufficiently different to warrant parental concern and bids for assistance. Initial diagnosis may be in the absence of a *comprehensive evaluation* by a team of child development and medical specialists. It is ideal to have a multidisciplinary comprehensive assessment team, and for the planning phase of the intervention program it is *crucial* to involve the parents and teachers in the process (see Chapter 17).

The evaluation team members can include a psychologist, who would perform an assessment of cognitive and adaptive functioning, a speech and language pathologist, who would perform an assessment of communicative functioning, a case worker (who may be a social worker or welfare officer), who would evaluate the needs of the family and the social context, and a medical specialist, who would contribute on the medical aspects of the disorder and development. The occupational therapist and early childhood teacher should be included in the assessment team as much as possible; together with the speech and language pathologist and the parents, they are indispensable members of the teaching team.

Some early identification tools for autism are available, among which are the *Checklist for Autism in Toddlers* (CHAT), which attempts to evaluate autism in infants and toddlers in their second year of life, by a parent questionnaire (Baron-Cohen, Allen & Gillberg, 1992). It probes the child's ability to engage in pretend play, protodeclarative pointing (e.g. 'Does your child ever use his/her index finger to point and indicate interest in something?'), joint attention (e.g. 'Does your child ever bring objects to you, or show you something?'), social relatedness to others, and social play (e.g. 'Does your child enjoy playing peek-a-boo?').

Others are the *Childhood Autism Rating Scale* (Schopler, Reichler, DeVellius, et al., 1980) and *Autism Diagnostic Interview* (LeCouteur, Rutter, Lord, et al., 1989).

Early intervention

Autism is a challenging disorder, and necessitates as early an intervention as possible, which should be intensive, ongoing, coordinated, and bring into the arena the skills of many professionals, as well as parents. Some intervention regimens may be prohibitively intensive and expensive, like the Lovaas (1993) program, which requires 40 hours a week for two to four years of intensive training on specific language, adaptive and social behaviours within a behavioural paradigm. This intervention claims a 50% recovery rate, as well as improved IQ scores, but at a cost of tens of thousands of dollars a year, remains both experimental and inaccessible for most families. Another curriculum for PPD is called Treatment and Education of Autistic and related Communication Handicapped Children (TEACCH) (Cox & Schopler, 1993). This is a comprehensive and behaviourally based program, with applications for classroom teaching as well as parent training to implement most objectives.

Some *general intervention principles* to facilitate adaptive behaviours in children with autism include the following:

- An educational environment that is *language-based,* which promotes communicative development and social interaction: modelling of functional conversations, reduction of echolalia, and teaching augmentative communication to children who do not yet use verbal means;
- *One-on-one* teaching and prompting, balanced with a sense of respect for and gradual elimination of the child's rituals;

■ Use of *behavioural strategies based on rewards*. The optimal means of avoiding tantrums may be by anticipating the trigger events (like changing from one activity to another), teaching the schedule of events, providing anticipation for change, and rewarding for successful transitions.

■ Empowering and supporting the *families*, as well as involving them both in planning and implementation of objectives to foster normal development.

■ Using an *inclusive normalised environment* as much as possible. Children with Asperger disorder are easily integrated in a normal classroom; more severely affected children should be integrated in the mainstream in all possible ways from which they derive benefit.

A child with autism is likely to present an interesting challenge to the early childhood teacher because, except for tantruming, most of the behaviours appear to be self-regulated. As long as the child's routine or rhythm is not tampered with, she may be perfectly content to drift on the fringes or be absorbed in a stereotypical activity. It is this self-sufficiency that is targeted by intervention: in fact, the challenge is to attempt to socially engage the child away from activities of interacting with the self. Careful planning and one-on-one attention are needed for effective programs for young children with autism. Community volunteers and retirees are sources of people power that may be useful when attracted into early childhood settings. Also, normal peers who exhibit high levels of empathy can be superb co-therapists in bonding with the loner child and cajoling her to participate in the events of the day (Talay-Ongan, 1991).

Families with children whose development is arrested with autism often find themselves grappling with the question of whether or not to pursue yet another possible 'cure' for the disorder. From mega-vitamin therapies to mirrored rooms, from sound therapies to steroid hormones, alternative therapies abound, some with anecdotal positive outcomes. Until there is sufficiently rigorous scientific support for such interventions, a healthy dose of scepticism may be in order. Nevertheless, treatment choices that families make need to be supported, unless they are clearly dangerous to the wellbeing of the child.

Outcome

As in most developmental disorders, outcomes in PDD are dependent on the level of intellectual impairment and language development. Many adults with autism function well in the community, although they may have family or group support needs. High-functioning individuals with Asperger disorder or PDD-NOS may show idiosyncrasies within the community at large, but can usually make successful adjustments. Children with degenerative disorders under the umbrella of PDD, Rett syndrome and CDD are reported not to survive beyond adolescence.

CONCLUSIONS

Children who fall under the umbrella of autism and other pervasive developmental disorders may show different levels of severity of impairment in intellectual and language functions. Early identification and intervention may facilitate the adaptive skills in these children. It is important to recognise the family's support needs as well: from infancy, children with autism present challenging behaviours which some parents find difficult to deal with. The central focus in early intervention and integration is the facilitation of social communicative skills.

16

Neurogenic and other impairments

Here we look at children with damage to the brain or the spinal cord, which results primarily in movement disorders, although such disabilities as sensory impairment, mental retardation or communication impairment often accompany the condition. You may find it helpful to review sections of Chapter 4, particularly those on motor systems, to consolidate your understanding of neurogenic disorders.

Some children are affected in their motor or movement systems alone, as with youngsters with *orthopaedic* impairments, involving muscles and bones (*musculoskeletal disabilities*). A child with an amputated leg or one who has suffered polio may have difficulties with ambulation or walking, running and sports; however, while challenges like these are likely to bring with them difficulties in making social-emotional adaptations most unimpaired children take for granted, they are not associated with cognitive or linguistic impairments *per se*. Others may have brain damage with more pervasive disabilities.

The degree of *neurological* motor involvement is likely to be on a continuum, similar to intellectual functioning: many children with motor disabilities have normal or above-average intelligence. Others may be multiply handicapped, with severe motor involvement and severe to profound mental retardation. Their communication skills span from being normal to having high support needs, requiring augmentative and alternative systems.

CEREBRAL PALSY

Cerebral palsy (CP) refers to a non-progressive neurological abnormality incurred prenatally or early in development. Although CP is a disorder of posture and movement, because developmental neurogenic disorders tend to involve many systems in the brain its effects may also be seen in cognitive and perceptual domains.

Causes of cerebral palsy

Causes can be summarised as follows (Nelson & Ellenberg 1986):

- *Prenatal causes.* In the first trimester these include teratogens, genetic syndromes, chromosomal abnormalities and brain malformations; in the remaining trimesters, intrauterine infections and problems with placental functioning account for nearly half of CP.
- *Perinatal causes.* Complications during labour and delivery, asphyxia and anoxia (lack of oxygen), nervous system infections (sepsis) and prematurity account for nearly a quarter of the cases of CP.
- *Postnatal causes.* Traumatic brain injury, toxins, encephalitis and meningitis present as potential causes of brain damage in babies and young children, accounting for about 5% of CP.
- One in four cases of CP are attributed to *unknown* causes.

The incidence of CP is reported to remain fairly stable over the years at 0.6–2.4 per 1000 live births and, of the prenatally acquired CP, half of the cases are attributed to *prematurity* (Hagberg Hagberg, & Olow, 1993). The reason for the high incidence of CP in prematurity is related to the vulnerability to injury of the brain's white matter in areas close to the lateral ventricles at 26–32 weeks' gestation (Volpe, 1990). Bleeds in these regions damage the fibres that are part of the pyramidal system and thus crucial to voluntary motor systems.

Types of cerebal palsy

There are two basic dimensions CP is described in. The first is with respect to the *limbs involved:*

- *Hemiplegia* refers to paralysis on either the right or the left side of the body, involving the upper and lower extremities on the affected side. As cortical motor control is contralateral (see Chapter 4), the side of the bodily symptoms implies a brain damage on the opposite side of the cortical hemisphere.
- *Diplegia* refers to the legs being more affected than the arms; the symptoms are evident in both lower extremities. The cortical damage suggested by diplegia is bilateral lesions from the midline out, as the feet and the legs are represented on the medial (towards the centre) portion of the primary motor area of the frontal cortex.
- *Quadriplegia* refers to involvement of all four limbs, and implies a considerably more extensive cortical damage. The trunk muscles as well as those for the oral musculature may be involved, resulting in communication difficulties and feeding problems. Severity of brain damage may result in various medical complications, mental retardation, associated sensory impairments such as hearing and vision loss, and seizures.

With respect to *type of neuromotor impairment:*

■ *Spasticity* is attributed to an impairment of the *pyramidal* system (see Chapter 4 for different motor systems), which originates from the pyramidal motor neurons in the primary motor cortex. The motor output flows down the fibres (axons) through the white matter and the brainstem, exiting at the appropriate vertebral segments of the spinal cord to innervate the particular voluntary muscle groups. The pyramidal system is responsible for conscious, voluntary and refined movements. Spastic paralysis comes about when the synergy between the muscle groups necessary to the smooth execution of movement is disrupted, which usually results in excessive muscle tone and contractures.

■ *Extrapyramidal* motor system regulates muscle tone, posture and balance. Extrapyramidal disorders in CP are also known as *dyskinesias,* and can include the following:

   ■ *Athetosis* (or athetoid CP) is characterised by involuntary slow writhing movements of the neck and the limbs in particular, and is associated with damage to the *basal ganglia.*

   ■ *Choreiform* CP is characterised by rapid, jerky involuntary movements of the upper limbs.

   ■ *Dystonia* refers to abnormal muscle tone, and is characterised by rigidity of the trunk and neck.

   ■ *Hypotonia* (reduced muscle tone) or *atonia* (lack of muscle tone; depending on the extent of the damage) may imply damage to the lower motor neurons, which actually supply the motor messages.

   ■ *Ataxia* is associated with disorders of the cerebellum, and is characterised by balance deficits. *Ataxic gait* refers to the wide-spaced feet adopted to better maintain balance in walking. In the arms and hands, it may reflect as imprecise control in timing as well as coordination of distance and reach in judging location, such that the objects aimed at may be overshot (passed in reaching and holding).

■ *Mixed* CP may contain a combination of these symptoms.

> Close your eyes and touch the tip of your nose with your index finger. Successful execution of this event tells you two things: (i) that you are not drunk; (ii) that you have adequate cerebellar functioning, which allows for sensorimotor integration! A person who has ataxia may find this difficult to execute with precision.

Identification of cerebral palsy

Early diagnosis of CP may have important early intervention implications, although as many as 50% of the infants suspected for being at risk of CP at 12 months were in fact found not to be neurologically impaired by two years of age (Piper, Mazer, Silver, et al., 1988). Some early signs of CP include the following:

- Children with CP may sleep excessively or be irritable when they are awake.
- They may have weak cries or a weak sucking reflex, and show little interest in their surroundings.
- Their resting position may be floppy (rag-doll position, typical of the hypotonic infant), or arched with too much muscle tone.
- Asymmetrical reflexes between two sides of the body or persistence of primitive reflexes (see below) are evident.
- They may have persistent clenched fists, or too early hand preference.
- There is discrepancy between the rates of cognitive and motor development, where children with mild neuromotor involvements meet expected milestones linguistically and cognitively, but not via motor skills.

Reflexive development and cerebral palsy

In Chapter 5 we review some of the primitive reflexes normally exhibited by infants. Reflexive development is particularly important in understanding children with CP, as retention of these reflexes contributes to the symptomatology. Furthermore, there are treatment methods, long and laborious though they may be, which are based on motor reflexive development in infancy. Let us take a brief look at reflexive development from a neuroevolutionary perspective.

According to this perspective, the nervous system has four levels of reflexes, or *sensorimotor integration*, which are hierarchically organised such that each emerging level subsumes and supersedes the previous one, until the final level is reached, which remains for life. The first three levels contain primitive reflexes which are not compatible with walking, whereas the fourth level allows for balance reactions which allow for *bipedal motion* (walking); nevertheless, for the final stage to be reached, all the previous levels need to come on line, serve their purpose, then become extinct or inhibited, so the next level of integration can become operative.

The reflexive sensorimotor integration is completed by 12–18 months of age in children developing normally, after which motor skills are refined through interactions of biological skill and environmental opportunity, encouragement and practice. Retained early reflexes result in changes in muscle tone and position of limbs, interfering with normal standing and walking, and development of voluntary motor activity. The four levels of sensorimotor integration in reflexive development are:

1. spinal cord level
2. brainstem level
3. midbrain level
4. cortical level.

Children are born at the *spinal level* of sensorimotor integration. At this level, the following reflexes are evidenced (Mysak, 1980):

■ *flexor withdrawal,* where the stimulation of the sole of the foot precipitates flexion of that leg;
■ *extensor thrust,* where similar stimulation of the flexed limb precipitates it to extend;
■ *crossed extension,* the flexion of the second leg precipitates the extension of the first leg.

If in evidence beyond two months of age, these reflexes are considered to be an indication of central nervous system (CNS) dysmaturity.

At the *brainstem level,* the following reflexes are evidenced:

■ *asymmetrical tonic neck reflex,* where turning the head to one side precipitates extension of the arm and leg on that side and flexion of the limbs on the opposite side (also known as 'fencing position');
■ *symmetrical tonic neck reflex,* where bending the head forward precipitates flexion of the arms and extension of the legs, while bending the head backwards precipitates extension of the arms and flexion of the legs;
■ *supporting reaction,* where bouncing the baby on the balls of his feet precipitates sufficient increase in extensor tone in the legs to support his own weight.

These reflexes are postural, and effect changes to the distribution of muscle tone throughout the body. Persistence of these reflexes beyond six months may be an indication of CNS dysmaturity.

At the *midbrain level,* the following reflexes are evidenced:

■ *neck-righting reflex,* where rotation of the head to one side now precipitates rotation of the body as a whole in that direction;
■ *head labyrinthine reflex,* where, regardless of the position of body tilt in space, the head rights itself, with a vertical face and horizontal mouth orientation;
■ *amphibian reaction,* where stimulation of the pelvis when the baby is lying in a prone position elicits a flexion of the arm and leg on the same side.

These reflexes establish a normal head and body relationship, and their combined action enables the child to roll over, sit up and stand up. The absence of righting reflexes after six months is a sign of CNS dysmaturity.

At the *cortical level,* the *equilibrium reactions* (or balance reactions) are evidenced:

■ in crawling, sitting and standing, when the centre of gravity in the body changes as in being tilted to one side, the opposite side limbs extend to maintain balance;

- these reactions emerge from the time of crawling, and are a prerequisite to walking; they are retained for life.

Many children with CP exhibit retained spinal, brainstem and midbrain-level reflexes, which interfere with assuming an independent walking position.

Associated impairments in cerebral palsy

By definition, CP implies a primary deficit with posture and movement. All children with CP have some degree of motor involvement, but most have accompanying impairments as well. Table 16.1 summarises some common associated symptoms (Robinson, 1973).

Type of CP	Associated deficit (%)			
	Seizures	Mental retardation	Visual impairment	Auditory impairment
Quadriplegia	45	67	55	22
Hemiplegia	12	38	23	8
Diplegia	12	56	38	17
Extrapyramidal	45	92	50	17
Mixed	12	79	64	21

TABLE 16.1

Common symptoms associated with cerebral palsy

As you can see, *hemiplegic spastic CP* has the most favourable overall outcome; given that this is the most common type of the disorder, the chances of children and adults having *no other* handicapping conditions are pretty high. However, most individuals with CP are likely to have associated impairments.

- Children born prematurely are prone to developing *spastic diplegia*, have a substantial risk of mental retardation, and retinopathy of prematurity may contribute to the visual impairments (see Chapter 3).
- Extrapyramidal forms of CP involving the whole body appear to have higher incidence of associated impairments.
- Visual impairments include homonymous hemianopia (visual field loss; see Chapter 14) in children with hemiplegia, consistent with damage to one cerebral hemisphere.
- Most children with CP have *strabismus* (unaligned eyes); ataxia is often associated with involuntary oscillating eye movements (*nystagmus*).
- Hearing, speech and language impairments occur with varying severity in about a third of children with CP. Children subjected to maternal intrauterine viral infections or rubella tend to have a high incidence of hearing loss.
- In terms of communication skills, CP is often characterised by *dysarthria* (see Chapter 10), which comes about as a result of damage to the voluntary control over systems coordinating and regulating speech. It includes impairment in the motor processes of respiration, phonation,

articulation and resonance, resulting in an inability to speak with normal muscular speed, strength, precision or timing and ranging from mild problems to severe communication impairment with poor intelligibility (LaPointe, 1990).

- Children with general-pattern spasticity with heightened muscle tone and stiff, tight and overactive muscles typically demonstrate slow, laboured speech.
- Children with athetoid patterns with fluctuating muscle tone and uncontrolled writhing movements tend to have jerky speech.
- Children with ataxic patterns with awkward, clumsy and poorly coordinated movements tend to have a tremorous, quivering voice (McCormick, Loeb & Schiefelbusch, 1997).

■ Seizures develop in 50% of children with CP, with spastic CP having the highest incidence (Aksu, 1990).

■ Problems such as low muscle tone, weak sucking reflex, poor swallowing coordination, overactive biting and gag reflexes may lead to poor nutrition and feeding difficulties, which have growth repercussions (Jones, 1989).

Intervention

The term often used in delivery of services to children with CP is *habilitation,* as opposed to *re*habilitation, because CP treatment does not imply a restoring of a lost function but a maximising of existing functioning, while minimising disability-related disadvantages (Pellegrino, 1995):

> *Habilitation* is an intervention strategy that is community-based, and family-centred; it is conceived and implemented as a comprehensive program designed to facilitate adaptation to and participation in an increasing number and variety of societal settings, including home, school, clinic, childcare, neighbourhood, and day treatment programs.

The intervention team for a child with CP needs to include interdisciplinary participation, with full family participation and communication between all involved parties. A coordinator for the intervention efforts (i.e. case manager, care coordinator—many titles, one role) is crucial to ensure communication and facilitate the integration of services. This role can be assumed by the early childhood teacher, a social worker, or any other team member who can interact across a wide variety of settings and persons to keep all focused on the goals for the child and the family.

Early intervention and family support and involvement are the keys to successful habilitation. Encouraging parent participation in planning for the service delivery and educational facilitation are crucial in empowering them, so they can develop competence and advocacy for their child. Programs must be individualised to the needs of each child and family. Often such planning will include a variety of services, including consultations by professionals and home-based as well as educational-centre-based activities.

Neurodevelopmental therapy

As noted earlier, many children with CP exhibit reflexes that interfere with assuming an independent walking position. (If, for example, the arm and the leg flex each time the head turns to one side (asymmetrical tonic neck reflex), walking is made quite difficult, as we constantly scan the environment through head movements in walking.) Facilitating sensorimotor development along neuroreflexive lines to promote the evolution of higher levels, and inhibition of lower level reflexes are the basic goals of neurodevelopmental therapy. The Bobath method (Bobath, 1980) seeks the emergence of equilibrium reactions, which allow the child to gain the balance and stability to walk. Many physiotherapists and occupational therapists use intervention techniques aimed at increasing mobility and the range of motion based on such principles.

Other treatment approaches

CP is not a progressive disease; however, often the musculoskeletal complications associated with it need to be attended to in order to prevent further impairment.

■ *Orthotic devices* are used to increase the range of motion, provide stability and prevent contractures. Physical therapists and occupational therapists integrate their treatment strategies in the use of such facilitative devices, which may include leg braces, splints to position the thumb and fingers, or arm rests, and 'inhibitive casts', which improve gait and weight-bearing as well as enhance range of motion and functional hand use (Yasukawa, 1990).
■ Some *medical procedures* include medications, which seem to have a limited usefulness and undesirable side-effects when compared with benefits in children with spasticity and rigidity (Pranzatelli, 1996).
■ Spasticity can be treated by injection of agents into muscle groups to create a *nerve block*, which can reduce spasticity for four to six months, although some of these procedures remain experimental (Denislic & Meh, 1995).
■ Selective *posterior rhizotomy* refers to severing of the *afferent* (sensory) fibres that most saliently contribute to spasticity, which results from an overactive stretch reflex. The procedure reduces muscle tone and improves sitting, standing and walking abilities in some cases (Peacock & Staudt, 1990).
■ A new technique is reported whereby antispastic medication is delivered directly to the *cerebrospinal fluid*, by placing a pump under the skin in the lumbar region and computerised regulation of the flow of the

medication. Although the procedure requires intensive medical follow-up at this stage, dramatic improvements in spasticity are reported (Albright, 1996).

■ *Orthopaedic surgery* aims at reducing the permanent shortening of muscles, reducing the range of motion by lengthening a tendon by cutting through a muscle or by moving its point of attachment on the bone. This allows children to walk and sit more freely (Binder & Eng, 1989).

Overcoming limitations

Functional mobility for children in which CP interferes with walking may require a combination of physical therapy and assistive devices such as crutches or wheelchairs. Motorised wheelchairs can enhance the independence of the affected children, and can be driven via a joystick or other switches. The head, trunk and postural supports needed make it imperative to custom-tailor the devices to each child's current and evolving needs.

Technology-assisted communication and other forms of assistive technology have made significant positive contributions to the quality of life of children and adults with CP. Multi-use computers become a window to the world, a teaching and learning tool, a communication device and an entertainment centre (Cole & Dehtashti, 1990).

Sport and physical exercise are important not only in strengthening the muscles and bones, reducing contractures and enhancing motor skills—they also offer great opportunities to excel in competitive sports through such events as the Special Olympics. Obviously, the benefits of such participation span considerably more than the mere physical enhancement: they include a sense of personal accomplishment few children without disabilities embrace, and a social network of like-minded peers.

Most children with CP can be successfully educated in *inclusive classrooms*, provided that their associated disabling conditions such as specific learning disabilities, visual or auditory impairment, communication deficits and attention and behaviour problems are properly addressed. Education within the least restrictive environment should be the goal for all children, and the use of 'multiply handicapped' as an expedience category should be rethought.

SEIZURE DISORDERS

Seizures ('fits' in colloquial language) occur because some abnormal locus of the brain's electrical activity escalates and spreads into an area of cortex. Behavioural responses to this invasion are evidenced to the extent that the areas corresponding to motor and sensory functions represented on the brain are involved. Having a seizure is similar to a severe stress reaction of the brain: even normally functioning brains can have a seizure if they are overheated (too high body temperature), deprived of sleep for prolonged periods, or have an abnormally low levels of nutrients (hypoglycaemia).

In infancy, the brain's threshold for seizures is lower. *Febrile convulsions* may occur in children aged three months to three years when they have a high fever associated with a viral condition, such as middle ear infections or upper respiratory illnesses; they are not related to brain infections or conditions associated with epilepsy. Combined with seizures related to head injury, more than 5% of children are likely to have a single seizure episode in their lives (O'Donohoe, 1994). But a single seizure does not constitute a *seizure disorder* or *epilepsy,* which is a chronic condition associated with brain pathology and the repeated random/unprovoked occurrence of electrical storms in the brain.

Seizures are also a manifestation of the less-than-intact nervous system, and may be caused by developmental brain abnormalities or developmental disabilities.

- About half the population with seizure disorders has subnormal intelligence.
- The incidence of seizure disorders in populations with existing brain damage is significantly higher: 16% in mental retardation, 25% in cerebral palsy, and 25% in spina bifida (Wallace, 1990).
- For the children who have a febrile convulsion with a normal EEG (electroencephalogram) the risk of recurrence is 26% in the next three years, whereas for the child with an abnormal EEG (suggesting a brain abnormality) after the first seizure the risk jumps to 56% (Shinnar, Berg, Moshe, et al., 1990).
- Seizure disorders predispose the child to a higher incidence of learning disabilities and various behavioural and psychosocial problems (Aldenkamp, Alpherts, Dekker, et al., 1990).

In young children whose seizures have been controlled by medication, a common practice is to stop the medication if no seizures have occurred in two years; more than two-thirds of this population remains free of seizure activity for five years (Shinnar et al., 1994). Factors that contribute adversely to a positive outcome include the existence of mental retardation, early onset, high familial incidence of epilepsy, and severity and frequency of seizures.

Classification of seizure disorders

Seizure disorders have been classified by the Commission on Classification and Terminology of the International League Against Epilepsy (1981), and more neutral terms describing the underlying pathology have been put in place.

Generalised seizures
In these, both hemispheres of the brain are involved simultaneously; the more serious type, they account for nearly half of all cases of epilepsy. Tonic–clonic

seizures, absence seizures, myoclonic seizures and atonic seizures are all forms of generalised epileptic seizures.

Tonic–clonic seizures (grand mal seizures) involve the entire body. The tonic (rigidity) phase is followed by a clonic (oscillating, jerking) phase. From a stiff posture to cessation of convulsions may take two to four minutes. The person may experience an *aura* (a warning sign, like seeing coloured flashing lights) briefly prior to an attack, with no memory of the attack itself and a state of deep restful sleep afterwards. A child who remains in a state of convulsion for more than 15 minutes is said to be in *status epilepticus*, and will need emergency treatment to avert a life-threatening or further damage-inducing condition.

Absence seizures (petit mal seizures) take only seconds, and may be quite difficult actually to see in the child, as the body posture and muscle tone remain the same. The eyes appear somewhat glazed and the child is literally absent in mind from the situation he is in; nor can his unawareness be disrupted by prompting. Such interruptions in consciousness occur dozens of times a day in some children, giving them a fragmented input of experiences around them, particularly since they are not aware of the episodes.

Myoclonic seizures are characterised by powerful abrupt contractions of muscles, which may involve the entire body or a part of it. *Atonic seizures* involve just as sudden a loss of muscle tone, such that the child may need to wear a helmet to avoid head injury in case of an inevitable fall.

Partial seizures

These are more common than generalised seizures. The brain abnormality is usually restricted to one hemisphere, and most of the children affected have some prenatal brain insult. Partial seizures can be categorised as simple or complex.

Simple partial seizures are those in which the child retains consciousness. The symptoms include twitching, or oscillation of the hand, arm or leg. If the abnormal discharge of electrical activity occurs in sensory areas of the cortex, visual, auditory or olfactory sensations may also be present.

Complex partial seizures (temporal, or psychomotor seizures) are those in which the child is unaware of the seizure activity, which may last up to several minutes. Some characteristic symptoms are staring, blinking, lip-smacking, finger-tapping, grimacing or other rapid automatic actions. The child looks confused and tired after an episode.

Management of seizure disorders

In the first instance management of seizure disorders is achieved by antiepileptic medication administered over several years, until it is viable to terminate it under medical supervision. However, all medications have some side-effects and negative interactive effects (e.g., with other medication, with alcohol), and may show varying responses from child to child. Medications may need to be manipulated in dose and kind to get the optimal result. Nevertheless, they make life normal for most affected children, adolescents and adults who learn to live with the condition. The consensus on living with epilepsy seems to be doing it all rather than curtailing activities, although some activities such as swimming need to be carried out with adequate precaution.

Successful adaptation and best outcomes are again usually the result of a team effort of many professionals and parents. As children with seizure disorders can be as diverse as the population itself (ranging from gifted to profoundly delayed), their needs for planning, adaptation and support are also diverse. In a mainstream classroom the teacher needs to understand the parameters of the disorder to be able to contribute to the multidisciplinary team, on frequency of seizures for example, and hence in its medical management, as well as to know what to do in the event of a generalised tonic–clonic seizure. Both the child and his peers need to be educated in dealing with the disorder, and replacing fear and stigma with knowledge about and preparedness for the disorder.

SPINA BIFIDA

Spina bifida is a part of the group of congenital disorders known as *neural tube defects*, in which the bony structures of the spinal cord, the vertebrae, fail to fuse properly during embryonic development. In contrast to cerebral palsy, which has a diffuse spectrum of neurological dysfunction, dysfunctions associated with spina bifida are relatively localised.

The precise causes underlying spina bifida are unknown, although folic acid deficiency, alcoholism and antiepileptic medication use in the mother have been implicated. Some genetic predisposition influences seem at play: the incidence of having a second child with spina bifida is 50 times higher than the normal incidence, and people of Irish descent are four times more likely to have the disorder (Noetzel, 1989). During pregnancy, alpha-fetoprotein in the amniotic fluid as determined by amniocentesis (see Chapter 2) is a reliable indicator of the fetus having the disorder.

There are three types of spina bifida; only the third one has serious neurological repercussions: spina occulta, meningocoele and myelo-meningocoele.

Spina bifida occulta is the 'hidden' type, in which the meninges covering the spinal cord are intact and the spinal cord not damaged, although the vertebra are not completely joined. Children may have no motor symptoms, or a mild weakness in the lower limbs. A tuft of hair grows on the site, and may be the only sign of the disorder.

Meningocoele is a condition, where the vertebrae have an opening from which the meningeal sac protrudes, filled with cerebrospinal fluid, although the spinal cord itself is normal. The sac is removed and the opening is usually repaired shortly after birth.

Myelomeningocoele involves both meninges and spinal cord, where the spinal cord is pushed into the protruding meningocoele sac. The nerves below the opening fail to develop, resulting in loss of motor control and tactile, proprioceptive and pain sensation in those parts of the body innervated by the nerves below the level of the lesion.

- Neurological deficits associated with myelomeningocoele depend on how high up on the spinal column the lesion is located, with higher lesions having more extensive paralysis and loss of sensation.
- Common symptoms include paralysis of the legs and lack of bowel control. Physiotherapy and assistive devices such as callipers, crutches or a walking frame are used for ambulation.
- Incontinence is managed by a surgical procedure known as *catheterisation,* in which a tube is inserted into the bladder to drain the urine and into the large intestine for bowel control (Shandling & Gilmour, 1987).
- Lack of pain sensation presents as another problem, as the child's safety needs, which would otherwise be signalled by pain (e.g. a burn on the legs because of a heater being too close or in contact with the skin), may be compromised.
- *Hydrocephalus* may result in myelomeningocoele if the brainstem and part of the cerebellum are displaced downwards towards the neck region, leading to blockage of the cerebrospinal fluid circulation. Hydrocephalus occurs in 60%–95% of children with myelomeningocoele, and is more common in lesions higher up in the spinal cord (Griebel, Oakes & Worley, 1991).
- A *ventriculo-peritoneal shunt,* through which the fluid is drained by a small catheter from the ventricles to the abdominal cavity, is a common treatment procedure to alleviate the building up of extra pressure and fluid in the brain. Shunts have potential blockage and infection problems, and need to be monitored closely.
- Other conditions associated with spina bifida include musculoskeletal deformities in the hips and other joints. Spinal curvature (*scoliosis*) and spinal hump (*kyphosis*) may also be present.

Educational implications for the child with spina bifida are centred around concerns with mobility and orthopaedic problems, as well as continence and urinary issues. Medical needs of the child may necessitate further knowledge and care from the teacher and the adults in the learning environment. The incidence of learning difficulties seems higher in these children than in the general population; sometimes verbal chattiness, known as the *cocktail party syndrome,* where big words are used with limited understanding of their meaning, is evidenced.

The interdisciplinary team, with its medical specialist, occupational and physical therapists, speech and language clinician, psychologist or social worker, as well as the special education specialist and teacher, are crucial in planning with family and child for optimal placement and forward-looking outcomes.

TRAUMATIC BRAIN INJURY

Statistics given by the NSW Roads and Traffic Authority (1998, statistical database) highlight the significance of road and passenger safety in early childhood. For example, in 1996, in the Australian state of New South Wales (population 6 200 000), 13 children were killed in road accidents and 92 seriously injured in the age group 0–4 years; in the 5–9 years age group, 13 were killed and 169 seriously injured.

As the most common cause of *acquired* disability of childhood, traumatic brain injury includes cases of precipitous falls, road accidents, sports injuries, self-inflicted injuries, and child assault and abuse. Major factors contributing to the damage are the *impact* forces, which occur on contact of the head with a hard surface as in a fall from a height, and *inertial* forces, which include acceleration/deceleration forces acting on the head as in a car accident, which may have much more grievous consequences. Injuries include the following (Bathshaw & Perret, 1992):

- *Scalp and skull injuries* may cause considerable blood loss but not necessarily brain damage, although a depressed skull fracture where the bone is pressing on cortical tissue is more serious.
- *Brain contusion* results in direct impact to the brain, where the tissue is bruised. Symptoms may appear a few days after the injury, and surgical intervention may be warranted.
- *Epidural haematoma*, which is a blood clot in the space between the brain and its meninges (i.e. dura), is potentially lethal but surgically treatable. Vein bleeds are less serious than arterial bleeds; initial symptoms may be absent until the haematoma becomes sufficiently severe to present symptoms ranging from a headache to coma. Swift surgical intervention reduces the risk of sustained damage.
- *Subdural haematoma* is the more severe type of brain bleed. It occurs on the brain surface, and is usually attributed to tremendous movement forces acting on the head that displace it with sufficient violence to rupture veins or arteries that are otherwise protected by the multilayer meninges of the brain and the fluid it bathes in. Surgical removal of the clot is usually not sufficient to ameliorate the symptoms, as the damage to the brain itself may be extensive.

- *Concussion* leads to a brief period of loss of consciousness, but does not get worse over time. Symptoms such as headache, drowsiness, confusion and irritability usually clear within a few days.
- *Diffuse axonal injury* refers to more severe concussion symptoms, where nerve fibres are torn with impact or mechanical motion. Common in road accidents, it results in coma in severe cases, and difficulty with breathing and maintaining blood pressure in milder cases. Subdural haematoma may be present, as other body parts can also suffer injury in such accidents, exacerbating the condition.

The *severity* of brain injury in cases of lost consciousness is assessed by the *Glasgow Coma Score* (Jennett & Teasdale, 1981), which evaluates the response to eye-opening, best motor response, and verbal response on a numerical scale for each; higher scores indicate *milder* damage. The responses evaluated include:

- *eye opening* (4 to 1)—spontaneous, to speech, to pain, nil;
- *best motor response* (6 to 1)—obeys, localises, withdraws, abnormal flexion, extensor response, nil;
- *verbal response* (5 to 1)—oriented, confused conversation, inappropriate words, incomprehensible sounds, nil.

Severe head injury has a score of 8 or less, while minor head injury has 13 or more.

Management and rehabilitation

A multidisciplinary team is essential in the management and rehabilitation of brain trauma, particularly in cases where global damage has been sustained. Recovery from coma usually presents multiple neurological problems, which include motor, communication, cognitive, behavioural and sensory deficits, calling on the skills of the psychologist, speech and language pathologist, physical and occupational therapists, as well as the special education consultant and teacher (Hall, Johnson & Middleton, 1990). The aims of rehabilitation are:

- aversion of complications that may arise from immobilisation, disuse, and neurological dysfunction;
- augmentation of the use of abilities regained after recovery from coma;
- teaching adaptive compensation for impaired or lost function;
- alleviation of the effect of chronic disability on the growth and development processes (Molnar & Perrin, 1983).

OTHER DISEASES AND CONDITIONS: A BRIEF GLOSSARY

The following diseases and syndromes are congenital. (Some of them are mentioned in Chapter 2 on genetics and heredity.) Some are progressive; most have a neurological involvement, and hence may carry sensory, motor, learning and/or adaptive implications. They are a sample of the many such syndromes, and are compiled for your reference because they are the ones with relatively high incidence (based on Bathshaw & Perret, 1992):

Apert syndrome: primary difficulty is associated with premature fusion of the sutures of the head, resulting in such deformities as high forehead, flattened head, downward-slanting widely spaced eyes, sometimes with cleft palate and crowded teeth. Attributed to genetic mutations, hydrocephalus, hearing defects and developmental delay may be present. Surgical correction reduces the risk of mental retardation.

Batten disease: a progressive neurodegenerative disease, where the child grows normally in the first six to 18 months, followed by loss of motor and cognitive skills, onset of seizures, mental retardation and sensory losses.

CHARGE association: the acronym is derived from the symptoms of the disease, which include *C*oloboma (failure of fusion of the eye socket), *H*eart defect, *A*rtesia chonae (blockage of the nose), *R*etarded growth and development, and *G*enital abnormalities. Variable degrees of mental retardation, as well as visual and auditory impairments, may also be present.

Cornelia de Lange syndrome: children have a characteristic facial appearance, with downward-slanting eyes, heavy eyebrows and long eyelashes. Short stature and microcephaly are common. Autistic-like behaviours and hearing impairment may be observed; speech and language may be delayed as a part of the global developmental delay.

Duchenne muscular dystrophy: caused by a mutation of the X chromosome, the disease is characterised by progressive pelvic muscle weakness and wasting, enlargement of thigh muscles, and tight heel cords. As the myelin sheath dissolves, respiratory effort increases and heart problems are common. Affected children are usually wheelchair-dependent before puberty. Learning difficulties and mental retardation may be observed. Survival expectancy is to young adulthood.

Galactosaemia: inborn metabolical error where the natural sugar found in milk cannot be tolerated; neonates often have jaundice, enlarged liver, vomiting, lethargy and increased risk of infection. If infants are treated with a controlled diet, IQ is minimally affected. Abnormal visual perception, cerebellar ataxia and tremors are common.

Huntington disease (chorea): a progressive neurological disease, it can occur during childhood (although its typical onset is in adulthood), especially if this genetically transmitted disorder has been passed on from the father. It is characterised by tic-like movements which gradually involve large muscle groups, seizures and speech abnormalities.

Hurler syndrome: motor and cognitive development usually peak at about two years of age and subsequently deteriorate in this disease of inborn metabolical error. Associated deficits include visual and hearing impairment, progressive joint mobility limitation and cardiac failure.

Hypothyroidism (congenital cretinism): these infants are noted to be large for gestational age, with low muscle tone, a large tongue and a hoarse cry. If thyroid supplementation is initiated before six weeks, developmental delays can be averted. However, such delays are inevitable if treatment has not occurred beyond the first year of life; these include mental retardation and delayed bone and dental maturation.

Kernicterus: due to accumulation of excessive bilirubin in Rh incompatibility between fetus and mother, it results in athetoid cerebral palsy, with stained teeth, upward-gaze paralysis, high-frequency hearing loss and mental retardation. Its incidence has decreased significantly due to postnatal therapy.

Marfan syndrome: attributed to a genetic abnormality, it is characterised by a tall, thin stature, spidery limbs, hypermobile joints, chest deformities and loss of vision. Learning disabilities and ADHD are commonly observed, although intelligence is normal.

Neurofibromatosis (type I): multiple darkened spots ('café-au-lait' splatters) on the body are typical, and are associated with nerve tumours (neurofibromas) in the body and on the skin. Cognitive ability is not affected, although disfigurement may result in some cases. Type II is associated with tumours on the auditory nerve only.

Noonan syndrome: characterised by a short stature, congenital heart defects, widely spaced downward-slanting eyes, low-set ears and chest deformity, the affected children also show mild mental retardation, motor delays, hearing deficits and articulation defects.

Osteogenesis imperfecta: also known as brittle bone disease, the disease process involves an underlying abnormality of collagen formation, so the child is highly susceptible to bone fractures. It may result in bony deformities. Affected children also have bluish eyeballs, translucent skin, and possible hearing impairment.

Pediatric AIDS (acquired immune deficiency syndrome): the virus causing the disorder, HIV (human immunodeficiency virus), causes a breakdown in the immune system by destroying T4 and CD4 cells, which allows opportunistic diseases to attack the body. Some children with chronic conditions such as haemophilia who rely on blood transfusions have been known to contract the disease, although 80% of children have acquired the virus from their mothers: the infected mother has a one in three chance of infecting the fetus. Aggressive pharmacological treatments have improved the longevity in infected children.

Prader-Willi syndrome: as infants, these children show poor muscle tone, feeding and temperature control. Tone improves with age, but a disproportionate appetite and severe obesity follows. Other characteristics include small hands and feet, small genitalia and short stature. Associated with the deletion of chromosome 15, children develop serious behavioural problems (with food as the focus) and mental retardation.

(Congenital) rubella syndrome: attributed to the mother's contraction of rubella prior to the 17th week of pregnancy; affected children suffer intrauterine growth retardation, microcephaly, cataracts, sensorineural hearing loss and congenital heart disease. Mental retardation, deafness and cerebral palsy are common developmental problems.

Torsion dystonia (dystonia musculorum deformans): a progressive involuntary movement disorder with normal intelligence; the limbs show contractures. Ashkenazi populations are affected.

Treacher-Collins syndrome: characterised by a facial appearance with low-set ears with malformations, widely spaced eyes, flattened cheekbones, absence of lower eyelashes, cleft palate, and frequent conductive hearing loss; affected children are of normal intelligence. During infancy, feeding problems, nasal obstruction, apnoea and language delay due to hearing loss may be observed.

Trisomy 13: associated with microcephaly, brain malformations, cleft lip and palate, congenital heart defects, multifingers, and eye, kidney and digestive system malformations. Affected children also show profound mental retardation and cerebral palsy.

Trisomy 18: associated with severe birth defects; these children are small for gestational age, with low-set ears, clenched hands and overriding fingers, and congenital heart defects; few survive beyond the first year of life.

Trisomy 21: better known as Down syndrome (see Chapter 11).

Tuberous sclerosis: associated with underpigmented areas and acne-like facial lesions in young children, other characteristics include infantile spasms and calcium deposits on the brain. Malignancies, hydrocephalus, and tumours of the heart are common. Children may have mild to moderate mental retardation.

Waardenburg syndrome: characterised by congenital deafness; affected children have an unusual facial appearance, with irises of different colours and a white forelock of hair. Developmental disabilities are related to hearing loss.

William syndrome (elfin facies syndrome/hypercalcaemia): characterised by a short stature, full lips and cheeks, a star-like pattern to the iris and a hoarse voice; affected children may suffer heart and kidney complications. Hyperactivity, temperament abnormalities and mild to moderate mental retardation may be observed, although, curiously, language development and competence does not seem to be affected.

CONCLUSIONS

We have reviewed some neurogenic and congenital disabilities of early childhood. Most children with such disabilities are successfully integrated into mainstream classrooms; others with high support needs may require home or institutional care.

Traumatic brain injury in young children incurred by accidents may be prevented by astute safety and security measures. Home, school, playground and road safety are paramount in ensuring the prevention of loss of life and function.

17

Preferred practice: working with the families

In this final chapter, let us consider how to deal with young children with special needs: Are we to follow the medical model, where the causes and classification of conditions are in the forefront, and the professional is at the helm when it comes to making decisions for the child and the family? Or shall we consider more contemporary approaches, in which professionals work in teams, families are empowered to make the decisions that work best for them and their child, and children with special needs are seen on a continuum of development, difference and disability, where their strengths are augmented and needs are facilitated?

Most professionals working with young children with disabilities or exceptionalities prefer to engage in a practice where the child and the family are seen as a unit, while they themselves are a member of a team facilitating the decisions and progress of the child and family. Let us take a closer look, and review the theory that interfaces with such practice.

FAMILY AS A SOCIAL SYSTEM

The ecological perspective on families views them as dynamic, interrelated subsystems, in which a change in one component will have an impact on all other components. Families do not exist in isolation but are embedded within a wider sociological matrix. Similarly, the developing child is embedded within the social system, and will be greatly influenced by the forces acting upon her as she will influence the interactive constellation that she is a part of (Bronfenbrenner, 1977). (You may recall our review of family systems in Chapter 9, as we looked at psychopathology.)

The family systems conceptual framework has four components, a change in any one of which affects all the others (Turnbull, Summers & Brotherson, 1986):

- family resources, which are the psychological and monetary means available;
- family interactions, which define the patterns of relatedness and nurturing;
- family functions, which describe decision-making mechanisms and role expectancies;
- family life cycle, which describes the process of growth and transitions of families as they move through time.

The arrival of a new child in the family system is bound to affect these components. A child with a disability is likely to introduce unexpected variables, which need to be assimilated into the system; what is important to appreciate is that *all* members and components of the family system will be affected by a single adjustment. To illustrate, consider the following excerpt.

> The birth of a child may alter the responsibilities of other family members, as well as the allocation of resources to meet new or different family functions. If the child is born with or develops a disability, this may further stress the family system. The family may be introduced to an early intervention program or to a set of providers to assist with the new baby. The ramifications of particular treatments or interventions will likely extend beyond the effects upon the baby. For example, the mother may devote her time and physical and emotional energy to specialised feeding procedures and therapeutic exercises several times a day. This takes time away from her husband, the other children and herself. Some specialised treatments may strain the family's financial resources. Others may require numerous appointments and creative solutions to childcare. Even relatively simple interventions (from the professional team's perspective) may have ripple effects on the other family members. (Widerstrom, Mowder & Sandall, 1991, p.177)

Effects of disability on the family

It is not unusual for families to go through a grieving process before they come to grips with a child with a disability. Often, the birth of a new baby is an opportunity for the parents to relive their childhood with the benefit of hindsight. The aspirations, expectancies and motivations for the infant may have to be re-evaluated; at times there is a serious battle to be won for the infant's life. There may be overpowering feelings of guilt, shame, anger and rebellion. Coping with a disability is a lifelong endeavour, and many families learn the ropes while they are actually in the journey.

Each family is a complex social system, with many different characteristics, values, belief systems, relational structures, and material and psychological resources. With such diversity, each family may react to and cope with having a child with a handicapping condition quite differently. Some factors influencing the family's reaction are the following (Turnbull & Turnbull, 1986):

Disability characteristics.   Although parents' initial reaction may be stronger to a child with a congenital and readily identifiable disability such as spina bifida or Down syndrome, the more 'invisible' conditions such as a learning disability may be considerably more difficult to get the appropriate services for.

Family characteristics.   Larger families with adequate financial resources seem to adjust better to a child with a disability. Single-parent families often have greater difficulty than nuclear families. Families of lower socioeconomic status may already be stressed with limited resources and inadequate health care, and the arrival of an infant with a handicap (the incidence of which is higher in that population due to poor prenatal care) may present as a crisis, and even reduce their capacity to take advantage of community support programs.

Balance of the extent of the problems with available resources.   Families' resilience and coping skills are related to how well they can negotiate the system around them to get a good match between the demands of a disability and the resources needed to deal with it. The family's feelings of isolation and stress may be compounded when there is lack of synchrony with the rest of the community.

Principles to guide professionals working with families include the following (Paul & Simeonsson, 1993):

- Develop an appreciation for the developmental life course of the family with a child with a disability.
- Take a central interest in the family's experiences.
- Respect ethnicity as an organising framework for understanding families.
- Focus on the ethical implications of all aspects of professional decisions affecting families.
- Develop particular emphasis on the social and cultural complexity of providing care for and with families who have children with disabilities.
- Have a commitment to sharing the vision of diversity, and sensitivity to the spiritual and social lives of families.

PARADIGM SHIFTS IN INTERVENTION: FAMILY-CENTRED CARE

We are all in the middle of a substantial change of attitude, or a paradigm shift in early intervention: intervention revolves around the family, instead of the child or the professionals. There have been some powerful influences bringing about the approach where families are at centre stage, collaboration among professionals is paramount, and both families and professionals are equal partners in the assessment, planning and implementation of services for children with disabilities. No longer are the paternalistic, authoritarian professional models, largely engendered by the medical model, viable—nor are restrictive environments for children in special schools or institutions: inclusive education aims at providing educational experiences to all children. Assessment and intervention, too, take place in naturalistic environments, rather than in those alien to the child. In the USA this approach is mandated before funding is made available to agencies; in Australia it is preferred practice. We examine how some of these applications affect our attitudes and practices with young children with disabilities and their families.

One of the most vocal influences affecting the family-centred approach is that of Dunst and his colleagues (Dunst, Trivette & Deal, 1988), who have challenged us to rethink the ways in which we view families and the helping relationships we have with them. Two terms they have introduced are important contributors to the paradigm shift:

- *Enabling families* implies creating means and opportunities for families to apply their present abilities and competencies, as well as acquiring novel ones that are necessary to meet their needs and those of their children.
- *Empowering families* implies interacting with them in ways that allow families the maintenance or acquisition of control over their own lives, as well as attributing positive changes that result from early intervention to their own strengths, abilities and actions.

In order to achieve family enablement and empowerment, the tone of communications between professionals and families needs to change from a condescending one to a partnership mode, where feelings of trust and respect are conveyed to the families. Professionals do not 'treat the deficit'; families are capable of making the decision that best suits their child's and their own needs. Such practices emphasise supporting the augmentation of the capabilities and existing social networks of the family in its quest to optimise the development of its child with special needs.

Family-centred approaches

The practice of *family-centred care* is founded on family systems theory, which views families as interacting systems, appreciating the impact that the role and responsibility of any member of the family unit will have on all parts of the system. As already mentioned, *family-centred care* is a concept that shifts decision-making from the professionals to the family members, a quite revolutionary concept given the traditional paradigms.

The principal elements of family-centred care for all professionals involved with families of young children with disabilities can be summarised as follows (Shelton, Jeppson & Johnson, 1987, p.71):

- recognition that the family is the constant in the child's life while the service systems and service-providers within those systems are variable;
- facilitation of parent–professional collaboration at all levels of health care, including the care of the child, development, implementation and evaluation of programs for her, and policy formation;
- sharing of unbiased and complete information with parents about their child's care on an ongoing basis with appropriate and supportive communicative styles;
- implementation of appropriate policies and programs that are comprehensive, and supplying of emotional and financial support to meet the family needs;
- recognition of family strengths and individuality, and respect for different methods of coping;
- understanding and incorporating the developmental needs of infants, children, adolescents and their families into health care delivery systems;
- encouragement and facilitation of parent-to-parent support;
- assurance that the design of health care delivery systems is flexible, accessible and responsive to family needs.

Given the diversity of communities, cultures and societies, the elements given above may be benchmarks: the implementation of some of these may be limited or not possible universally, unless it has protection under the law, as in the USA. Nevertheless, at the baseline *attitudinal* level, preferred practice mandates that we come to understand and accept that professionals are in partnership with families. Here are some basic tenets in working with families (Crais, 1991):

- Families are equal partners in assessment and intervention.
- The primary professional role is to support the family in making decisions and stating individual preferences regarding services for their children.
- Families are individual systems, and professionals need to be aware of and responsive to this.
- Families are community members first, so services need to fit into natural settings.

Multicultural service delivery

The challenges to professionals working with young children and their families often include understanding and respecting the diverse cultural values, preferences and child-rearing styles present in our multicultural societies. Some guidelines are suggested for professionals to enhance their cultural competence in supporting families (Hanson, Lynch & Wayman, 1990):

■ Describe the ethnic group with which the family identifies, including the family's country of origin, language, and the size of the ethnic community in the local area.

■ Identify the social organisation of the ethnic community, particularly those structures which may be a source of support and resource to the family.

■ Determine how the members of that community gain access to the use of social services.

■ Understand the family's belief systems, ceremonies, symbols, values and attitudes towards seeking help.

■ Seek information about the history of the ethnic group, and the past and present events that have an impact on family life.

CLOSER LOOK: LANGUAGE FACILITATION AND FAMILY INVOLVEMENT

Language, probably more than any other domain of development, appears to be a central construct in child development. It is a tool that shapes learning, facilitates problem-solving, negotiates social relations, expresses the self and emotions, manifests positive interactions between caregivers and children; and, more often than not, speech and language are affected in atypical development. Most intervention or facilitation programs are likely to have a language component, and language and literacy skills are crucial to positive academic outcomes in school. Particularly in the early years, the family crucible is where most language exchange takes place, the early childhood setting and school following as a close second in later years. It therefore makes sense to use the setting most readily available (i.e. family) to put into place the strategies to enhance communicative skills.

In earlier chapters (5 and 6), we examine how communication develops within the mother–child interactive matrix, and how such interactivity is also the genesis of sound social emotional development. Professionals working with families, too, have substantial support and responsivity responsibilities towards the families, whose emotional energies may be sapped by the acceptance and care of a child with a handicap.

There is increasing evidence that adult interaction with young children has a significant effect on the prelinguistic and emerging language skills of young children with developmental delays, including non-verbal communication, vocabulary, and early semantic relations. Adults were found to communicate with children in similar ways, regardless of the children's ability to communicate. However, children with language delays were found to be less capable to maintain conversations with caregivers. This represents a mismatch and many lost opportunities, as adults were found to speak for the child, or to limit the variety of responses to the child.

Research indicates that the models of language intervention professionals develop with families have a significant positive impact on facilitating children's communicative skills:

- Teaching adults to increase their responsiveness to young children with developmental delays demonstrates positive effects in enhancing communicative skills in the children (Warren, Yoder, Gazdag, Kim & Jones, 1993).
- Positive effects were found when parents used *milieu approaches,* where they were instructed to use contingent imitation, responsivity, following the child's lead, linguistic mapping and social routines.
- Prelinguistic skills were found to improve when parents (i) elicited child communication behaviours through the use of the above techniques; (ii) provided language models through naming objects and actions that the child attended to; and (iii) embedded teaching within developmentally appropriate routines.
- Adults' use of milieu techniques was found to produce *generalised effects* in eliciting more *intentional* behaviours from children, where they looked, pointed and vocalised significantly more towards their parents (Yoder, Warren & Gazdag, 1994).
- With preschool-aged children, the employment of a naturalistic environmental arrangement of toys, elevated their responsiveness to adults, and the employment of incidental teaching techniques as a part of *enhanced milieu teaching*, also resulted in enhanced communicative utterances and vocabulary (Kaiser & Hester, 1994).

The degree of adult responsiveness to young children, as determined by the caregivers' ability to recognise the child's behavioural cues and provision of contingent, appropriate and consistent responses to those cues, enhances the child's ability to understand and use communicative signals. Parents often benefit from training aimed at sharpening their awareness of such behavioural cues. Many family–professional team partnerships enhance the family's skills of attunement, which then result in positive child outcomes, not only in terms of communicative skills but also in attachment and psychosocial development. The primary goals for the early intervention professional are (Bailey & Simeonsson, 1988):

- to support families to care for their children;
- to enhance child development outcomes; and
- to facilitate positive interactions between caregivers and children in the family context.

Supporting families in facilitating their children's communicative development seems the perfect opportunity to meet these goals.

In summary, family members have crucial roles in facilitation; they in turn may need to be facilitated themselves by the professionals to elicit positive child outcomes.

ASSESSMENT, PLANNING, INTERVENTION, EVALUATION

Assessment

Assessment is the procedure by which information is collected for the child's intervention needs. Assessment *overlaps* with planning and intervention; it needs to be an ongoing, daily process, where the child and all her adaptive skills in all developmental domains are observed and critically analysed as a matter of course.

In the preceding chapters some *formal* or standardised tools of assessment are mentioned that target particular domains of development. Also mentioned is that *norm-referenced testing*, which compares an individual's performance to a large group of the same age, is not appropriate for children with special needs. *Criterion-referenced measures* are those assessment tools which evaluate performance against a target or criterion; these are often more suitable. *Naturalistic observation* when performed competently can be as informative as any other measure, and forms the basis for *play-based assessment*. The assessment procedure would not be complete unless *contextual* variables were considered and accounted for as well. The brief of the team is to use all approaches appropriately and then frame them within an *ecological* perspective.

Ecological assessment takes into account the environments the child is expected to function in, so the child's chances for successful adaptation are

Table 17.1		Traditional assessment	Ecological assessment
Ecological vs traditional assessment	*Reference*	Child's test performance is judged against comparable data from other children or norm	Child's performance is compared to demands and expectations of tasks in her environment
	Focus	Developmental ages and stages that are representative of the child's age	Child's ability to participate in natural settings and to meet task expectations in those settings
	Procedures	Child's response is elicited to a set of standardised tasks which are believed to represent skills and abilities in that domain	Child's behaviour is observed in relevant activities and contexts, and persons who know the child well are interviewed
	Context	Independent assessments are made by representatives of different professions in alien settings	Coordinated assessments are made by a team of professionals, and family members, in naturalistic settings
	Use of results	Child's status is determined relative to peers, with a view to placement and eligibility for services	Child's individualised goals and objectives are generated to plan for specialised instruction for optimal adaptation

maximised within those environments. Ecological versus traditional assessment is compared and contrasted in Table 17.1 (based on McCormick, Loeb & Schiefelbusch, 1997, p.228).

Teams are a central concept in preferred practices of service delivery to young children and their families. Models for teams have evolved, with the *transdisciplinary team* being the most favoured one. In a transdisciplinary team, team members collaborate in assessment and planning as well as sharing skills in the implementation of intervention, and professionals and parents become trainers and consultants for one another (Rainforth, York & MacDonald 1992).

Transdisciplinary play-based assessment (Linder, 1993) is one such contemporary practice, which utilises a team approach in a joint assessment arena. Assessment is performed by all collaborating discipline members simultaneously, while the child is being observed in a naturalistic environment at play. Parents contribute to the information collected, and questions asked encourage the observation of qualitative aspects of *how* the child performs certain tasks. It provides for an ecological and holistic assessment, while avoiding the redundancy inherent in individual assessments.

Collaborative consultation involves two professionals working together to provide special instruction or intervention, based on joint planning, shared responsibility, resources and accountability, and a willingness to invest time and energy in becoming familiar with one another's viewpoints, values and vocabulary. Both believe that two heads is better than one and that sharing increases the probability of desired outcomes (Thousand & Villa, 1992).

Planning and inclusion

The Individualised Family Service Plan (IFSP) is the written *program* and record of the culmination of the efforts of the team towards providing a very young child and her family with appropriate services. It is mandated by the *Individuals with Disabilities Education Act* (IDEA, 1990), the sequel to Public Law 99–457 in the USA, which provides funding to state and local service agencies to assist with the cost of serving children with disabilities. Here are some of characteristics of an IFSP:

- It is appropriate for children *birth to three years* of age, and specifies the services needed for the child and the family.
- It is a process of sharing and consolidating information, and is intended to be an *ongoing*, dynamic process, geared to establish working relationships between the professionals and the family.
- It does not have a particular format, and families are encouraged to write it out; however, there are components that *must* be included in this document:

- a statement of the young child's current level of functioning in physical, cognitive, communicative, social-emotional and adaptive development, based on acceptable objective criteria;
- a statement of the family's strengths and needs related to enhancing the development of the child;
- a statement of the major intervention outcomes, including the criteria by which they are judged, the procedures to be employed, and the time lines in which progress is expected, so that necessary modifications can be made;
- a statement regarding the specific early intervention services necessary to meet the unique needs of the child and the family;
- the projected date for initiation of services and their expected duration, as well as the naturalistic environments in which such services will be provided;
- the procedures to be employed to ensure successful transition from infant to preschool or school services;
- The name of a service coordinator (case manager) from the profession most immediately relevant to the identified needs of the family, who will be responsible for the implementation of the plan and for coordination with other agencies and persons.

- The *service coordinator* is a team member who brings together all the elements in an IFSP, as well as promoting family independence by assisting the family to mobilise its resources to better meet their needs.
- A *multidisciplinary assessment* must be provided, where at least two disciplines are involved in the provision of integrated and coordinated assessment activities.
- The IFSP meetings may include all the individuals the family deems necessary, including extended family members, friends and advocates. They should be held at a place and time convenient to the family, and is to be reviewed every six months unless the family wishes for an earlier review.

The Individual Education Plan (IEP) provides for the needs of the older child under IDEA legislation, and has provisions for educational and special services. It is the document which shows the agreement between the school and the family as to the nature, extent and manner of delivery of services to the child within the least restrictive environment.

- It comes about as a team decision, the participants being the family members, the school representatives and special service-providers.
- The parents are invited to participate in developing an IEP at a time and place convenient to them.
- The contents of the IEP should address the following items (IDEA, 1990):
  - a statement regarding the child's present levels of performance in all developmental areas;

- identification of annual and short-term instructional goals and objectives in all targeted areas;
- a statement regarding the appropriate objective criteria, evaluation procedures and methods of determining the child's progress towards the goals and objectives;
- a statement of the special educational and related services to be provided to achieve these goals and objectives;
- a statement of the child's participation in the least restrictive environment;
- projected dates for initiation, and duration of services;
- a statement regarding the community transition for students by 16 years of age.

- Parental consent is necessary for the implementation of special services or placement, although IEP goals can be implemented without parental consent. The mandate provides that the parents have access to legal protection and due process if the IEP agreement or its implementation is disagreeable to them.
- While all children with special needs within the public school systems are required to have an IEP and are entitled to due process, in Australia this may be a less formal process, as it is not mandatory and does not carry legal clout.

Least restrictive environment and inclusion means that children with disabilities have the opportunity to be educated with the rest of the population to the maximum extent appropriate. In the continuum of placements from the least restrictive (i.e. normal classroom) to the most restrictive (i.e. a special education centre or school), being placed in a normal class is the preferred option. The learning environment needs to adapt to the needs of *all* children by restructuring classrooms and schools such that individual differences can be supported and nurtured (Stainback & Stainback, 1990).

In Australia today, through national policies of inclusion, schools are moving to cater for the needs of all children in their neighbourhood, regardless of any disabilities or special needs that individual children may possess. Some special schools remain, although most are closely associated with local schools, providing opportunities for integration and inclusion for children with and without disabilities (Cowley, 1996).

Inclusion is *not* episodic visits to the general education classroom for art, music, and/or circle time . . . Inclusion is *'belonging'*. It is *every* child (whether eligible for special services or not) having whatever resources and supports she needs, *and* a challenging educational program that is geared to her abilities, needs and interests . . . It is everyone (children and adults alike) welcoming and valuing abilities as well as disabilities and learning to respect and depend on one another. (McCormick, Loeb & Schiefelbusch, 1997, p.231)

Intervention

Intervention in the past has been in a clinic, a therapy room or a corner of the classroom, by the representative of a discipline, such as a speech and language pathologist, occupational therapist, psychologist, physical therapist or special education consultant/teacher. The rationale underlying the isolated therapy model was that children acquired skills most efficiently when taught in a highly structured, distraction-free environment, with access to specialised tools and equipment. We have moved towards an *integrated intervention* approach within naturalistic environments, with good reasons for the shift (Cirrin & Penner, 1995):

- Children have difficulty in the generalisation of acquired skills from the therapy room to the natural environment.
- Particularly in language therapy, the roles of social interaction and literacy are seen as a contextually bound whole with language, and thus adult-directed, systematic instruction became incompatible with our current notions of facilitation.
- Withdrawing children from classrooms meant that not only was attention drawn to them, they also missed classroom learning.
- Fragmentation, redundancy and lack of coordination were inevitable, as the classroom teacher or the family were not fully informed of the intervention process or contents.

Integrated intervention in naturalistic environments by collaborative teams has required the members of a collaborative team to redefine their professional goals and responsibilities, and has been endorsed by the professional organisations of the disciplines that work in school settings. In return, it has yielded a contemporary model of effective communications, a shared vision for the child and the family, and skills that are much more likely to generalise and become functional in the 'real' world in which the child lives.

Program evaluation

Evaluation is essential to determine the efficacy of intervention. Traditionally, effectiveness of evaluation has been determined by measuring the child's progress. More contemporary views include not only child progress but the family's satisfaction with the program, and the long-term benefit to society. In order to attribute the progress in the child to the intervention, and not to maturation or other extraneous variables, the following criteria need to be met (Fey & Cleave, 1990):

- Areas to be targeted for intervention need to be specified. Well-written IEPs will have included this information in the stated objectives.
- Behaviours believed to be valid representations of the target areas need to be selected. Again, IEPs should specify this attribute.
- Measurements must be made reliably and objectively.

To illustrate these points, consider the following IEP objectives. Have the evaluation criteria been worked in well?

> By the review date in six months, Lily will maintain eye contact for five seconds at the beginning of a conversation when she is prompted 50% of the time.
> or
> By the review date, Jasmine will indicate her desire to go to the toilet by signalling the caregiver consistently.
> or
> By the review date, Kara's parents will be able to read her a short bedtime story while she listens attentively without getting out of bed, three evenings a week.

Another method for evaluating the efficacy of an intervention program may be through the employment of *social validity* measures, which obtains qualitative information from individuals who are within the social system of the child regarding the targeted outcomes. A set of questions may be given before and after the intervention to see parents' and others' opinions on the effectiveness of the intervention or facilitation provided. The use of both the objective and the qualitative measures may be called for in evaluating treatment and intervention outcomes (Olswag & Bain, 1994).

CHALLENGES FOR EARLY CHILDHOOD TEACHERS

As teachers of young children embrace the challenge of inclusion, they need to be as knowledgeable about normal child development and developmentally appropriate practice (DAP) (Bredecamp, 1987) as about atypical development and development of children with special needs and their families. While all the other members of the professional team are *trained* in atypical development and conditions, the baseline for practice for the early childhood teacher is normal populations. Yet, as we reviewed above, these lines of distinction have now been blurred: *all* children, with their myriad of individual differences, share the learning environment, albeit with modifications to ensure successful adaptations for a few. How is one to cope?

One can argue that early childhood teachers have been suffused with the 'developmentally appropriate practice' endorsed by the National Association for the Education of Young Children (Bredecamp, 1987) in their professional training, which prepares them for inclusive education. The basic tenets of DAP are the following:

Age appropriateness.   The knowledge base derived from developmental theory and research on universal, predictable sequences of growth and change that occur in the first eight years of life in all domains of development, including the physical, emotional, social and cognitive–linguistic domains, forms the framework on which appropriate learning activities are structured.

Age-appropriate practice emphasises those aspects of development which are considered to be applicable to all children uniformly, with an assumption of a maturational model of development.

Individual appropriateness. This is even more pertinent to inclusive education. Individual appropriateness stresses aspects of development that are *unique* to each child, such as rate of development, individual personality characteristics such as temperament, and factors that may be influenced by the different cultural and social circumstances in which the child is living (Elkind, 1989). The curriculum is responsive to *each child's growing abilities,* at the same time as challenging the child's interest and understanding.

Another concern is for teachers who have not had child development in their professional preparation but who nevertheless work with children. Indeed, the focus of training in most elementary and secondary school teacher preparation programs is more on curriculum than on development. Thus, the early childhood teacher has a distinct advantage in planning for and accommodating successful inclusive education applications.

Early childhood educators as team coordinators

Having come to the end of the book, I wish to make my biases for early childhood educators (ECEs) quite clear. I argue that ECEs are uniquely qualified and placed to be not only case managers/service coordinators but pivotal members of the service-providers' team for young children with disabilities and their families.

- ECEs have a sound knowledge of typical development, and are familiar with atypical child development; thus they are well placed to plan inclusive educational settings.
- Early childhood settings, particularly in preschool years, are much more naturalistic and child-centred in their approach. As such, they are ideal grounds for early intervention.
- ECEs maintain developmentally appropriate practice, which allows an inherent commitment to inclusive education.
- ECEs have ample opportunity to liaise and maintain contact with the families, which allows for the maturation of a professional, supportive and empowering relationship.
- After home, children spend more time at an early childhood setting or school than any other facility. School becomes a substantive chunk of the young child's life, presenting an ideal opportunity for implementation of the intervention goals and objectives in that naturalistic setting with the assistance of the ECE.
- ECEs are relatively easy to access, for communication purposes, by the rest of the transdisciplinary team members. The early childhood setting is

also suitable for family and other team member consultations, making it a viable venue for ongoing points of contact.

- The role of the teacher has been clearly delineated in IEP meetings as absolutely essential in the planning and review process.
- The profession of early childhood has matured in its standing to make such a critical contribution to the assessment, planning, intervention and evaluation of services for young children with disabilities and their families.
- In cases of less obvious disabilities, such as learning disabilities or attention-related deficits, ECEs are the professionals who may identify children at risk for school failure before any other referral has been made, based on their knowledge of development and the child's comparison with the norm.
- The professional role of the ECE is inherently trans- and interdisciplinary; the various professional hats an ECE wears include, but are not limited to, those of:
  - an administrator and manager of an educational centre or setting,
  - a guidance counsellor, with the families who often seek assistance for their support needs,
  - a social worker and community liaison officer, in the capacity of providing resources and information to the parents towards enabling and empowering them,
  - an adult facilitator, in providing support and supervision for untrained teaching staff at the setting,
  - a teacher, in educating young children in developmentally appropriate ways,
  - a special educator and service-provider, as a transdisciplinary team member,
  - a first aid officer, in cases of accidents and minor emergencies, and
  - an occasional cook, cleaner, handyperson and gardener.
- ECEs are trained to be flexible in their approach and to utilise lateral thinking in problem-solving. They can often recruit the additional resources called for in successful adaptation which may be necessitated by the individual attention required by some children.[1]
- And, last but not the least, ECEs seem to possess the temperament and professional commitment for *going the extra mile* for the welfare of young children and their families.

Towards the new millennium . . .

The fact that there has been such a substantial change in attitudes and practices in the delivery of services to children with atypical development deserves a standing ovation but not complacency.

---

1   Many come to mind, but one stands out. During the course of my supervision visits to students in guided practice in Sydney, I found out that one preschool director had recruited a reliable pool of volunteer teachers from the Seniors Village next door.

- In many countries of the world, even those that are developed, like Australia, the rights of the child and family to a free and appropriate education in the least restrictive environment is not a legal mandate; it is thus a privilege, and not a right.
- There are subpopulations even in the USA where poverty, remoteness of the community or its minority status have a negative impact on the family's ability to negotiate the system effectively to obtain optimal services for their child with a disability.
- Family-centred practice calls for reflective skills on the part of its practitioners, which may have implications for further self-awareness training. Old habits die painfully slowly; abandoning the paternalistic model in favour of a democratic and egalitarian one may appear to be threatening to the professional roles.
- Inclusive education is recognised as having as much potential benefit for children without handicaps as for those with special needs. However, it may also serve an expedient motive driven by monetary rationalisation. Inclusion is not dumping the child without adequately preparing the learning environment for her needs; it is not a sink-or-swim approach, and is not meant to be a cost-cutting device for governing bodies.

> The balance of vulnerability and resilience is seen as fundamental in the effort to produce innovative models of early developmental services that both address the needs of children, families and communities and enhance their capacity to cope in a model where
>
> *difference is the norm*
> *change is constant, and*
> *context is central*
>
> (Hayes, 1997).

CONCLUSIONS

Children and families are the very essence of society. Some require more support than others to participate fully in community life. And all of us are getting better at feeling, thinking, knowing, communicating, delivering and reflecting on what we have done in contributing to that process of being a valued member of the community. This we must perform responsibly and sensitively, so we can do it better with each new and special child and her family.

References

Abidin, R. (1990). *Parenting Stress Index manual* (3rd ed.). Charlottesville, VA: Pediatric Psychology Press.

Achenbach, T.M. (1978). The child behavior profile: I < boys aged 6–11. *Journal of Consulting and Clinical Psychiatry, 46,* 478–488.

——(1991). *Manuals for Child Behavior Check List (4–18) and Teachers Report Form.* Burlington, VT: University of Vermont.

Achenbach, T.M., & Edelbrock, C.S. (1983). *Manual for the Child Behavior Checklist and Revised Child Behavior Profile.* Burlington, VT: University Associates in Psychiatry.

Adams, R.J. (1987). An evaluation of color preference in early infancy. *Infant Behavior and Development, 10,* 143–150.

Adesman, A.R., Altshuler, L.A., Lipkin, P.H., & Walce, G.A. (1990). Otitis media in children with learning disabilities and in children with attention deficit disorder with hyperactivity. *Pediatrics, 85* (3) 442.

Ainsworth, M.D.S. (1973). The development of infant-mother attachment. In B.M. Caldwell & H.N. Ricciutti (Eds.), *Review of child development research (Vol. 3): Child development and social policy.* Chicago, IL: University of Chicago Press.

——(1989). Attachments beyond infancy. *American Psychologist, 44,* 709–716.

Ainsworth, M.D.S., Blehar, M.C., Waters, E., & Wall, S. (1978). *Patterns of attachment.* Hillsdale, NJ: Erlbaum.

Aksu, F. (1990). Nature and prognosis of seizures in patients with cerebral palsy. *Developmental Medicine and Child Neurology, 351,* 549–558.

Albright, A.L. (1996). Intrathecal baclofen in cerebral palsy movement disorders. *Journal of Child Neurology, 11* (1), S29–S35.

Aldenkamp, A.P., Alpherts, W.C., Dekker, M.J. et al. (1990). Neuropsychological aspects of learning disabilities in epilepsy. *Epilepsia, 31* (Suppl. 4), S9–S20.

Allen, D.A. (1989). Developmental language disorders in preschool children: Clinical subtypes and syndromes. *School Psychology Review, 18,* 442–451.

Allen, D.A., & Rapin, I. (1992). Autistic children are also dysphasic. In H. Naruse & E.M. Ornitz (Eds.), *Neurobiology of infantile autism* (pp.157–168). Amsterdam: Excerpta Medica.

Allen, M.C., Donohue, P.K., & Dusman, A.E. (1993). The limit of viability: Neonatal outcome of infants born at 22 to 25 weeks' gestation. *New England Journal of Medicine, 329,* 1597–1601.

American Humane Association (1985). *Highlights of official child neglect and abuse reporting.* Denver, CO: Author.

American Speech-Language-Hearing Association (1990). Audiologic screening of infants who are at risk for hearing impairment. *ASHA, 31,* 89–91.

Andersen, E.S., Dunlea, A., & Kekelis, L.S. (1984). Blind children's language: Resolving some differences. *Journal of Child Language, 11,* 645–664.

Anderson, K.L., & Matkin, N.D. (1991). Hearing conservation in the public schools revisited. *Seminars in Hearing, 12,* 340–364.

Andre, T., & Phye, G.D. (1986). Cognition, learning and education. In G.D. Phye & T. Andre (Eds.), *Cognitive classroom learning: Understanding, thinking and problem solving.* Orlando, FL: Academic Press.

ASHA Committee on Language, Speech and Hearing Services in the Schools (April 1980). Definitions for communicative disorders and differences. *ASHA, 22,* 317–318.

Aslin, R.N. (1981). Experiential influences and sensitive periods in perceptual development: A unified model. In R.N. Aslin, A.J. Alberts & M.R. Petersen (Eds.), *Development of perception: Psychobiological perspectives, Vol. 2: The visual system* (pp. 45–93). New York: Academic Press.

Astington, J.W., & Gopnik, A. (1991). Theoretical explanations of the children's understanding of the mind. In G.E. Butterworth, P.L. Harris, A.M. Leslie & H.M. Wellman (Eds.), *Perspectives on the child's theory of mind* (pp.7–31). New York: Oxford University Press.

Australian Bureau of Statistics (1994). *Childcare arrangements.* Canberra: ABS.

Badian, N.A. (1995). Predicting reading ability over the long term: The changing roles of letter naming, phonological awareness, and orthographic processing. *Annals of Dyslexia, 40,* 79–96.

Bailey, D., & Bricker, D. (1986). A psychometric study of criterion-referenced assessment instrument for infants and young children. *Journal of the Division for Early Childhood, 10,* 124–134.

Bailey, B.D., & Simeonsson, R.J. (1988). *Family assessment in early intervention.* Columbus, OH: Merrill.

Baine, D. (1986). *Memory and instruction.* Englewood, NJ: Educational Technical Publications.

Baker-Ward, L., Ornstein, P.A., & Holden, D.J. (1984). The expression of memorization in early childhood. *Journal of Experimental Child Psychology, 37,* 555–575.

Balaban, M.T. (1995). Affective influences on startle in five-month-old infants: Reactions to facial expressions of emotion. *Child Development, 66,* 28–36.

Ballard, J.L., Khoury, J.C., Wedig, K. et al. (1991). New Ballard score, expanded to include extremely premature infants. *Journal of Pediatrics, 119,* 417–423.

Bandura, A. (1989). Social cognitive theory. *Annals of Child Development, 6,* 1–60.

Banks, M.S., & Salapatek, P. (1983). Infant visual perception. In M.S. Banks & P. Salapatek (Eds.), *Handbook of child psychology, Vol. 2: Infancy and developmental psychobiology* (4th ed) (pp.436–571). New York: Wiley.

Barkley, R.A. (1990). *Attention deficit hyperactivity disorder: A handbook for diagnosis and treatment.* New York: Guilford Press.

——(1991). The ecological validity of laboratory and analogue assessment methods of ADHD symptoms. *Journal of Abnormal Child Psychology, 19,* 149–178.

——(1995). A closer look at the DSM-IV criteria for ADHD: Some unresolved issues. *ADHD Report, 3* (3), 1–5.

Barnett, L.A., & Fiscella, J. (1985). A child by any other name . . . A comparison of the playfulness of gifted and non-gifted children. *Gifted Child Quarterly, 29* (2), 61–66.

Baron-Cohen, S. (1995). *Mindblindness: An essay on autism and theory of mind.* Cambridge, MA: MIT Press.

Baron-Cohen, S., Allen, J., & Gillberg, C. (1992). Can autism be detected at 18 months? The needle, the haystack and the CHAT. *British Journal of Psychiatry, 161,* 839–843.

Barrios, B.A., & O'Dell, S. (1989). Fears and anxieties. In E.J. Mash & R.A. Barkley (Eds.), *Treatment of childhood disorders* (pp.167–221). New York: Guilford.

Barton, D.P. (1980). Phonemic perception in children. In G. Yeni-Komshian, J.F. Kavanagh, & C.A. Ferguson (Eds.), *Child phonology, Vol. 2: Perception* (pp.97–116). New York: Academic Press.

Bates, E. (1976). *Language and context: The acquisition of pragmatics.* New York: Academic Press.

Bates, J.E., Marvinney, D., Kelly, T., Dodge, K.A., Bennett, D.S., & Pettit, G.S. (1994). Child-care history and kindergarten adjustment. *Developmental Psychology, 30,* 690–700.

Bateson, M.D. (1975). Mother–infant exchanges: The epigenesis of conversational interaction. In D. Aronson & R. Rieber (Eds.), *Annals of the New York Academy of Sciences, Vol. 363: Developmental psycholinguistics and communication disorders* (pp.101–113).

Bathshaw, M.L. (1998). *Children with disabilities: A medical primer* (4th Ed.) Baltimore, MD: Brookes.

Bathshaw, M.L., & Perret, Y.M. (1992). *Children with disabilities: A medical primer* (3rd ed.). Baltimore, MD: Brookes.

Baumrind, D. (1971). Current patterns of parental authority. *Developmental Psychology Monograph, 4* (No.1 Sec.2).

Bavin, E. (1993). Socialisation in a Walpiri community. In M. Walski & C. Yallop (Eds.), *Language and culture in Aboriginal Australia.* Canberra: Aboriginal Studies Press.

Bayley, N. (1969). *Bayley Scales of Infant Development.* New York: Psychological Development.

Bayley, N. (1993). *Bayley Scales of Infant Development* (2nd ed.) New York: The Psychological Corporation.

Beckwith, L., & Parmalee, A.H. (1986). EEG patterns of preterm infants: Home environment and later IQ. *Child Development, 57,* 777–789.

Bee, H.L. (1997). *The developing child* (8th ed.). New York: Longman.

Bee, H.L., Barnard, K.E., Eyres, S.J., Gray, C.A., Hammond, M.A., Spietz, A.L., Snyder, C., & Clark, B. (1982). Prediction of IQ and language skill from perinatal status, child performance, family characteristics, and mother–infant interaction. *Child Development, 53,* 1135–1156.

Behrman, R. (1992). *Textbook of pediatrics* (14th ed.). Philadelphia, PA: Saunders.

Bell, S.M., & Ainsworth, M.D.S. (1972). Infant crying and maternal responsiveness. *Child Development, 43,* 1171–1190.

Belsky, J. (1992). Consequences of child care for children's development: A deconstructionist view. In A. Booth (Ed.), *Child care in the 1990s: Trends and consequences* (pp.83–94). Hillsdale, NJ: Erlbaum.

——(1993). Etiology of child maltreatment: A developmental-ecological analysis. *Psychological Bulletin, 114,* 413–434.

Belsky, J., & Rovine, M. (1988). Nonmaternal care in the first year of life and the security of infant–parent attachment. *Child Development, 59,* 157–167.

Bem, S. (1989). Genital knowledge and gender constancy in preschool children. *Child development,* 60, 649–662.

Bender, L. (1946). *Instructions for the use of Visual Motor Gestalt Test.* New York: American Orthopsychiatric Association.

Bender, L. (1947). Childhood schizophrenia: Clinical studies of 100 schizophrenic children. *American Journal of Orthopsychiatry, 17,* 40–56.

Bendersky, M., & Lewis, M. (1994). Environmental risk, biological risk, and developmental outcome. *Developmental Psychology, 30,* 484–494.

Bennett, E.L., Diamond, M.C., Krech, D., & Rosenzweig, M.R. (1964). Chemical and anatomical plasticity in the brain. *Science, 146,* 610–619.

Berg, W.K., & Berg, K.M. (1987). Psychophysiological development in infancy: State, startle and attention. In J. Osofsky (Ed.), *Handbook of infant development* (2nd ed.) (pp.238–317). New York: Wiley.

Berliner, L., & Stevens, D. (1982). Clinical issues in child sexual abuse. *Journal of Social Work and Human Sexuality, 1,* 93–108.

Bernstein, D.K., & Tiegerman, E. (1993). *Language and communication disorders in children* (3rd ed.). New York: Merrill.

Bess, F.H., & Tharpe, A.M. (1984). Unilateral hearing impairment in children. *Pediatrics, 74,* 206–216.

Bettison, S. (1996). The long-term effect of auditory training on children with autism. *Journal of Autism and Developmental Disorders, 26,* 361–375.

Binder, H., & Eng, G.D. (1989). Rehabilitation management of children with spastic diplegic cerebral palsy. *Archives of Physical Medicine and Rehabilitation, 70,* 482–489.

Biswas, M.K., & Craigo, S.D. (1994). The course and conduct of normal labor and delivery. In A.H. DeCherney & M.L. Pernoll (Eds.), *Current obstetric and gynecologic diagnosis and treatment* (pp.202–227). Norwalk, CT: Appleton & Lange.

Blakemore, C. (1982). Developmental plasticity in the brain: A parable for education. In *The brain sciences and education.* Symposium conducted in January at the American Association for the Advancement of Science, Washington, DC.

Bloom, L. (1970). *Language development: Form and function in emerging grammars.* Cambridge, MA: MIT Press.

Bloom, L., & Lahey, M. (1978). *Language development and language disorders.* New York: Macmillan.

Bluestone, C.D. (1989). Modern management of otitis media. *Pediatric Clinics of North America, 36,* 1371–1387.

Bobath, K. (1980). A neurophysiological basis for the treatment of cerebral palsy. *Clinics in Developmental Medicine, 75,* 77–87.

Bonner, B.L., Kaufman, K.L., Harbeck, C., & Brassard, M.R. (1992). Child maltreatment. In C.E. Walker & M.C. Roberts (Eds.), *Handbook of clinical child psychology* (2nd ed.). New York: Wiley.

Borghgraef, M., Fryns, J.P., & van der Berghe, H. (1990). The female and the fragile X syndrome: Data on clinical and psychological findings in 7 fra X carriers. *Clinical Genetics, 37,* 341–346.

Borghi, W.R. (1990). Consonant, phoneme, and distinctive feature error patterns in speech. In D.C. VanDyke, D.J. Lang, F. Heide, S. VanDuyne & M.J. Soucek (Eds.),

Clinical perspectives in management of Down syndrome (pp.147–152). New York: Springer Verlag.

Borland, J.H. (1986). IQ tests: Throwing out the bath water, saving the baby. *Roeper Review, 8* (3), 163–167.

Bornstein, M.H., & Sigman, M.D. (1986). Continuity in mental development from infancy. *Child Development, 57,* 251–274.

Bouchard, T.J. Jr., & McGue, M. (1981). Familial studies of intelligence: A review. *Science, 212,* 1055–1059.

Bowlby, J. (1969). *Attachment and loss, Vol. 1: Attachment.* New York: Basic Books.

——(1980). *Attachment and loss, Vol. 3: Loss, sadness, and depression.* New York: Basic Books.

Braden, J.P. (1994). *Deafness, deprivation and IQ.* New York: Plenum Press.

Bradley, R.H., Whiteside, L., Mundfrom, D.J., Casey, P.H., Kelleher, K.J., & Pope, S.K. (1994). Early indications of resilience and their relation to experiences of the home environments of the low birthweight, premature children living in poverty. *Child Development, 65,* 346–460.

Braggett, E. (1994). The gifted and talented children. in A. Ashman & J. Elkins (Eds.), *Educating children with special needs* (pp.105–167). Sydney: Prentice Hall.

Bredecamp, S. (Ed.) (1987). *Developmentally appropriate practice in early childhood programs serving children from birth through age 8.* Washington, DC: National Association for the Education of Young Children.

Breitmayer, B.J., & Ramey, C.T. (1986). Biological nonoptimality and quality of postnatal environment as codeterminants of intellectual development. *Child Development, 57,* 1151–1165.

Brent, R.L. (1986). Evaluating the alleged teratogenicity of environmental agents. *Clinics in Perinatology, 13,* 121–150.

Bretherton, I., & Waters, E. (1985). Growing points of attachment theory and research. *Monographs of the Society for Research in Child Development, 50* (209), 1–211.

Bronfenbrenner, U. (1977). Toward an experimental ecology of human development. *American Psychologist, 4,* 513–531.

——(1989). Ecological systems theory. *Annals of Child Development, 6,* 187–249.

Brown, A.L., & Campione, J.C. (1972). Recognition memory for perceptually similar pictures in preschool children. *Journal of Experimental Psychology, 95,* 55–62.

Brown, A.M., Clark, G.M., Dowell, R.C., Martin, L.F., & Seligman, P.M. (1985). Telephone use by a multichannel cochlear implant patient: An evaluation using open-set CID sentences. *Journal of Laryngology and Otology, 99,* 231–238.

Brown, R. (1973). *A first language: The early stages.* Cambridge MA: Harvard University Press.

Brown, W.T., Jenkins, E.C., Cohen, I.L. et al. (1986). Fragile X and autism: A multicenter survey. *American Journal of Medical Genetics, 23,* 341–352.

Bruner, J. (1974/75). From communication to language: A psychological perspective. *Cognition, 3,* 225–287.

——(1978). Learning how to do things with words. In J. Bruner & A. Gorton (Eds.), *Wolfson College Lectures 1976: Human growth and development.* Oxford: Oxford University Press.

——(1983). Formats and contexts. Paper presented at the Australian New Zealand Association for the Advancement of Science, Perth.

Bullock, M., & Lutkenhaus, P. (1990). Who am I? Self-understanding in toddlers. *Merrill-Palmer Quarterly, 36,* 217–238.

Buncic, J.R. (1987). The blind child. *Pediatric Clinics of North America, 34,* 1403–1414.

Burns, A., & Goodnow, J.J. (1985). *Children and families in Australia.* Sydney: Allen & Unwin.

Bushnell, E.W. (1985). The decline of visually guided reaching during infancy. *Infant Behavior and Development, 8,* 139–155.

Bussey, K. (1983). A social cognitive appraisal of sex-role development. *Australian Journal of Psychology, 35,* 135–143.

Butterworth, G., & Harris, M. (1994). *Principles of developmental psychology.* Hove: Erlbaum.

Buyse, M.L. (Ed.) (1990). *Birth defects encyclopedia.* Dover, MA: Center for Birth Defects Information Services.

Byng-Hall, J. (1991). The application of attachment theory to understanding and treatment in family therapy. In C.J. Murray Parkes & J. Stevenson-Hinde (Eds.), *The place of attachment theory in human behaviour.* London: Tavistock.

Calvert, S.L., & Huston, A.C. (1987). Television and children's gender schemata. *New Directions in Child Development, 38,* 75–88.

Campbell, F.A., & Ramey, C.T. (1994). Effects of early intervention on intellectual and academic achievement: A follow-up study of children from low income families. *Child Development, 65,* 684–698.

Campbell, S.B. (1990). *Behavior problems in preschool children: Clinical and developmental issues.* New York: Guilford.

——(1995). Behavior problems in preschool children: A review of recent research. *Journal of Child Psychology and Psychiatry, 36,* 113–149.

Campione, J.C., Brown, A.L., Ferrera, R.A., Jones, R.S., & Steinberg, E. (1985). Breakdowns in flexible use of information: Intelligence-related differences in transfer following equivalent learning performance. *Intelligence, 9,* 297–315.

Cantwell, D.P. (1982). Childhood depression: A review of current research. In B.B. Lahey & A.E. Kazdin (Eds.), *Advances in clinical child psychology* (Vol. 5). New York: Plenum.

Capps, L., Sigman, M., & Mundy, P. (1994). Attachment security in children with autism. *Development and Psychopathology, 6* (2), 249–261.

Carver, R.P. (1990). Intelligence and reading ability in grades 2–12. *Intelligence, 14,* 449–455.

Catell, P. (1940/1960). *Cattell Infant Intelligence Scale.* San Antonio. TX: The Psychological Corporation.

Cattell, R.B. (1971). *Abilities: Their structure, growth, and action.* Boston, MA: Houghton Mifflin.

Catts, H. (1991). Facilitating phonological awareness: Role of speech-language pathologists. *Language, Speech, and Hearing Services in Schools, 22,* 196–203.

Caughy, M.O., DiPietro, J.A., & Strobino, D.M. (1994). Day-care participation as a protective factor in the cognitive development of low-income children. *Child Development, 65,* 457–471.

Centers for Disease Control (1994). Recommendations of the U.S. Public Health Service task force on the use of zidovudine to reduce perinatal transmission of human immunodeficiency virus. *Morbidity and Mortality Weekly Report, 43,* 1–20.

Cernoch, J.M., & Porter, R.H. (1985). Recognition of maternal axilliary odors by infants. *Child Development, 56,* 1593–1598.

Chamrad, D.L., & Robinson, N.M. (1986). Parenting the intellectually gifted preschool child. *Topics in Early Childhood Special Education, 6* (1), 74–87.

Chapman, R. (1978). Comprehension strategies in children. In J. Kavanagh &

W. Strange (Eds.), *Speech and language in the laboratory, school and clinic* (pp.308–327). Cambridge, MA: MIT Press.

Chapman, J. (1979). Confirming children's use of cohesive ties in text: Pronouns. *The Reading Teacher, 33* (3), 317–332.

Chomsky, N. (1965). *Aspects of the theory of syntax.* Cambridge, MA: MIT Press.

Christofersen, E.R. (1988). *Little people: Guidelines for common sense child rearing.* Kansas City, MO: Westport.

Chudley, A.E., & Hagerman, R.J. (1987). Fragile X syndrome. *Journal of Pediatrics, 110,* 821–831.

Cicchetti, D., & Aber, J.L. (1986). Early precursors of later depression: An organizational perspective. In P. Lipsitt & C. Rovee-Collier (Eds.), *Advances in infancy research* (Vol. 4) (pp.87–137). Norwood, NJ: Ablex.

Cicchetti, D., & Beeghly, M. (Eds.). (1990). *Children with Down syndrome: A developmental perspective.* Cambridge, MA: Cambridge University Press.

Cicchetti, D., & Cohen, D.J. (1995). Perspectives on developmental psychopathology. In D. Cicchetti & D.J. Cohen (Eds.), *Developmental psychopathology, Vol. 1: Theory and methods* (pp.3–20). New York: Wiley.

Cicchetti, D., & Sroufe, L.A. (1976). The relationship between affective and cognitive development in Down's syndrome infants. *Child Development, 47,* 920–929.

Cicchetti, D., Toth, S.L., & Lynch, M. (1995). Bowlby's dream comes full circle: The application of attachment theory to risk and psychopathology. *Advances in Clinical Child Psychology, 17,* 1–75.

Cirrin, F.M., & Penner, S.G. (1995). Classroom-based and consultative service delivery models for language intervention. In E.M. Fey, J. Windsor & S.F. Warren (Eds.), *Language intervention: Preschool through the elementary years* (pp.333–362). Baltimore: Brookes.

Clark, B. (1988). *Growing up gifted* (3rd ed.). Columbus, OH: Merrill.

Clark, D.B., & Uhry, J.K. (1995). *Dyslexia theory and practice and theory of remedial instruction* (2nd ed.). Baltimore: York Press.

Clark, E.V. (1983). Meanings and concepts. In J.H. Flavell & E.M. Markman (Eds.), *Handbook of child psychology, Vol. 3: Cognitive development* (pp.787–840). New York: Wiley.

Clarke-Stewart, K.A. (1992). Consequences of child care for children's development. In A. Booth (Ed.), *Child care in the 1990s: Trends and consequences* (pp.63–82). Hillsdale, NJ: Erlbaum.

Clarke-Stewart, K.A., Gruber, C.P., & Fitzgerald, L.M. (1994). *Children at home and in day care.* Hillsdale, NJ: Erlbaum.

Clay, M.M. (1991). *Becoming literate: The construction of inner control.* Auckland, NZ: Heinemann.

Cohen L.B., DeLoache, J.S., & Strauss, M.S. (1979). Infant visual perception. In J.D. Osofsky (Ed.), *Handbook of infant development.* New York: Wiley.

Cole, E., & Dehtashti, P. (1990). Interface design as a prosthesis for an individual with brain injury. *Special Interest Group on Computer and Human Interaction Bulletin, 22,* 28–32.

Cole, M. (1987). An analysis of stress and coping in mothers of young handicapped children and normal children. Unpublished thesis, Murdoch University.

Colombo, J. (1993). *Infant cognition: Predicting later intellectual functioning.* Newbury Park, CA: Sage.

Combrinck-Graham, L. (1983). The family life cycle and families with young children.

In H. Liddle (Ed.), *Clinical implications of the family life cycle* (pp.35–53). Rockville, MD: Aspen.

Commission on Classification and Terminology of the International League Against Epilepsy (1981). Proposal for revised clinical and electroencephalographic classification of epileptic seizures. *Epilepsia, 22,* 489–501.

Conners, C.K. (1976). Conners' Teacher Questionnaire. In W. Guy (Ed.), *Assessment manual for psychopharmacology.* Rockville, MD: US Department of Health, Education and Welfare, NIHM.

——(1989). A drug for dyslexia. In K. Klivington (Ed.), *The science of the mind* (pp. 216–218).

——(1992). *Conners' Continuous Performance Test. User's manual.* New York: Multi-Health Systems.

Connolly, J., & Doyle, A.B. (1984). Relations of social fantasy play to social competence in preschool children. *Developmental Psychology, 20,* 797–806.

Cook, E.H., Stein, M.A., Krasowski, M.D. et al. (1995). Association of attention-deficit disorder and the dopamine transporter gene. *American Journal of Human Genetics, 56,* 993–998.

Coplan, J. (1989). *ELM Scale: The early language milestone scale (revised).* Austin, TX: Pro-Ed.

Corrigan, R. (1987). A developmental sequence of actor-object pretend play in young children. *Merrill-Palmer Quarterly, 33,* 87–106.

Courchesne, E. (1991). Neuroanatomic imaging in autism. *Pediatrics, 87,* 781–790.

Cowley, J. (1996). Inclusive practices. In P. Foreman (Ed.). *Integration and inclusion in action* (pp.81–113). Sydney: Harcourt Brace.

Cox, R.D., & Schopler, E. (1993). Aggression and self-injurious behaviors in persons with autism: The TEACCH (Treatment and Education of Autistic and related Communications Handicapped Children) approach. *Acta Paedopsychiatrica, 56,* 85–90.

Craig, H. (1991). Pragmatic characteristics of the child with specific language impairment. In T. Gallagher (Ed.), *Pragmatics of language: Clinical practice issues.* (pp.163–198). San Diego, CA: Singular Press.

Crais, E. (1991). Moving from family involvement to family-centered services. *American Journal of Speech-Language Pathology, 1,* 5–8.

Cratty, B.J. (1981). *Movement and spatial awareness in blind children and youth.* Springfield, IL: Charles C. Thomas.

Creer, T.L., Harm, D.L., & Marion, R.J. (1988). Childhood asthma. In D.K. Routh (Ed.), *Handbook of pediatric psychology* (pp.162–185). New York: Guilford.

Crick, N.R., & Grotpeter, J.K. (1995). Relational aggression, gender, and social-psychological adjustment. *Child Development, 66,* 710–722.

Cross, T.G. (1978). Motherese: Its association with syntactic development in young children. In N. Waterson & C. Snow (Eds.), *The development of communication: Social and pragmatic factors in language acquisition.* London: Wiley.

——(1981). Parental speech as primary linguistic data: some complexities in the study of the effect of the input on language acquisition. In P. Dale & D. Ingram (Eds.), *Child language.* Baltimore: University Park Press.

Cross, T.G., Nienhuys, T.G., & Kirkman, M. (1983). Parent–child interaction with receptively disabled children: Some determinants of maternal speech style. In K. Nelson (Ed.), *Children's language* (Vol. 5). New York: Gardner Press.

Curtis, S. (1977). Genie: A psycholinguistic study of a modern day 'wild child'. Orlando, FL: Academic Press.

Dagna-Bricarelli, F.D., Pierluigi, M., Grasso, M. et al. (1990). Origin of extra chromosome 21 in 343 families: Cytogenic and molecular approaches. *American Journal of Medical Genetics, 7,* 129–132.

Das, J.P., & Varnhagen, C.K. (1986). Neurophysiological functioning and cognitive processing. In J.E. Obrzut & G.W. Hynd (Eds.), *Child neuropyschology: Vol. 1. Theory and research.* Orlando, FL: Academic Press.

Davidson, P.S. (1983). *Mathematics viewed from a neurobiological model for intellectual functioning,* Report No. G–79–0089. Washington, DC: National Institute of Education.

Davidson, R. (1994). Asymmetric brain function, affective style, and psychopathology: The role of early experience and plasticity. *Development and Psychopathology, 6,* 741–758.

DeCasper, A.J., & Fifer, W.P. (1980). Of human bonding: Newborns prefer their mothers' voices. *Science, 208,* 1174–1176.

DeCasper, A.J., & Spence, M.J. (1986). Prenatal maternal speech influences newborns' perception of speech sounds. *Infant Behavior and Development, 9,* 133–150.

Delisle, J.R. (1992). *Guiding the social and emotional development of gifted youth: A practical guide for educators and counsellors.* New York: Longman.

DeLoache, J.S., & Brown, A.L. (1987). Differences in the memory-based searching of delayed and normally developing young children. *Intelligence, 11,* 277–289.

DeLoache, J.S., & Todd, C.M. (1988). Young children's use of spatial categorization as a mnemonic strategy. *Journal of Experimental Child Psychology, 46,* 1–20.

DeLong, R. (1994). Children with autistic spectrum disorder and a family history of affective disorder. *Developmental Medicine and Child Neurology, 36,* 674–687.

DeMaio, R.X. (1995). Helping families become places of healing: Systemic treatment of intrafamilial sexual abuse. In L. Combrinck-Graham (Ed.), *Children and families at risk: maintaining the connections* (pp.125–149). New York: Guilford Press.

Dempster, F.N. (1981). Memory span: Sources of individual and developmental differences. *Psychological Bulletin, 89,* 63–100.

DeMyer, M.K. (1975). Research in infantile autism: A strategy and its results. *Biological Psychiatry, 10,* 433–440.

Denckla, M.B., & Reader, M.J. (1993). Education and psychosocial interventions: Executive dysfunction and its consequences. In R. Kurlan (Ed.), *Handbook of Tourette's syndrome and related tic and behavioral disorders* (pp.431–451). New York: Marcel Dekker.

Denckla, M.B., & Rudell, R.G. (1976). Rapid automatatized naming (RAN): Dyslexia differentiated from other learning disabilities. *Neuropsychologia, 14,* 471–479.

Denislic, M., & Meh, D. (1995). Botulinum toxin in the treatment of cerebral palsy. *Neuropediatrics, 26,* 249–252.

Dermody, P. (1990). Intervention in auditory receptive language disorders. In S. Butler (Ed.), *The exceptional child* (pp.324–326). Sydney: Harcourt Brace Jovanovich.

DeRosier, M.E., Kupersmidt, J.B., & Patterson, C.J. (1994). Children's academic and behavioral adjustment as a function of chronicity and proximity of peer rejection. *Child Development, 65,* 1799–1831.

Dishion, T.J. (1990). The family ecology of boys' peer relations in middle childhood. *Child Development, 61,* 874–892.

Dodge, K.A., & Feldman, E. (1990). Issues in social cognition and sociometric status. In S. Asher & J.D. Coie (Eds.), *Peer rejection in childhood* (pp.119–155). Cambridge: Cambridge University Press.

Dollfus, C., Patetta, M., Siegel, E. et al. (1990). Infant mortality: A practical approach to the analysis of the leading causes of death and risk factors. *Pediatrics, 86,* 176–183.

Donaldson, M. (1987). The origins of inference. In J. Bruner & H. Haste (Eds.), *Making sense: The child's construction of the world,* London: Methuen.

Dore, J. (1974). A pragmatic description of early language development. *Journal of Psycholinguistic Research, 3,* 343–350.

——(1975). Holophrases, speech acts, and language universals. *Journal of Child Language, 2,* 21–40.

Douglas, J. (1989). Training parents to manage their child's sleep problem. In C.E. Schaefer & J.M. Briesmeister (Eds.), *Handbook of parent training: parents as co-therapists for their child's behavior problems* (pp.13–37). New York: Wiley.

Dowell, R.C., Mecklenburg, D.J., & Clark, G.M. (1986). Speech recognition for forty patients receiving multichannel cochlear implants. *Archives of Otolaryngology, 112,* 1054–1059.

DSM IV (American Psychiatric Association) (1994). *Diagnostic and statistical manual of mental disorders* (4th ed.). Washington, DC: American Psychiatric Association.

DuBose, R.F. (1983). Working with sensorily impaired children. In S.G. Garwood (Ed.), *Educating young handicapped children: A developmental approach* (2nd ed) (pp. 235–276). Rockville, MD: Aspen.

Duffy, F.H., Denckla, M.B., McAnulty, G., & Holmes, J.A. (1988). Neurophysiological studies in dyslexia. In F. Plum (Ed.), *Language, communication, and the brain.* (pp.149–170). New York: Raven Press.

Dunn, J., & Shatz, M. (1989). Becoming a conversationalist despite (or because of) having an older sibling. *Child Development, 60,* 399–410.

Dunst, C.J., Trivette, C.M., & Deal, A. (1988). *From enabling to empowering families: Principles and guidelines for practice.* Cambridge, MA: Brookline Books.

During, S.M., & McMahon, R.J. (1991). Recognition of emotional facial expressions by abusive mothers and their children. *Journal of Clinical Child Psychology, 20,* 132–139.

Durkin, K. (1985). Television and sex role acquisition. *British Journal of Social Psychology, 24,* 101–113.

Dykens, E., Hodapp, R., & Evans, D. (1994). Profiles and development of adaptive behavior in children with Down syndrome. *American Journal on Mental Retardation, 98* (5), 580–587.

Earls, F. (1982). Application of DSM-III in an epidemiological study of preschool children. *American Journal of Psychiatry, 139,* 242–243.

Edwards, M.L., & Shriberg, L. (1983). *Phonology: Applications in communicative disorders.* San Diego, CA: College Hill Press.

Egeland, B., Jacobovitz, D., & Sroufe, L.A. (1988). Breaking the cycle of abuse: Relationship predictors. *Child Development, 55* (3), 753–771.

Eisenberg, N. (1986). *Altruistic emotion, cognition, and behavior.* Hillsdale, NJ: Erlbaum.

Eisenson, J., & Ogilvie, M. (1983). *Communicative disorders in children* (5th ed.). New York: Macmillan.

Elkind, D. (1989). Developmentally appropriate practice: Philosophical and practical implications. *Phi Delta Kappa, 71* (20), 113–117.

Emmitt, M., & Pollack, J. (1992). *Language and learning.* Mebourne: Oxford.

Epstein, H.T. (1980). Some biological bases of cognitive development. *Bulletin of the Orton Society, 30,* 46–62.

Erikson, E. (1950). *Childhood and society.* New York: Wiley.

Eysenck, M.W. (1982). *Attention and arousal.* New York: Springer-Verlag.

Fagan, J.F. III, & Singer, L.T. (1979). The role of simple feature differences in infants' recognition. *Infant Behavior and Development, 2,* 39–45.

Fagot, B.I., & Hagan, R. (1991). Observations of parent reactions to sex-stereotyped behaviors: Age and sex effects. *Child Development, 62,* 617–628.

Fagot, B.I., & Leinbach, M.D. (1993). Gender-role development in young children: From discrimination to labeling. *Developmental Review, 13,* 205–224.

Faraone, S.V., & Biederman, J. (1994). Genetics of attention-deficit hyperactivity disorder. *Child and Adolescent Psychiatric Clinics of North America, 3,* 285–301.

Farnham-Diggory, S. (1992). *The learning disabled child.* Cambridge: Harvard University Press.

Federal Register (1992). Washington, DC: US Government Printing Office, 29 September 1992.

Fein, G. (1981). Pretend play in childhood: An integrative view. *Child Development, 52,* 1095–1118.

Feldman, S.S. (1987). Predicting strain in mothers and fathers of 6-month-old infants: A short-term longitudinal study. In P.W. Berman & F.A. Pedersen (Eds.), *Men's transition to parenthood* (pp.13–36). Hillsdale, NJ: Erlbaum.

Feldhusen, J.F. (1986). A conception of giftedness. In K.A. Heller & J.F. Feldhusen (Eds.), *Identifying and nurturing the gifted* (pp.19–32). Toronto: Hans Huber.

Fenson, L., Dale, P.S., Reznick, J.S., Bates, E., Thal, D.J., & Pethick, S.J. (1994). Variability in early communicative development. *Monographs of the Society for Research in Child Development, 59* (5, Serial No. 242).

Fenson, L., Dale, P., Reznick, J.S., Thal, D., Bates, E. et al. (1993). *MacArthur communicative development inventories.* San Diego, CA: Singular Publishing.

Ferber, R. (1989). Sleeplessness in the child. In M.H. Kyger, T. Roth, & W.C. Dement (Eds.), *Principles and practice of sleep medicine* (pp.633–639). Philadelphia: Saunders.

Fergusson, D.M., Horwood, L.J., & Lynskey, M.T. (1993). Maternal smoking before and after pregnancy: Effects on behavioural outcomes in middle childhood. *Pediatrics, 92,* 815–822.

Feuerstein, R. (1979). *The dynamic assessment of retarded performers.* Baltimore, MD: University Park Press.

Fey, D. (1986). *Language intervention with young children.* London: Taylor & Francis.

Fey, M.E., & Cleave, P.L. (1990). Early language intervention. *Seminars in Speech and Language, 11,* 165–181.

Fielder, A.R., Best, A.B., & Bax, M.C.O. (Eds.) (1993). *The management of visual impairment in childhood.* London: MacKeith Press.

Filipek, P.A. (1995). Neurobiological correlates of developmental dyslexia: How do dyslexics' brains differ from those of normal readers? *Journal of Child Neurology, 10* (Suppl. 1), S62–S69.

Fisk, A.D., & Schneider, E. (1984). Memory as a function of attention, level of processing and automatization. *Journal of Experimental Psychology, 10,* 181–197.

Flavell, J.H. (1985). *Cognitive development* (2nd ed.). Englewood Cliffs, NJ: Prentice Hall.

——(1992). Cognitive development: Past, present, and future. *Developmental Psychology, 28,* 998–1005.

Flavell, J.H., Green, F.L., & Flavell, E.R. (1990). Developmental changes in young children's knowledge about the mind. *Cognitive Development, 5,* 1–27.

Flavell, J.H., Green, F.L., & Flavell, E.R. (1989). Young children's ability to differentiate appearance-reality and level 2 perspectives in the tactile modality. *Child Development, 60,* 201–213.

Flavell, J.H., Green, F.L., & Flavell, E. (1995). Young children's knowledge about thinking. *Monographs of the Society for Research in Child Development, 60* (1, Serial No. 243).

Fodor, J. (1983). *Modularity of mind.* Cambridge, MA: MIT Press.

Francis, P.L., Self, P.A., & Horowitz, F.D. (1987). The behavioral assessment of the neonate: An overview. In J.D. Osofsky (Ed.), *Handbook of infant development* (2nd ed.) (pp.723–779). New York: Wiley-Interscience.

Frankenburg, W.K., & Dodds, J.B. (1969). *Denver Developmental Screening Test.* Denver. CO: University of Colorado Press.

Frea, W.D. (1995). Social communicative skills in higher-functioning children with autism. In R.L. Koegel & L.K. Koegel (Eds.), *Teaching children with autism: Strategies for initiating positive interactions and improving learning opportunities* (pp.53–66). Baltimore: Brookes.

Freeman, J. (1995). Annotation: Recent studies of giftedness in children. *Journal of Child Psychology and Psychiatry, 36* (4), 531–547.

Freiberg, S. (1974). Blind infants and their mothers: An examination of the sign system. In M. Lewis & L.A. Rosenblum (Eds.), *The effect of the infant on its caregiver* (pp.215–232). New York: Wiley.

——(1977). *Insights from the blind.* New York: Meridian.

Freud, S. (1920). *A general introduction to psychoanalysis* (J. Riviere, Trans.). New York: Washington Square Press.

Frey, K.S., & Ruble, D.N. (1992). Gender constancy and the cost of sex-typed behavior: A test of the conflict hypothesis. *Developmental Psychology, 28,* 714–721.

Frith, U. (1989). *Autism: Explaining the enigma.* Oxford: Basil Blackwell.

——(Ed.), (1991). *Autism and Asperger's syndrome.* Cambridge: Cambridge University Press.

Frodi, A.M., & Lamb, M.E. (1980). Child abuser's reactions to infant smiles and cries. *Child Development, 51,* 238–241.

Gadow, K.D. (1992). Pediatric psychopharmacotherapy: A review of recent research. *Journal of Child Psychology and Psychiatry, 33,* 153–195.

Gallagher, J.J. (1991). Educational reform, values and gifted students. *Gifted Child Quarterly 35,* 12–19.

Gandini, L. (1993). Fundamentals of the Reggio Emilia approach to early childhood education. *Young Children, 49,* 4–8.

Gange, F. (1985). Giftedness and talent: Re-examining a reexamination of the definitions. *Gifted Child Quarterly, 29,* 103–112.

Gardner, H. (1983). *Frames of mind: The theory of multiple intelligence.* New York: Basic Books.

——(1987). *Frames of mind: The theory of multiple intelligences.* London: Palladin.

——(1997). *Extraordinary minds.* London: Weidenfeld & Nicolson.

Garfinkle, P.E., & Garner, D.M. (1982). *Anorexia nervosa: A multidimensional perspective.* New York: Brunner/Mazel.

Garvey, C. (1977). *Play.* Cambridge, MA: Harvard University Press.

Gelman, R. (1969). Conservation acquisition: A problem of learning to attend to relevant attributes. *Journal of Experimental Child Psychology, 7,* 167–187.

——(1972). Logical capacity of very young children: Number invariance rules. *Child Development, 43,* 75–90.

——(1979). Preschool thought. *American Psychologist, 34* (10), 900–905.

Gerber, A. (1993). *Language-related learning disabilities: Their nature and treatment,* Baltimore, MD: Brookes.

Gerson, E.S., Hamovit, J., & Guroff, J.J. (1983). A family study of schizoaffective, bipolar I, bipolar II, unipolar, and normal control probands. *Archives of General Psychiatry, 39,* 1157–67.

Gesell, A. (1929). Maturation and infant behavior pattern. *Psychological Review, 36,* 307–319.

Gesell, A., & Amatrada, C.S. (1947). *Developmental diagnosis.* New York: Paul B. Holden.

Gibbs, D.P., & Cooper, E.B. (1989). Prevalence of communication disorders in students with learning disabilities. *Journal of Learning Disabilities, 29,* 60–63.

Gibson, E.J., & Walk, R.D. (1960). The 'visual cliff'. *Scientific American, 202,* 64–71.

Gillberg, C. (1991). The treatment of epilepsy in autism. *Journal of Autism and Developmental Disorders, 21,* 61–77.

Gillberg, C. & Coleman, M. (1996). Autism and medical disorders: A review of literature. *Developmental Medicine and Child Neurology, 38,* 191–202.

Gilstrap, L.C. (1990). Pathophysiology of preeclampsia. *Seminars in Perinatology, 14,* 147–151.

Glenn, N.D. (1990). Quantitative research on marital quality in the 1980s: A critical review. *Journal of Marriage and the Family, 52,* 818–831.

Goble, J.L. (1984). *Visual disorders in the handicapped child.* New York: Marcel Dekker.

Goldberg, G.L., & Craig, C.L. (1983). Obstetric complications in adolescent pregnancies. *South African Medical Journal, 64,* 863–864.

Goldfield, B.A. (1987). The contributions of child and caregiver to referential and expressive language. *Applied Psycholinguistics, 8,* 267–280.

Goldman, R.J., & Goldman, J.D.G. (1982). *Children's sexual thinking.* Melbourne: Routledge & Kegan Paul.

Goodman, Y.M. (1987). Children coming to know literacy. In W. Teale & E. Sulzby (Eds.), *Emergent literacy: Writing and reading.* NJ: Ablex.

Goodnow, J.J. (1969). Problems in research on culture and thought. In D. Elkind & J. Flavell (Eds.), *Studies in cognitive development: Essays in honour of Jean Piaget.* Oxford: Oxford University Press.

Goodnow, J.J., Cashmore, J., Cotton, S., & Knight, R. (1984). Mother's developmental timetables in two cultural groups. *International Journal of Psychology, 19,* 193–205.

Gopnik, A., & Astington, J.W. (1988). Children's understanding of representational change and its relation to the understanding of false belief and the appearance-reality distinction. *Child Development, 59,* 903–910.

Gopnik, A., & Meltzoff, A.N. (1987). Language and thought in the young child: Early semantic developments and their relationships to object permanence, means-end understanding, and categorization. In K. Nelson & A. Van Kleeck (Eds.), *Children's language* (Vol. 6) (pp.191–212). Hillsdale, NJ: Erlbaum.

Gopnik, A., & Wellman, H.M. (1994). The theory on theory. In L. Hirschfield & S.A. Gelman (Eds.), *Mapping the mind* (pp.257–293). Cambridge: Cambridge University Press.

Gottesman, I.I., & Goldsmith, H.H. (1994). Developmental psychopathology of antisocial behavior: Inserting genes into its ontogenesis and epigenesis. In C.A. Nelson (Ed.), *The Minnesota Symposia on Child Psychology* (Vol. 27) (pp.69–104). Hillsdale, NJ: Erlbaum.

Gottman, J.M. (1986). The world of coordinated play: Same- and cross-sex friendships in young children. In J.M. Gottman & J.G. Parker (Eds.), *Conversations of friends:*

Speculations on affective development (pp.139–191). Cambridge: Cambridge University Press.

Gow, L., & Ward, J. (1985). The use of verbal self-instruct training for enhancing generalisation outcomes with people with an intellectual disability. *Australian and New Zealand Journal of Developmental Disabilities, 11,* 157–188.

Goyco, P.G., & Beckerman, R.C. (1990). Sudden infant death syndrome. *Current Problems in Pediatrics, 20,* 863–864.

Graham, J.M. Jr., Hanson, J.W., Darby, B.L. et al. (1988). Independent dysmorphology evaluation at birth and 4 years of age for children exposed to varying amounts of alcohol in utero. *Pediatrics, 81,* 772–778.

Grandin, T. (1992). An inside view of autism. In E. Schopler & G.B. Mesibov (Eds.), *High functioning individuals with autism* (pp.105–126). New York: Plenum Press.

Grant, D.A., & Berg, E.A. (1993). *Wisconsin Card Sorting Task.* Psychological Assessment Resources, USA.

Graziani, L.J., Pasto, M., Stanley, C. et al. (1986). Neonatal neurosonography correlation of cerebral palsy in preterm infants. *Pediatrics, 78,* 88–95.

Greenberg, L. (1990). *Test of Variables of Attention.* Los Alamitos, CA: Universal Attention Disorders, Inc.

Greenbough, W. (1996). Your child's brain. *Newsweek,* February (pp.55–62).

Greenhill, L.L. (1992). Pharmacotherapy: stimulants. *Child and Adolescent Psychiatric Clinics of North America, 1,* 411–447.

Greif, E.B., & Berko Gleason, J. (1980). Hi, thanks, and goodbye: More routine information. *Language in Society, 9,* 159–166.

Griebel, M.L., Oakes, W.J., & Worley, G. (1991). The Chiari malformation associated with myelomeningocele. In H.L. Rekate (Ed.), *Comprehensive management of spina bifida* (pp.67–92). Boca Raton, FL: CRC Press.

Griffiths, R. (1978). *Griffiths Mental Developmental Scales.* Sarasota, FL: Test Center.

Gross, M.U.M. (1993). *Exceptionally gifted children.* London: Routledge.

Grusec, J.E., & Goodnow, J.J. (1994). Impact of parental discipline methods on the child's internalization of values: A reconceptualization of current points of view. *Developmental Psychology, 30* (1), 4–19.

Guilford, J.P. (1967). *The nature of human intelligence.* New York: McGraw Hill.

Gunn, P. (1985). Speech and language. In D. Lane & B. Stratford (Eds.), *Current approaches to Down syndrome* (pp.260–277). London: Cassell Education.

Guralnick, M.J., & Paul-Brown, D. (1984). Communicative adjustments during behavior-request episodes among children at different developmental levels. *Child Development, 55,* 911–919.

Gustafson, G.E., & Harris, K.L. (1990). Women's responses to young infants' cries. *Developmental Psychology, 26,* 144–152.

Hack, M., Taylor, C.B.H., Klein, N., Eiben, R., Schatschneider, C., & Mercuri-Minich, N. (1994). School-age outcomes in children with birth weights under 750g. *New England Journal of Medicine, 331,* 753–759.

Hagberg, B. (1995). Rett syndrome: Clinical peculiarities and biological mysteries. *Acta Paediatrica, 84,* 971–976.

Hagberg, B., Harberg, G., & Olow, I. (1993). The changing panorama of cerebral palsy in Sweden: Prevalence and origin during the birth year period 1983–1986. *Acta Paediatrica, 82,* 387–393.

Hainline, L. (1985). Occulomotor control in human infants. In R. Groner, G.W. McConkie & C. Menz (Eds.), *Eye movements and human information processing* (pp.71–84). Amsterdam: Elsevier.

Haith, M.M. (1990). Progress in the understanding of sensory and perceptual processes in early infancy. *Merrill-Palmer Quarterly, 36,* 1–26.

Halford, G.S. (1993). *Children's understanding: The development of mental models.* London: Erlbaum.

Hall, E.G., & Skinner, N. (1980). *Somewhere to turn: Strategies for parents of gifted and talented children.* New York: Teachers College Press.

Hall, D.M., Johnson, S.L., & Middleton, J. (1990). Rehabilitation of head injured children. *Archives of Disease in Childhood, 65,* 553–556.

Halliday, M.A.K. (1975). *Learning how to mean: Explorations in the development of language.* London: Edward Arnold.

Hamilton, A. (1981). *Nature and nurture.* Canberra: Australian Institute of Aboriginal Studies.

Hanshaw, J.B., Scheiner, A.P., Moxley, A.W., Gaev, L., Abel, V., & Scheiner, B. (1976). School failure and deafness after silent congenital cytomegalovirus infection. *New England Journal of Medicine, 295,* 468–470.

Hanson, M.J. (1987). *Teaching the infant with Down syndrome: A guide for parents and professionals* (2nd ed.). Austin, TX: Pro-Ed.

Hanson, M., Lynch, E.W., & Wayman, K. (1990). Honoring cultural diversity of the family when gathering data. *Topics in Early Childhood Special Education, 10,* 112–131.

Harris, J. (1980) *Report No. 27,* Educational Research and Development Council (Australia), 15.

Harris, M. (1992). *Language experience and early language development: from input to uptake.* Hove, UK: Erlbaum.

Harris, S., Kasari, C., & Sigman, M. (1996). Joint attention and language gains in children with Down syndrome. *American Journal on Mental Retardation, 100* (6), 608–619.

Harrison, C. (1995). *Giftedness in early childhood.* Sydney: KU Children's Services.

Harrison, R., & Edwards, J. (1983). *From child abuse.* Portland, OR: Ednick Publications.

Harter, S. (1990). Processes underlying adolescent self-concept formation. In R. Montemayor, G.R. Adams & T.P. Gullotta (Eds.), *From childhood to adolescence: A transitional period* (pp.205–239). Newbury Park, CA: Sage.

Hartup, W.W. (1992). Peer relations in early and middle childhood. In V.B. Hasselt & M. Hersen (Eds.), *Handbook of social development: A lifespan perspective* (pp.257–281). New York: Plenum Press.

Hay, D.A. (1986). Children at risk. *Australian Journal of Early Childhood, 11,* 6–10.

Hayes, A. (1997). *Child development in the balance: From child focused and family centred intervention to community development and prevention.* Plenary session held at the launch of the Centre for Child Development, Macquarie University, Sydney, 20 June 1997.

Heibeck, T., & Markman, E. (1987). Word learning in children: an examination of fast mapping. *Child Development, 58,* 1021–34.

Helmstetter, E., & Durand, V.M. (1991). Non-aversive intervention for severe behavior problems. In L. Meyer, C. Peck & L. Brown (Eds.), *Critical issues in the lives of people with severe disabilities* (pp.559–600). Baltimore: Brookes.

Hinde, R.A., Titmus, G., Easton, D., & Tamplin, A. (1985). Incidence of friendships and behaviour toward strong associates versus nonassociates in preschoolers. *Child Development, 56,* 234–245.

Hinshaw, S.P. (1992). Externalizing behavior problems and academic underachievement in childhood and adolescence: Causal relationships and underlying mechanisms. *Psychological Bulletin, 111,* 127–155.

Hobson, P.R. (1989). On sharing experiences. *Development and Psychopathology, 1* (3), 197–203.

Hoffman, M.L. (1988). Moral development. In M.H. Bornstein & M.E. Lamb (Eds.), *Developmental psychology: An advanced textbook* (2nd ed.) (pp.497–548). Hillsdale, NJ: Erlbaum.

——(1994). Discipline and internalization. *Developmental Psychology, 30,* (1), 26–28.

Holden, E.W., Willis, D.J., & Corcoran, M.M. (1992). Preventing child maltreatment during the prenatal/perinatal period. In D. Willis, E.W. Holden & M. Rosenberg (Eds.), *Prevention of child maltreatment: developmental and ecological perspectives* (pp.17–46). New York: Wiley.

Hollins, M. (1989). *Understanding blindness: An integrative approach.* Hillsdale, NJ: Erlbaum.

Holmes, L.B. (1988). Teratogenic effects of anticonvulsant drugs. *Journal of Pediatrics, 112,* 576–581.

Honzig, M.P., MacFarlane, J.W., & Allen, L. (1948). The stability of mental test performance between two and eighteen years. *Journal of Experimental Education, 17,* 309–329.

Hook, E.B., & Fabia, J.J. (1978). Frequency of Down syndrome in live births by single-year maternal age interval: Results of a Massachusetts study. *Teratology, 17,* 223–228.

Horowitz, F.D. (1990). Developmental models of individual differences. In J. Colombo & J. Fagen (Eds.), *Individual differences in infancy: Reliability, stability, prediction* (pp.3–18). Hillsdale, NJ: Erlbaum.

Howes, C. (1988). Peer interactions in young children. *Monographs of the Society of Child Development, 53* (1, serial no. 217).

Howes, C. & Stewart, P. (1987). Child's play with adults, toys, and peers: An examination of family and child-care influences. *Developmental Psychology, 23,* 423–430.

Hubbard, F.O.A., & van IJzerdoorn, M.H. (1987). Maternal unresponsiveness and infant crying: a critical replication of the Bell & Ainsworth study. In L.W.C. Tavecchio & M.H. van IJzerdoorn (Eds.), *Attachment in social networks* (pp.339–378). Amsterdam: Elsevier/North Holland.

Hurst, J.A., Baraitser, M., Auger, E., Graham, F, & Norell, S. (1990). An extended family with dominantly inherited speech disorder. *Developmental Medicine and Child Neurology, 32,* 352–355.

Huttenlocher, F.H. (1991). Early vocabulary growth: Relationship to language input and gender. *Developmental Psychology, 27* (2), 236–248.

Huttonlocher, P.R. (1994). Synaptogenesis, synapse elimination, and neural plasticity in human cerebral cortex. In C.A. Nelson (Ed.), *The Minnesota Symposia on Child Psychology* (Vol. 27, pp.35–54). Hillsdale, NJ: Erlbaum.

IDEA (1990). USC Secs. 1400–85.

Jacobson, R., & Halle, M. (1956). *Fundamentals of language.* The Hague: Mouton.

Janos, P.M. (1987). A fifty-year follow-up of Terman's youngest college students and IQ matched agemates. *Gifted Child Quarterly, 31,* 55–58.

Jennett, B., & Teasdale, G. (1981). *Management of head injuries.* Philadelphia: F.A. Davis.

Johnson, C.M. (1991). Infant and toddler sleep: a telephone survey of parents in one community. *Developmental and Behavioral Pediatrics, 12,* 108–14.

Johnson, W. (1961). *Stuttering and what you can do about it*. Minneapolis, MN: University of Minnesota Press.

Jones, K.L., Smith, D.W., Ulleland, C.N. et al. (1973). Pattern of malformation in offspring of chronic alcoholic mothers. *Lancet, 1*, 1267–1271.

Jones, P.M. (1989). Feeding disorders in children with multiple handicaps. *Developmental Medicine and Child Neurology, 31*, 404–406.

Kail, R., & Hall, L.K. (1994). Processing speed, naming speed, and reading. *Developmental Psychology, 30*, 949–954.

Kaiser, A.P., & Hester, P.P. (1994). Generalized effects of enhanced milieu teaching. *Journal of Speech and Hearing Research, 37*, 1320–1340.

Kalland, M. (1995). Psychosocial aspects of cleft lip and palate: implications for parental education. *Research Report No. 138*. Helsinki: University of Helsinki.

Kanner, L. (1943). Autistic disturbances of affective contact. *Nervous Child, 2*, 217–250.

Kashani, J.H., Holcomb, W.R., & Orvaschel, H. (1986). Depression and depressive symptoms in preschool children from the general population. *American Journal of Psychiatry, 143* (9), 931–934.

Katz, P. & Ksansnak, K. (1994). Developmental aspects of gender role flexibility and traditionality in middle childhood and adolescence. *Developmental Psychology, 30*, 272–82.

Katz., D., & Kahn, R.L. (1969). Common characteristics of open systems. In F.E. Emery (Ed.), *Systems thinking*. Harmondsworth, UK: Penguin.

Kaufman, A.S., & Kaufman, N.L. (1993). *Kaufman Assessment Battery for Children*. Circle Pines, MN: American Guidance Service.

Kaye, K. (1982). *The mental and social life of babies: How parents create persons*. Chicago, IL: University of Chicago Press.

Kazdin, A.E. (1990). Childhood depression. *Journal of Child Psychology and Psychiatry, 31* (1), 121–160.

Kearins, J. (1981). Visual spatial memory of Australian Aboriginal children of desert regions. *Cognitive Psychology, 13*, 434–460.

Keeny, T.J., Cannizzo, S.R. & Flavell, J.H. (1967). Spontaneous and induced verbal rehearsal in a recall task. *Child Development, 38*, 935–966.

Kendall-Tackett, K.A., Williams, L.M., & Finkelhor, D. (1993). Impact of sexual abuse on children: A review and synthesis of recent empirical studies. *Psychological Bulletin, 113*, 164–180.

Kessler, C. (1988). Language acquisition in bilingual children. In N. Miller (Ed.), *Bilingualism and language disability: Assessment and remediation* (pp.26–54). London: Chapman & Hall.

Kestenbaum, R., Farber, E.A., & Sroufe, L.A. (1989). Individual differences in empathy among preschoolers: Relation to attachment history. *New Directions in Child Development, 44*, 51–64.

Khatena, J. (1992). *Gifted challenge and response for education*. Itasca, IL: Peacock.

Kibrick, S. (1980). Herpes simplex infection at term: What to do with the mother, newborn, and nursery personnel. *Journal of the American Medical Association, 243*, 157–160.

Kilminster, M., & Laird, E. (1978), Articulation development in children aged 3–9 years. *Australian Journal of Human Communication Disorders, 6*, 23–29.

King, P.M. (1985). Formal reasoning in adults: A review and critique. In R. A. Mines & K.S. Kitchener (Eds.), *Adult cognitive development*. New York: Praeger.

Kirk, S. (1958). *Early education of the mentally retarded*. Urbana, IL: University of Illinois Press.

Kitzinger, M. (1984). The role of repeated and echoed utterances in communication with a blind child. *British Journal of Disorders of Communication, 19,* 135–146.

Klein, S.K., Kurtzberg, D., Brattson, A., Kreuzer, J.A. et al. (1995). Electrophysiologic manifestations of impaired temporal lobe auditory processing in verbal auditory agnosia. *Brain and Language, 51,* 383–405.

Klin, A.(1994). Asperger syndrome. *Child and Adolescent Psychiatric Clinics of North America, 3* (1), 131–148.

Knobloch, H., & Pasamanick, B. (1974). *Developmental diagnosis.* Hagerstown, MD: Harper & Row.

Kohlberg, L. (1964). The development of moral character and moral ideology. In M. Hoffmann & L. Hoffmann (Eds.), *Review of child development research.* New York: Russell Sage Foundation.

——(1976). Moral stages and moralization: The cognitive-developmental approach. In T. Lickona (Ed.), *Moral development and behavior: Theory, research and social issues* (pp.31–53). New York: Holt.

——(1981). *Essays on moral development, Vol. 1: The philosophy of moral development.* New York: Harper & Row.

Korn, S.J. (1984). Continuities and discontinuities in difficult temperament: Infancy to young adulthood. *Merrill-Palmer Quarterly, 30,* 189–199.

Korner, A.F., Hutchinson, C.A., Koperski, J.A., Kramer, H.C., & Schneider, P.A. (1981). Stability of individual differences in neonatal motor and crying patterns. *Child Development, 52,* 83–90.

Kotelchuck, C.M. (1980). Nonorganic failure to thrive: The status of interactional and environmental etiologic theories. In B. Camp (Ed.), *Advances in behavioral pediatrics.* Greenwich, CT: JAI Press.

Kreutzer, M.A., Leonard, C., & Flavell, J.H. (1975). An interview study of children's knowledge about memory. *Monographs of the Society for Research in Child Development, 40,* 1–57.

Kuhl, P.K. (1993). Infant speech perception: A window on psycholinguistic development. *International Journal of Psycholinguistics, 9* (1), 33–54.

Kupersmidt, J.B., & Coie, J.D. (1990). Preadolescent peer status, aggression and school adjustment as predictors of externalizing problems in adolescence. *Child Development, 65,* 1350–1362.

Lamb, M.E., Sternberg, K.J. & Prodromidis, M. (1992). Non-maternal care and the security of mother–infant attachment: A reanalysis of the data. *Infant Behavior and Development, 15,* 71–83.

Landau, B., & Gleitman, L. (1985). *Language and experience: Evidence from the blind child.* Cambridge, MA: Harvard University Press.

Langley, M.B. (1980). The teachable moment and the handicapped infant. Reston, VA: ERIC Clearinghouse on Handicapped and Gifted Children.

LaPointe, L.L. (1990). Neurogenic disorders of speech. In G.H. Shames & G.H. Wiig (Eds.), *Human communication disorders* (3rd ed.), (pp.463–496). Columbus, OH: Merrill.

Lawrence, B.M. (1984). Conversation and cooperation: Child linguistic maturity, parental speech, and helping behavior of young children. *Child Development, 55,* 1926–35.

Leaper, C. (1991). Influence and involvement in children's discourse: Age, gender, and partner effects. *Child Development, 62,* 797–811.

LeCouteur, A., Rutter, M., Lord, C. et al. (1989). Autism diagnostic interview: A standardized investigator-based instrument. *Journal of Autism and Developmental Disorders, 19,* 363–387.

Lenneberg, E.H. (1969). On explaining language. *Science, 164,* 635–643.

Leonard, L. (1982). The nature of specific language impairments in children. In S. Rosenberg (Ed.), *Handbook of applied psycholinguistics: major thrusts of research and theory* (pp.295–327). Hillsdale, NJ: Erlbaum.

Lerner, R.M. (1985). Adolescent maturational changes and psychosocial development: a dynamic, interactional perspective. *Journal of Youth and Adolescence, 14,* 355–72.

Lester, B.M. (1987). Prediction of developmental outcome from acoustic analysis in term and preterm infants. *Pediatrics, 80,* 529–534.

Lewis, M. (1991). Ways of knowing: objective self-awareness of consciousness. *Developmental Review, 11,* 231–43.

Lewis, M., Allesandri, S.M., & Sullivan, M.W. (1992). Differences in shame and pride as a function of gender and task difficulty. *Child Development, 63,* 630–8.

Lewis, M., & Brooks, J. (1978). Self-knowledge and emotional development. In M. Lewis, & L.A. Rosenblum (Eds.), *The development of affect* (pp.205–226). New York: Plenum Press.

Licht, B.G., & Dweck, C. (1984). Determinants of academic achievement: The interaction of children's achievement orientations with skill area. *Developmental Psychology, 20,* 628–636.

Liebman, R., & Ziffer, R.L. (1985). Case consultation within family systems framework. In R.L. Ziffer (Ed.), *Adjunctive techniques in family therapy* (pp. 185–186). New York: Grune & Stratton.

Light, J.G., & DeFries, J.C. (1995). Comorbidity of reading and mathematical disabilities: Genetic and environmental etiologies. *Journal of Learning Disabilities, 28,* 69–106.

Lindamood, C.H., & Lindamood, P.C. (1979). *The Lindamood Auditory Conceptualization Test.* Chicago, IL: Riverside.

Linder, T.W. (1993). *Transdisciplinary play-based assessment: a functional approach to working with young children* (Revised ed.). Baltimore: Brookes.

Loeber, R., Green, S.M., Lahey, B.B., Christ, M.A., & Frick, P.J. (1992). Developmental sequences in the age of onset of disruptive child behaviors. *Journal of Child and Family Studies, 1,* 21–41.

Loiselle, D.L., Stamm, J.S., Matinsky, S., & Whipple, S.C. (1980). Evoked potential and behavioral signs of attentive dysfunctions in hyperactive boys. *Pyschophysiology, 17,* 193–201.

Lord, C., Schopler, E., & Revicki, D. (1982). Sex differences in autism. *Journal of Autism and Developmental Disorders, 12,* 317–30.

Lou, H.C., Henriksen, L., & Bruhn, C.P. (1984). Focal cerebral hyperfusion in children with dysphasia and/or attention deficit disorder. *Archives of Neurology, 41,* 825–829.

Lovaas, O.I. (1993). The development of a treatment-research project for developmentally disabled and autistic children. *Journal of Applied Behavior Analysis, 26* (4), 617–630.

Lowe, D. (1990). Visual impairment: Overview. In S.R. Butler (Ed.), *The exceptional child* (pp.207–222). Sydney: Harcourt Brace Jovanovich.

Lyman, R.D., & Hembree-Kigin, T. (1994). *Mental health interventions with preschool children.* New York: Plenum Press.

Lyon, G.R. (1995). Toward a definition of dyslexia. *Annals of Dyslexia, 45,* 3–31.

McCall, R.B. (1993). Developmental functions for general mental performance. In

D.K. Detterman (Ed.), *Current topics in human intelligence, Vol. 3: Individual differences and cognition* (pp.3–30). Norwood, NJ: Ablex.

Maccoby, E.E. (1990). Gender and relationships: A developmental account. *American Psychologist, 45,* 513–520.

Maccoby, E.E., & Martin, J.A. (1983). Socialization in the context of the family: Parent-child interaction. In P.H. Mussen & E.M. Hetherington (Eds.), *Handbook of child psychology, Vol 4: Socialization, personality and social development* (pp.1–101). New York: Wiley.

Maccoby, E.E., Snow, M.E., & Jacklin, C.N. (1984). Children's dispositions and mother child interaction at 12 and 18 months: A short term longitudinal study. *Developmental Psychology, 20,* 459–472.

McConkey, K. (1995). Hypnosis, memory, and the ethics of uncertainty. *Australian Psychologist, 30,* 1–10.

McCormick, L., Loeb, D.F., & Schiefelbusch, R.L. (1997). *Supporting children with communication difficulties in inclusive settings.* Boston, MA: Allyn & Bacon.

McCormick, L. & Schiefelbusch, R. (1990). *Early language intervention: An introduction.* Columbus, OH: Merrill.

McDade, H.L., & Adler, S. (1980). Down syndrome and short-term memory impairment: A storage or retrieval deficit? *American Journal of Mental Deficiency, 84,* 561–567.

MacFarlane, J.W. (1977). *Psychology of childbirth.* Cambridge, MA: Fontana.

McKenzie, B.E., Tootell, H.E., & Day, R.H. (1980). Development of visual size constancy during the first year of human infancy. *Developmental Psychology, 16,* 163–174.

McLean, J., & Snyder-McLean, L. (1978). *A transactional approach to early language training.* Columbus, OH: Merrill/Macmillan.

Main, M., Kaplan, N., & Cassidy, J. (1985). Security in infancy, childhood and adulthood: A move to the level of the representation. *Monographs of the Society for Research in Child Development, 50* (1–2 Serial No. 209).

Mann, V. (1994). Phonological skills and the prediction of early reading problems. In N.C. Jordan & J. Goldsmith-Phillips (Eds.), *Learning disabilities: New Directions for assessment and intervention* (pp.67–84). Boston, MA: Allyn & Bacon.

Marcell, M., & Jett, D. (1985). Identification of vocally expressed emotions by mentally retarded and non-retarded individuals. *American Journal of Mental Deficiency, 89,* 537–545.

Marland, S.P. (1972). Education of the gifted and the talented. *Report to the Congress of the United States by the US Commissioner of Education, Vol. 1.* Washington, DC: Government Printing Office.

Marschark, M. (1993). *Psychological development of deaf children.* New York: Oxford University Press.

Martin, C.L. (1991). The role of cognition in understanding gender effects. In H.W. Reese (Ed.), *Advances in child development and behavior* (Vol. 23, pp.113–150). San Diego: Academic Press.

Martin, G.B., & Clark, R.D. III (1982). Distress crying in neonates: Species and peer specificity. *Developmental Psychology, 18,* 3–9.

Martin, J.R. (1985). *Factual writing: Exploring and challenging social reality.* Geelong, VIC: Deakin University.

Maurer, D. (1985). Infants' perception of facedness. In T. Fields & N. Fox (Eds.), *Social perception in infants* (pp.73–100). Norwood, NJ: Ablex.

Mazella, C., Durkin, K., Cerini, E., & Buralli, P.L. (1992). Sex role stereotyping in Australian television advertisements. *Sex Roles, 26,* 243–259.

Mecklenburg, D.J. (1988). Cochlear implants in children: Nonmedical considerations. *American Journal of Otolaryngology, 9* (2), 163–168.

Mecklenburg, D.J., & Brimacombe, J.A. (1985). An overview of the nucleus cochlear implant program. *Seminars in Hearing, 6* (1), 41–51.

Mehler, J., Morton, J., & Jusczyk, P. (1984). On reducing language to biology. *Cognitive Neuropsychology, 1,* 83–116.

Meltzoff, A.N., & Moore, M.K. (1977). Imitation of facial and manual gestures by human neonates. *Science, 198,* 75–78.

Mercugliano, M. (1995). Neurotransmitter alterations in attention deficit hyperactivity disorder. *Mental Retardation and Developmental Disorders Research Reviews, 1,* 220–226.

Meyers, L.F. (1990). Language development and intervention. In D.C. VanDyke, D.J. Lang, F. Heide, S. VanDuyne & M.J. Soucek (Eds.), *Clinical perspectives in the management of Down syndrome* (pp.153–164). New York: Springer Verlag.

Miller, J.F. (1981). *Assessing language production in children: Experimental procedures.* Austin, TX: Pro-Ed.

——(1988). Development of asynchrony of language development in children with Down syndrome. In L. Nadel (Ed.), *Psychobiology of Down syndrome* (pp.167–198).

——(1992). Development of speech and language in children with Down syndrome. In I. Lott, & E. McCoy (Eds.), *Down syndrome: Advances in medical care* (pp.39–52). New York: John Wiley & Sons.

Minde, K.K., & Minde, R. (1981). Psychiatric intervention in infancy. *Journal of the American Academy of Child Psychiatry, 20,* 217–238.

Minner, S. (1990). Teacher evaluations of case descriptions of LD gifted children. *Gifted Child Quarterly, 34,* 37–39.

Minuchin, S. (1980). *Structural family therapy: Activating alternatives within a thera-peutic system.* Philadelphia, PA: Smith, Kline & French Laboratories report no. 3.

Minuchin, S., Rosman, B.L., Baker, L., & Liebman, R. (1978). *Psychosomatic families: anorexia nervosa in context.* Cambridge, MA: Harvard University Press.

Mirenda, P. & Iacono, T. (1988). Strategies for promoting augmentative and alternative communication in natural contexts with students with autism. *Focus on Autistic Behaviour, 3,* 1–16.

Mitchell, P.R., & Kent, R.D. (1990). Phonetic variation in multisyllable babbling. *Journal of Child Language, 17,* 247–265.

Molnar, G.E., & Perrin, J.C.S. (1983). Rehabilitation of the child with head injury. In K. Shapiro (Ed.), *Pediatric head trauma* (pp.241–269). Mt Kisco, NY: Futura Publishing.

Moore, K.L., & Persaud, T.V.N. (1993). *The developing human: Clinically oriented embryology* (5th ed.). Philadelphia, PA: W.B. Saunders.

Morelock, M.J., & Morrison, K. (1996). *Gifted children have talents too: Multi-dimen-sional programs for the gifted in early childhood.* Melbourne, VIC: Hawker Brownlow Education.

Morgan, M. (1987). Television, sex-role attitudes, and sex-role behavior. *Journal of Early Adolescence, 7,* 269–282.

Moser, H.M. (1985). *Prenatal/perinatal factors associated with brain disorders.* NIH publication T5–1149. Washington, DC: US Government Printing Office.

Mrazek, P.J., & Mrazek, D.A. (1987). Resiliency in child maltreatment victims: A conceptual exploration. *Child Abuse and Neglect, 11,* 357–366.

Mundy, P. (1995). Joint attention and social-emotional approach behavior in children with autism. *Development and Psychopathology, 7* (1), 63–82.

Myers, B.J. (1987). Mother–infant bonding as a critical period. In M.H. Bornstein (Ed.), *Sensitive periods in development: Interdisciplinary perspectives* (pp.223–246). Hillsdale, NJ: Erlbaum.

Mysak, E.D. (1980). *Neurospeech therapy for the cerebral palsied.* New York: Teachers College Press.

National Center on Child Abuse and Neglect (1978). *Child sexual abuse: incest, assault, and sexual exploitation. A special report.* Washington, DC: National Center on Child Abuse and Neglect.

——(1988). *Study of national incidence and prevalance of child abuse and neglect: 1988.* Washington, DC: National Center on Child Abuse and Neglect.

National Joint Committee on Learning Disabilities (1994). Learning Disabilities: Issues on definition. A position paper of the National Joint Committee on Learning Disabilities. In *Collective perspectives on issues affecting learning disabilities: Position papers and statements.* Austin, TX: Pro-Ed.

Nelson, K. (1973). Structure and strategy in learning to talk. *Monographs of the Society for Research in Child Development, 38* (1–2, no. 149).

——(1983). The derivation of concepts and categories from event representations. In E. Kofsky (Ed.), *New trends in conceptual representation: challenges to Piaget's theory?* (pp.129–149). Hillsdale, NJ: Erlbaum.

——(1986). *Event knowledge.* Hillsdale, NJ: Erlbaum.

Nelson, K. & Gruendel, J. (1981). Generalized event representations: basic building blocks of cognitive development. In M. Lamb & A. Brown (eds), *Advances in developmental psychology* (Vol. 1, pp. 131–58). Hillsdale, NJ: Erlbaum.

Nelson, K.B. (1989). Relationship of intrapartum and delivery room events to long-term neurologic outcome. *Clinics in Perinatology, 16,* 995–1007.

——(1991). Prenatal and perinatal factors in the etiology of autism. *Pediatrics, 87,* 761–766.

Nelson, K.B., & Ellenberg, J.H. (1986). Antecedents of cerebral palsy: Multivariate analysis of risk. *New England Journal of Medicine, 315,* 81–86.

Newborg, J., Stock, J.R., Wnek, L., Guidubaldi, J., & Svinicki, J. (1984). *Battelle Developmental Inventory.* Allen, TX: Teaching Resources.

Newcomb, A.F., & Bagwell, C.L. (1995). Children's friendship relations: a meta-analytic review. *Psychological Bulletin, 117,* 306–347.

Newman, C.G. (1985). Teratogen update: Clinical aspects of thalidomide embryopathy—A continuing preoccupation. *Teratology, 32,* 133–144.

Newport, E., Gleitman, A., & Gleitman, L. (1977). Mother, I'd rather do it myself: Some effects and non-effects of maternal speech style. In C. Snow & C. Ferguson (Eds.), *Talking to children: Language input and acquisition.* New York: Cambridge University Press.

Nicholls, G.A. (1988). *Cochlear implants: Results with teenagers and children.* Proceedings of the Australian and New Zealand Conference for Educators of the Deaf: Christchurch, NZ.

Nienhuys, T.G., Cross, T.G., & Horsborough, K.M. (1984). Child variables influencing maternal speech style. *Journal of Communication Disorders, 17,* 189–207.

Nienhuys, T.G., Horsborough, K.M., & Cross, T.G. (1985). A dialogic analysis of interaction between mothers and their deaf and hearing preschoolers. *Applied Psycholinguistics, 6,* 121–140.

Ninio, A., & Bruner, J. (1978). Achievement of antecedents of labelling. *Journal of Child Language, 5,* 1–15.

Noetzel, M.J. (1989). Myelomeningocele: Current concepts in management. *Clinics in Perinatology, 16,* 311–329.

Nordin, V., & Gillberg, C. (1996). Autism spectrum disorders in children with physical or mental disability or both, I: Clinical and epidemiological aspects. *Developmental Medicine and Child Neurology, 38,* 297–313.

Northern, J.L., & Downs, M.P. (1991). *Hearing in children* (4th ed). Baltimore, MD: Williams & Wilkins.

O'Brien, M. (1992). Gender identity and sex roles. In V.B. Van Hasselt & M. Hersen (Eds.), *Handbook of social development: A lifespan perspective* (pp.325–345). New York: Plenum Press.

O'Connor, N., & Hermelin, B. (1991). Talents and preoccupations in idiot-savants. *Psychological Medicine, 21,* 959–964.

O'Donohoe, N.V. (1994). *Epilepsies of childhood* (3rd ed.). Oxford: Butterworth-Heinemann.

O'Kearney, R. (1996). Attachment disruption in anorexia nervosa and bulimia nervosa: A review of theory and empirical research. *International Journal of Eating Disorders, 20* (2), 115–127.

Olegard, R., Sabel, K.G., Aronsson, M. et al. (1979). Effects on the child of alcohol abuse during pregnancy: Retrospective and prospective studies. *Acta Paediatrica Scandinavica, 275* (Suppl.), 112–121.

Ollendick, T.H., & King, N.J. (1991). Fears and phobias of childhood. In M. Hervert (Ed.), *Clinical child psychology: Social learning, development and behavior* (pp.309–329). Chichester, UK: Wiley.

Olshan, A.F., Baird, P.A., & Teschke, K. (1989). Paternal occupational exposures and the risk of Down syndrome. *American Journal of Human Genetics, 44,* 646–651.

Olson, R.A., Huszti, H.C., Mason, P.J., & Seibert, J.M. (1989). Pediatric AIDS/HIV infection: An emerging challenge to pediatric psychology. *Journal of Pediatric Psychology, 14,* 1–21.

Olswag, L., & Bain, B. (1994). Data collection: Monitoring children's treatment progress. *American Journal of Speech-Language Pathology, 3,* 55–66.

Orvaschel, H., Walsh-Allis, G., & Ye, W. (1988). Psychopathology in children of parents with recurrent depression. *Journal of Abnormal Child Psychology, 16,* 17–28.

Orwin, L. (1984). Language for absent things: Learning from visually handicapped children. *Topics in Language Disorders, 4* (4), 24–37.

Osterling, J., & Dawson, G. (1994). Early recognition of children with autism: A study of first birthday home videotapes. *Journal of Autism and Developmental Disorders, 24* (3), 247–257.

Owens, R. (1993). Mental retardation: Difference or delay. In D. Bernstein & E. Tiegerman (Eds.), *Language and communication disorders in children* (3rd. ed.). (pp.366–430). New York: Macmillan.

Owens, R., & MacDonald, J. (1982). Communicative uses of the early speech of nondelayed and Down syndrome children. *American Journal of Mental Deficiency, 86,* 503–511.

Palfrey, J.S., Levine, M.D., Walker, D.K., & Sullivan, M. (1985). The emergence of attentional deficits in early childhood: A prospective study. *Journal of Developmental and Behavioral Pediatrics, 6,* 339–348.

Papousek, H. (1974). The course of conditioning in newborns. In L.J. Stone, H.T. Smith & L.B. Murphy (Eds.), *The competent infant.* London: Tavistock.

Paris, S. (1986). Teaching children to guide their reading and learning. In T. Raphael (Ed.), *The context of school-based literacy.* New York: Random House.

Park, K., Shallcross, R., & Anderson, R. (1980). Differences in coverbal behavior between blind and sighted persons during dyadic communication. *Journal of Visual Impairment and Blindness, 74,* 142–146.

Parten, M. (1932). Social participation among preschool children. *Journal of Abnormal and Social Psychology, 27,* 243–269.

Passman, R.H., & Longeway, K.P. (1982). The role of vision in maternal attachment: Giving 2-year-olds photograph of their mother during separation. *Developmental Psychology, 18,* 530–533.

Paul, J., & Simeonsson, R. (1993). *Children with special needs: Family culture and society* (2nd ed.). New York: Harcourt Brace Jovanovich.

Pavlov, I.P. (1927). *Conditioned reflexes* (G.V.Anrep, Trans.). London: Oxford University Press.

Pavuluri, M.N., Luk, S.L., Clarkson, J., & McGee, R. (1995). A community study of preschool behaviour disorders in New Zealand. *Australian and New Zealand Journal of Psychiatry, 29,* 454–462.

Peacock, W.J., & Staudt, L.A. (1990). Spasticity in cerebral palsy and the selective posterior rhizotomy procedure. *Journal of Child Neurology, 5,* 179–185.

Peckham, C.S. (1986). Vision in childhood. *British Medical Bulletin, 42* (2), 150–154.

Pellegrini, A. (1984). The effects of classroom ecology on preschoolers' functional uses of language. In A. Pellegrini & T. Yawkey (Eds.), *The development of oral and written language in social contexts.* Norwood, NJ: Ablex.

Pellegrino, L. (1995). Cerebral palsy: A paradigm for developmental disabilities. *Developmental Medicine and Child Neurology, 37,* 834–839.

Pennington, B.F., Groisser, D., & Welsh, M.C. (1993). Contrasting cognitive deficits in attention deficit hyperactivity disorder versus reading disability. *Developmental Psychology, 29,* 391–404.

Perlman, M., Claris, O., Hao, Y. et al. (1995). Secular changes in the outcomes to 18 to 24 months of age of extremely low birth weight infants, with adjustment for changes in the risk factors and severity of illness. *Journal of Pediatrics, 126,* 75–87.

Perlmutter, M. (1984). Continuities and discontinuities in early human memory: Paradigms, processes, and performances. In R.V. Kail, Jr. & N.R. Spear (Eds.), *Comparative perspectives on the development of memory* (pp.253–287). Hillsdale, NJ: Erlbaum.

Peters, S.D., Wyatt, G.E., & Finkelhor, D. (1986). Prevalence. In D. Finkelhor & Associates (Eds.), *A sourcebook on child sexual abuse* (pp.15–59). Beverly Hills, CA: Sage.

Peterson, C.C. (1995). Husbands' and wives' perceptions of global equity in marriage over the family life cycle. In J. Hendricks (Ed.), *The ties of later life.* New York: Baywood.

——(1996). *Looking forward through the lifespan. Developmental psychology.* Sydney: Prentice Hall.

Peterson, C.C., Peterson, J.L., & Carroll, J. (1983). Children's attitudes towards imagination. Paper presented at 53rd Australian and New Zealand Association for Advancement of Science Conference, Perth, May.

Peterson-Falzone, S. (1995). Speech outcomes in adolescents with cleft lip and palate. *Cleft Palate—Craniofacial Journal, 31* (6), 446–451.

Phillips, D. (1984). The illusion of incompetence among academically competent children. *Child Development, 55,* 2000–2016.

Piaget, J. (1929/1973). *Child's conception of the world.* Frogmore, UK: Paladin.

——(1932/1965). *The moral judgement of the child*. New York: Free Press.

——(1952). *The origins of intelligence in children*. New York: International Universities Press.

——(1970). Piaget's theory. In P.H. Mussen (Ed.), *Carmichael's manual of child psychology* (Vol. 1, 3rd ed.) (pp.703–732). New York: Wiley.

Pietratoni, M., & Knuppel, R.A. (1991). Alcohol abuse in pregnancy. *Clinics in Periantology, 18*, 93–111.

Pinker, S., Lebeaux, D.S., & Frost, L.A. (1987). Productivity and constraints in the acquisition of the passive. *Cognition, 26*, 195–267.

Piper, M.C., Mazer, B., Silver, K.M. et al. (1988). Resolution of neurological symptoms in high-risk infants during the first two years of life. *Developmental Medicine and Child Neurology, 30*, 26–35.

Plomin, R. (1995). Genetics and children's experiences in the family. *Journal of Child Psychology and Psychiatry, 36*, 33–68.

Polka, L., & Werker, J.F. (1994). Developmental changes in perception of nonnative vowel contrasts. *Journal of Experimental Psychology: Human Perception and Performance, 20*, 421–435.

Porter, L. (1997). *Young gifted children: Meeting their needs*. AECA Resource Book Series, 4 (1). ACT: Australian Early Childhood Association.

Pranzatelli, M.R. (1996). Oral pharmacotherapy for the movement disorders of cerebral palsy. *Journal of Child Neurology, 11* (1), S13–S22.

Prizant, B.M. (1996). Brief report: Communication language, social and emotional development. *Journal of Autism and Development Disorders 26*, (2), 173–178.

Prizant, B.M., & Rydell, P.J. (1984). Analysis of functions of delayed echolalia in autistic children. *Journal of Speech and Hearing Research, 27*, 183–192.

Purpura, D.P. (1974). Dendritic spine dysgenesis and mental retardation. *Science, 186*, 1126–1128.

Putallaz, M. (1983). Predicting children's sociometric status from their behavior. *Child Development, 54*, 1417–1426.

——(1987). Maternal behavior and children's sociometric status. *Child Development, 58*, 324–340.

Rainforth, B., York, J., & MacDonald, C. (1992). *Collaborative teams for students with severe disabilities*. Baltimore, MD: Brookes.

Randhawa, B.S., DeLacey, P.R. & Saklofske, D.H. (1986). Personality and behavioural measures: Gender, age, and race contrasts in an Australian setting. *International Journal of Psychology, 21*, 389–402.

Rapin, I. (1996). Practitioner review: Developmental language disorders—A clinical update. *Journal of Child Psychology and Psychiatry, 37*, (6) 643–655.

Rauscher, H.H. (1994). Music and spatial task performance. A causal relationship. Paper presented at the Annual Meeting of the American Psychological Association, Los Angeles, CA (12–16 August, 1994).

Reisman, J.E. (1987). Touch, motion, and proprioception. In P. Salapatek & L. Cohen (Eds.), *Handbook of infant perception, Vol. 11: From sensation to perception* (pp.265–303). Orlando, FL: Academic Press.

Reiss, A.L., & Freund, L. (1990). Fragile X syndrome. *Biological Psychiatry, 27*, 223–240.

Renzulli, J.S. (1978). What makes giftedness? Reexamining a definition. *Phi Delta Kappa, 60* (3), 180–184.

Reynell, J. (1978). Developmental patterns of visually handicapped children. *Child: Care, Health and Development, 4*, 291–303.

Reynolds, A.M., Elksnin, N., & Brown, F.R., III (1996). Specific reading disabilities:

Early identification and long term outcome. *Mental Retardation and Developmental Disabilities Research Reviews, 2,* 21–27.

Rhodes, W.C. (1967). The disturbing child: A problem of ecological management. *Exceptional Children, 33,* 449–455.

Rice, M.L., & Woodsmall, L. (1988). Lessons from television: Children's word learning when viewing. *Child Development, 59,* 420–429.

Ricks, D. (1979). Making sense of experience to make sensible sounds. In M. Bullowa (Ed.), *Before speech.* New York: Cambridge University Press.

Rimland, B. (1991). Improving the auditory functioning in autistic persons: A comparison of the Bernard auditory training approach with the Tomatis audio-phonology approach. *Autism Research Review International, 5,* (3), 1–4.

Roberts, J., Cairns, S. & Treolar, R. (1990). *Communication skills assessment and goal setting guide.* Sydney: Autistic Association of NSW.

Roberts, M.C. (1986). *Pediatric psychology: psychological interventions and strategies for pediatric problems.* New York: Pergamon.

Robertson, M.M. (1994). Gilles de la Tourette syndrome: An update. *Journal of Child Psychology and Psychiatry, 35,* 597–611.

Robinson, R.O. (1973). The frequency of other handicaps in children with cerebral palsy. *Developmental Medicine and Child Neurology, 15,* 305–312.

Rochat, P. (1989). Object manipulation and exploration in 2- to 5-month-old infants. *Developmental Psychology, 25,* 871–884.

Roedell, W.C. (1989). Early development of gifted children. In J.L. Van Tassel-Baska & P. Olszewski-Kubilius (Eds.), *Patterns of influence on gifted learners.* New York: Teachers College Press.

Roffwarg, H.P., Muzio, J.N., & Dement, W.C. (1966). Ontogenetic development of the human sleep-dream cycle. *Science, 152,* 321–331.

Rogers, M.T., & Silverman, L.K. (1988). Recognising giftedness in young children. *Understanding Our Gifted, 1* (2).

Roggman, L.A., Langois, J.H., Hubbs-Tait, L., & Rieser-Danner, L.A. (1994). Infant day-care attachment, and the file drawer problem. *Child Development, 65, 1429–1443.*

Rondal, J.A. (1995). *Exceptional language development in Down syndrome: implications for the cognition–language relationship.* Cambridge, MA: Cambridge University Press.

Rose, S.A., & Ruff, H.A. (1987). Cross-modal abilities in human infants. In J.D. Osofsky (Ed.), *Handbook of infant development* (2nd. ed.) (pp.318–362). New York: Wiley Interscience.

Rosenak, D., Diamant, Y.Z., Yaffe, H. et. al. (1990). Cocaine: Maternal use during pregnancy and its effects on the mother, the fetus, and the infant. *Obstetrical and Gynecological Survey, 45,* 348–359.

Rosenblith, J.F. (1992). *In the beginning: development in the first two years of life* (2nd ed.). Newbury Park, CA: Sage.

Rosenstein, D.S., & Horowitz, H.A. (1996). Adolescent attachment and psychopathology. *Journal of Consulting and Clinical Psychology, 64* (2), 244–253.

Rosenthal, R. (1994). Interpersonal expectancy effects: A 30-year perspective. *Current Directions in Psychological Science, 3,* 176–179.

Rovee-Collier, C.K. (1984). The ontogeny of learning and memory in human infancy. In R. Kail & N.E. Spear (Eds.), *Comparative perspectives on the development of memory* (pp.103–134). Hillsdale, NJ: Erlbaum.

Rubin, K.H. (1982). Nonsocial play in preschoolers: Necessarily evil? *Child Development, 53,* 651–657.

Rubin, K.H., Fein, G.G., & Vandenberg, B. (1983). Play. In E.M. Hetherington (Ed.), *Handbook of child psychology: Socialisation, personality and social development* (Vol. 4, pp.693–774). New York: Wiley.

Rubin, K.H., Watson, K.S., & Jambor, T.W. (1978). Free-play behaviors in preschool and kindergarten children. *Child Development, 49,* 534–536.

Ruble, D.N. (1987). The acquisition of self-knowledge: A self-socialization perspective. In N. Eisenberg (Ed.), *Contemporary topics in developmental psychology* (pp. 243–270). New York: Wiley-Interscience.

Rutter, M., & Garmezy, N. (1983). Developmental psychopathology. In E.M. Hetherington (Ed.), *Handbook of child psychology, Vol. 4: Socialization, personality, and social development* (pp.775–912). New York: Wiley.

Saccuzzo, D.P., Johnson, N.E., & Guertin, T.L. (1994). Information processing in gifted versus nongifted African American, Latino, Filipino, and White children: Speeded versus nonspeeded paradigms. *Intelligence, 19,* 219–243.

St George, A. (1983). Teacher expectations and perceptions of Polynesian and Pakeha pupils and the relationship to classroom behaviour and school achievement. *British Journal of Educational Psychology, 53,* 48–59.

Sameroff, A.J. (1995). General systems theories and developmental psychopathology. In D. Cicchetti & D.J. Cohen (Eds.), *Developmental psychopathology, Vol. 1: Theory and methods* (pp.659–695). New York: Wiley.

Sandlin, R.E. (Ed.) (1988). *Handbook of hearing amplification.* Boston: College Hill.

Sanson, A., Prior, M., & Oberklaid, F. (1985). Normative data on temperament in Australian infants. *Australian Journal of Psychology, 37,* 185–191.

Satterfield, J., Swanson, J., Schell, A., & Lee, F. (1994). Prediction of antisocial behavior in attention-deficit hyperactivity disorder boys from aggression/defiance scores. *Journal of the American Academy of Child and Adolescent Psychiatry, 33,* 185–190.

Sawyer, D.J. (1987). *Test of awareness of language segments.* Austin, TX: Pro-Ed.

Sayler, M. (1994). *Investigation of talented students.* Denton, TX: University of North Texas.

Scarborough, H.S. (1990). Very early deficits in dyslexic children. *Child Development, 61,* 1728–1743.

Scarr, S., & Eisenberg, M. (1993). Child care research: Issues, perspectives, and results. *Annual Review of Psychology, 44,* 613–644.

Schiff-Myers, N. (1992). Considering arrested language development and language loss in the assessment of second language learners. *Language, Speech, & Hearing Services in Schools, 23,* 28–33.

Schneider, W., & Bjorklund, D.F. (1992). Expertise, aptitude, and strategic remembering. *Child Development, 63,* 461–473.

Schopler, E., Reichler, R.J., DeVellius, R. et al. (1980). Toward objective classification of childhood autism: Childhood Autism Rating Scale (CARS). *Journal of Autism and Developmental Disorders, 10,* 91–102.

Schore, A.N. (1996). The experience-dependent maturation of regulatory system in the orbital prefrontal cortex and the origin of developmental psychopathology. *Development and Psychopathology, 8* (1), 59–87.

Schroeder-Kurth, T.M., Schaffert, G., Koeckritz, W. et al. (1990). Quality of life of adults with trisomy 21 living in mental retardation homes compared with those staying under parental care. *American Journal of Medical Genetics, 7 (suppl.),* 317–321.

Schwartz, R.G., & Leonard, L.B. (1982). Do children pick and choose? An examination of phonological selection and avoidance in early lexical acquisition. *Journal of Child Language, 9,* 319–336.

Seigel, B. (1996). *The world of the autistic child.* New York: Oxford University Press.

Selman, R.L. (1980). *The growth of interpersonal understanding.* New York: Academic Press.

Semel, E., Wiig, E., & Secord, W. (1995). *Clinical evaluation of language functions—revised.* San Antonio, TX: Psychological Corporation.

Shandling, B., & Gilmour, R.F. (1987). *The enema continence catheter in spina bifida: Successful bowel management.* Paper presented at 33rd Annual Congress of the British Association of Paediatric Surgeons, Birmingham, July 16–18.

Shapiro, B.K., & Gallico, R.P. (1993). Learning disabilities. *Pediatric Clinics of North America, 40,* 491–505.

Shelton, T., Jeppson, E., & Johnson, B. (1987). *Family centered care for children with special health care needs.* Washington, DC: Association for the Care of Children's Health.

Sheppard, J.J., & Mysak, E.D. (1984). Ontogeny of infantile oral reflexes and emerging chewing. *Child Development, 55,* 831–843.

Shinnar, S., Berg, A.T., Moshe, S.L., et al. (1990). Risk of seizure recurrence following a short unprovoked seizure in childhood: A prospective study. *Pediatrics, 85,* 1076–1085.

Shinnar, S., Berg, A.T.T., Moshe, S.L. et al. (1994). Discontinuing antiepileptic medication in children with epilepsy: A prospective study. *Annals of Neurology, 35,* 534–545.

Shreibman, L. (1988). *Autism.* Newbury Park, CA: Sage.

Siegal, M (1985). *Children, parenthood, and social welfare in the context of developmental psychology.* Oxford: Oxford University Press.

——(1987). Are sons and daughters treated more differently by fathers than by mothers? *Developmental Review, 7,* 183–209.

Siegal, M. & Storey, R.M. (1985). Daycare and children's conceptions of moral and social rules. *Child Development, 56,* 1001–1008.

Siegel, B. (1996). *The world of the autistic child.* New York: Oxford University Press.

Silcock, A. (1984). Crises in parents of prematures: An Australian study. *British Journal of Developmental Psychology, 2,* 257–268.

Silverman, L.K. (1993). *Counselling the gifted.* Denver, CO: Love.

Simko, A., Hornstein, L., Soukup, S. et al. (1989). Fragile X syndrome: Recognition in young children. *Pediatrics, 83,* 547–552.

Singer, J.L. (1973). *The child's world of make-believe: Experimental studies of imaginative play.* New York: Academic Press.

Singer, J.L., & Singer, D.G. (1981). *Television, imagination, and aggression: A study of preschoolers.* Hillsdale, NJ: Erlbaum.

Skinner, B.F. (1957). *Verbal behavior.* New York: Prentice Hall.

Slaby, R.G., & Frey, K.S. (1975). Development of gender constancy and selective attention to same-sex models. *Child Development, 46,* 849–856.

Slobin, D.I. (1973). Cognitive prerequisites for the development of grammar. In C.A. Ferguson, & D.I. Slobin (Eds.), *Studies of child language development* (pp 175–208). New York: Holt, Rinehart & Winston.

Smilansky, S. (1968). *The effects of sociodramatic play on disadvantaged children: Preschool children.* New York: Wiley.

Smith, C.L., & Tager-Flusberg, H. (1982). Metalinguistic awareness and language development. *Journal of Experimental Child Psychology, 34,* 449–468.

Snow, C. (1977). The development of conversation between mothers and babies. *Journal of Child Language, 4,* 1–22.

——(1991). The theoretical bases for relationships between language and literacy in development. *Journal of Research in Childhood Education, 6* (1), 5–10.

Sodian, B., Schneider, W. & Perlmutter, M. (1986). Recall, clustering, and metamemory in young children. *Journal of Experimental Child Psychology, 41,* 395–410.

Sonksen, P.M., Petrie, A., & Drew, K.J. (1991). Promotion of visual development in severely visually impaired babies: Evaluation of a developmentally based programme. *Developmental Medicine and Child Neurology, 33,* 320–335.

Spelke, E.S., & Owsley, C.J. (1979). Intermodal exploration and knowledge in infancy. *Infant Behavior and Development, 2,* 13–27.

Spitz, R.A. (1945). Hospitalism: An inquiry into the genesis of psychiatric conditions in early childhood. *Psychoanalytical Study of the Child, 1,* 53–74.

Springer, S.P., & Deutsch, G. (1984). *Left brain, right brain.* New York: W.H. Freeman.

Sroufe, L.A. (1983). Infant–caregiver attachment and patterns of adaptation in pre-school: The roots of maladaptation and competence. In M. Perlmutter (Ed.), *Minnesota symposium on child development.* Hillsdale, NJ: Erlbaum.

——(1985). Attachment classification from the perspective of infant-caregiver relationships and infant temperament. *Child Development, 56,* 1–14.

Sroufe, L.A., & Fleeson, J. (1986). Attachment and construction of relationships. In W. Hartup & Z. Rubin (Eds.), *Relationships and development.* Hillsdale, NJ: Erlbaum.

Stainback, W., & Stainback, S. (1990). *Support networks for inclusive schooling.* Baltimore, MD: Brookes.

Stanovich, K.E., & Stanovich, P.J. (1995). How research might inform debate about early reading acquisition. *Journal of Research in Reading, 18,* 87–105.

Steiner, J.E. (1979). Human facial expressions in response to taste and smell stimulation. In H.W. Reese & L.P. Lipsitt (Eds.), *Advances in child development and behavior* (Vol. 13, pp.257–296). New York: Academic Press.

Stelhi, A. (1991). *The sound of a miracle.* Doubleday: New York.

Sternberg, R.J. (1986). *Intelligence applied.* New York: Harcourt Brace Jovanovich.

Sternberg, R.J., & Davidson, J.E. (1986). *Conception of giftedness.* New York: Cambridge University Press.

Stevenson, J., Richman, N., & Graham, P. (1985). Behavior problems and language abilities at three years and behavioral deviance at eight years. *Journal of Child Psychology and Psychiatry, 26,* 215–230.

Stipek, D., & Gralinski, H. (1991). Gender differences in children's achievement—related belief and emotional responses to success and failure in math. *Journal of Educational Psychology, 83,* 361–371.

Streissguth, A.P., Barr, H.M., Sampson, P.D. et al. (1986). Attention, distraction, and reaction time at age 7 years and prenatal alcohol exposure. *Neurobehavioral Toxicology and Teratology, 8,* 717–725.

Streissguth, A.P., Aase, J.M., Clarren, S.K., Randells, S.P., LaDue, R.A., & Smith, D.F. (1991). Fetal alcohol syndrome in adolescents and adults. *Journal of the American Medical Association, 265,* 419–442.

Sudhalter, V., Cohen, I., Silverman, W., & Wolf-Schein, E. (1990). Conversational analysis of males with Fragile X, Down syndrome, and autism: Comparison of the emergence of deviant language. *American Journal on Mental Retardation, 99,* 431–441.

Sullivan, K., Zaitchik, D., & Tager-Flusberg, H. (1994). Preschoolers can attribute second order beliefs. *Developmental Psychology, 30,* 395–402.

Super, C.M., & Harkness, S. (1982). The infant's niche in rural Kenya and metropolitan America. In L.L. Adler (Ed.), *Cross-cultural research at issue* (pp.247–255). New York: Academic Press.

Sutherland, G.R., & Mulley, J.C. (1990). Diagnostic molecular genetics of the fragile X. *Clinical Genetics, 37,* 2–11.

Szatmari, P. (1991). Asperger's syndrome: Diagnosis, treatment and outcome. *Psychiatric Clinics of North America, 14,* 81–93.

Taber's Cyclopedic Medical Dictionary (16th ed.) (1991). Philadelphia: F.A. Davis.

Talay (Senkal), A. (1978). Development of asymmetry of brain function for language activity in children as reflected by performances on a listening and viewing task. *Hacettepe University Bulletin of Social Sciences, 11,* 135–147.

Talay-Ongan, A. (1991). A comprehensive, transdisciplinary, centre-based model of early intervention. *Early Child Development and Care, 72,* 69–81.

——(1994). Preventive intervention: Preschoolers at risk for learning difficulties. *Austalasian Journal of Special Education, 18* (2), 11–20.

——(1996). Infants' phonemic awareness and receptive language profiles: A follow-up study. *Child Language Teaching and Therapy, 12,* 99–112.

——(1997). *Contextual variables in ADHD.* Paper presented at 5th Conference on Australian Research in Early Childhood Education, Canberra, 26 January 1997.

Tallal, P., Miller, S.L., Bedi, G. et al. (1996). Language comprehension in language-learning impaired children improved with acoustically modified speech. *Science, 271,* 81–84.

Tallal, P. & Piercy, M. (1978). Defects of auditory perception in children with developmental aphasia. In M.A. Wyke (Ed.), *Developmental dysphasia.* New York: Academic Press.

Tannenbaum, A. (1992). Early signs of giftedness: Research and commentary. In P. Klein & A. Tannenbaum (Eds.), *To be young and gifted.* Norwood, NJ: Ablex.

Tanner, J.M. (1978). *Education and physical growth.* New York: International Universities Press.

Teller, D.Y., McDonald, M.A., & Preston, K. (1986). Assessment of visual acuity in infants and children. *Developmental Medicine and Child Neurology, 28,* 779–789.

Thelen, E. (1981). Rhythmical behavior in infancy: An ethological perspective. *Developmental Psychology, 17 I,* 237–257.

——(1989). The (re)discovery of motor development: Learning new things from an old field. *Developmental Psychology, 25,* 946–949.

Theorell, K., Prechtl, H., & Vos, J. (1974). A polygraphic study of normal and abnormal newborn infants. *Neuropaediatrie, 5,* 279–317.

Thomas, A., & Chess, S. (1977). *Temperament and development.* New York: Brunner/Maazel.

Thomas, A., Chess, S. & Birch, H. (1963). *Behavioral individuality in early childhood.* New York: University Press.

Thomson, S.K. (1975). Gender labels and early sex role development. *Child Development, 46,* 339–347.

Thorndike, R.L., Hagen, E.P., & Sattler, J.M. (1986). *The Stanford-Binet Intelligence Scale: A guide for administering and scoring* (4th ed.). Chicago: Riverside Publishing.

Thousand, J.S., & Villa, R.A. (1992). Collaborative teams: A powerful tool in school restructuring. In R.A. Villa & J.A. Thousand (Eds.), *Restructuring and caring and effective education* (pp.73–108). Baltimore, MD: Brookes.

Timmer, S.G., Eccels, J., & O Brien, K. (1985). How children use time. In F.T. Juster & F.P. Stafford (Eds.), *Time, goods and well-being* (pp.353–369). Ann Arbor, MI: University of Michigan.

Torgesen, J.K., & Bryant, B.R. (1994). *Test of phonological awareness.* Austin, TX: Pro-Ed.

Touwen, B.C.L. (1984). Primitive reflexes: Conceptual or semantic problem? In H.F.R. Prechtl (Ed.), *Continuity of neural functions from prenatal to postnatal life* (Clinics in Developmental Medicine, No. 94, pp.115–125). Philadelphia, PA: Lippincott.

Trehub, S.E., & Rabinovitch, M.S. (1972). Auditory-linguistic sensitivity in early infancy. *Child Development, 6,* 74–77.

Trybus, R. D. (1980). National data on rated speech intelligibility of hearing impaired children. In J.D. Subtelny (Ed.), *Speech assessment and speech improvement for the hearing impaired.* Washington, DC: A.G. Bell.

Tseng, W., & Hsu, J. (1991). *Culture and family: Problems and therapy.* Binghamton, NY: Haworth.

Tuchman, R.F., Rapin, I., & Shinnar, S. (1991). Autistic and dysphasic children, II: Epilepsy. *Pediatrics, 88,* 1219–1225.

Tulving, E. (1972). Episodic and semantic memory. In E. Tulving & W. Donaldson (Eds.), *Organization of memory* (pp.382–403). New York: Academic Press.

Turnbull, A.P., & Turnbull, H.R., III (1986). *Families, professionals, and exceptionality: A special partnership.* Columbus, OH: Merrill.

Turnbull, A.P., Summers, J.A., & Brotherson, M.J. (1986). *Working with families with disabled members: A family systems approach.* Lawrence, KS: University of Kansas.

Uchida, I.A., Freeman, V.C., Jamro, H. et al. (1983). Additional evidence for fragile X activity in heterozygous carriers. *American Journal of Genetics, 35,* 861–868.

Underwood, M.K., Coie, J.D., & Herbsman, C.R. (1992). Display rules for anger and aggression in school-age children. *Child Development, 63,* 366–80.

Upfold, L.J. (1988). Children using hearing aids in the 1980s: Etiologies and severity of impairment. *Ear and Hearing, 9,* 75–80.

Usher, R. (1987). Extreme prematurity. In G.B. Avery (Ed.), *Neonatology* (3rd. ed.) (pp.264–298). Philadelphia, PA: J.B. Lippincott.

Valdes-Dapena, M.A., & Arey, J.B. (1970). The causes of neonatal mortality: An analysis of 501 autopsies on newborn infants. *Journal of Pediatrics, 77,* 366–375.

Victorian Infant Collaborative Study Group (1991). Eight-year outcome in infants with birth weights of 500–999 grams: Continuing regional study of 1979 and 1980 births. *Journal of Pediatrics, 118,* 761–767.

Volkmar, F., & Rutter, M. (1995). Childhood disintegrative disorder: Results of the DSM-IV autism field trial. *Journal of the American Academy of Child and Adolescent Psychiatry, 34,* 1092–1095.

Volpe, J.J. (1990). Brain injury in the premature infant. Is it preventable? *Pediatric Research, 27,* S28–S33.

Vygotsky, L.S. (1930/1978). *Mind in society: The development of higher mental processes.* Cambridge, MA: Harvard University Press.

——(1934/1962). *Thought and language.* Cambridge, MA: MIT Press.

——(1988). The genesis of higher mental functions. In K. Richardson & S. Sheldon (Eds.), *Cognitive development to adolescence.* Hove, UK: Erlbaum.

Walden, T.A. (1991). Infant social referencing. In J. Garber & K.A. Dodge (Eds.), *The* development of emotion regulation and dysregulation (pp.69–88). Cambridge: Cambridge University Press.

Waldrop, M.F., & Halverson, C.F., Jr, (1975). Intensive and extensive peer behavior: Longitudinal and cross-sectional analysis. *Child Development, 46,* 19–26.

Walker, C.E., Bonner, B.L., & Kaufman, K.L. (1988). *The physically and sexually abused child: Evaluation and treatment.* New York: Pergamon.

Walker, L.J., deVries, B., & Trevathan, S.D. (1987). Moral stages and moral orientations in real life and hypothetical dilemmas. *Child Development, 58,* 842–958.

Wallace, S.J. (1990). Risk of seizures (Annotation). *Developmental Medicine and Child Neurology, 32,* 645–649.

Warren, S.F., Yoder, P.J., Gazdag, G., Kim, K., & Jones, H. (1993). Facilitating communication skills in young children with developmental delay. *Journal of Speech and Hearing Research, 36,* 83–97.

Wechsler, D. (1974). *Manual for the Wechsler Intelligence Scale for Children—Revised.* New York: Psychological Corporation.

——(1991). *Wechsler Intelligence Scale for Children (3rd ed.)* San Antonio, TX: Psychological Corporation.

——(1992). *Wechsler Individual Achievement Test.* San Antonio, TX: Psychological Corporation.

Weisenfeld, A.R., Malatesta, C.Z., & DeLoach, L.L. (1981). Differential parental response to familiar and unfamiliar infant distress signals. *Infant Behavior and Development, 4,* 281–296.

Wellman, H.M. (1977). Preschoolers' understanding of memory-relevant variables. *Child Development, 48,* 1720–1723.

Wellman, H.M., & Hickling, A.K. (1994). The mind's I: children's conception of the mind as an active agent. *Child Development, 65,* 1564–1580.

Wenar, C. (1982). On negativism. *Human Development, 25,* 1–23.

——(1990). *Developmental psychopathology: From infancy through adolescence* (2nd ed.). New York: McGraw Hill.

Werner, L.A., & Gillenwater, J.M. (1990). Pure tone sensitivity of 2- to 5-week old infants. *Infant Behavior and Development, 13,* 355–375.

White, B.L. (1975a). *The first three years of life.* Englewood Cliffs, NJ: Prentice Hall.

——(1975b). Critical influences in the origins of competence. *Merrill-Palmer Quarterly, 22,* 165–175.

Whitmore, J. (1980). *Giftedness, conflict and underachievement.* Boston, MA: Allyn & Bacon.

Widerstrom, A.H., Mowder, B.A., & Sandall, S.R (1991). *At-risk and handicapped newborns and infants: Development, assessment, and intervention.* Englewood Cliffs, NJ: Prentice Hall.

Wiig, E.H. (1990). Language disabilities in school-age children and youth. In G.H. Shames & E.H. Wiig (Eds.), *Human communication disorders* (3rd ed.) (pp.193–320). Columbus, OH: Merrill.

Wilkinson, L., & Rembold, K. (1982). Communicative context of early language development. In S. Kuczaj (Ed.), *Language development, Vol. 2: Language, thought and culture.* Hillsdale, NJ: Erlbaum.

Williams, D. (1994). *Nobody, nowhere.* London: Doubleday.

Wittrock, M.C. (1978). Education and the cognitive process in the brain. In J.C. Chall & A.F. Mirsky, (Eds.), *Education and the brain.* Chicago, IL: National Society for the Study of Education.

Wolff, P.H. (1987). *The development of behavioral states and emotional states in infancy.* Chicago: University of Chicago Press

Wolfle, J. (1990). Gifted preschoolers within the classroom. *Early Childhood Development and Care, 63,* 83–93.

Wood, K., & Talay-Ongan, A. (forthcoming). Unusual sensory sensitivities in autism: an empirical account.

Woodcock, R.W., & Johnson, M.B. (1989). *Woodcock-Johnson Psycho-Educational Battery—Revised.* Allen, TX: DLM Teaching Resources.

Woody-Ramsey, J., & Miller, P.H. (1988). The facilitation of selective attention in preschoolers. *Child Development, 59,* 1497–1503.

Wright, L. (1977). Conceptualizing and defining psychosomatic disorders. *American Psychologist, 32,* 625–628.

Wurtele, S.K., Kast, L.C., Miller-Perrin, C.L., & Kondrick, P.A. (1989). A comparison of programs for teaching personal safety skills to preschoolers. *Journal of Consulting and Clinical Psychology, 57,* 505–511.

Wurtele, S.K., & Miller-Perrin, C.L. (1992). *Preventing child sexual abuse: sharing the responsibility.* Lincoln, NE: University of Nebraska Press.

Wyver, S.R. (1997). Play of 3–5 year old children with a visual impairment. *Proceedings of the Australian and New Zealand Association of Educators of the Visually Handicapped 1997 Biennial Conference.* Adelaide, South Australia: ANZAEVH.

Wyver, S.R., & Livesey, D.J. (1997). Kinaesthetic acuity and motor skills of preschool children with a congenital visual impairment: Preliminary findings. *The Australian Educational and Developmental Psychologist, 14,* 72–79.

Yasukawa, A. (1990). Upper extremity casting: Adjunct treatment for a child with cerebral palsy hemiplegia. *American Journal of Occupational Therapy, 44,* 840–846.

Yoder, P.J., Warren, S.F., & Gazdag, G.E. (1994). Facilitating prelinguistic communication skills in young children with developmental delay, II. Systematic replication and extension. *Journal of Speech and Hearing Research, 37,* 841–851.

Yonas, A., & Owsley, C. (1987). Development of visual space perception. In P. Salapatek & L. Cohen (Eds.), *Handbook of infant perception, Vol. 2: From sensation to perception* (pp.80–122). Orlando, FL: Academic Press.

Zigler, E., & Styfco, S.J. (1993). Using research and theory to justify and inform Head Start expansion. *Social Policy Report, Society in Research in Child Development, 7* (2), 1–21.

Index